ECONOMICS:
Meeting People's Needs

ECONOMICS:
MEETING PEOPLE'S NEEDS

George G. Watson, Jr.
Peter H. Dublin
Robert M. Harrington
Betty L. S. Bardige
Jacqueline H. Walsh

Economic Consultants:

Richard Morgenstern
Queens College

Everett Erlich
Congressional Budget Office

®

SCIENCE RESEARCH ASSOCIATES, INC.
Chicago, Palo Alto, Toronto
Henley-on-Thames, Sydney, Paris

A Subsidiary of IBM

ACKNOWLEDGEMENTS

26 Excerpted from *Patterns of Culture* by Ruth Benedict. © Reprinted with permission of Houghton Mifflin Company. **36** Excerpted from *Life in a Turkish Village* by Joe E. Pierce. © Reprinted with permission of Holt, Rinehart and Winston. **47** Excerpted from *The Russians* by Hedrick Smith. © 1976 by Hedrick Smith. Reprinted with permission of Quadrangle Press. **67** Excerpted from "Mom Goes to Law School," by Marilyn Smith. Reprinted with permission of MS Magazine. **98** Copyright 1977 by Newsweek, Inc. All rights reserved. Reprinted by permission. **107** "The Verger," copyright 1929 by W. Somerset Maugham from *The Complete Short Stories of W. Somerset Maugham.* Used by permission of Doubleday & Company, Inc. **117** Extracts from *The Economic Organization of a P.O.W. War Camp* by R. A. Radford. *Economica* November 1945. **128** "The Parable of the Parking Lots," by Henry G. Manne. Reprinted with the permission of the author from *The Public Interest,* No. 23 (Spring 1971), pp. 10–13. © by National Affairs Inc. **147** Adaptation by permission of G. P. Putnam's Sons from *Pink Collar Workers* by Louise Kapp Howe. Copyright © 1977 by Louise Kapp Howe. **158** Excerpt from *Clockwork* by Richard Balzer. Copyright © 1976 by Richard Balzer. Used by permission of Doubleday & Company, Inc. **177** Copyright 1977 by Newsweek, Inc. All rights reserved. Reprinted by permission. **188** Excerpted from "This Sporting Life," by Kenneth Boulding. © 1977 by the Alumni Association of M.I.T. Reprinted by permission of *Technology Review.* **221** From *Income Distribution* (Allen Lane, The Penguin Press, 1971) pp. 48–53. Copyright © Jan Pen, 1971. Translation copyright © Trevor S. Preston, 1971. Reprinted by permission of Penguin Books Ltd. **231** Reprinted by permission of Scholastic Magazines, Inc. from *Senior Scholastic.* Copyright © 1957 by Scholastic Magazines, Inc. **241** "Caught in the Organ Draft," by Robert Silverberg, copyright © 1972 by Robert Silverberg. Reprinted by permission of the author. **256** Excerpt from *The Gospel According to the Harvard Business School: The Education of America's Managerial Elite* by Peter Cohen. Copyright © 1973 by Peter Cohen. Used by permission of Doubleday & Company, Inc. **277** Excerpt from "What GNP Doesn't Tell Us." Reprinted by permission of The Saturday Review. **285** From *Yellow Gentians and Blue* by Zora Gale. By permission of Hawthorn Books, Inc. All rights reserved. **298** From *Talley's Corner* by Elliot Liebow. Copyright © 1967 by Little, Brown and Company, Inc. **309** Copyright 1976 by Newsweek, Inc. All Rights Reserved. Reprinted by permission. **327** From *The Grapes of Wrath* by John Steinbeck. Copyright 1939 © 1967 by John Steinbeck. Reprinted by permission of The Viking Press. **339** Reprinted from "U.S. News & World Report." Copyright 1975 U.S. News and World Report, Inc. **348** Reprinted from "U.S. News & World Report." Copyright 1975 U.S. News & World Report, Inc. **367** Reprinted by permission of the Federal Reserve Bank of Philadelphia. **377** Reprinted by permission of Harold Ober Associates Incorporated. Copyright © 1942 by Collier's Magazine. **391** "A Cautious Approach to Doomsday," by Ian Menzies, October 5, 1977. Courtesy of the Boston Globe. **394** Adapted from Part Three, "James Cotswold," of *The*

VISUAL CREDITS

ABOUT THE AUTHORS

George G. Watson, Jr. is Director of the Economic Education Center at Tufts University and a high school economics teacher in Winchester, Massachusetts. He is a director of the Joint Council on Economic Education and is the President of the National Council for the Social Studies.

Peter H. Dublin is Director of the Curriculum Center at the Institute of Open Education/ Antioch Graduate Center in Cambridge, Massachusetts. He has taught in the New Haven, Connecticut, and New York City public schools.

Robert M. Harrington is an administrator in the Boston public schools. He has taught in Boston and has chaired numerous city-wide social studies curriculum committees.

Betty L. S. Bardige is associated with the Harvard University Graduate School of Education's human development program. She has taught and has edited and authored social studies materials.

Jacqueline H. Walsh is teaching in the Brookline, Massachusetts, public schools. She has also taught in Marblehead, Massachusetts, and has conducted curriculum workshops at many area colleges.

Economics: Meeting People's Needs has been developed by Intentional Educations, Inc., in cooperation with the editorial staff of Science Research Associates, Inc. Intentional Educations is a nonprofit educational group with headquarters in Cambridge, Massachusetts.

Designer: Martha Scotford Lange

Visual Coordinator: Rick Colson/Educational Images

Editor: Eleanor Gates

Permissions Editor: Margaret Harrington

Testers: Jim Campagna, Stoneham High School
Ted Martin, Cambridge High School
John McGloughlin, Chelmsford High School

Reading Consultants: Selma Abinader, Steve Conroy, Jane Cutter, Karla Delites, Marilyn Gigliotti

TABLE OF CONTENTS

UNIT TWO   MICRO-ECONOMICS

UNIT THREE   MACRO-ECONOMICS

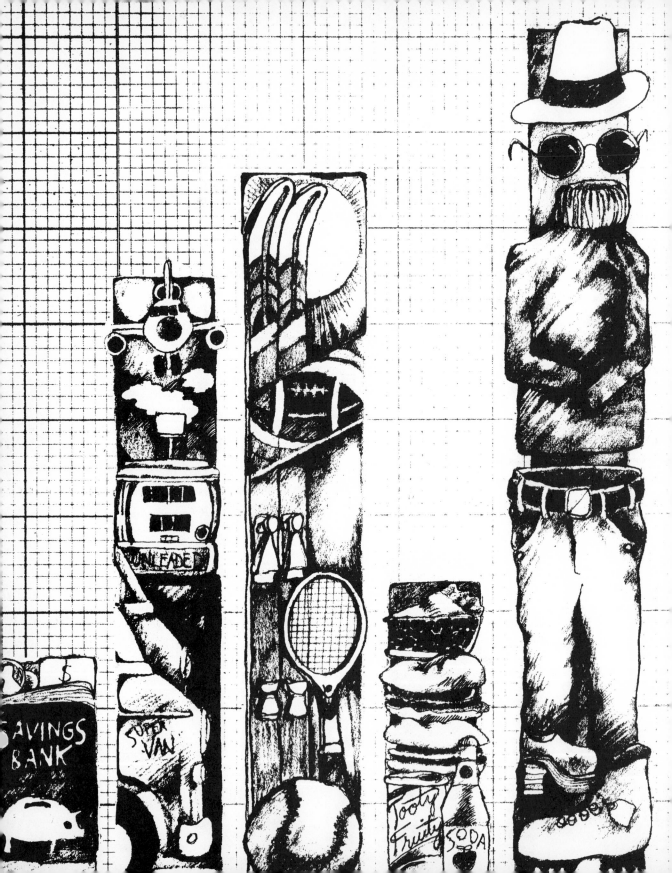

ONE

INTRODUCTION TO ECONOMICS

CHAPTER 1 THE ECONOMIST'S VIEW OF THE WORLD

Scarcity: Unlimited Wants and Limited Resources

Economics is a subject that people begin to learn about when they are still very young. Even before they start school, they make two very important economic discoveries. They find that there are lots of things in the world they want to have. They also find that they can't have them all. There is a gap between what they want and what they can have.

Later on young people learn another lesson. When they watch television commercials, they discover that there are thousands of things they or their parents could buy. Little by little, they settle into one of the two major economic roles people have, the role of *consumer*. A consumer is a person who uses *goods* (products) and *services*. Some of these goods, like food and drink, are actually consumed (eaten). Others, like soap or paper towels, are used up. Still others, like TV sets or cars, last a long time, but are used up sooner or later. Services are actions like haircutting, operations, or teaching, which are "used up" at the time they are provided.

Later on young people may work after school or during the summer to earn money to buy some of the things they want—records, or books, or maybe a bicycle. If so, they are learning about the other major economic role people have, the role of *producer*. A producer is someone who makes the goods or provides the services that consumers use. If a person shovels snow during the winter, or is a clerk in a store, she is providing a service. If a person makes something and then sells it, she is producing a good.

In order to produce something, however, a person must first have the right amount of *productive resources.* These are the materials from which goods and services are made. There are three kinds of productive resources: human resources, natural resources, and capital resources. *Human resources* are people and the physical and mental effort they put into their work. *Natural resources* are raw materials such as land, water, oil, timber, iron ore, gold, coal, and so on. *Capital resources* are goods that are used to produce other goods or services—things like tools and buildings.

People's ability to be producers depends on what kinds of productive resources they have. If they don't have enough of the right kind of resources, they will not be able to produce what they want to produce. For example, to shovel snow, two kinds of resources would be needed: human (a person's own labor) and capital (a good snow shovel). If a person catches cold and can't work for a while, her level of production will go down. And if the snow shovel breaks, she won't be able to produce at all. In the first case, the problem is a lack of human resources. In the second case, it is a lack of capital resources.

The same is true for the economy as a whole. No economy can produce the things people want if it does not have enough of the right kind of resources. And no economy has an unlimited supply of resources. Another way of saying this is to say that resources are *scarce. Economics* is the study of how people use their

What kinds of things might this child be learning? What does this have to do with economics?

productive resources to make the things they need and want and of how they decide who will get them. Human wants tend to be unlimited, but human, natural, and capital resources are, unfortunately, limited.

Human wants are unlimited for two reasons. First, there are some things, such as food, clothing, and shelter, that people never stop needing as long as they live. These things get consumed (used up) pretty fast and have to be replaced. Second, no matter how much people have, they always seem to want more. If they have plenty of the basic necessities of life, then they want other things, luxuries like record players or motorbikes. And if they get those things, then they want still more. Even the very rich somehow manage to find new things to buy.

A society can deal with this problem of unlimited wants and limited resources in four ways:

1. People can simply do without some of the things they want. Selecting the most important goods and services and doing without the others is by far the most widespread method.
2. People can create more resources. New natural resources, such as oil fields, can be located. Workers can be taught new skills. Better tools can be invented. All these things make it possible to produce more goods and services so that people can have more of what they want.

3. People can produce more by making better use of the resources they already have. Using supermarket cash registers to keep inventory as well as to collect money is one example.
4. People can redistribute goods and services so that everyone has enough but no one has too much or too little. Taxing adults to provide schools for children is a simple form of redistribution.

Individuals, like societies, must deal with the problem of scarcity. You probably want many things—clothes, entertainment, friends, independence, status. You may also have a number of resources—time, energy, money, talent, knowledge and skills, charm, intelligence, imagination. Yet your resources are limited. Your dreams are often bigger than you can satisfy.

Scarcity forces you to make choices. You have to decide what you want most. At the same time, you must find ways to use your resources wisely, in order to get what you want. The same is true for society. Each economy has a certain amount of human, natural, and productive resources. But there are even more wants and needs. People need food, clothing, housing, transportation, and many other things. When you study economics, you study how it is decided what will be produced, and who will get them when they are.

"Oh...oh!"

☐ The reading for this lesson comes from a short story by O. Henry. The people in it have very few resources. They must decide how to use them. Because they want more than they can have, they must make some hard choices. As you read it, ask yourself these questions:
1. What resources do Della and Jim have? How do they use them?
2. In what sense were Della's and Jim's choices foolish? In what sense were they wise?
3. What do you want? What and how much can you have?

THE GIFT OF THE MAGI

One dollar and eighty-seven cents. That was all. And sixty cents of it was in pennies. To-morrow would be Christmas Day. She had been saving every penny she could for months, with this result. Twenty dollars a week doesn't go far. Expenses had been greater than she had calculated. They always are. Only $1.87 to buy a present for Jim. Her Jim. Many a happy hour she had spent planning for something nice for him. Something fine and rare and sterling—something worthy of the honour of being owned by Jim.

Now, there were two possessions of the James Dillingham Youngs in which they both took a mighty pride. One was Jim's gold watch that had been his father's and his grandfather's. The other was Della's hair. Had the Queen of Sheba lived in the flat across the airshaft, Della would have let her hair hang out the window some day to dry just to depreciate Her Majesty's jewels and gifts. Had King Solomon been the janitor, with all his treasures piled up in the basement, Jim would have pulled out his watch every time he passed, just to see him pluck at his beard from envy.

So now Della's beautiful hair fell about her, rippling and shining like a cascade of brown waters. It reached below her knee and made itself almost a garment for her. And then she did it up again nervously and quickly. Once she faltered for a minute and stood still while a tear or two splashed on the worn red carpet.

On went her old brown jacket; on went her old brown hat. With a whirl of skirts and with the brilliant sparkle still in her eyes, she fluttered out the door and down the stairs to the street.

Where she stopped the sign read: "Mme. Sofronie. Hair Goods of All Kinds." One flight up Della ran, and collected herself, panting. Madame, large, too white, chilly, hardly looked the "Sofronie."

"Will you buy my hair?" asked Della.

"I buy hair," said Madame. "Take yer hat off and let's have a sight at the looks of it."

Down rippled the brown cascade.

"Twenty dollars," said Madame, lifting the mass with a practised hand.

"Give it to me quick," said Della.

Oh, and the next two hours tripped by on rosy wings. Forget the hashed metaphor. She was ransacking the stores for Jim's present.

She found it at last. It surely had been made for Jim and no one else. It was a platinum fob chain simple and chaste in design. As soon as she saw it she knew that it must be Jim's. It was like him. Quietness and value—the description applied to both. Twenty-one dollars they took from her for it, and she hurried home with the 87 cents. With that chain on his watch Jim might be properly anxious about the time in any company. Grand as the watch was, he sometimes looked at it on the sly on account of the old leather strap that he used in place of a chain.

When Della reached home, she looked at her reflection in the mirror long, carefully, and critically.

"If Jim doesn't kill me," she said to herself, "before he takes a second look at me, he'll say I look like a Coney Island chorus girl. But what else could I do—oh! what could I do with a dollar and eighty-seven cents?"

The door opened and Jim stepped in and closed it. He looked thin and very serious. Poor fellow, he was only twenty-two—and to be burdened with a family! He needed a new overcoat and he was without gloves.

Jim stopped inside the door, as immovable as a setter at the scent of quail. His eyes were fixed upon Della, and there was an expression in them that she could not read, and it terrified her. It was not anger, nor surprise, not disapproval, nor horror, nor any of the sentiments that she had been prepared for. He simply stared at her fixedly with that peculiar expression on his face.

Della wriggled off the table and went for him.

"Jim, darling," she cried, "don't look at me that way. I had my hair cut off and sold it because I couldn't have lived through Christmas without giving you a present. It'll grow out again—you won't mind, will you? I just had to do it. My hair grows awfully fast."

"You've cut off your hair?" asked Jim.

"Don't you like me just as well, anyhow? I'm me without my hair, ain't I?"

Out of his trance Jim seemed quickly to wake. He enfolded his Della.

Jim drew a package from his overcoat pocket and threw it upon the table.

"Don't make any mistake, Dell," he said, "about me. I don't think there's anything in the way of a haircut or a shave or a shampoo that could make me like my girl any less. But if you'll unwrap that package you may see why you had me going a while at first."

White fingers and nimble tore at the string and paper. There lay The Combs—the set of combs, side and back, that Della had worshipped for long in a Broadway window. Beautiful combs just the shade to wear in the beautiful vanished hair. Her heart had simply craved and yearned over them without the least hope of possession. And now, they were hers, but the tresses that should have adorned the coveted adornments were gone.

But she hugged them to her bosom, and at length she was able to look up with dim eyes and a smile and say: "My hair grows so fast, Jim!"

And then Della leaped up like a little singed cat and cried, "Oh, oh!"

Jim had not yet seen his beautiful present. She held it out to him eagerly upon her open palm. Jim tumbled down on the couch and put his hands under the back of his head and smiled.

"Dell," said he, "let's put our Christmas presents away and keep 'em a while. They're too nice to use just at present. I sold the watch to get the money to buy your combs. And now suppose you put the chops on."

The magi, as you know, were wise men—wonderfully wise men—who brought gifts to the Babe in the manger. They invented the art of giving Christmas presents. Being wise, their gifts were no doubt wise ones, possibly bearing the privilege of exchange in case of duplication. And here I have lamely related to you the uneventful chronicle of two foolish children in a flat who most unwisely sacrificed for each other the greatest treasures of their house. But in a last word to the wise of these days let it be said that of all who give gifts these two were the wisest. Of all who give and receive gifts, such as they are wisest. Everywhere they are wisest. They are the magi.

What do you think makes objects like these so valuable?

ACTIVITIES

This activity will help you to look at some of the ways scarcity develops and at the kinds of choices it can force you to make.

1. Imagine you have just received $2,000 to spend on any of the following goods and services.

Number available	Goods and services for sale	Cost for each unit
3	used sports car	$1,400
5	someone to do your homework	500
10	ability to jump off the ground 3 feet	100
4	clothing store credit card	1,000
1	all A's on your report card	2,000
2	apartment of your own	1,700
3	popular girl/boy friend	750
2	college expenses	900
5	your choice of an important responsibility	500
1	old car	350
7	somebody to do all your home chores for you	50
3	acquisition of a saleable skill	400

(Note: Unspent money returns to teacher.)

2. Split into groups of ten to twelve students each. As a group, first decide which items on the list are scarce and why.
3. Then all members of each group make a list of how they personally would spend the $2,000.
4. One person in each group is chosen to tally the individual lists. Then each group discusses which of the items on the list are scarce and what makes them scarce.

5. All of the goods and services are available to members of each group, but only as many as appear on the list and only at the price given. As a group, decide how each member can spend the $2,000. No member can spend more than $2,000, and the group cannot purchase more than what is on the list.

6. Discussion questions
   a. How did you decide what you wanted to buy before you knew the choices made by others in the group? after you knew their choices?
   b. What influenced the scarcity of a particular item?
   c. Did you have to give up anything to gain something you really wanted more? Explain.
   d. Suppose five people wanted a used sports car. How might it be decided which two of the five people must do without one?

What kinds of things might these people produce or consume? In what ways might they adjust to the resources available?

Choice-Making: Opportunity Costs and Tradeoffs

All production involves a cost. This is counted not simply in terms of money but also in terms of the resources used. In building a bridge, for example, the *real costs* of the bridge are the human, capital, and natural resources it uses up. To build a bridge requires the labor of many people and the use of many tools and machines. It also requires natural resources: the iron to make the steel to make the bridge.

Since resources are limited and human wants are unlimited, people and societies must make choices as to what they want most. Each choice involves costs, which economists call *opportunity costs*. For example, a person might have a choice between spending an evening at the movies or staying at home to study. The opportunity cost of going to the movies is the studying that could have been done in the same time. If a person has more than two choices, then there is also more than one opportunity cost. He could earn money baby-sitting or he could watch television. If any one of these things is done, the opportunity costs of doing it are the other things that could have been done instead.

Likewise, when steel is used to make a bridge instead of a hospital, the loss in hospitals is the opportunity cost of making the bridge. In fact, whatever resources are used for the bridge are then no longer available for something else.

When people make a choice between two possible uses of their resources, they

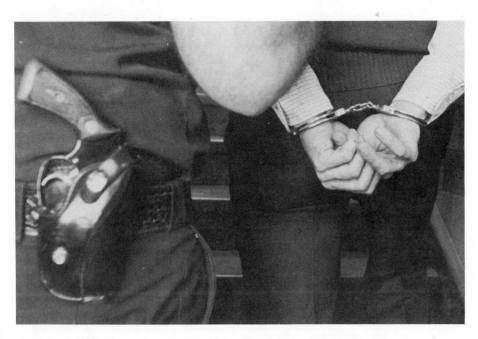

What might some of the real costs of this situation be?

are making a *tradeoff* between them. A person who goes to the movies instead of studying is making a tradeoff between two uses of his time (a valuable resource). But tradeoffs seldom involve only two choices. For instance, steel can be used for things other than bridges and hospitals. Steel can also be used for sports arenas, coat hangers, screwdrivers, skyscrapers, and a thousand other things. So the tradeoff between using steel for bridges and hospitals could just as easily have been stated as a tradeoff between coat hangers and skyscrapers, or sports arenas and screwdrivers.

Making choices that best satisfy human wants requires that people be aware of what all the tradeoffs are. That way the society will understand the true costs of making one decision as opposed to another. It can then make the decision that best fits its values and goals.

How can the concepts of opportunity costs and tradeoffs be used to make sense of the economy? One way is to construct a simple plan of the economy called an *economic model.* An economic model is a little bit like a model airplane. It helps explain how the real thing works, even if it doesn't fly. When models are used to help solve economic problems, their usefulness depends on the assumptions made about the world.

A useful economic model for opportunity costs is a *production possibilities* model. This model can be used to explain the production choices open to a nation. What are the assumptions of the model? First, only two goods or two kinds

Table 2-1
Production Possibilities
in Alpha

POSSIBILITIES	ICE CREAM (MILLIONS OF GALLONS)	MISSILES (THOUSANDS)
A	0	100
B	2.5	75
C	5	50
D	7.5	25
E	10	0

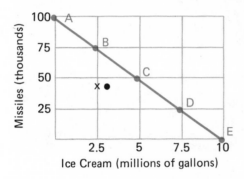

Figure 2-1

of goods can be produced. Second, the country's resources can be used to produce either good.

For example, assume that a make-believe country called Alpha can produce only two kinds of goods: missiles and ice cream. (This is an extremely simple model, but it will show how economic models work.) Now, if Alpha uses all of its resources to produce missiles, it can make 100,000. If it uses all of its resources to produce ice cream, it can produce 10,000,000 gallons. If Alpha uses half of its resources to produce missiles and half to produce ice cream, it can make 50,000 missiles and 5,000,000 gallons of ice cream. Table 2-1 shows these and other possibilities.

These possibilities are shown graphically in Figure 2-1, with ice cream measured on the horizontal axis and missiles on the vertical axis. The same possibilities, A, B, C, D, and E, listed in Table 2-1 are shown as points on the graph in Figure 2-1. The line joining these points includes all the other ways in which Alpha could produce using all its resources. Alpha can also produce any combination below the line, such as Point X. Producing at Point X would give Alpha 25,000 missiles and 5,000,000 gallons of ice cream. Any point below the line shows a combination that does not use all of Alpha's resources.

Now, using this model and the concepts of opportunity costs and tradeoffs shows what choices face the leaders of Alpha. Suppose for the moment that

Alpha is producing 5,000,000 gallons of ice cream and 50,000 missiles (possibility C in Table 2-1). Alpha's leaders decide that they need a stronger armed force. They will need more missiles. So they change their production plans. They now will produce 2,500,000 gallons of ice cream and 75,000 missiles (possibility B in Table 2-1). Looking at their situation carefully, Alpha's leaders see that the opportunity cost of those 25,000 extra missiles will be 2.5 million gallons of ice cream. In other words, Alpha will have traded off 2.5 million gallons of ice cream for 25,000 missiles.

What is true for make-believe Alpha is true of countries in the real world. A million dollars spent on a guided missile cannot be spent on a school. On the other hand, a million dollars spent on a school cannot be spent on a guided missile. The economic model allows such tradeoffs to be measured so that the country can make sound choices as to how it will use its resources. But first it must decide which it needs more: schools or missiles.

You may not always be aware of the opportunity costs of what you want. When you analyze these costs, you can make better choices. Once you have seen the opportunity costs of your goal, you must choose between your conflicting wants. Which is more important for now? What about the future?

If you are unwilling to make the tradeoff, you may be able to find another option. Perhaps you can compromise, taking some of each. Maybe you can find a way to get both by giving up something else.

What are some of the opportunity costs associated with this use of resources?

The reading for this lesson looks at a political issue in economic terms. It presents some of the tradeoffs that a society must consider in choosing what kind of an army to have. As you read it, ask yourself the following questions:

1. What are the opportunity costs of a volunteer army? of the draft?
2. How should the society decide in this situation? What factors are most important?
3. How do you decide when you want conflicting things?

WHICH IS THE CHEAPER ARMY?

For many years, there has been an argument over what kind of army the United States should have. Many people want to do away with the draft and have an all-volunteer army instead. Others say that an all-volunteer army would be too expensive. The army would have to offer high salaries to attract new recruits. This would add greatly to its cost.

In the early 1970's, Congress ended the draft, but the argument goes on.

On the surface, it seems that an all-volunteer army does cost more. Without the draft, the army must compete with the civilian careers people go into. It does this by paying higher salaries than it would pay draftees. But there are costs to the army and to society over and above salaries. Society as a whole must pay certain costs if it uses the draft to create an army. Because these costs are not as clear as wages they are often overlooked.

First, a draft army may be larger than an all-volunteer army, which naturally increases its cost. This happens because the draft allows the army to pay artificially low wages. People are required to serve even if the army pays them less than they could earn at a civilian job. Since extra people come so cheaply, the army may draft large numbers of recruits. These people do what machines would ordinarily do at a lower cost. This is an important cost because it drains people away from civilian jobs for which they might be more qualified.

A second cost to society has to do with the length of time people serve in the army. In most jobs, an employer invests time and money in training new people. The same is true of the army. In regular civilian jobs, an employer wants to hold on to the people who have been trained in order to keep *turnover costs* (the costs of replacing workers who leave with new workers) as low as possible. But this doesn't happen with the draft. The draft is usually for a short period of time, say two or three years. Just as people finish their training, they leave the army. The army then has to train new people all over again. The cost to society can thus be measured in terms of wasted machines and time spent on the constant training of new soldiers.

A third overlooked cost of the draft is the waste of talent that occurs when all people are forced to do the same job. Society spends a lot of money training an engineer. If that engineer is drafted and washes dishes for two years, society isn't getting the services it paid for. The same would be true of a high school dropout who was good at electronics. If that person served in the military police, society would lose the contribution he might have made had he been able to use his talents in his specialty.

There was a draft during the American Civil War. This was not a pure draft or a lottery draft. It was possible for wealthy men who were drafted to pay others to replace them. For example, a lawyer who was drafted could pay someone else to take his place in the army. This was possible because the lawyer could make more money practicing law than it cost him to hire a substitute to join the army. Even the man

What might be some of the tradeoffs illustrated here?

who served in the army was better off because of the amount he got for replacing the lawyer.

There was, of course, a cost to the worker if he quit a job to serve in the army. This cost is called an *opportunity cost*. In this case, it is the money the person lost in not being able to work at his old job. But the man would have earned less than the lawyer. Economists would say that it was efficient for this man to replace the lawyer. The man with the lowest opportunity cost fought in the army. The man with the highest opportunity cost could use his knowledge and skills in civilian life where they were most needed.

The same is true today. If a person who earns $10,000 a year is drafted, the economy is giving up $10,000 worth of services. In return, society gets a smaller amount of military services from that person. Thus, the wages paid this person in the army are not the true cost of drafting him. Just as important is the difference between the lost value of his civilian services and the value of his military services. Society as a whole suffers because civilian output is lower when people do not work at their regular jobs.

So, is an all-volunteer army really more expensive? It is true that wages to people in the army are now higher to attract enough new recruits. But the size of the army is smaller, and that saves some money. There are also enough people available to fill jobs in civilian life. Today, many more soldiers are placed in jobs where they are more productive. It has become expensive to waste their abilities. Society as a whole benefits when each soldier contributes more efficiently to the national defense.

Of course, there is more to the army than just economics. Many people feel that a draft, at least one that requires everyone to serve, is fairer. Others feel that the army can be an important experience for all young men and women. Often, a country can want conflicting things. It wants the cheapest, but it also wants the best. The most efficient, and the most fair. How does a country decide when it wants conflicting things?

Select from this text or any other source at least five photographs that demonstrate energy, material, and human resources. What might these images have looked like 100 years ago? What might they look like 100 years from now? Who are these resources available to? What are some of the real costs associated with their use?

VISUAL
ACTIVITY

ACTIVITIES

In this activity, you must make a choice between two goals that may or may not conflict.

1. Imagine that you want to become popular. You must decide whether you will spend your time on activities that will make you popular with teachers or on activities that will make you popular with other students. You must plan activities for five hours. You may choose to divide your time between the two kinds of activities. But, whatever your choice, you must consider both its positive and negative aspects.

2. Use an economic model to better understand the nature of your choice:
   a. Time is the unit of measure.
   b. Time spent on activities intended to make you popular with your peers is on the vertical axis.
   c. Time spent on activities intended to make you popular with your teachers is on the horizontal axis.

3. Place your point (the decision as to how to spend your time) on the graph in the Workbook or copy the following graph on a separate sheet of paper.

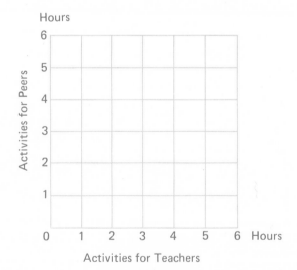

4. Now imagine situations that would require you to change how you spent your time. As you think of other possibilities, place them on the graph and record them in the chart in the Workbook. If you don't have a Workbook, copy the chart in the text on a separate piece of paper.

Possibilities	Time with Peers	Time with Teachers

Compare the opportunity costs of the various possibilities.

5. Discussion questions
    a. What assumptions did you make when you decided how to spend your time?
    b. Would it be possible for someone to pick the point 4,4 on the graph? Why?
    c. What assumptions does the economic model make?

The Questions Economists Ask

Economics is the study of how scarce resources are used to produce goods and services that will satisfy human wants and needs. Every country faces the basic problem of scarcity. Economists are interested in how people deal with this problem. In studying an economy they will ask: What answers does this country give to the basic economic questions? And how does it arrive at them?

The following are economic questions that every country must answer for itself.

1. What goods and services will be produced?
2. How will they be produced?
3. Who will get them?
4. How much will be produced for now and how much for later?

There are many possible mixtures of goods and services that can be produced with a country's human, natural, and capital resources. Thus, the first question raises many others. For instance, are more goods and services for consumers wanted? If so, which consumer goods are needed the most? Is it better to produce more shoes or more electric dishwashers? Does the country want more capital resources? If so, then what tools and machines must be produced? Which public policies are favored? Do people want more national defense or better health care, more roads or better schools?

The answer to the "How will they be produced?" question depends on the resources available to the country and on the knowledge and skills of its work force. Not all cultures have the same mix of human, natural, and capital resources. For example, a country might have plenty of workers but few natural resources. Or it might have plenty of natural resources, such as minerals or timber, but few capital resources, such as tools. Without the tools needed to get at its minerals, those resources are of little value.

The first two questions deal with the production of goods and services. The "Who will get them?" question deals with the way goods and services are distributed to consumers. Does the country want to help certain groups, or does it want goods and services to be shared equally by all? Should a person's share of the goods and services be based on her contribution to production? Or should it be based on some other factor, like need? And how is a person's "contribution" measured in the first place? Each society will come up with a different answer to these questions, based on its own unique customs and values.

The "How much will be produced for now and how much for later?" question involves two decisions. First, the country will have to decide whether its natural resources should be used now or conserved for later use. Second, it must decide what mix of consumer goods and capital goods (goods used to produce other goods later) it wants. This is an extremely important decision, for it will shape the economy for years to come. By creating more capital goods (machines, tools, factories, and so on), the country is adding to its capital. With more capital resources, the country is making it possible to produce more goods and services in the future.

How does this image relate to the questions on the facing page?

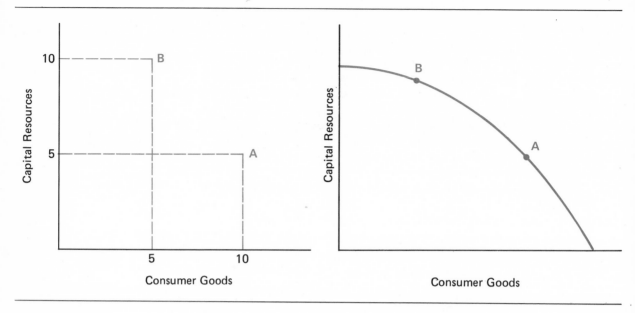

Figure 3-1 (left)
Figure 3-2 (right)

On the other hand, by deciding to produce more *consumer* goods, the country will be able to satisfy the immediate needs and wants of its population.

An economic model can be used to show the tradeoffs between capital goods and consumer goods. The graph in Figure 3-1 shows this tradeoff.

The x-axis of the graph measures the number of consumer goods, and the y-axis measures the number of capital resources. Point A shows that ten consumer goods and five capital resources are produced in a certain year. Point B shows just the opposite: ten capital resources and five consumer goods.

Many other points could be put on the graph to show how much of one kind of good there could be if there were so much of another. The line connecting these points tells what amounts of production of the two goods are possible. Figure 3-2 represents this *production possibilities model.*

Figure 3-3 is a production possibilities model for a poor farming country during a period of time that can be labeled Period I. Three mixtures of consumer goods and capital goods that might be produced have been marked A1, A2, and A3. A1 represents a decision to produce only consumer goods. A2 represents a reduction in consumer goods as a tradeoff for some capital goods. A3 represents a decision to sacrifice even more consumer goods in order to have more capital goods.

Figure 3-4 shows the results, at a later period (Period II), of each of the deci-

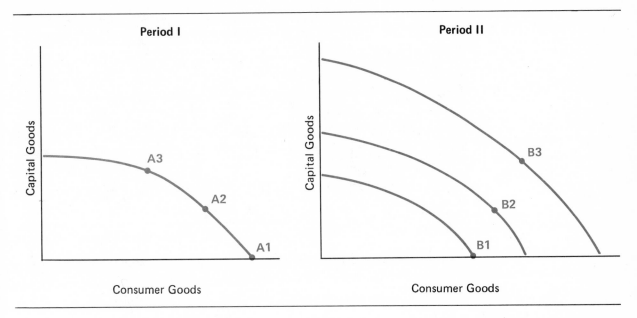

Period I   Period II

Capital Goods

A3
A2
A1

Consumer Goods

Capital Goods

B3
B2
B1

Consumer Goods

Figure 3-3   Period I (left)

Figure 3-4   Period II (right)

sions shown in Figure 3-3. If the country chose point A1, it did not produce any capital goods. Thus, its total production of goods and services could not increase. The line that B1 is on shows this situation. The line that B2 is on shows the results of decision A2. By slightly increasing its production of capital goods and reducing its production of consumer goods, the country has been able to increase its total production. The line that B3 is on shows the result of decision A3. In return for sacrificing even more consumer goods during Period I, the country has enjoyed a great increase in consumer goods and capital goods in Period II.

However, decision A3 represents a big sacrifice in consumer goods, especially for a country that is already poor. Governments that ask their people to make such huge sacrifices often do not last from Period I to Period II.

The questions economists ask reflect their views of the important choices countries must make. They do not always ask questions that others may think are important. Why, for instance, do people want certain goods and services? What do people really want? And what are they taught to want? How do people feel about their resources? What values do production choices reflect? Is the system fair? These questions could be asked by people who think differently from economists.

Economics, then, provides one useful way of looking at the world. Throughout this book, you will also be developing other ways. You will see that the way you view the world determines the choices you make.

How vital is this
"product"? Who pays
for it?

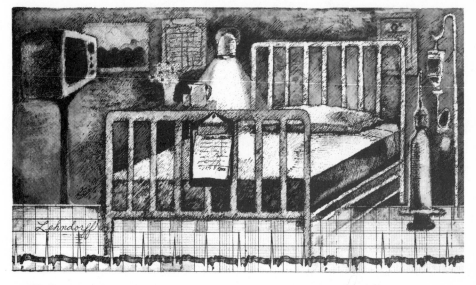

☐ The reading for this lesson is adapted from a study by the
anthropologist Ruth Benedict. It describes the Kwakiutl, an Indian
tribe living in British Columbia, Canada. The reading describes a
special kind of contest once important in their society. This contest
takes on different meanings depending on who is viewing it. As you
read the selection, ask yourself the following questions:
1. How would an economist view this event?
2. How do you think the people involved viewed this event?
3. How does your way of looking at a situation affect your choices.

THE KWAKIUTL AND THEIR POTLATCH

The Kwakiutl were a North American Indian tribe living on Vancouver
Island, on the west coast of Canada. They are one of the few
Northwest Coast Indian tribes that anthropologists in the twentieth
century have been able to study.

In many ways, the Kwakiutl were a wealthy tribe: They fished from
the sea and the sea was kind to them. They were well-known for their
vast amounts of possessions. They had two general kinds of
possessions. They owned material things, especially land and fishing
rights. Some families had to travel for miles to find a stretch of beach
from which they could dig clams.

The other kind of possession is harder to describe. Wealth for the Kwakiutl had become more than mere economic goods. Songs, myths, names of chiefs' house-posts, their dogs, their canoes, were all considered to be wealth. Valued privileges, like the right to tie a dancer to a post, were considered wealth, too, and were handed down from parents to children. One could see the change in a person's status from a change in his name. Every child was given a name at birth, but it only indicated where he was born. Throughout his life he tried for better and better names. Names depended on economic status. Did a man repay his loans with one hundred percent interest? How much did he give away at the potlatch ceremonies?

The Kwakiutl did not use wealth to get for themselves something of equal value in goods or services. They saw wealth as symbols of fixed values in a game they played to win. They saw life as a ladder of which the rungs were the names with their status and prestige. Each new step up the ladder required them to give away great amounts of wealth.

In the end, the reason the Kwakiutl cared about the names and the wealth was that they were used in a contest to shame their rivals. Each person, according to his means, vied with all others to outdistance them in giving away wealth. Since the chiefs were the major decision-makers in the culture, their ceremonies were the greatest examples of this.

In the contests between great chiefs the violence and the rivalry that were the heart of this culture found free scope. The story of the conflict of Fast Runner and of Throw Away, chiefs of the Kwakiutl, shows the way in which these contests become open enmity. The two chiefs were friends. Throw Away invited the clan of his friend to a feast of salmon berries and carelessly served the grease and berries in canoes that had not been cleaned sufficiently to do them honour. Fast Runner chose to take this as a gross insult. He refused the food, lying down with his black bear blanket drawn over his face, and all his relatives, seeing he was displeased, followed his example. The host urged them to eat, but Fast Runner had his speaker address him, complaining of the indignity: 'Our chief will not eat the dirty things you have offered, O dirty man.' Throw Away scornfully replied: 'Let it be as you say. You speak as if you were a person of very great wealth.' Fast Runner replied, 'Indeed I am a person of great wealth,' and he sent his messengers to bring his copper Sea Monster. They gave it to him, and he pushed it under the fire, 'to put out the fire of his rival.' Throw Away sent also for his copper. His attendants brought him Looked at Askance and he pushed it also under the fire in the feasting-place, 'to keep the fire burning.' But Fast Runner had also another copper,

Crane, and he sent for that and placed it upon the fire 'to smother it.' Throw Away had no other copper, so he could not add more fuel to keep his fire going and was defeated in the first round.

The following day Fast Runner returned the feast and sent his attendants to invite Throw Away. Throw Away meanwhile had pledged property enough to borrow another copper. Therefore when the crabapples and grease were set before him, he refused in the words which Fast Runner had used the day before, and sent his attendants to bring the copper Day Face. With this he extinguished his rival's fire. Fast Runner rose and addressed them: 'Now is my fire extinguished. But wait. Sit down again, and see the deed that I shall do.' He put on the excitement of the Dance of the Fools, of whom he was a member, and destroyed four canoes of his father-in-law's. His attendants brought them to the feasting-house and heaped them on the fire to take away the shame of having had their fire extinguished by Throw Away's copper. His guests at all costs had to remain where they were or admit defeat. The black bear blanket of Throw Away was scorched, and below his blanket the skin of his legs was blistered, but he held his ground. Only when the blaze had begun to die down, he arose as if nothing had happened and ate of the feast in order to show his complete indifference to the extravagance of his rival.

Fast Runner and Throw Away were now in open enmity. They chose, therefore, to give rival initiations into the secret societies, using their religious privileges rather than their secular. Throw Away secretly planned to give this Winter Ceremonial, and Fast Runner, hearing of it through his informers, determined to outdo him. Throw Away initiated a son and a daughter, but Fast Runner two sons and two daughters. Fast Runner now had outdistanced his rival.

Fast Runner had still another triumph. His daughters were being initiated as war dancers, and they asked to be put upon the fire. A

Who is this product produced for? How much is it needed?

great wall of firewood was raised about the fire, and the daughters were tied to boards ready to be committed to the flames. Instead, two slaves dressed like true war dancers and similarly tied to boards were put into the fire. For four days the daughters of Fast Runner remained in hiding, and then, from the ashes of the slaves which had been preserved, they apparently returned to life. Throw Away had nothing to match this great demonstration of privilege, and he and his men went off to fight the Nootka. Only one man returned to tell of the defeat and death of the war party.

This is told as a true story, and there are eye-witness accounts of other contests that vary only in the acts which the rival chiefs performed to demonstrate their greatness. On one occasion within the lifetime of men now living, the chief tried to 'put out' the fire of his rival with seven canoes and four hundred blankets, while his host poured oil upon the fire in opposition. The roof of the house caught fire and the whole house was nearly destroyed, while those who were concerned kept their places with assumed indifference and sent for more possessions to heap upon the fire. 'Then those who went to get the two hundred blankets returned, and they spread them over the fire of the host. Now they "put it out." '

Such contests were the peak of ambition. Their picture of the ideal man was drawn up in terms of these contests, and all the motivations proper to them were reckoned as virtue. An old chieftainess, addressing her son at a potlatch, admonished him: 'My tribe, I speak particularly to my son. Friends, you all know my name. You knew my father, and you know what he did with his property. He was reckless and did not care what he did. He gave away or killed slaves. He gave away or burned his canoes in the fire of the feast-house. He gave away sea-otter skins to his rivals in his own tribe or to chiefs of other tribes, or he cut them to pieces. You know that what I say is true. This, my son, is the road your father laid out for you, and on which you must walk. Your father was no common man. He was a true chief among the Koskimo. Do as your father did. Either tear up the button blankets or give them to the tribe which is our rival. That is all.' Her son answered: 'I will not block the road my father laid out for me. I will not break the law my chief laid down for me. I give these blankets to my rivals. The war that we are having now is sweet and strong.' He distributed the blankets.

ACTIVITIES

I. This activity has been organized into two parts. In each, you will have the chance to view an event within a society from two different perspectives.

1. The Kwakiutl had a unique way of choosing how their natural resources were best used. Analyze their society from an economic perspective by answering the four basic economic questions described in the narrative of this lesson. Complete the charts in the Workbook or copy the charts in the text onto another piece of paper.

Questions an Economist Would Ask
What is produced?
How is it produced?
For whom is it produced?
How much is produced?

2. Now analyze the Kwakiutl society from the perspective of a decision-maker by answering the following questions.

Questions a Decision-Maker Would Ask
What situations created the need for decisions?
Who has the power to make decisions?
What are the decisions meant to accomplish?
What are the consequences of these decisions?

3. Discussion questions
   a. How might this economic system affect this society?
   b. How might this way of making decisions affect this society?
   c. Did these people use their resources efficiently?
   d. Did these people use their resources wisely?
   e. How might your perspective affect the choices you make?

II. In this activity you will analyze the American family as an economic unit and as a decision-making unit.

1. Analyze the activities of your family as an economist would by answering the four basic questions on the chart in the Workbook or on a separate sheet of paper.

Questions an Economist Would Ask
What is produced?
How is it produced?
For whom is it produced?
How much is produced?

2. Now analyze the activities of your family from the point of view of a decision-maker by filling in this chart in the Workbook or on a separate sheet of paper.

Questions a Decision-Maker Would Ask
What situations created the need for decisions?
Who has the power to make decisions?
What are the decisions meant to accomplish?
What are the consequences of these decisions?

3. Discussion questions
   a. How were the perspectives of the economist and the decision-maker similar? How were they different?
   b. Which perspective was most useful? most interesting?
   c. What other points of view might you have used?

CHAPTER 2 THE NATURE AND TYPES OF IDEAL ECONOMIC SYSTEMS

Traditional Systems

In studying an economic system, economists look at two things, the answers given to the basic economic questions and how these answers are reached. The way a society makes economic decisions says a great deal about the pattern of its culture. It also tells about the society's politics, religion, and even its family life. Economics is only one part of a society's life. It influences, and is influenced by, all the other parts.

Economist Robert L. Heilbroner has found a simple way to look at the different methods of making economic decisions. He has said that economic systems can be classed into three main types or some mix of these types. These are economies run by *tradition,* by *command,* and by the *market.*

Traditional economic systems make decisions the way they have always been made in the past. Command systems permit a group of planners to answer the basic economic questions. Market systems rely on exchange or barter and a network of prices to determine what, how, for whom, and how much.

Tradition is by far the most widespread approach to economics. Traditional economies are tied to methods that grew up long ago by trial and error. They produce what has always been made in the same way it has always been. Jobs are handed down from parents to children so that skills can be kept up and the economy can survive. In some African countries, for example, most boys are taught to

Figure 4-1   Traditional Economy
How do people, culture, and resources affect the way decisions are made in a traditional economy?

build, plow, milk cattle, and sew skins. Most girls are taught to hoe, thatch roofs, and weave mats and baskets.

Answers to the "for whom" and "how much" questions are fixed by custom, habit, religion, or law in traditional cultures. Traditional hunting societies, like that of the Bushmen of the Kalahari Desert in southern Africa, follow custom in making economic decisions. They have rules for sharing their kills among the hunters and their families. The largest share usually goes to the best hunter. In this way, the best hunters survive when game is scarce. But in times of plenty the favored hunters share their portions so that no one eats more than any other.

Traditional cultures are conservative. When change does come, it is not always welcomed and may even be bitterly opposed. The fight of the Plains Indians against the building of the railroads across the United States was an example of such resistance. The Iron Horse and the white settlers who traveled on it were a

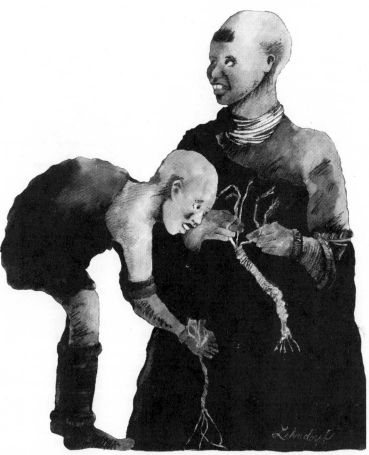

How might the skill this young girl learns affect her tribe's economy?

threat to the Plains Indian economy. They were rapidly killing off the buffalo, the Indians' most important natural resource.

One of the best known traditional cultures is found in North America. The Eskimos today are changing or losing many of the old ways as they mix more with other people from the United States and Canada. The following account, written by an explorer in 1913, shows the role that tradition then played in the Eskimo economy.

> It was the vanishing of the caribou from the inland coastal plain that drove down the Eskimo to the coast. Now it seems that the caribou are having a slight chance. In large districts where formerly they had to face the hunter, their only enemy is now the wolf. . . . (T)he Eskimo expects to find everything next year as he found it last year; and so the belief dies hard that the foothills had an endless supply of caribou. But when starvation had year after year taken off families by groups, the Eskimo finally realized that the caribou in large numbers were a thing of the past. They were so firmly impressed with the fact that now they are sure that no caribou are in the interior. They had once thought they would be there forever.

Wars, climate, and other outside forces can cause traditional countries to change. In the 1860's, Japan depended almost wholly on farming. Then came contact with Western nations and the rapid growth of Japanese industry and trade in the twentieth century. World War II and military occupation by U.S. forces after the war followed. All these helped transform Japan's economic system into one based more on the market than on tradition.

Many other countries in Asia, Africa, and Latin America are now subject to outside influences. Some of the changes that come—like improved seed and plows—are easily accepted. Others, like women working outside the home, are fought because they conflict with deeply held values of the culture.

In a traditional culture, then, economic choices are limited. People do things "the way they are supposed to be done," because these ways have meant survival in the past. They do not know any other way.

A person in a traditional economy is to some extent like a member of a family. The family member may disagree with other members but must go along just the same. Similarly, people in traditional economies see their way of doing things and their elders' choices as right. It is hard for them to believe that there may be other or better methods.

As a young child, you probably did not question your parents' teachings. However, even as an adult, you will find that many of your choices are made for you by the traditions of your family, group, or society. In many cases, it may not even occur to you to do things in new ways. You may take certain jobs, go to certain kinds of schools, get married, have children, live in certain places without ever seriously looking at alternatives.

"Dean Bozo is big on tradition."

☐ The reading for this lesson comes from a book by Joe E. Pierce. It describes work and marriage in a traditional economy. It shows how tradition shapes, and even eliminates, some basic life choices. As you read it, ask yourself the following questions:
1. How does tradition answer the basic economic questions in this society?
2. What alternatives do Mahmud and his family not have because of their traditions?
3. What traditions eliminate choices for you?

— LIFE IN A TURKISH VILLAGE —

The cold hard winter passed, and most of the people had enough to eat and lived to see the spring. Some died, of course, but the villagers rarely knew why. So far as the people could see there were no solutions to these problems, for it had always been so, and when anyone asked why, they were always given the answer that it was the will of Allah.

One morning, after the snows had gone, but the bitter cold winds were still blowing across the hills, his father was fastening the heavy wooden yoke onto the oxen when Mahmud came into the room that was reserved for the animals.

"Let's go together and plow this morning, my son," the older man said.

"What can I do, my father?" the boy responded with enthusiasm.

"You can best watch today, my son, but soon you must help, for you will some day have to plow the fields alone."

As they walked along, Mahmud examined the plow very carefully, because he knew that one day he would probably have to make one like it. This was the only piece of equipment that they would need that day, as it would take about a month, working from sunup till sundown, to plow the four acres that his father had decided he would cultivate this year. Whenever he finished turning the soil, he would replace the plow with a heavy log and ride this, behind the same pair of oxen, over the field several times to break up the heavy clods and shake stones loose from the dirt. However, the first and most difficult job was to break the hard-packed, rocky ground so that the seeds could take root and grow.

It took the two of them well over an hour to reach the spot to be planted, and the sun was well up in the sky when they arrived. They did not begin to plow immediately, because the ground had to be cleared of the larger rocks first. This made it much easier for the oxen to pull the dull wooden plowshare through the very hard earth. Picking up the stones, which ranged in size from that of an acorn to a small melon and which lay scattered thickly over the surface of the ground, they made neat piles of rock outside the area to be plowed. These stacks began to look like small buildings, and Mahmud liked to pretend that these structures were the houses of a village of little people, and he made up all kinds of stories about what happened to these people.

By shortly after the noon hour they had cleared nearly half an acre, which was twice as much as a man could plow up in one day, so Mahmud sat down to rest, and his father took up the plow and began the long hard job of following the oxen back and forth across what would soon be his wheat field.

Days passed, each very much like the first, and all of the rocks were cleared from the surface. The ground was broken, and Mahmud followed his father and picked up many more stones that had been turned up during the plowing. Finally, after all this had been done, and his father had decided that they had broken all the land that he and his family could properly tend that year, Mahmud was allowed to ride on the clod-breaking log (harrow). His body added weight to the implement, which made it more efficient, and also gave father and son a chance to work more closely together so that Mahmud could learn how to be a man.

As the weeks and months went by Mahmud grew older and entered school, just as his parents had said that he would. Each morning he walked the two kilometers to the city in company with the other school-age children, taking half a loaf of bread and some fruit for lunch, and returned in the evening. School life was very different from that in the village, but when he was at home things went on pretty much as they always had.

Even in the village, however, things new to Mahmud happened occasionally, and one evening he heard his father and mother talking softly in the hallway between the two living rooms. They were whispering so that no one could understand what they were saying, but this only made him want more than ever to hear, and so he edged nearer to where they were standing and listened intently, in the shadows near the doorway. The conversation concerned his older sister who was nearly sixteen and old enough to be married.

''What will you tell them?'' his mother said.

''I don't know just yet,'' his father answered.

''But they will come tomorrow, and you know that they have been here twice already. They will want to know tomorrow, and you cannot wait until then to decide,'' the wife insisted.

How was this resource lost to the Plains Indians? How did this affect their economy?

In what ways might these people participate in a traditional economy?

This reminded Mahmud of the two special visits in recent weeks by the mother and father of one of his friends who lived just down the street. He had not understood their purpose then, but the family had come to look over his sister as a prospective wife for their son who would soon be old enough to go into the army and should be married before he left. Thinking back on the visits, Mahmud remembered how his sister had each time been told well in advance that they were coming and that she had spent hours getting dressed, preparing fruits and nuts for the visitors, and asking her mother if she should do this or that when they arrived.

At the very first knock she ran to the door. As they came in, she kissed first the back of the hand of the man and lifted it to her forehead, then did the same to the woman. Mahmud's mother and father had also welcomed the guests. Then the men had gone into the men's room and the women into the women's. As they sat talking, the visitors would call in and ask for this or that, and Mahmud's sister would run to bring what they asked for as quickly as she could. On the second visit the mother had asked her to make some coffee, and she had very carefully and skillfully demonstrated her ability to handle cooking utensils. They had seemed pleased, and his sister appeared to be happy, but he did not quite understand it all.

Now it became clear, as he listened to the talk of his mother and father. The visitors had thought his sister would make a good wife for their son or they would not have come back again. Now that they were coming a third time, it meant that they might very well ask for a final decision about the arrangements. If they were not completely satisfied, they might come once more, but Mahmud's mother felt that they should have an answer ready before tomorrow, just in case the boy's parents did want to settle it all then.

The prospective husband was of good family. He was quite nice looking, a hard worker, and the daughter liked him, from a distance of course, as she was not allowed to talk with boys his age. There

How might these people have known how and what to grow?

seemed to be no obvious reason for not accepting, but Mahmud's father was worried about how much money the family would give. He realized that his daughter was an unusually pretty girl and that this was only the first family to ask. He wondered if they should accept if the man offered them 5000 lira, bargain for more, or just wait for a better offer, but Mahmud's mother said that almost any girl in the village was worth that much, and Fatma should be worth much more.

This was not a sale of their daughter, because all the money would be used to buy furniture for the couple after they were married and to pay for the wedding feast. Still, the more they could get, the better their daughter would be able to outfit her household. After much discussion it was decided that they would not accept less than 6000 lira, but that would be a fair amount considering that Fatma would go into a fine family and, after all, she was getting an exceptional husband out of the deal too.

Mahmud wondered why no one in the village ever married people from the city, or other villages, but he knew that for some reason this was forbidden. Someone said that there was a village somewhere, where the people were also their relatives, to which young people could go to marry, but he had never known of anyone who had done it. He wondered also if there really were such a place, and if so where it was, but these things he did not know.

Late in the day a knock was heard on the door sounding their arrival. Again he watched as his sister went to the door, kissed the hands of the visitors respectfully, and jumped to serve their every wish. Finally, after a rather long visit, the man asked Mahmud's father what he thought of arranging a marriage between the two young people. He had been cautious, approving with some hesitancy, until the man offered 7000 lira in payment to cover the wedding costs. With the amount proffered it would have been almost impossible for anyone not to enter wholeheartedly into the agreement, and it was settled that within a few weeks the couple would be married.

ACTIVITIES

I. Like people living in a traditional economic system, you have probably accepted some family traditions without question. This role play activity focuses on the origins of holiday traditions within the family and on the possibility of creating new traditions.

1. Split into two groups. The first group meets briefly to devise a role play about what a family would do at a gift-giving holiday. Be sure to include specific holiday traditions that have been observed by group members' families.
2. The second group observes the first group's role play and analyzes it by answering the following questions:
   a. What traditions were observed? What was the purpose of each tradition?
   b. Where did the traditions come from?
   c. What was the purpose of each tradition?
   d. Could these same purposes be better fulfilled in other ways?
   e. How are people limited by these traditions?
3. The second group meets briefly to devise a role play about another family at a gift-giving holiday. The goal of this role play situation is to think up different customs that would fulfill the same purposes behind the traditions in the first role play.
4. The first group watches this second role play and analyzes it using the questions listed in point 2.
5. Both groups share their observations and discuss the following questions:
   a. Which traditions would be easiest to accept?
   b. Which traditions permit the most freedom? Which the least?
   c. Which traditions strike you as having most meaning?
   d. What other purposes could different traditions fulfill?

II. This activity will help you to see how your expectations of the future have been shaped by tradition. You will have the chance to compare your work with that of your classmates and to study the similarities and differences in your predictions.

1. Think of three times in your life when you expect certain events to happen. You may be specific in selecting an age, or you may choose three general age ranges (for example, 20–25, 45–50, 70–75).

20–25	45–50	70–75

2. Cut pictures from newspapers, magazines, greeting cards, etc., to show the events that you predict will take place in your future. Make a visual life line by pasting the pictures on a chart patterned after the one shown next to the time when you expect certain events to occur.
3. Exchange your life line chart with that of a classmate. Then analyze the situation by answering the following questions:
   a. Which events have been shaped by tradition?
   b. What kind of people might have influenced the predictions you made?
   c. What might occur that would cause a change in expectations? How might a person deal with this change?
4. Display the charts around the room. Then discuss the following questions:
   a. Which traditions are most commonly mentioned by the class?
   b. Which traditions are most unique?
   c. Which events could not be considered traditional?

Command Systems

In a command economic system, the basic economic questions are answered by a group of planners. They have the power to make economic decisions for the society as a whole. Many of the great cultures of the past, such as Egypt, China, and Rome, were command economies. In modern times, the Soviet Union, Cuba, and the People's Republic of China almost always use the command system. Other nations, like Great Britain, Sweden, and even the United States, use the command system in part.

Command economies answer the "what to produce" question in a number of ways. The leaders may decide to produce what they themselves want—things like palaces or works of art. The rulers of ancient Egypt, for example, built huge pyramids in honor of dead kings and queens. On the other hand, the leaders may decide to produce what they believe is good for the people—modern weapons or schools. Or they may decide to produce what they think the people want—low-cost housing or cheap food, for example.

In command economies, the leaders also answer the "how to produce" question. They decide how many people will work, which workers will get jobs, and where they will work. In the Soviet Union, for example, there is a central planning agency called the Gosplan. It assigns to each factory or farm its production goals, its machinery and supplies, and its work force.

Who decides what food is available in this economy?

By setting wages, the leaders of a command economy also answer the "for whom" question. That is, they decide how much of the country's goods and services each worker will be able to buy. Leaders can decide to provide some goods and services (such as housing or medical care) to everyone. They can deny other goods (such as cars) to all but a favored few. They can also control who can buy goods and services by the way they set prices and fix production goals.

A hard problem faced by most command economies is to decide how much of each good or service will be wanted at the prices that are set. If the planners do not predict buyers' wants, or if factories do not meet production goals, there will be either shortages or surpluses of goods. People may have to wait a long time for some goods to be delivered. Other goods may have to be stored because the demand for them is smaller than the supply.

Punishments and rewards are often used in command economies to back up the decisions of the planners. Often the social value of work is stressed to make people work harder and to give them a sense of pride. Sometimes material rewards—more pay or a promotion—are used. Punishments can range from giving workers the silent treatment or cutting their wages to political terror.

Command economies are able to act quickly. War, famine, natural disasters, and other emergency situations can be met with prompt action. Economic change too can be brought about much faster than in traditional economies. The two problems of overcoming the opposition of those who do not want to change their traditional ways and of organizing the society's resources to achieve such tasks could be much more easily solved by a command economy.

It is important to understand that a command economy does not have to be a dictatorship. Many democratic countries make some of their major economic decisions this way. Important industries in Great Britain, France, Sweden, and Japan are government-owned. Government planners in these countries make many of the decisions on how to invest in capital goods and how many consumer goods to produce. The important difference between a democracy and a dictatorship is not an economic one. It is a political one. The difference is that in a democracy, the people have some influence on planning. They can remove the planners if their decisions turn out to be foolish or unfair.

Even in market economies some decisions are made by command. In the United States, some decisions are made by command. For example, the federal government has controlled prices and wages in wartime and sometimes in peacetime as well. State governments and cities and towns have zoning laws that restrict the use of private property. There are antipollution laws that regulate the dumping of wastes into the air and water. All these laws represent commands

Figure 5-1 Command Economy
How does a central planner decide what should be produced?

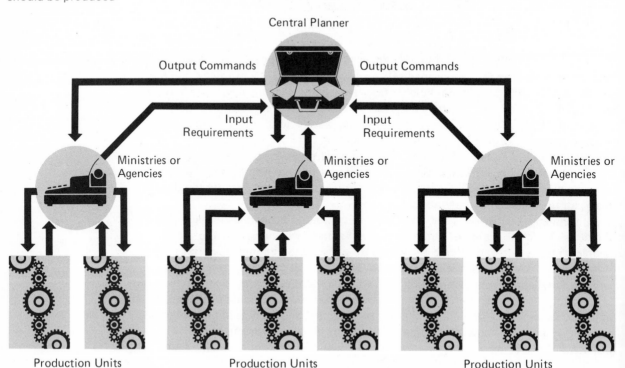

from the government to private businesses. They are told that they must do some things and may not do other things.

In every economy, people allow others to make their decisions for them. In a traditional culture, the right to make a decision that will affect others is based on strong, shared social values and beliefs. In a command economy, the right to make decisions is based on political power. People may feel that they have no choice but to obey the commands of those in power. They may also feel that their leaders are better able to choose for the common good than they are.

As a young child, you believed that parents, teachers, and others in authority were always right. Later you came to question some of the decisions that these people made for you. Sometimes you have to obey, even when you disagree. Otherwise you will be punished. Sometimes you are willing to obey, even though you disagree. You accept your teachers' right to decide how students should behave in school. You accept your parents' right to decide when you have to be in at night. You accept the police's duty to enforce the law. You therefore allow certain people, in certain situations, to tell you what to do.

☐ The reading for this lesson comes from *The Russians* by Hedrick Smith. The story is about queues, or lines. It shows how consumers shop in the Soviet Union, one country with a command economy. There, the government decides what and how much will be produced and for whom. Consumers buy whatever is available. They have very little choice. As you read the article, ask yourself the following questions:
1. Why do you think consumer goods are so scarce in the Soviet Union?
2. Why do you think Russian consumers are willing to wait in such long lines, with so little choice about what they buy?
3. When do you let others make choices for you?

———— THE ART OF QUEUING ————

The urge for a touch of class, for something better than others have, has put new pressure on that classic Russian institution—the queue. Customers the world-over wait in lines, but Soviet queues have a dimension all their own, like the Egyptian pyramids. They reveal a lot about the Russian predicament and the Russian psyche. And their operation is far more intricate than first meets the eye. To the passerby they look like nearly motionless files of mortals doomed to

Who determines the amount of time allotted
for this kind of activity?

some commercial purgatory for their humble purchases. But what the
outsider misses is the hidden magnetism of lines for Russians, their
inner dynamics, their special etiquette.

The only real taste of stoical shopping vigils in recent American
history were the pre-dawn lines at service stations during the gasoline
crisis in the winter of 1973–74. That produced a wave of national self-
pity in America. But it was temporary and only for one item. Imagine it
across the board, all the time, and you realize that Soviet shopping is
like a year-round Christmas rush. The accepted norm is that the
Soviet woman daily spends two hours in line, seven days a week, daily
going through double the gauntlet that the American housewife
undergoes at her supermarket once, maybe twice a week.

Personally, I have known of people who stood in line 90 minutes to

Who might have wanted
this building and why?
Who determined its cost?

buy four pineapples, three hours for a two-minute roller coaster ride,
three and a half hours to buy three large heads of cabbage only to
find the cabbages were gone as they approached the front of the line,
18 hours to sign up to purchase a rug at some later date, all through a
freezing December night to register on a list for buying a car, and then
waiting 18 more months for actual delivery, and terribly lucky at that.
Lines can run from a few yards long to half a block to nearly a mile,
and usually they move at an excruciating creep. Some friends of ours,
living in the southwest part of Moscow, watched and photographed a
line that lasted two solid days and nights, four abreast and running all
through an apartment development. They guessed there were 10,000–
15,000 people, signing up to buy rugs, an opportunity that came only
once a year in that entire section of Moscow. Some burned bonfires to
keep warm out in the snow and the crackling wood and din of
constant conversation kept our friends awake at night.

Yet despite such ordeals the instinctive reaction of a Russian
woman when she sees a queue forming is to get in line immediately—
even before she knows what is being sold. Queue-psychology has a
magnetism of its own. Again and again, I have been told by Russians
that anyone's normal assumption on seeing people up front hurrying
to get in line is that there must be something up there worth lining up
for. Never mind what it is. Get in line first and ask questions later.
You'll find out when you get to the front of the line, or perhaps they'll
pass back word before then. A lady lawyer told me she once came

upon an enormous line stretching all through the Moskva Department Store, and when she asked those at the end of the line what was on sale, "they said they didn't know or else snarled at me and told me not to interfere. I walked up 20 or 30 yards asking people and no one knew. Finally I gave up asking."

Nina Voronel, a translator of children's literature, said she happened to be at an appliance counter one day buying an ordinary hand mixer for 30 rubles, when a clerk carried in a box of East German wall-lamps. "I told the salesgirl, 'I'll take one. Put me down for one and I'll go pay the cashier.' And while I went to the cashier, a line of about 50 people formed. How they found out about it, I don't know, word spreads—that is the way we always learn here. Practically everyone in the store was there. It didn't matter whether they needed the lamps or not. People here don't just buy what they need, but whatever they see that is worth having. Some may sell those lamps. Some may give them to friends. But mostly they keep them on the shelf. A lamp is always needed. Good fabrics are always needed, fur coats, fur hats, good winter boots, bright summer dresses, floor rugs, dishes, enamel pots and pans, kettles, good woolen cardigan

Who might these goods be produced for? How is this determined?

sweaters, umbrellas, a decent purse, a nice writing table, a typewriter, a good woman's bra—not a floppy, ugly Soviet one with no support and no adjustments, made for big-bosomed country girls. But a Czech bra or a Polish one, white and pretty instead of blue and baggy with rose buds. That is why people are so quick to join a line. It might be any of those things.''

Once formed, moreover, Soviet lines are more fluid than they appear. Eddies and undercurrents work within them. In most stores, for example, the shopper's ordeal is prolonged by the requirement to stand in not one, but three lines for any purchase—the first to select her purchase, find out its price and order it; the second to pay a cashier somewhere else in the store and get a receipt; and the third, to go pick up her purchase and turn in her receipt.

But in a dairy store one Saturday morning, I found out that the game is both simpler and more complex than that. I went in to buy some cheese, butter and bologna sausage which were, unfortunately, in three separate departments, each with its own line. *Nine lines!* I groaned inwardly. But rather quickly, I noticed that veteran shoppers were skipping the first stage. They knew what most items cost, so they went directly to the cashier for their receipts. After a bit of studying prices, that was what I did, too. Then, receipts in hand, I went to the cheese line, the longest—probably 20 people—to get the worst over with first. But I was in line less than a minute when the lady in front of me turned around and asked me to hold her place. She darted off to the butter-and-milk line. The cheese line was moving so slowly that she got her butter and milk and returned before we had moved forward three feet. I decided to take the risk, too, and got back with my butter while the cheese line was still inching along. Then it dawned on me that the entire store was churning with people getting into line, holding places, leaving, returning. Everyone was using the cheese line as home base. That was why it was barely moving: it kept expanding in the middle. So once again, I got the elderly gentleman behind me to hold my place and went off to buy my bologna. Once again, it worked. In the end it took me 22 minutes to buy butter, sausage and cheese and instead of being furious, I felt oddly as if I had somehow beaten the system with all those shortcuts.

ACTIVITIES

I. This activity has been designed to recreate some of the experiences of working within a command economic system.

1. Split the class into groups of five or six students each. Each group should look upon itself as a planning committee, with full planning responsibility for the class.
2. Each group must select a goal for the class to reach. The goal can be in any of the following areas:
   a. class trips
   b. academic achievement
   c. ways in which students relate to each other
   d. raising money for class projects
   e. deciding what is most important for the class to do
3. After a goal has been chosen, the group must decide on the means for achieving that goal. These should be described as a series of steps toward the goal.
4. Keep in mind that each group is a planning committee for the entire class. For the purposes of this activity, assume that the class is a command economic system. In other words, everyone must follow your plan. Each committee has a chance to share its plan with the rest of the class.
5. After each plan is presented, answer the following questions:
   a. How did each of the plans answer the four basic economic questions?
   b. Which groups did each plan benefit?
6. Discussion questions
   a. How would these plans be carried out in a command system?
   b. How did you react to being planned for?
   c. What did you gain? What did you lose?
   d. How did you feel about planning for others?

II. In a command economic system, many choices are made for you. Many decisions in your own life are made for you as well. This activity will help you think about how you make decisions.

1. This is a card-sorting activity making use of twenty-four cards. The cards do not represent the kind of decisions made in a command economy. They include the kinds of decisions you might be required to make. Sort the cards in

the Workbook or ones you have made yourself into the following three
categories:

a.   Situations where YOU DECIDE.

b.   Situations where OTHERS DECIDE FOR YOU.

c.   Situations where YOU DECIDE WITH THE HELP OF OTHERS.

2.   When you are finished, share the results with others in your class. As a class,
     discuss these questions:

a.   How does the way you make decisions affect the control you have over
     your life?

b.   Who or what is most influential when you make a choice?

c.   Are there ways other than the three ways listed above in which you make
     decisions? If so, what are they?

what clothes to buy	whether to go to college	whether to have surgery	where to live
which skills to develop	how to finance further education	decisions on foreign policy	how to comb your hair
whether to break the law	what TV channel to watch	what holidays to observe	how to earn extra money
how to vote in elections	which athletic team to join	who your friends will be	whether to marry
whether to attend or skip classes	whether to sleep late in the morning	how much to spend on living expenses	what to do after graduation
where a new school is built	what prices are charged in the supermarket	what you do on a job you have	who your doctor is

Market Systems

In a *market economy,* the basic economic questions are answered by the interplay of buyers and sellers. There is no overall planning, as with command systems. The guiding principle of market systems is self-interest. Sellers want to sell at the highest prices. Buyers want to buy at the lowest prices. The bargains that buyers and sellers make give the answers to the questions.

With so many people making decisions, what prevents chaos? What ensures that there will be enough coffee, milk, and meat for consumers to buy? How can there be enough trucks for merchants to ship their goods? Can there be enough workers to produce what customers want? How can there be any order when people make these decisions without the help of leaders or traditions?

In 1776, a British economist named Adam Smith wrote *The Wealth of Nations.* This is now considered the first great book on the market system. To explain how the system worked, Smith said that it seemed as if an "invisible hand" were controlling things. His "invisible hand" ensured that people would always try to earn as much income as they could. It also made sure that buyers and sellers would compete against one another. This competition would mean that producers would make what the most customers would buy, and that they would do so as cheaply as possible.

How does the market system answer the basic economic questions? The "what to produce" question is answered by producers and consumers together. Producers compete for the business of consumers in order to earn *profits*. Profit is the difference between what it costs to make something and the price for which it sells. If producers think that profits will be higher if they switch to making different goods and services, then they will switch. Consumers, in turn, seek the best goods at the lowest prices.

The producers and owners of resources answer the "how to produce" question. Owners of human resources sell their labor for the highest wages. Owners of natural and capital resources also seek the highest prices they can get. Producers are seeking profits, so they want to produce goods and services at the lowest cost. Those who find a more efficient method will be able to sell their goods at lower prices than others. People will buy from them, and so they will make profits. Other producers, if they want to stay in business, will have to copy their methods. In this way, the most efficient methods quickly spread through an entire industry.

The "for whom to produce" question is answered at the same time as the "what" and "how" questions. The income that people get as profits, wages, rent, or interest determines their ability to buy the goods and services that have been produced.

The "how much now" and "how much in the future" questions are answered at the same time as the "what" question. If producers are willing to pay more for tools, machines, factories, and other capital goods than consumers are willing to pay for consumer goods, then more capital goods will be produced. The reverse is also true. If consumers pay more for consumer goods than producers pay for capital goods, then more consumer goods will be made.

A market system requires the presence of four things in order to work: private property, freedom of exchange, the profit motive, and competition.

How do these currencies work? Who determines their respective values?

Which of these two
merchants might you
have gone to? How do
you decide?

In market economies, resources are the *private property* of their owners. They do not belong to the culture as a whole, as they might in a traditional or command system. A market economy can come about only when buyers and sellers are *free to exchange* goods and services for whatever prices they can agree upon.

The importance of the *profit motive* and *competition* have already been shown. They are Adam Smith's "invisible hand." Competition gives consumers a choice of goods and services. It also provides firms with a choice of human, natural, and capital resources. The profit motive leads producers to seek the best bargains with consumers. It also leads consumers to seek the lowest prices. Competition assures that the most efficient producers will get the most business. And it gives consumers the power to get the products they are willing to pay for.

In a pure market economy, people choose for themselves. They freely decide what to buy, how much to spend, and what to work at. They make bargains with others who are also free to choose. Trade is fair in that everyone has the right to turn down an unfair deal. Each person can choose what is best for himself.

Fair bargains can be made with nonmaterial things as well. People who see each other as equals often make deals, even without stating them outright. "I'll help you now, and I expect you to help me when I need it," they may say, or, "I'll stay out of your way if you stay out of mine."

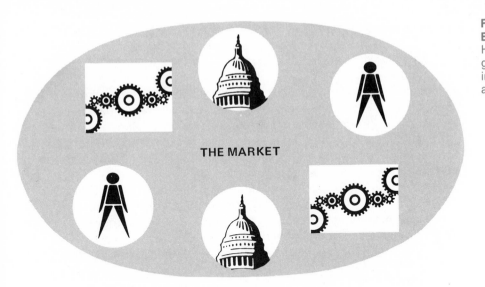

Figure 6-1   Market Economy
How are people, government, and industries interrelated in a market economy?

THE MARKET

☐ The reading for this lesson is a story that sketches the career of a man who came to the United States early in the twentieth century. He was free to sell his labor and to spend the money he earned. The reading describes some of the choices he was able to make. As you read, ask yourself the following questions:

1. What free choices did Horatio make in his career?
2. What assumptions does the idea of a pure market economy make about people's relations with one another?
3. What economic choices do you make freely? Which choices will you make freely when you enter the labor market?

THE TRUE STORY OF
HORATIO HISS

This is the story of a poor immigrant's son whose family left Russia when he was eight years old. He came to New York City knowing not a word of English. In the short space of thirty years, he raised himself by his own efforts to a position of leadership and great wealth. It is a romantic story in that it pictures the sunnier side of capitalism: through abilities and hard work, Horatio Hiss, like many fictional heroes before him, rose straight to the top.

Horatio was born in a small Russian village outside of Kovna. The boy was put to studying the Talmud at age six, two thousand words a day, six days a week. He had mastered as much as his age would permit by the time he came to America at the beginning of the twentieth century.

These were bad days for the Jews in Russia. Life in the ghettos was stifling. Horatio's father decided that his children should have a better chance in life than he had had. By saving and borrowing, he scraped enough money together to pay for his own trip to America. Then, after two years of hard work in the New World, he was able to save enough to bring the rest of his family over to join him.

America was different for Horatio, very different from the Russia he knew. The mounted police in New York didn't carry whips, as the Cossacks had. More light and air filled their rooms than they were used to. Best of all, there were public schools.

Horatio went off to school each day, but he had to work to help support his family too. Every waking moment when he wasn't studying, he was on the streets, delivering meat for the corner butcher, selling papers, running errands. He liked selling papers best. He read them, and in this way came in contact with the broader world of which he had known nothing. At first, his parents had hoped he would become a rabbi. But now Horatio had a secret dream that he might work some day for a newspaper. That's how he would make his fortune in this land of opportunity.

When he was fourteen, his father died. Horatio was then forced to find a regular job. He went first to the Tribune Building and was amazed at how big the building was. He was told to go to the twenty-sixth floor. When he got to the newsroom, he was even more amazed to find such a large room and so many people all working frantically.

"I would like a job," he said to the man who ran the newsroom.

"We have a personnel office," the man said.

"I want a newspaper job," Horatio replied. "You are a newspaper man, so I want to talk to you."

"Well, then," the man chuckled. "What kind of job would you like? Delivering newspapers?"

"I have delivered newspapers for many years," Horatio said seriously. "That is not what I want to do. I want to write in newspapers."

"And what makes you think," the man asked, "that you can write in newspapers?"

"It is what I want," replied Horatio, "and I have been told that one can do whatever one wants in this land of opportunity."

"It is not always quite that simple. You must have ability. And you must work hard."

"I have worked hard all my life," Horatio answered. "I know nothing comes easy. I will start at the bottom and work my way up."

Horatio had spunk. People found it hard to deny him when he went after something he really wanted. It was a trait that would last throughout his life.

Horatio did start at the bottom: as a messenger. But he spent as much time as he could with the reporters. He watched them write and often picked up the stories they threw away. He worked on them, always trying to improve them . . . and himself. When he finally got his chance to write a small story, he was ready. It had taken him over a year, but he didn't fail when given the opportunity. His first story was small, but it was accepted. Horatio was on his way to the top.

The outlines of success may seem simple. But it wasn't simple for Horatio at all. He spent hours working on the stories that others had discarded. And all that hard work was on top of his regular job as

Who, in a market economy, might own these lands? How are they obtained?

messenger. What made Horatio different from other people was that he knew what he wanted and knew what he had to do to get it.

Horatio wanted to be rich. He had been poor and had lived poor all his life. His father had died poor and Horatio wanted to make sure that such a fate would never be his. Horatio had choices, but so did other people his age. Horatio was different because he knew he had choices.

"I could have been anything," Horatio once said, looking back on his youth. "I could have had any one of ten different jobs. But I knew from my school days that I had a flair for language. I didn't just walk into the Tribune office. I knew what they wanted from a reporter and I knew that I could learn to produce it.

"You know, I didn't make much more as a messenger than I did as a delivery boy. But I did make more, and that was important. All I had to sell was my labor, and I made sure I sold it to the highest bidder. But I also chose a profession I felt confident I could succeed in. It wasn't luck I walked into that office, I can tell you that."

Over the next few years, Horatio won many promotions. Each time he got a new position with the newspaper, his salary went up. Within three years, he was supporting his whole family. He was able to fulfill one of his promises to his mother. They moved out of the Lower East Side into a bigger and brighter apartment. He was still living at home and still responsible for his younger brothers and sisters. He made sure that they could continue at school. Like his father before him, he wanted those younger than himself to have a better chance in life than he had had.

Horatio wasn't doing too badly for himself either. By twenty-five, he had become managing editor of the Tribune. By thirty he had become editor-in-chief. And by thirty-five, Horatio Hiss had bought the paper. It was a swift rise from messenger boy to publisher.

There are many today who think people of great wealth are lucky. The story of Horatio Hiss proves just the opposite. There was no luck involved. Sure, he had a great many choices, but so does everyone. The difference is that Horatio Hiss chose wisely. He knew what his skills were and he knew who would pay the most money for them. Many have the ability to get rich in America, but Horatio Hiss also had the determination and willingness to work hard.

"As I look back on my life," Horatio remarked a few years ago, "I am most struck by the number of choices I had. I could choose my profession. I could choose to work or go back to school. I could choose where my mother would live. I could choose how much I wished to work. And I chose freely. No one told me what to do. And they still don't."

Select from any source, other than this book, at least five photographs or drawings that demonstrate economic interactions. At least three of these visuals should involve foreign economies. What type of economy is represented in each? Are there visual clues that indicate this? If so, what are they? Who makes economic decisions in each of these images? What parts of each image would have to change so that each image would represent another type of economy?

VISUAL
ACTIVITY

ACTIVITIES

I. This research activity is designed to test the hypothesis that there is a market economy in the United States.

1. Make a shopping list of six or seven of the food items your family uses most often. Enter them in the chart in the Workbook or copy the chart in the text onto a separate sheet of paper.
2. Assume that there is a market economy in the United States. Imagine that you check the prices of these items at a number of different stores. How similar or different would you expect the prices of these items to be? Why? Keep your guesses in mind as you do your research.
3. Test the hypothesis that there is a market economy in the United States. Visit two local supermarkets and two small neighborhood stores to compare the prices of the six or seven items. Fill in the chart with your findings.

| SHOPPING LIST | Supermarkets | | | | Neighborhood stores | |
| | #1 | | #2 | | | |
	House Brand	National Brand	House Brand	National Brand	#1	#2

4. Share your findings with the class. Then discuss these questions:
   a. Do the data you gathered support the hypothesis that there is a market economy in the United States? Why or why not?
   b. What other hypotheses could your data be used to support?
   c. How do you explain the differences in price between national brands and house brands of the same item?
   d. How do you explain the differences in price between the stores?

II. This activity will help you to explore the economic choices open to you and to decide which ones you make freely.

1. Each of the categories in the chart below describes a place where food can be bought. Within each category, you have a number of choices, in terms of price, brand, quality of product, and convenience of shopping.
2. Begin with the supermarket and list the choices you have in terms of the four categories given. List also the advantages of shopping in a supermarket and the choices that are not available when you shop in only one supermarket. Use the chart in the Workbook or copy the chart in the text.
3. When certain choices are not available to you in your usual supermarket, you might decide to shop in a competing supermarket. Fill in those choices, along with the advantages and choices not available.
4. As you write the choices not available in a given situation, go on to the next category until you have filled in the entire chart.

CHOICES

	Price	Brand	Quality	Convenience	Advantages	Disadvantages
SUPERMARKET						
COMPETING SUPERMARKET						
NEIGHBORHOOD STORE						
FOOD CO-OP						
GROW YOUR OWN FOOD						

5. When you have finished, discuss as a class the following questions:
   a. What choices are realistically available to you and your family when you purchase food?
   b. What considerations are most important in shopping for food? How might you change your habits to better meet your needs?
   c. Are you free to choose the kind of food you buy? Are you free to choose how you obtain food?
   d. What other choices do you make freely?

CHAPTER 3 AN OVERVIEW OF THE
AMERICAN ECONOMY

A Mixed Economy

The traditional, command, and market economies described so far are models. They are simple versions of real economies. Economists use such models to study the real world. The models bring out what is most important. For example, in the rural areas of many Asian and African nations, tradition is most important. Command is central in the Soviet Union, China, and Cuba. The market economy is most important in the United States, Canada, Japan, and Western Europe.

But in no country or region is the major economic form the only form. Command and market systems also exist within traditional countries. Some goods and services are bought and sold in the market even in the Soviet Union and China. And features of both tradition and command can be found in the United States and Western Europe. In other words, most countries, unlike models, are mixtures of all three elements.

Tradition has never been missing from the American economy. One tradition is that children often take the same kinds of jobs as their fathers or mothers. Another is that people whose parents have worked in offices seldom like to work in factories. Leaving tips in restaurants and giving allowances to children are other American traditions. Closing stores on Sundays is traditional in some parts of the country. So is discriminating against members of minority groups and women. Another tradition is that of working without pay for charities or worthy causes.

Does the government have any say in what happens in this classroom? In what ways?

How does this image represent a tradition in the American economy? How might this tradition have evolved?

There are also important elements of command in the American economy. The federal government, for instance, has always played a large role. By giving land to the railroads in the nineteenth century, it allowed private companies to build a vast network of rail lines. It has helped American business by taxing goods made abroad. This reduces the competition for American firms.

Government has a say over many parts of the economy. For instance, zoning laws in most American towns limit the way land can be used. The draft, from time to time, has kept men from controlling their own labor by forcing them into the army. Laws that forbid the use of child labor keep young people from working. Food and drug laws and government regulation of oil affect what and how much will be produced.

Other government actions affect the distribution of goods and services. Laws against discrimination try to increase the share of income going to women and minorities. Social security payments, unemployment insurance, and public welfare programs provide resources to people who, for the most part, cannot support themselves. Public education attempts to improve the skills of everyone who goes to school.

All of these government programs have one thing in common. They try to increase the resources of people who might otherwise be left with few or none. In a pure market system, such programs would not exist. People without money might very well starve to death or be forced to leave the country. These programs exist because most Americans do not want to live in an economy that is run solely by the market. They would rather have some elements of tradition and command mixed in.

And yet the market remains the major form of economic organization in the United States. If you have ever turned down a job because the pay was too low, you saw the market at work. You saw the market working if you decided not to buy something because its price was too high. If someone in your family got laid off because "business was bad," that too was the market at work.

Americans like to feel that in their economy all choices are free. Yet many choices that seem to be free are in fact made by others or by tradition. For instance, it may be easier just to fall into a way of life that others have "chosen" than to look at all your options. And it is often easier to obey rules than to question them. A free choice is one that seems best to you, no matter what others think. But free choices are not always responsible choices. What is best for you may not be best for others, or for the society as a whole. That is why a choice governed by tradition or by command may sometimes be better than a free choice.

☐ The reading for this lesson comes from an article by Marilyn Smith. It shows some of the problems people face in choosing and starting their careers. It tells how two people tried to sort out what they wanted to be from what they were told to be. They had to balance freedom and responsibility. As you read the story, ask yourself the following questions:

1. In what ways were Marilyn and Randy's choices influenced by tradition? by command?
2. How were Marilyn and Randy's choices free? How were they responsible?
3. How free are your choices? How free do you want them to be?

MOM GOES TO LAW SCHOOL

From the time that I decided to be a lawyer during my freshman year of college, people have told me not to. "You'll turn into a hard woman," one friend said. No one had ever asked Randy, my husband, whose undergraduate degree was similar to mine, why *he* wanted to go to law school. In fact, after he decided *not* to go to law school, people asked him why.

At the time I applied in the fall of 1972, I had been following Randy around for two years. He was in the Army, due to be discharged in the summer of 1973, and we had assumed he would begin graduate school right away. However, he hadn't decided what he wanted to do and wasn't motivated to apply to graduate school. I, on the other hand, had been unhappy for a long time and was anxious to go to law school.

That was how we fell into our "revolutionary" arrangement: I would start law school, Randy would take care of our children and we would live off our savings for a year. We were not sure where the money would come from after the first year, except for Randy's G.I. Bill. I felt guilty and scared. How could I explain it to the people who expected Randy to be going on to a brilliant career? How dare I set him back?

I entered law school in September, 1973. Lori was two, and Kathy was seven months old.

For much of my first year I was happier than I could remember having been since college. Yet, even with Randy supporting me, life as a law student and mother had problems. Inevitably, Kathy would wake me up crying on the night before an exam, and I couldn't go back to sleep until Randy had quieted her.

When my legal methods instructor called a sudden, late-night meeting, he justified it by reminding us that lawyers are constantly faced with last-minute deadlines, changes in court dates, and unforeseeable emergencies. In real life, however, you are being paid to cope with surprise.

Lack of sleep, scheduling pressures, and tight finances began to take their toll. Every time there was an additional expense, no matter how justifiable, I thought of it in terms of children's shoes. I could not even afford to go out for lunch.

Having children and following my husband around for three years made me feel that I was no longer in control of my life. I'd lost my undergraduate self-confidence and the belief that my future was golden.

A few months after the school year began, I realized our arrangement was not working out well for Randy. He was already unhappy and spent hours on the telephone. Normally quiet, he became talkative. He spent a lot of time listening to sports talk shows, and his conversation with company consisted of children and sports. He didn't enjoy my conversations with other law students. His part-time job started taking more time. He wanted to go out a lot; I was happy to stay home. He began criticizing me for trivial reasons.

However, our arrangement had long-range, beneficial results.

Randy learned to cook meals quickly and efficiently while entertaining two hungry children. After years of denying its usefulness, he was anxious to buy a dishwasher. We discovered that his housecleaning was no better than mine. He knew Kathy as a baby better than he had known Lori and he developed close relationships with both. He found himself yelling at them and feeling distraught when they were ill. When I came home at dinnertime, he was anxious to have me take over; I only wanted dinner and a chance to read the newspaper.

By the end of my first year, Randy was ready to enter Harvard's Kennedy School of Government. A generous scholarship, his G.I. Bill, and a loan for my tuition were going to pay our second-year expenses. We couldn't afford full-time child care for our children. I had two choices—stay home for a year and let Randy go to school, or try to do second-year law school, all the housework, and take care of the children half a day. I chose the latter. My beautifully worked-out schedule of afternoon courses was shattered by a last-minute change and I took on too heavy a load.

I spent my mornings doing breakfast dishes, laundry or shopping, fixing lunch for the children, preparing dinner, and getting us all bundled into the car to arrive at school by 2:30. The children got little of my time. Some days I sat through four straight hours of classes, hardly having time for a cup of coffee.

I desperately wanted some recognition for trying so hard. I never got it. Only women with children ever expressed admiration. I think

this was because people who haven't kept house and raised children can't understand how difficult it is.

Nobody seemed to think I could be a lawyer. Nobody seemed to care whether I became a lawyer or not, no family pride hung in the balance. I was a burden to my husband (who routinely and sincerely denied it). Only my children, who needed me, kept me alive.

I entered my third year of law school with relief. The end was near. Our children were healthy. Our car was going to last. Because Randy could get a job as a teaching assistant, we could afford to put our children in the child-care center full-time. It worked out better than we had hoped; they thrived on it.

We agreed to split the housework. We drew up two sets of tasks, one centered around the kitchen, one centered around cleaning, and alternated weeks doing each.

I have occasionally sensed that people were looking at me and thinking, "You see, *she's* doing it. It can be done." But at what price! The physical exhaustion, short tempers, arguments over who should do the dishes, resentment of anyone who could afford to buy lunch every day, the days I wanted to fling myself on my bed and cry but couldn't because there was work to be done, the avoidance of movies or books that would start me crying. And, most of all, my loss of self-respect. I would give almost anything to regain my self-control and a sense of well-being, both of which seem to have vanished.

I could never push someone to do what I have done. Yet, in most respects, I would do it again. It needs doing.

In what ways do these people compete as shoppers? as vendors?

ACTIVITIES

This activity will help you to look at the part played by tradition, command, and market economic systems in one area of your school life.

1. Split up into two groups. Each group should sit in a circle, with the members facing inward.
2. Group A writes a brief safety code for the school. Group B writes a brief hygiene code for the school. A spokesperson for each group stands and reads its code to the other group.
3. Group A must decide which features of the hygiene code result from market conditions. Group B must decide which features of the safety code result from market conditions. Use the chart in the Workbook or copy the one in the text to record your answers.
4. The following discussion questions will help you think about what you have done:
   a. What was the difference between the two codes in terms of tradition, command, and market elements?
   b. How do the three economic systems relate to other parts of your life?
   c. In what ways are you free to decide?

Safety or Hygiene Code Aspect (circle one)	Tradition?	Command?	Market?	Response

Specialization, Division of Labor, and Interdependence

People can deal with the problem of scarcity in three ways. They can do without; they can create more resources; or they can use their resources in better ways. A society might use any of these approaches. Normally, the poorer farming regions of the world have simply done without. The richer nations, on the other hand, have been able to use both the second and third methods.

Even in the United States, doing without is sometimes used. After floods or severe snow storms, for example, many towns find that there is not enough food, clothing, or shelter to go around. *Rationing* is then set up to decide how these scarce resources will be used. Government steps in to pass out the necessities on the basis of need.

Increasing the supply of resources is usually a long-term solution. A shortage of workers, for example, can be solved by immigration, by retraining, or by population growth. All of these take time. The supply of capital resources (such as factories and tools) can be increased if business thinks the prospects for profits look good. Natural resources can be increased over the long run if new supplies of minerals are found or if farm land is increased through irrigation.

The third way of dealing with scarcity is to use existing resources more wisely. The most common way to do this is to *specialize*. For example, New England farms grow crops like apples and potatoes. With the help of greenhouses, oranges could be grown as well. But it is much cheaper to import oranges from warmer regions, such as Florida or California. This is called *geographic specialization.*

Occupational specialization means that it is simpler for one person to be a doctor, a plumber, or a farmer than to be all these things at once. People can produce more goods and services by specializing than they could if each tried to do all the jobs done by the others.

The third type of specialization is called *resource specialization.* A doctor who likes children may choose to specialize and become a pediatrician. A steel company that invented a process for making rolled steel might specialize in making that kind of steel. A city that has mostly skilled workers will try to attract those industries that need skilled workers.

When each worker on a job does the one task that he is trained for, then the total job will be done faster than if each worker did a lot of jobs. This is known as *division of labor.* An auto assembly line is an extreme example of the division of labor. Division of labor also makes it possible to take advantage of the special skills some workers may have. It can also create new problems. The auto worker who does the same task again and again often gets bored with the work.

Specialization and division of labor increase total production. Consumers not only have a wider range of goods and services to choose from. They also have more of these goods and services than they could produce for themselves. Think of all the things people use during the course of a single day. Then imagine how much time it would take for people to make all of these things themselves: clothes, cars, books, dishes, food, houses, and so on.

Specialization and division of labor force people to get most of the goods and services they need from others. This makes for social *interdependence,* which has its costs as well as its benefits. A drought in the wheat belt can cause bread prices to go up elsewhere. A coal miners' strike may increase consumers' electric bills. When everything is connected, it is not possible to deal with economic problems separately. One small change in the economy can change everything.

Specialization occurs because each of us is different. You have your own talents, strengths, weaknesses, and personality. When you choose freely, you base your choice on your own traits and desires. At the same time, others too are choosing freely. Everybody is trying to get what they want by doing what they like and are good at.

Sooner or later these choices are bound to conflict. Too many people will want the same things. There will be some jobs that have to be done that nobody wants to do. Those who like to be different may find that others are cramping their style. If others do not want what you can give, you may not be able to do what you most want to do. You must often adjust your choices because of the choices others make.

This industry is prominent in most coastal areas. How might some other areas specialize? Is this kind of specialization an advantage?

How does the training of employees in highly specific tasks contribute to the American economy?

☐ The reading for this lesson comes from Adam Smith, a British economist who wrote at the time of the American Revolution. He was the first economist to describe a market economy. He believed that free and fair exchange among equals, with everyone acting in his own best interest, could produce an ideal economy. The following passage explains how specialization and the division of labor are natural in any human society. As you read it, ask yourself the following questions:

1. Why and how do specialization and division of labor come about? In the modern world, what factors hinder the specialization described by Adam Smith?
2. In the tribe that Adam Smith describes, everyone ends up with the occupation he prefers. What could happen to change that?
3. How are your choices affected by others' choices?

ON THE PROPENSITY TO TRUCK

This division of labour, from which so many advantages are derived, is not originally the effect of any human wisdom, which foresees and intends that general opulence to which it gives occasion. It is the necessary, though very slow and gradual, consequence of a certain propensity in human nature which has in view no such extensive utility; the propensity to truck, barter, and exchange one thing for another.

Whether this propensity be one of those original principles in human nature, of which no further account can be given; or whether, as seems more probable, it be the necessary consequence of the faculties of reason and speech, it belongs not to our present subject to enquire. It is common to all men, and to be found in no other race of animals, which seem to know neither this nor any other species of contracts. Two greyhounds, in running down the same hare, have sometimes the appearance of acting in some sort of concert. Each turns her towards his companion, or endeavours to intercept her when his companion turns her towards himself. This, however, is not the effect of any contract, but of the accidental concurrence of their passions in the same object at that particular time. Nobody ever saw a dog make a fair and deliberate exchange of one bone for another with another dog. Nobody ever saw one animal by its gestures and natural cries signify to another, this is mine, that yours; I am willing to give this for that. When an animal wants to obtain something either of a man or of another animal, it has no other means of persuasion but to gain the favour of those whose service it requires. A puppy fawns upon its dam, and a spaniel endeavours by a thousand attractions to engage the attention of its master who is at dinner, when it wants to be fed by him. Man sometimes uses the same arts with his brethren, and when he has no other means of engaging them to act according to his inclinations, endeavours by every servile and fawning attention to

obtain their good will. He has not time, however, to do this upon every occasion. In civilised society he stands at all times in need of the co-operation and assistance of great multitudes, while his whole life is scarce sufficient to gain the friendship of a few persons. In almost every other race of animals each individual, when it is grown up to maturity, is entirely independent, and in its natural state has occasion for the assistance of no other living creature.

But man has almost constant occasion for the help of his brethren, and it is in vain for him to expect it from their benevolence only. He will be more likely to prevail if he can interest their self-love in his favour, and shew them that it is for their own advantage to do for him what he requires of them. Whoever offers to another a bargain of any kind, proposes to do this. Give me that which I want, and you shall have this which you want, is the meaning of every such offer; and it is in this manner that we obtain from one another the far greater part of those good offices which we stand in need of. It is not from the benevolence of the butcher, the brewer, or the baker, that we expect our dinner, but from their regard to their own interest. We address ourselves, not to their humanity but to their self-love, and never talk to them of our own necessities but of their advantages. Nobody but a beggar chuses to depend chiefly upon it entirely. The charity of well-disposed people, indeed, supplies him with the whole fund of his subsistence. But

In what ways might these people be dependent on each other?

though this principle ultimately provides him with all the necessaries of life which he has occasion for, it neither does nor can provide him with them as he has occasion for them. The greater part of his occasional wants are supplied in the same manner as those of other people, by treaty, by barter, and by purchase. With the money which one man gives him he purchases food. The old cloaths which another bestows upon him he exchanges for other old cloaths which suit him better, or for lodging, or for food, or for money, with which he can buy either food, cloaths, or lodging, as he has occasion.

As it is by treaty, by barter, and by purchase, that we obtain from one another the greater part of those mutual good offices which we stand in need of, so it is this same trucking disposition which originally gives occasion to the division of labour. In a tribe of hunters or shepherds a particular person makes bows and arrows, for example, with more readiness and dexterity than any other. He frequently exchanges them for cattle or for venison with his companions; and he finds at last that he can in this manner get more cattle and venison, than if he himself went to the field to catch them. From a regard to his own interest, therefore, the making of bows and arrows grows to be his chief business, and he becomes a sort of armourer. Another excels in making the frames and covers of their little huts or moveable houses. He is accustomed to be of use in this way to his neighbours, who reward him in the same manner with cattle and with venison, till at last he finds it his interest to dedicate himself entirely to this employment, and to become a sort of house-carpenter. In the same manner a third becomes a smith or a brazier; a fourth a tanner or dresser of hides or skins, the principal part of the cloathing of savages. And thus the certainty of being able to exchange all that surplus part of the produce of his own labour, which is over and above his own consumption, for such parts of the produce of other men's labour as he may have occasion for, encourages every man to apply himself to a particular occupation, and to cultivate and bring to perfection whatever talent or genius he may possess for that particular species of business.

ACTIVITIES

I. This activity requires that you work as a group toward common goals. You will have to decide how to divide your labor. In the process you will learn how others' choices affect your own.

1. Your goal is to design a self-contained society. For this purpose, pretend that your class is lost in the mountains for a month and that you must make a plan showing how the class will function during that time. One object of your month-long venture is to develop skills that will be useful to you as a person and to your community.

2. The following questions will help you to organize your plans:
   a. What are fitting and realistic goals for the group?
   b. What jobs will be needed and who will fill them?
   c. What special skills do members of the group have to offer?
   d. What practical arrangements must be made?
   e. How will the group measure its success?

3. It may be helpful if the class divides into committees after a goal has been chosen. That way each group can take over a more specialized task.

4. Discussion questions
   a. Was it easier to work as a whole class or in committees?
   b. How did people decide what committee to be on? What problems came up in assigning committees?
   c. What kinds of specializations were called for by your plan? by the division in the committees?
   d. What were the advantages and disadvantages of specialization in each case?

II. Arizona Indians call this game *Pon chochtl* or *Coyotes and Chicken.* As you play the game, think of your strengths and weaknesses in terms of your role in the game and the rules you have to follow.

1. GAME RULES
   a. Two can play. The Chicken player has one counter; the Coyote player has twelve.
   b. Counters must be arranged as shown on the board.

c. The Chicken player may move his counter to any adjoining empty space. He may capture a Coyote by a short jump or by a series of short jumps in any direction, as in checkers.

d. The Coyote player may move only one counter per turn one space in any direction. He may not jump or capture.

e. The Chicken wins by capturing so many Coyotes that they can no longer block him. The Coyotes win if they block the Chicken so that he cannot move.

2. After the game, reverse roles and play again.

3. Discussion questions

a. What was the Coyote's specialty? What was the Chicken's specialty?

b. How did your partner's decisions affect yours?

c. How did your guesses about what your partner would decide affect your decision?

d. How do other people's choices and your guesses about what they will choose affect your real-life choices?

COYOTE		CHICKEN		COYOTE
COYOTE	COYOTE	COYOTE	COYOTE	COYOTE
COYOTE	COYOTE	COYOTE	COYOTE	COYOTE

The Role of Economic Institutions

Economic institutions are the formal organizations, the customs, and the basic beliefs and traditions of a culture. In the United States, the most important formal organizations in the economy are the *household* and the *private business firm.* A household can consist of a whole family, adults without children, or people living alone. A private business firm may be an *individual proprietorship* (owned by a single person), a *partnership* (owned by two or more people), or a *corporation* (owned by a large number of people).

Figure 9-1 shows the relationships between households and business firms. Households provide the resources that businesses turn into products. These products are then sold to households. Put more simply, a person who has a job is providing labor to a business. In return, the firm pays a wage. That wage is used to buy needed goods and services. That permits businesses to earn profits. And this in turn allows them to make more goods and services.

Other organizations play a vital role too. Government buys and produces goods and services on behalf of the community or nation as a whole. Labor unions work to help their members by getting higher wages and better working conditions. Banks aid in the transfer of money.

The economy is also influenced by social customs, such as the use of money as a means of exchange. Private property is another customary institution in the United States. Still another is collective bargaining between unions and employers.

Among the beliefs that affect the American economy is the connection made between job and social status. Americans place a great deal of stress on having a "good" job, one that can earn respect from others. Americans also stress the importance of working hard.

No two countries have just the same kinds of economic institutions. Besides, institutions change over time, in response to changing values and needs. The history of the American corporation is an example of this process.

In the beginning of the nation's history, most firms were owned and run by one person, or by a small group of equal partners. Both forms of organization tended to limit the size of the business. A single person could invest only a limited amount of money. A group of partners could invest more, but if there were too many partners, it was hard for all of them to agree on how the firm should be run. What's more, these forms of business came to an end if the individual owner died or retired, or if one of the partners decided to sell out.

The corporation was a solution to these problems: (1) A corporation is owned by many separate investors, who vote to elect a board of directors. The board has the power to run the corporation as it sees fit. (2) Because there are so many owners, corporations can raise huge sums of money. They do this by selling pieces of the corporation (in the form of *shares of stock*). They can also borrow money through the sale of *bonds* (which are promises to pay the money back with

Figure 9-1 The Flow of Economic Activity

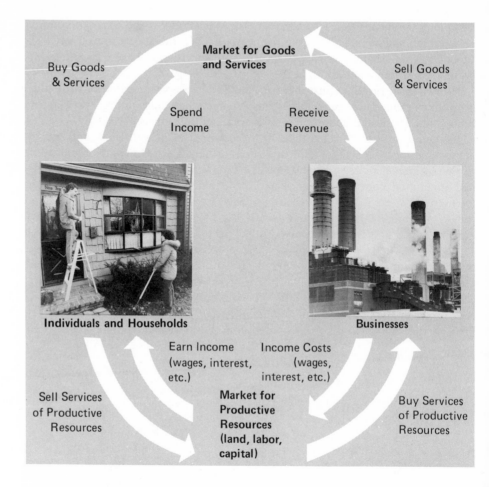

interest). (3) The U.S. corporation is by law a thing quite apart from the people who own it. Therefore, the owners cannot be forced to pay debts owed by the corporation if it were to become bankrupt. This is called *limited liability* (or limited risk). (4) Finally, because stocks and bonds can be transferred from one person to another, a corporation does not cease to exist when one of its owners leaves. It can exist as long as it makes a profit.

Once social institutions are set up, it becomes harder to do things in other ways. In the same way, you develop your own habits and ways of doing things, or personal institutions. Usually these are the ways that have worked for you in the past. You feel comfortable and confident about using them. Sometimes, however, these personal institutions blind you to options that might be better.

☐ The reading for this lesson is from the French novel *Candide* by François Voltaire. It describes the journey of Candide and his friend Cacambo through a mythical land in South America. By describing the social institutions of El Dorado—this mythical land—Candide helps us look at our own economic and social institutions. As you read the story, ask yourself the following questions:

1. What economic and social institutions limit Candide's choices?
2. What habitual ways of acting (personal institutions) limit Candide's choices?
3. How are your choices shaped by social and personal institutions?

CANDIDE

Candide landed with Cacambo near the first village to which they came, at the entrance of which some children, clad in gold brocade, but all in tatters, were playing at quoits. Our two inhabitants of the other world amused themselves with looking on; the quoits were pretty large round objects, yellow, red, and green, which shone with remarkable brilliance. The travellers were seized with a desire to pick up some of them, and found that they were gold, emeralds, and rubies, the smallest of which would have formed the chief ornament of the throne of the Great Mogul.

"Doubtless," said Cacambo, "these children who are playing here are the sons of the king of the country."

The village schoolmaster appeared at that moment to call them into school again.

"That," said Candide, "must be the tutor of the royal family."

The ragged little urchins immediately stopped their game, leaving their quoits on the ground, with all their other playthings. Candide picked them up, and running to the tutor, humbly presented them to him, giving him to understand by signs that their royal highnesses had forgotten their gold and precious stones. The village pedagogue with a smile threw them on the ground, regarded Candide for a moment from head to foot with considerable surprise, and then walked on.

The travellers did not fail to gather up the gold, the rubies, and the emeralds.

"Where are we?" exclaimed Candide. "The children of the kings of this country must be very well brought up, when they are taught to despise gold and precious stones."

Cacambo was as much astonished as Candide.

How does this image represent an American institution?

At length they reached the first house in the village itself, which was built as a palace would be in Europe. A great crowd was thronging at the door, and a still larger number were inside; most exquisite strains of music were heard, and a tempting smell proceeded from the kitchen. Cacambo went up to the door, and heard those within speaking in the language of Peru; it was his mother tongue, for everybody knows that Cacambo was born in Tucuman, at a village where no other language was known.

"I will act as your interpreter," said he to Candide; "let us enter; this is evidently an inn."

When the meal was done, both Candide and Cacambo thought they were paying handsomely for their share by laying on the table two or three of the large pieces of gold which they had picked up, but the host and hostess burst out laughing, and held their sides for a good while before they could recover their gravity.

"Gentlemen," said the innkeeper at last, "it is very evident that you are strangers, and we are not in the habit of seeing such; you must forgive us if we could not help laughing when you offered us for payment the stones which are found upon our high roads. Doubtless you have none of the money of the country, but it is not necessary for you to have any in order to dine here. All the inns established for the convenience of trade are supported by government."

Cacambo expressed all his curiosity to the landlord, and the latter said:

"I am very ignorant, and I find it all the better for me that I am so; but we have in our village an old gentleman, retired from Court, who is the most learned man in the kingdom, and the most ready to impart information."

Therewith he conducted Cacambo to the old man's house. Candide only played second fiddle, and accompanied his servant. They entered a house that was very unpretending, for the front door was only silver, and the panels of the rooms were merely gold, but worked with so much taste that the most sumptuous wainscoting could not have eclipsed them. The entrance hall, indeed, was incrusted with nothing more valuable than rubies and emeralds.

The conversation that followed was a long one, and turned on the form of government, the manners of the people, their women, their public shows, and the state of the arts among them. At last Candide, who always had a taste for metaphysics, inquired through Cacambo if there was any religion in their country.

The old man blushed a little at being asked such a question.

"Pray, can you doubt it?" said he. "Do you take us for wretches incapable of gratitude?"

Candide had the curiosity to wish to see some of their priests, and he bade Cacambo ask where they were to be found. The good old man said with a smile: "My friends, we are all of us priests; the King and all the heads of families solemnly sing hymns of thanksgiving every morning, and five or six thousand musicians accompany them."

"What! Have you no monks among you, who teach, and wrangle, and govern, and intrigue, and have people burned who do not agree with their opinions?"

"We should have to lose our senses first," said the old man; "we are all of the same way of thinking here, and we do not understand what you mean by your monks."

After this long conversation the kind old gentleman ordered a coach and six sheep to be got ready, and lent the services of a dozen of his domestics to escort the two travellers to Court.

A score of beautiful girls who were on guard received Candide and Cacambo as they alighted from the coach and ushered them into the presence of His Majesty.

"The custom," said the high official, "is to embrace the King and kiss him on both cheeks."

What is the function of this brokerage office? How do its transactions affect the economy?

Candide and Cacambo accordingly threw their arms round His Majesty's neck, who received them most graciously, and politely invited them to sup with him.

In the meantime they were taken to see the town—the public buildings, that seemed to touch the clouds; the market-places, beautified with a thousand columns; the fountains of pure water, the fountains of rose water, and those from which the juice of sugar-canes flowed constantly through the great squares, paved with a kind of precious stone which diffused an odour like that of cinnamon and cloves. Candide asked permission to see the Courts of Justice, or Parliament House; he was told that there were none, and that they never had any law-suits. He inquired if there were any prisons, and was answered in the negative. What surprised him yet more, and gave him most pleasure, was the Palace of Science, in which he saw a gallery two thousand feet long, all full of mathematical and philosophical instruments.

After they had spent the whole afternoon in inspecting hardly the thousandth part of the town, they were conducted back to the King.

"To tell you the truth once more, the castle where I was born bears no comparison with the country where we are now. If we stay here we shall be no better than others around us, whereas if we return to our own world with only a dozen sheep laden with the stones of El Dorado, we shall be richer than any king or all put together."

"You are doing a foolish thing," the Sovereign said to them; "I am well aware that my country is insignificant, but when one is tolerably well off anywhere, there one had best remain."

"We only ask Your Majesty," said Cacambo, "for a few sheep laden with provisions, and the stones and clay of the country."

The King answered with a smile: "I cannot comprehend the taste which your people of Europe have for our yellow clay; but take away as much of it as you like, and great good may it do you!"

Select from this text, or any other source, at least three photographs that show American economic institutions. What is it in each that shows you this is an institution? Can the people in these images be interchanged? Why? How might this change the meaning of each photograph? Are there traditional, command, or market elements in these institutions? How is this demonstrated in the photos?

ACTIVITIES

I. This activity will help you to look at two important institutions, the business corporation and the family.

1. The two series of boxes that follow describe the business corporation. One series shows how the institution is formed. The other describes the structure of the corporation and the decisions the people involved make. There are parallel boxes for describing the family.
2. Your first task is to fill in the first series of boxes for the family. Use the boxes in the Workbook. If you don't have a Workbook, copy the boxes on a separate sheet of paper. Assume that the family is organized like a corporation. What, for example, would the charter in the family be? One suggestion has been included.
3. Your next task is to fill in the second series of boxes for the corporation. What do the people do and how are they involved?
4. Finally, fill in the second series of boxes for the family. Assume that the structure of the family is the same as the structure of a corporation. Who in a family would be like the board of directors in a corporation? What do they do and how are they involved?
5. When you are finished, discuss as a class the following questions:
    a. Was it useful to look on the corporation and the family from the same point of view? In what ways are families and corporations the same? In what ways are they different?
    b. Who has power in each institution and how is that power used?
    c. Why has each institution survived? How has each survived?

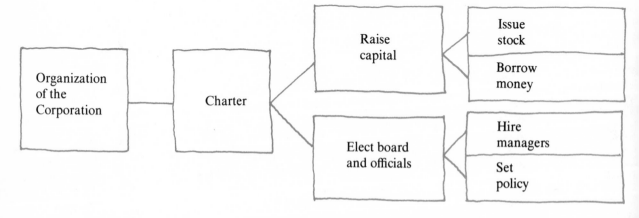

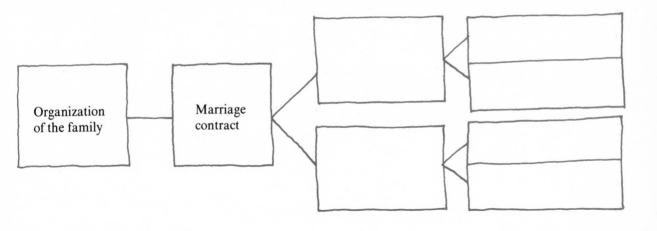

STRUCTURE OF THE CORPORATION	Stockholders:	Directors/Officers:	Managers:

STRUCTURE OF THE FAMILY			
	Make decisions		

II. This activity is about the way certain behaviors become so habitual that they seem to become institutionalized as part of you.

1. If you don't have a Workbook, write the letters from a-q down the left-hand column of a piece of paper. As you read through the list below, decide whether you behave in the described way as a result of habit (mark an H next to it in the Workbook, or the appropriate letter on your piece of paper), because you are convinced that that is the best way (mark a C), or for other reasons (mark an O and explain). Draw a line through the types of behaviors that do not apply to you in the Workbook or the appropriate letters on your piece of paper.

a. laughing when someone makes a joke

b. waiting in line for your turn

c. not disagreeing with a person in authority

d. standing when an important person enters the room

e. ignoring tragic news on TV

f. shaking hands when you meet someone new

g. watching certain TV shows

h. lowering your voice in a place of worship

i. avoiding eye contact in crowded public places

j. how you answer the phone

k. kissing goodbye

l. sitting where you sit in class

m. picking the type of book you usually read

n. tapping your feet when nervous

o. being polite to people you don't like

p. changing the subject when you don't understand or like the topic

q. saying things you don't really mean

2. Circle the five types of behavior that are most important to you. Pick out one or two of these and think of a specific situation in which you might act this way. Describe the situation in the chart below. Now think of two or three other ways you could have acted in that situation.

Behavior	Situation	Alternatives
#1		
#2		
#3		
#4		
#5		

3. Discussion questions
   a. What kinds of behavior or choices are most important to you? Why?
   b. Which of your behaviors are personal institutions? Which are influenced by social institutions?
   c. Do your habits influence you in the way your strongest beliefs do?
   d. What other kinds of behavior could be added to the list as examples of personal or social institutions?
   e. How are the effects of institutions on your choices like the effects of economic institutions on the American economy? How are they different?

107

109

110

111

112

113

114

No. 115
THIS SIDE OUT

116

117

118

119

120

122

123

124

125

IN

241

242

243

244

252

No.   NOV 6
THIS SIDE OUT

265

No.   NOV 6

No.   NOV 6
THIS SIDE OUT

284

285

286

288

289

No.   NOV 6
THIS SIDE OUT

291

No. 292   NOV 6
THIS SIDE OUT

IN

No. 213   NOV 6
THIS SIDE OUT

215

216

219

No. 220
THIS SIDE OUT

221

222

223

224

No.   NOV 6

No. 226   Frank Ward
THIS SIDE OUT

227

No.

No. 230   NOV 6
THIS SIDE OUT

No. 31   NOV
THIS SIDE OUT

TWO

MICRO-ECONOMICS

CHAPTER 4 UNDERSTANDING A MARKET ECONOMY

Consumption and Demand

In a market economy, the basic economic questions—what? how? for whom? and how much?—are answered by buyers and sellers. It is the actions of buyers and sellers who set the prices of goods and services. The prices in turn determine what gets produced, how it is produced, who will buy it, and what the mix of consumer and capital goods will be. The "buyer side" of each transaction is called *demand*. The "seller side" is called *supply*. This lesson will focus on demand.

The demand for a product is the quantity consumers are willing to buy at each of its possible prices. Sellers will try to find the "one best price" that will allow them to make the most money. Buyers will try to find the "one best price" that will bring them the most value for the least cost. The best place to see this at work is an auction.

An auction is a market where goods are sold to the highest bidders. Because the items are sold one at a time, buyers must quickly decide what prices they want to pay. If not, they risk seeing the item go to someone else who is willing to pay more. Imagine now that you are at an auction with about a hundred other people. The auctioneer brings out a used electric popcorn maker and you decide you would like to own it. In order to get it you will have to outbid all the others who want it. How do you decide how high to bid?

Since you know you will have to pay for the popcorn maker right away, you

Table 10-1 Demand for Popcorn Makers	PRICE	QUANTITY DEMANDED
	$11	0
	10	1
	9	1
	8	3
	7	4
	6	4
	5	5
	4	5
	3	5
	2	5
	1	5

look into your wallet. There's nothing there but a $5 bill. You know that you have another $15 in your desk at home and that a friend will lend you that amount if you return it tomorrow. You decide you're willing to go as high as $10 but no higher. You know that a brand-new popcorn maker sells for $14. A used one isn't worth much more than $10. Besides, if you spend all your money, you won't have anything left to buy popcorn, oil, salt, and butter.

What factors so far have influenced you? Your decision is the result of your tastes (for popcorn), your income (the $5 you carry), and your wealth (the $15 at home). You have also had to think of the price of a substitute (a new popcorn maker) and the price of complements (things like popcorn and salt).

The bidding starts at $1 and five people take part in the bidding. The price then goes up to $5, and one person drops out. Five dollars is as much as that person wants to spend for the item. A second person drops out at $7 and two more drop out at $8. That leaves only you. The popcorn maker is yours for $9.

Economists use a tool called a *demand schedule* to study demand. A demand schedule showing what happened at the auction would look like that in Table 10-1. The demand schedule shows how many popcorn makers could have been sold at each of the possible prices (if there had been more than one for sale). Since all five bidders stayed in the auction through $5, five machines could have been sold at that price or anything less than $5. But when the price went up to $6, only four could have been sold. At $9, only one buyer remained—you. And you would have dropped out if the price had gone higher than $10. At $11 there was no demand at all for a used popcorn maker.

This demand schedule can also be placed on a graph, called a *demand curve* (Figure 10-1). This is basically what a demand curve looks like for most products. It slopes downward and to the right because more goods will be bought at lower prices than at higher ones.

Figure 10-1   Demand for Popcorn Machines

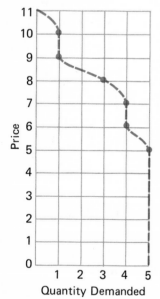

Quantity Demanded

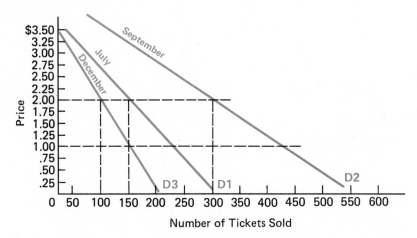

Figure 10-2   Demand for Movie Tickets on an Average Evening

Consumers are more sensitive to price changes for some products than for others. You may not want to buy a car if its price goes up by 10 percent. But if the price of salt goes up 10 percent, that's a different story. Chances are you'll pay the extra 10 percent rather than go without. Economists call this *elasticity of demand.* That is, the demand for cars changes. But the demand for salt is more *inelastic*— it stays very much the same.

The demand curve shown in Figure 10-1 is like a snapshot. It shows the relation between quantity demanded and price at one instant in time. If there is a change in any of the factors affecting demand, then the whole curve will change. If, for example, several people at the auction suddenly had an urge for a previously owned popcorn maker, they would have stayed in the auction and bid up the price.

Figure 10-2 shows the demand curve (D1) for movie tickets in a small town in Colorado during the month of July. In September, the local college reopens and demand shifts to D2. In December, the ski slopes open and demand shifts to D3. If the movie theater holds it prices constant at $2.00, there will be an average of 150 customers in July, 300 in September, and 100 in December. How many tickets would be sold each month if the ticket prices were $1.00?

The things you want to buy reflect your needs. You have material needs for food, clothing, and shelter. You also have psychological needs—for social acceptance, status, power, a sense of identity, and knowledge. You often want things because having them is one way you can meet these needs. For example, you might buy jeans because they form part of your image. Wearing jeans may give you a sense of belonging, set your group apart from other groups, or help you project a certain style. Jeans are important to you because they meet your psychological as well as material needs. You might therefore be willing to pay a higher price for them than you would for similar pants.

What kinds of factors might these people have considered in deciding how much to spend on a car?

☐ The reading for this lesson was written by Peter Carlson. It takes account of the worldwide surge in coffee prices in 1975–76. It shows why one item is so important to some people that they are willing to pay any price for it. As you read the article, ask yourself the following questions:

1. Based on the information in the article, what do you think the demand curve for coffee would look like?
2. What needs does coffee satisfy?
3. What are your most important needs and how do you satisfy them?

CONFESSIONS OF A COFFEE ADDICT

It looks like another foreign cartel has caused another American energy crisis. And this one really hurts.

The first crisis—the oil embargo—made it expensive to provide energy to our machines. This one—the coffee crisis—makes it expensive to provide energy to our nervous systems, which is a whole lot worse.

Nobody seems quite sure who is at fault. The supermarkets blame it on the wholesalers; the wholesalers blame it on the importers; the importers blame it on the growers, and the growers blame it on the weather. But whether it is caused by an act of God or an act of avarice or both, the problem is simple: the price of coffee is skyrocketing. And the social ramifications are horrible. Threatened addicts are never a pleasant sight.

Virtually all American adults are addicted to coffee. I am one of them. I didn't start out that way. Back in my prime—before the age of 10—I bounded out of bed at 6 in the morning, bursting with energy. As soon as my bare feet hit the cold floor, my engines were in high gear and I was off and running. In those days I hated coffee.

Now, after catching that wretched disease called adulthood, I can barely crawl out of bed. Before brushing my teeth, before washing my face, before taking out the dog, before even opening my second eye, I put the coffee water on the fire. I am the Creature from the Black Lagoon before I blast myself into consciousness with coffee. And I love it. I love the taste of coffee, the smell of coffee, the sound of coffee perking. Coffee is so good it makes getting out of bed worthwhile, which is saying something. But I not only *love* coffee, I *need* it metabolically. I need a quick fix in the morning to wake up and I need several more doses during the day to stay up. I am hopelessly addicted and so is almost everybody else.

The Brazilians know that, too. They must be gloating and grinning and carrying on like a team of World Series winners. After all those decades of taking it, now they are giving it out. The norte-americanos may have the money and the power and the Marines, but they have the coffee. And revenge is very sweet.

Realizing that, we should be thankful that they have only raised the price. What if they cut us off entirely? Addicts deprived of their drugs do terrible things. Coffee addicts probably wouldn't mug people or burglarize apartments like heroin addicts—for one thing they wouldn't have the energy—but the effect on our way of life could be worse.

Picture America without coffee:

At offices, clerks with coffeeless coffee breaks fall asleep at their desks. Typists with unstimulated nervous systems rip page after page of errors out of the typewriter. And nobody can stay awake through all those dull meetings.

At factories, production plummets. Products made by somnambulists fall apart. Hardest hit is the late-night ''graveyard shift'' where industrial accidents increase as workers fall asleep into their machines.

Transportation is treacherous. With nearly everybody asleep at the wheel, highways are like the bumper-car rinks at amusement parks.

Show business withers away. Without an after-dinner cup or two, people nod off on the couch after Walter Cronkite. Nobody can stay awake long enough for a night on the town. Bars are empty. Who dares risk a hangover without coffee to doctor them through the morning after?

Literature enters a dark age. Writers, who can't even look at a typewriter without slurping up four or five cups, stop creating new works. As for the classics, who can read Proust without artificial stimulation?

All in all, it's a dismal picture. Nobody wants to see it come true. So, what are the solutions?

Some people are talking about substitutes. Restaurants are pushing tea. It seems logical, being hot and supposedly containing caffeine. I've tried it, though, and it doesn't give me the kick I need. The only part of my body it stimulates is my bladder. Colas have caffeine, too, but the prospect of guzzling the Pause That Refreshes

How does the need for these products affect what people are willing to pay for them?

at 8 in the morning is too grisly to ponder. And I won't even dignify ersatz coffee with consideration.

Extreme measures will no doubt be proposed. During the oil crisis, some people suggested sending in the Marines to turn on the taps. Fortunately, nobody took that seriously. But an addicted public on the verge of panic would probably vote to invade Brazil. Not only would this be aggressive, immoral and nasty, but it would never work. Our sentries could never make it coffeeless through the night. At 3 the first morning, the entire American force would be captured in its sleep. So imperialism is out, too.

We could, I suppose, try to kick the habit cold turkey. Of course, work hours would have to be cut. Nobody could stagger into the office before 10 even if every neighborhood had a brass band parading the streets waking everybody up with Sousa marches. All workplaces would have to institute nap times, like kindergartens. As for the people providing vital services—police, firemen, emergency-room doctors— the government would have to shoot them up with amphetamines.

None of this sounds very appetizing. The only solution I can think of—and it's no solution at all—is to pay the price. Let's face facts, we are addicts. We need this human rocket fuel badly, and we can't grow it ourselves. We must inevitably succumb to what author and ex-junkie William Burroughs calls "the algebra of need." Three dollars a pound, $5 a pound, $10 a pound, whatever it costs, pay cheerfully. If it puts a strain on your wallet, addict, you can always give up some luxury item—like food.

What might the demand curve look like for these products in different seasons?

ACTIVITIES

I. Manufacturers of blue jeans have a varied demand for their product that is dependent on the season. In this activity, you will have the chance to predict and to graph shifts in demand for this product.

1. The tables below show the demand for jeans during the months of September and May in a school year.

TABLE 1   SEPTEMBER

Price	Quantity Demanded (in thousands)
$21	21
18	29
15	38
12	49
9	60
6	81
3	98

TABLE 2   MAY

Price	Quantity Demanded (in thousands)
$21	6
18	13
15	21
12	32
9	49
6	60
3	69

2. Graph the demand shifts using the figures from the table. Use the graph in the Workbook or copy the one in the text. Be sure to label each line.

DEMAND FOR BLUE JEANS—FEBRUARY

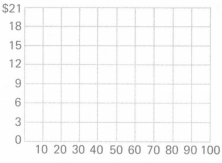

3. Predict what the demand for blue jeans was in February and record your figures on the graph. Label your line.
4. Discussion questions
   a. Why would people want to buy more blue jeans if the price were lower?
   b. How did the February curve compare with the September and May curves?
   c. In what other ways could you use the demand curve?

II. This activity will help you look at some of the psychological aspects of demand. It will help you gain insight into your own needs.

1. Make a list of the needs that owning the car of your dreams could satisfy for you. Explain briefly how it might satisfy each need.
2. Bring to class an ad from a magazine or a description of a television commercial showing the car you most want to buy. Study the ad and decide what is really being sold. What needs (material, economic, and psychological) does the advertiser imply this product could satisfy?
3. List the three most important selling features of the car, according to the ad. Opposite each, list one or two psychological needs that it might satisfy. Use the chart in the Workbook or copy the one in the text.

Features of the car	Needs they could satisfy
1.	
2.	
3.	

4. Now answer these three questions:
   a. Does the car satisfy the needs you first listed on your sheet of paper?
   b. What other needs does it satisfy?
   c. What is really being sold in the ad?
5. When you are finished, discuss these questions with the rest of the class:
   a. What needs do you share with others in your class?
   b. How else could you satisfy the needs that owning a car satisfies?
   c. How does advertising influence demand? Why is it usually so successful?

Production and Supply

The "seller" side of an economic exchange is called the *supply* side. It is the seller's job to supply what buyers demand. As with the buyer, the seller's actions are influenced by a number of things.

A major influence on sellers is the *profit motive*. The seller wants to make the highest profit possible on goods sold. It is not the only thing that affects sellers, but it is one of the most important. Some sellers, for example, would rather keep their profits lower than they could be than take risks. Others would rather work less hard and take a smaller profit. There are also laws that limit the pursuit of profits. These include laws against hiring children, laws that set maximum hours and minimum wages for workers, and safety rules.

Profit is defined as the difference between what it costs to make a good and the price that good sells for. The bigger the difference, the bigger the profit. Profits, therefore, are determined by two things: what it costs to make a product and the prices people are willing to pay for it. For each price offered by consumers, sellers will be willing to offer a different amount of a good or service. It is possible to show a supply schedule similar to the one made for demand.

Table 11-1 is a supply schedule for tennis rackets. It shows how many rackets sellers are willing to supply at each of several possible prices. No one is willing to supply any tennis rackets for only $5. At $10 a racket, sellers are willing to supply 10,000 rackets. At $50 a racket, they are willing to supply 115,000.

Usually, the higher the price offered, the more of a product sellers are willing to supply. This situation can be shown on a graph (Figure 11-1). Why does the supply curve slope upward? Imagine an increase in the price of tennis rackets from $25 to $35. The number sellers are willing to supply at the higher price goes up. At $25, they are willing to supply 40,000 rackets. At $35, they are willing to supply 70,000. The extra 30,000 rackets can come from two sources. Current suppliers can bring more rackets to market. Or new suppliers can enter the tennis racket business.

Some new suppliers, as shown on the graph, will not want to enter the market unless the price goes up to $35. Only at that price can enough profit be made to justify entering a new and strange business.

The same is true for those already in the business. At $25 a racket, they can bring 40,000 rackets to market and still make a profit. In order to bring more, they will need a higher price to meet their extra costs. Their expenses will go up for two reasons. First, making more rackets costs more money. That much is clear. But as the price of rackets starts to rise, and new suppliers get into the business, the competition for the resources needed for racket-making gets more intense. The resources get more scarce. So the price of these resources—lumber, machines, skilled workers—also goes up. These extra costs will be added on to the price of the tennis rackets. Only when the price people are willing to pay is high enough will the current suppliers be willing to increase their production.

In the graph in Figure 11-2, the supply curve, S1, shows how price and quantity relate at a given moment in time. S2 shows what would happen if factory

PRICE	QUANTITY SUPPLIED
$50	115,000
45	100,000
40	85,000
35	70,000
30	50,000
25	40,000
20	30,000
15	20,000
10	10,000
5	0

Table 11-1   Supply Schedule for Tennis Rackets

Figure 11-1 Supply of Tennis Rackets

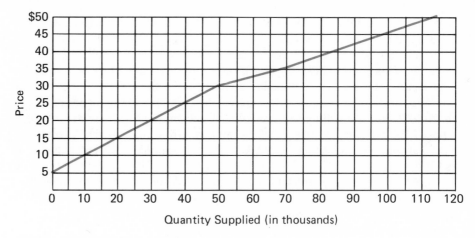

Figure 11-2

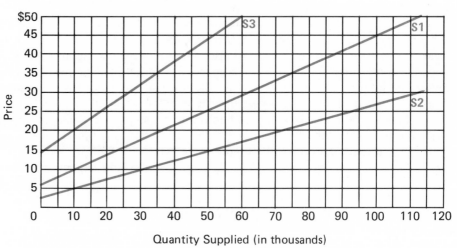

rents went up. S3 shows what would happen if a new, cheaper plastic racket became popular.

Producers are not the only ones who adjust their actions to meet others' needs. Any person who lives with others must learn to understand their needs and to take them into account. In order to have friends and gain the respect and support of others, you need to share. You must help others fulfill their needs as they help you fulfill yours. A producer can only meet the need for profit by fulfilling others' needs for goods or services. Likewise, you can satisfy some of your needs only by meeting the needs of others.

☐ The reading for this lesson is a short story by W. Somerset Maugham. It is about a verger, the person in charge of the interior of a church, in a fashionable neighborhood in London, England. Because of others' psychological needs, the verger is forced to make a hard decision. He finds himself without a job, and hence without income or status. He is able to build a new career for himself by finding something that others need and then providing it. As you read the story, ask yourself the following questions:

1. What is the economic moral of this story?
2. How did others' needs influence Albert Edward's actions as a verger? as a shopkeeper?
3. How do others' needs influence your actions?

What kinds of things do you think affect the profits on this person's craft?

THE VERGER

There had been a christening that afternoon at St. Peter's, Neville Square, and Albert Edward Foreman still wore his verger's gown. He wore it with complacence, for it was the dignified symbol of his office, and without it (when he took it off to go home) he had the disconcerting sensation of being somewhat insufficiently clad.

The verger busied himself quietly, replacing the painted wooden cover on the marble font, taking away a chair that had been brought for an infirm old lady, and waited for the vicar to have finished in the vestry so that he could tidy up in there and go home. Presently he saw him walk across the chancel, genuflect in front of the high altar and come down the aisle; but he still wore his cassock.

When the vicar had walked down the aisle so far that he could address the verger without raising his voice more than was becoming in a place of worship he stopped.

"Foreman, will you come into the vestry for a minute. I have something to say to you."

"Very good, sir."

The vicar preceded Albert Edward into the vestry. Albert Edward was a trifle surprised to find the two churchwardens there. He had not seen them come in. They gave him pleasant nods.

"Good-afternoon, my lord. Good-afternoon, sir," he said to one after the other.

The vicar began briskly.

"Foreman, we've got something rather unpleasant to say to you. You've been here a great many years and I think his lordship and the general agree with me that you've fulfilled the duties of your office to the satisfaction of everybody concerned.''

The two churchwardens nodded.

''But a most extraordinary circumstance came to my knowledge the other day and I felt it my duty to impart it to the churchwardens. I discovered to my astonishment that you could neither read nor write.''

The verger's face betrayed no sign of embarrassment.

''The last vicar knew that, sir,'' he replied. ''He said it didn't make no difference. He always said there was a great deal too much education in the world for 'is taste.''

''We don't want to be harsh with you, Foreman,'' said the vicar. ''But the churchwardens and I have quite made up our minds. We'll give you three months and if at the end of that time you cannot read and write I'm afraid you'll have to go.''

''I'm very sorry, sir, I'm afraid it's no good. I'm too old a dog to learn new tricks. I've lived a good many years without knowin' 'ow to read and write, and without wishin' to praise myself, self-praise is no recommendation, I don't mind sayin' I've done my duty in that state of life in which it 'as pleased a merciful providence to place me, and if I *could* learn now I don't know as I'd want to.''

''In that case, Foreman, I'm afraid you must go.''

''Yes, sir, I quite understand. I shall be 'appy to 'and in my resignation as soon as you've found somebody to take my place.''

Albert Edward was a non-smoker and a total abstainer, but with a certain latitude; that is to say he liked a glass of beer with his dinner and when he was tired he enjoyed a cigarette. It occurred to him now that one would comfort him and since he did not carry them he looked about him for a shop where he could buy a packet of Gold Flakes. He did not at once see one and walked on a little. It was a long street, with all sorts of shops in it, but there was not a single one where you could buy cigarettes.

''That's strange,'' said Albert Edward.

To make sure he walked right up the street again. No, there was no doubt about it. He stopped and looked reflectively up and down.

''I can't be the only man as walks along this street and wants a fag,'' he said. ''I shouldn't wonder but what a fellow might do very well with a little shop here. Tobacco and sweets, you know.''

He gave a sudden start.

''That's an idea,'' he said. ''Strange 'ow things come to you when you least expect it.''

He turned, walked home, and had his tea.

''You're very silent this afternoon, Albert,'' his wife remarked.

''I'm thinkin','' he said.

He considered the matter from every point of view and next day he went along the street and by good luck found a little shop to let that looked as though it would exactly suit him. Twenty-four hours later he had taken it and when a month after that he left St. Peter's, Neville Square, for ever, Albert Edward Foreman set up in business as a tobacconist and newsagent. His wife said it was a dreadful come-down after being verger of St. Peter's, but he answered that you had to move with the times, the church wasn't what it was, and 'enceforward he was going to render unto Caesar what was Caesar's. Albert Edward did very well. He did so well that in a year or so it struck him that he might take a second shop and put a manager in. He looked for another long street that hadn't got a tobacconist in it and when he found it, and a shop to let, he took it and stocked it. This was a success too. Then it occurred to him that if he could run two he could run half a dozen, so he began walking about London, and whenever he found a long street that had no tobacconist and a shop to let he took it. In the course of ten years he had acquired no less than ten shops and he was making money hand over fist. He went round to all of them himself every Monday, collected the week's takings and took them to the bank.

One morning when he was there paying in a bundle of notes and a heavy bag of silver the cashier told him that the manager would like to see him. He was shown into an office and the manager shook hands with him.

"Mr. Foreman, I wanted to have a talk to you about the money you've got on deposit with us. D'you know exactly how much it is?"

"Not within a pound or two, sir; but I've got a pretty rough idea."

"Apart from what you paid in this morning it's a little over thirty

If the owner of this service decided to increase production, what other things might be likely to happen?

thousand pounds. That's a very large sum to have on deposit and I should have thought you'd do better to invest it.''

The manager smiled. ''We'll do everything. All you'll have to do next time you come in is just to sign the transfers.''

''I could do that all right,'' said Albert uncertainly. ''But 'ow should I know what I was signin'?''

''I suppose you can read,'' said the manager a trifle sharply.

Mr. Foreman gave him a disarming smile.

''Well, sir, that's just it. I can't. I know it sounds funny-like, but there it is, I can't read or write, only me name, an' I only learnt to do that when I went into business.''

''And do you mean to say that you've built up this important business and amassed a fortune of thirty thousand pounds without being able to read or write? Good God, man, what would you be now if you had been able to?''

''I can tell you that, sir,'' said Mr. Foreman, a little smile on his still aristocratic features. ''I'd be verger of St. Peter's, Neville Square.''

How might this manufacturer make future changes in order to meet other people's needs?

ACTIVITIES

I. In this activity you will create supply curves for your services. You will look at the factors that affect what you are willing to supply.

1. The following seven jobs are available to you. Rank them in order, giving a (1) to the job you would most like to do and a (7) to the job you would least like to do.

exercise horses	clear and clean tables
serve as lifeguard at a beach club	act as radio disc jockey
	babysit
wash and wax cars	decorate clothing store windows

2. Imagine that you have twenty hours a week of free time over the next two months. You must decide how much of that spare time you will devote to working at a job. Choose the jobs at the top and bottom of the list you have just made. For each job, graph in a separate color how many of your twenty hours you would work if offered $1 an hour, $1.50 an hour, and so on. Use the graph in the Workbook or copy graph A on a piece of paper.

3. Discussion questions
   a. Were you willing to work longer at lower wages for one job than for another? Why?
   b. Were your decisions based on your needs? on others' needs? on market factors? How important was each factor?

4. Choose several of the more popular jobs. Make a class graph B showing the total number of hours that all students would work at each wage. What wage would you expect to receive for each job in your community?

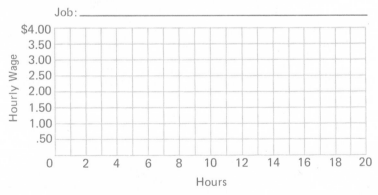

Job: _____   **GRAPH A**

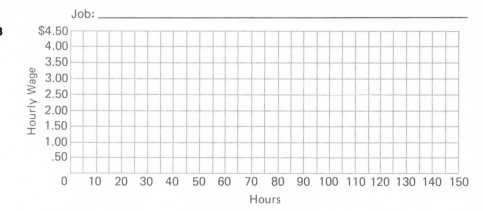

Job: _____

GRAPH B

II. In this activity, you will be the supplier. Your choices of what and how much to supply will depend on your reading of another person's needs.

1. Read the situation and pretend that you are the person making the decision.
2. Write down the need you think the other person has. Use column #1 in the Workbook or copy the chart in the text.
3. Think up and record one or two ways of satisfying the person's need. Use column #1 of the chart.
4. Imagine that your assessment of the situation is not as accurate as you had thought. Repeat the above process and think of a new need and ways of satisfying it. Use column #2 of the chart.

Situation A: An older couple has just moved into your neighborhood. When you call on them, they tell you there are a number of odd jobs around their house that need to be done. They ask you, "How much do you charge an hour?"

#1   #2

Person's need:	Person's need:
How can you satisfy it?	How can you satisfy it?

5.   Repeat the process for Situation B.

Situation B: A new student sits next to you in class.

#1   #2

Person's need:	Person's need:
How can you satisfy it?	How can you satisfy it?

6.   Situation C has been left blank so that you can record a situation in which you have personally taken part.

Situation C:

#1   #2

Need:	Need:
How can you satisfy it?	How can you satisfy it?

7.   Meet in small groups to discuss the effectiveness of the needs and strategies each of you thought up.
8.   Discussion questions
     a.   What happens when you misjudge another's needs?
     b.   How did you test the effectiveness of your choices?
     c.   How can others know what you need?

Equilibrium and Price Mechanisms

In a market economy, prices are the result of the needs of both buyers and sellers. Sellers want to supply more goods at higher prices than at lower ones. Buyers want to buy more goods at lower prices than at higher ones. Somewhere in between the highest price demanded and the lowest price offered is a price that is "just right." This is called the *equilibrium price*. At that price, the amount producers will supply and the amount consumers will buy are the same.

For example, Table 12-1 presents a supply and demand schedule for printed t-shirts. What does this schedule show? At $1 per t-shirt, consumers see a great bargain and are willing to buy 100,000 t-shirts. But suppliers don't see it that way. One dollar a t-shirt is no bargain for them. So, at that price they are not willing to supply any t-shirts. At $2 a t-shirt, they are willing to supply 2,000 t-shirts. But consumers, still sensing a bargain, would like to grab up as many as 80,000 t-shirts. The demand for t-shirts is clearly great enough to warrant a higher output and a higher price. As the price moves upward, the amount producers are willing to supply also goes up. But the amount consumers are willing to buy goes down. Eventually there is a price ($5) at which the number producers are willing to supply and the number consumers are willing to buy is the same— 15,000 t-shirts. This is the equilibrium price.

The supply and demand schedule can also be put on a graph. In this graph,

PRICE	QUANTITY SUPPLIED	QUANTITY DEMANDED
$10	100,000	1,000
9	70,000	3,000
8	50,000	6,000
7	35,000	9,000
6	25,000	12,000
5	15,000	15,000
4	9,000	25,000
3	5,000	50,000
2	2,000	80,000
1	0	100,000

Table 12-1   Supply and Demand Schedule for T-shirts

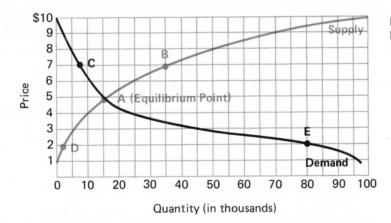

Figure 12-1   Supply and Demand for T-shirts

the equilibrium point is Point A—15,000 t-shirts at $5 a t-shirt. If t-shirt makers try to make more profits by raising the price to $7, they would want to supply 35,000 t-shirts (Point B). But consumers want to buy only 9,000 t-shirts at that price (Point C). So the suppliers are stuck with 26,000 unsold t-shirts. They have no choice but to roll the price back toward its equilibrium point. If, on the other hand, consumers were to offer only $2 a t-shirt, the suppliers would want to supply only 2,000 t-shirts (Point D). But at that price (Point E), they would be swamped by a demand for 80,000 t-shirts. This excess demand will drive the price back up toward its equilibrium point.

The market price also determines who will get the 15,000 t-shirts. They will go to those consumers who can and want to spend $5 on a t-shirt. The market price, then, serves to ration goods and services.

Sometimes a society decides that this is not the best way to share goods and services. This is often the case with very vital goods and services such as food, shelter, and medical care. People may try some other method of choosing who will have them. One method is to let people stand in line or put their names on a waiting list. *Price controls* are often used during wartime to make sure that the prices of important items such as food and gasoline do not go too high. The price of rental housing is controlled by law in some American cities today. During World War II, people were issued *ration stamps* for meat, butter, sugar, canned goods, and gasoline. Each person was thus able to get the minimum of these goods needed to survive. Price controls and ration stamps have also been discussed in recent years as a way of dealing with temporary shortages of gasoline and heating oil.

These alternatives to market prices all have side effects. When prices are not allowed to rise to their market level, suppliers will not supply as much of a good or service as consumers want. In other words, shortages develop. These shortages can sometimes become quite serious.

The market, then, coordinates the needs of producers and consumers. In some ways, groups of people are like market economies. You need things from others and others need things from you. Somehow you must find your own equilibrium point, so that everybody gets what they need. As a "producer," you try to help others as much as you can. In the process, you fulfill some of your own needs—

"Ah ... this must be the hotel group."

like friendship, belonging, and pride. At the same time, as a "consumer," you try to satisfy more selfish wants—for privacy, independence, and status. In both cases, you compete with others whose needs are like yours.

You often find that you and others make more demands on you than you can fulfill. Your time and energy are in short supply. You have to choose, for example, between helping a friend and having a good time. You develop your own ways of deciding who gets what.

☐ The reading for this lesson is from an article by R. A. Radford. It describes an unusual market economy that developed in a prisoner of war camp toward the end of World War II. The prisoners were given rations. Each man received less of some items than he wanted and more of others. The men had to find their own way of redistributing what they had so that all could most fully satisfy their needs. As you read this description, ask yourself the following questions:
1.   How was an equilibrium price for an item arrived at?
2.   How did the market enable the P.O.W.s to coordinate their own needs with others' needs?
3.   How do you coordinate your needs with others' needs?

THE ECONOMIC ORGANIZATION
OF A P.O.W. CAMP

There was active trading of all consumer goods and some services between prisoners. Most trading was in the form of food for cigarettes or other foods, but cigarettes soon grew in status from a normal commodity to currency. Our supplies were made up of rations provided by the Germans, plus the contents of Red Cross food parcels. These included tinned milk, jam, butter, cookies, meat, chocolate, sugar, and so forth, and cigarettes. So far, each person's supplies were equal and regular. Private parcels of clothes, toilet articles, and cigarettes were also received. Equality ended here because of the different amounts sent. All of these things were subject to trade.

Very soon after capture, people realized that, because of the limited size and inequality of supplies, it was not a good idea to give away or accept gifts of cigarettes or food. "Goodwill" turned into trading as a fairer way to bring about personal satisfaction.

How is the equilibrium
price for a product like
this determined?

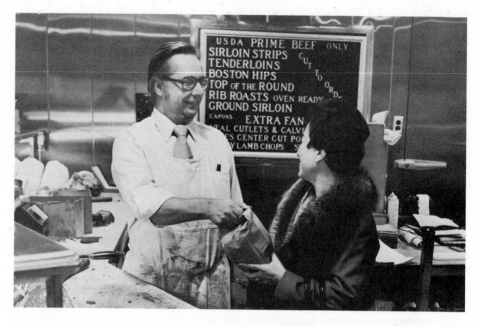

We reached a camp in Italy about two weeks after capture, and one
week later, each of us received one-quarter of a Red Cross food
parcel. At once, exchanges, which had already begun, grew in size.
Starting with simple direct trade—such as a nonsmoker trading a
smoker friend his cigarettes for a chocolate ration—more complex
exchanges soon became common. Stories were told of a chaplain
who started going around the camp with only a tin of cheese and five
cigarettes to trade. By the time he returned to his bed, his trading had
netted him a complete parcel of supplies, plus his original cheese and
cigarettes. Apparently, the market was not yet perfect.

Within a week or two, as the volume of trade grew, rough scales of
exchange values were set up. The Indian P.O.W.s had at first
exchanged tinned beef for almost any other foods. They soon began
to insist on jam and margarine. It was realized that a tin of jam was
worth a half-pound of margarine plus something else. A cigarette
issue was worth several chocolate issues. On the other hand, a tin of
diced carrots was worth almost nothing.

In this camp we did not visit other barracks very much, and prices
varied from place to place (hence the germ of truth in the story of the
shrewd chaplain). After a month, when we reached our permanent
camp, there was a lively trade in all goods. Their values were well-
known and were expressed not in terms of each other, but in terms of
cigarettes. Cigarettes became the standard of value. In the permanent

camp, people wandered through the barracks calling out their offers: "Cheese for seven" (cigarettes). And the hours after parcel issue were always bedlam. Because this system was inconvenient, it was soon replaced by an Exchange and Mart bulletin board in each barrack. Here, under the headings "Name," "Room Number," "Wanted," and "Offered," sales and wants were advertised. When a deal went through, it was crossed off the board. This public record of trades made cigarette prices well-known, and thus prices tended to be the same throughout the camp. But a clever trader could always make a profit from barter. With this development, everyone, including nonsmokers, was willing to sell for cigarettes, using them to buy at another time and place. Cigarettes became the normal currency, although barter never stopped.

General prices were affected by many factors. The arrival of new prisoners, always hungry, raised them. Heavy air raids in the neighborhood of the camp increased the demand for cigarettes and lowered prices. Good or bad war news had its effect, and the general waves of optimism and pessimism which swept the camp were reflected in prices. Before breakfast one morning in March of 1945, a rumor of the arrival of parcels and cigarettes went around. Within ten minutes, I sold a molasses ration for four cigarettes (hitherto offered in vain for three), and many similar deals went through. By 10 o'clock the rumor was denied, and molasses that day found no more buyers even at two cigarettes.

More interesting than changes in the general price level were changes in the price structure. Changes in the supply of a good, in

What kinds of things might affect supply and demand for this type of "product"?

the German ration scale, or in the makeup of Red Cross parcels would raise the price of one good compared to others. Tins of oatmeal, once a rare and much sought-after luxury in the parcels, became common in 1943, and the price fell. In hot weather, the demand for cocoa fell, while that for soap rose. A new recipe would be reflected in the price level. For instance, the discovery that raisins and sugar could be turned into an alcoholic liquor of awesome strength had a permanent effect on the dried fruit market. The invention of electric immersion heaters run off the power points made tea, a glut on the market in Italy, a certain seller in Germany.

VISUAL ACTIVITY

Select from any source at least ten images (photos, drawings, or paintings) of things that are wanted or needed by people. These can be either "products" or "services". Arrange them in order according to what you would be willing to pay for them. Then ask someone else to help you arrange them in order according to what you both think they might really cost. Is the order the same? Could you change anything in each image so that the order would be more nearly the same? If so, what? If not, why? What kinds of factors do you consider in this process?

If there is a greater shortage of this product, how might society "ration" its use?

ACTIVITIES

I. This activity is designed to let you see how supply and demand interact to determine the market price of a pair of blue jeans.

1. Divide into two groups. A small group of five students will represent the board of directors of a major blue jeans company. The rest of the students will play consumers. Each student in this group represents 100 people, although decisions are made as if everybody were acting for themselves.
2. The board meets to determine how much to sell a pair of blue jeans for if the jeans cost $8 to manufacture. The board must also decide how many pairs to manufacture.
3. The consumers decide how many pairs of blue jeans they will buy for that price. Each student can buy up to 500 pairs of jeans (since each student represents 100 consumers). Each student must decide alone and then announce this decision to the class.
4. If equilibrium hasn't been reached, the board must meet again. It must decide upon another price (higher or lower) and another quantity (higher or lower).
5. The consumers again decide, each by himself, how many pairs to buy at that price. If equilibrium is not reached, the board must meet again. This process continues until equilibrium is reached.
6. Discussion questions
    a. How hard was it to reach equilibrium? Why was it hard?
    b. How did consumers' choices influence the board? How did the board's choices influence consumers?
    c. What situations in your life are like this market? How do others' choices influence your choices?

II. In a market, the goal is to satisfy the needs of both producers and consumers. In this activity, you will be competing and trading with others.

1. Separate into groups of three students each. In this activity, each group will need to develop its own way of working together in choosing items and participating in the trading sessions.

2. Decide which items on the chart you most want. Rank the items from 1 (most desirable) to 20 (least desirable). The most desirable items are the ones most desirable to you. Record your answers on the chart in the Workbook. If you don't have a Workbook, copy this chart on a separate piece of paper.

Item	Rank by Value to Me	Rank by Market Value
season ticket to a sporting event		
10-speed bicycle		
new color TV		
farming tools		
Reader's Digest subscription		
set of oil paints		
new paint job for a car		
camping equipment		
museum membership		
slide rule		
complete set of Shakespeare		
8-week-old puppy		
pocket computer		
motorboat		
briefcase		
new winter coat		
chess game		
watch		
$100.00		
flying lessons		

3. Now decide which items would be most popular among your classmates. Rank the items from 1 (most popular) to 20 (least popular). Record your response on the chart. The most popular items are the ones most valuable in the classroom marketplace.
4. Have one student write the numbers from 1 to 10 on separate pieces of paper. Each group should pick a number from a hat or box.
5. Groups should refer to their original rankings and decide what strategy they will use to try to get the items they want. There will be two rounds of picking items, with a chance to trade numbers before the second round.
6. *First round:* The group with Number 1 picks first, the group with Number 2 picks second, and so on.
7. Groups may walk around the room for 15 minutes to trade numbers or items.
8. *Second round:* The group with Number 10 picks first, the group with Number 9 picks second, and so on.
9. Discussion questions
    a. How did you coordinate what you wanted with what others within your group wanted? How fair were the results?
    b. How did your group coordinate what it wanted with what other groups wanted? How fair were the results?

III. This activity will help you check your understanding of supply and demand. The following problems are based on the diagram at right.

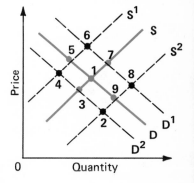

1. Point 1 represents the market equilibrium for margarine. If the price of butter suddenly drops 25 percent,
    a. what will happen to the demand curve?
    b. what will happen to the supply curve?
    c. at what point will the new market equilibrium be reached?
2. D and S represent the demand and supply curves for the product made by the XYZ industry. A new collective bargaining agreement has been signed, giving employees a 25 percent wage increase.
    a. What will happen to the demand curve?
    b. What will happen to the supply curve?
    c. At what point will the new market equilibrium be reached?
3. The laboratories of a major textile company were able to develop a new type of fiber that is much cheaper to make than the type now used. It has been proved that the new type has colors that will not fade and is thus superior to the old one. If the market for this kind of fiber was at equilibrium at Point 1,
    a. what will happen to the demand curve?
    b. what will happen to the supply curve?
    c. at what point will the new market equilibrium be reached?

CHAPTER 5 COMPETITION AND MARKET STRUCTURE

Perfect Competition

Economists use the term *perfect competition* to describe a model world. In such a world, competition would rule. Costs of production would be as low as possible. All resources would be put to uses that best satisfied people's demands. By comparing this model to the real world, certain features of real market economies stand out more sharply.

Think for a moment of what would be required for perfect competition to exist. First, for every good or service (like shoes, cars, and medical care), there would have to be many buyers and sellers. No one of them would be large enough to control prices. None of them would be able to influence the actions of the others, and none of them could cooperate. Influence and cooperation would interfere with competition, making it less than perfect. For instance, if two large producers, A and B, agreed to charge a certain price for their goods, other producers would be forced to do the same thing. If their price were higher than the market price, then all prices would be rigged upward. If it were lower than the market price, some firms would be forced out of business or would be taken over by producers A and B.

Second, all suppliers in the market would make identical products. Buyers would then make their decisions about who to buy from based only on market prices.

Figure 13-1
Which of the two firms
would never change its
price? Why?

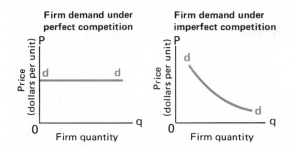

Third, all buyers and sellers would have to have full knowledge of all market conditions. Producers would have to know where the cheapest resources could be found. Consumers would have to know what stores charged the lowest prices. If a woman wanted to buy a new pair of shoes, for instance, she would have to know what every store near her was charging for the kind of shoes she liked. If she knew only what the store down the street charged, that store would have an advantage over the others. Competition then would no longer be perfect.

Fourth, there would be perfect mobility for buyers and sellers. This means that they would have to be free to move around in search of the highest profits or the best deal. A lumberjack in Maine, for instance, might find that higher wages were paid lumberjacks in Oregon. He would then have to be able to pick up and move to Oregon. Or a company might be making nails and find that hammers were selling at a higher profit this month. It would have to be free to switch production to hammers.

It is probably clear by now how hard it is to achieve these conditions. The reasons why it is so hard suggest what the restrictions on competition are in a real market economy:

1. Suppliers of goods and services are not all the same size. Luck, skill, and other factors permit some firms to grow larger than others. Also, some markets do not have a large number of suppliers. Some have only a few, while others, like telephone service, have but one.
2. Not all the producers in an industry make the same product. In fact this condition is met only in a few markets, such as the market for some farm products like wheat or soybeans, and the stock market.
3. Perfect knowledge of market conditions is hard to achieve in any economy. It might be possible to know the prices of goods and services in one part of the country. It would be very hard to know all prices everywhere. Even if such knowledge did exist, it might not be possible to take advantage of it.
4. The reason for this is that perfect mobility does not exist. People cannot move every time they hear of a chance to make more money. Nor can producers simply switch from one product to another. Changing production methods is costly and takes time.

Perfect competition is not only hard to achieve. It is often unpleasant as well. For this reason, most people try to avoid it. Perfect competition, it is true, would drive production costs down, as each producer tried to get goods to market at the lowest possible price. But it would also mean less money for the owners of the resources that go into making goods and services. Workers, for instance, would get the lowest possible wages. The owners of land, minerals, and capital would also get the lowest possible prices. And profits too would go down. In the past, therefore, when competition got too stiff, those who suffered from it organized trade unions or business groups. They forced the price of resources back up to higher levels. The tactics vary, but the goal is always the same. People try to reduce competition so they can make more money.

A purely competitive market, then, involves people acting alone, with everyone trying to gain as much for herself as possible. In human affairs, as in economics, this model is rarely achieved. You are an individual, but you are also a member of many groups. You belong to a family. You also belong to social, school, religious, and neighborhood groups. You want to help the members of your own group more than you do strangers. You and your friends thus tend to act as a group. You work together for common goals rather than competing against each other. You can build a sense of trust within the group so that you do not always have to be on guard.

Who pays the price for this kind of damage in a market economy?

☐ The reading for this lesson is from an article by Henry G. Manne. It describes how competition broke down when some people chose to act as a group. As you read it, ask yourself the following questions:

1. Was there perfect competition at the beginning of the story?
2. What did the members of APPLE gain by acting as a group? What did they lose?
3. How would you solve the new problem?
4. What groups do you belong to? How do they act as a group?

THE PARABLE OF THE PARKING LOTS

In a city not far away there was a large football stadium. It was used from time to time for various events, but the principal use was for football games played Saturday afternoons by the local college team. The games were tremendously popular, and people drove hundreds of miles to watch them. Parking was done in the usual way. People who arrived early were able to park free on the streets. Latecomers had to pay to park in regular and improvised lots.

In the neighborhood of the stadium there were about 25 parking lots. The lots closer to the stadium received more football business than those farther away. Some of the very close lots actually raised their price on Saturday afternoons. But they did not raise the price much, and most did not change prices at all. The reason was not hard to find.

For something else happened on football afternoons. A lot of people who lived nearby went into the parking lot business. It was not a hard thing to do. Typically, a young boy would put up a crude, homemade sign saying "Parking $3." He would direct a couple of cars into his parents' driveway, tell the driver to take the key, and collect the three dollars. The whole system seemed to work fairly smoothly. Though traffic just after a big game was terrible, there were no significant delays parking cars or retrieving parked cars.

But one day the owner of a chain of parking lots called a meeting of all the commercial parking lot owners. They formed an organization known as the Association of Professional Parking Lot Employers, or APPLE. And they were very concerned about the Saturday parking business. One man who owned four parking lots pointed out that honest parking lot owners had heavy capital investments in their businesses, that they paid taxes, and that they employed individuals who supported families. There was no reason, he alleged, why these lots should not handle all the cars coming into the area for special events like football games. "It is unethical," he said, "to engage in cutthroat competition with irresponsible fender benders. After all, parking cars is a profession, not a business." This last remark drew loud applause. Ethical car parkers, he said, understand their obligations not to dent fenders, to employ only trustworthy car parkers, and to pay decent wages.

Others at the meeting related various tales of horror about nonprofessional car parkers. One homeowner, it was said, actually allowed his fifteen-year-old son to move other peoples' cars around. Another said that he had seen an $8,000 Cadillac parked on a dirt lawn where it would have become mired in the mud had it rained that day. He felt that a professional group such as APPLE had a duty to protect the public from their folly in using those parking spaces. Still another speaker reminded the audience that these "fly-by-night" parking lot operators generally parked a string of cars in their driveways so that a driver had to wait until all cars behind his had been removed before he could get his out. "Clearly," he said, "driveway parking constitutes unfair competition."

Emotions ran high at this meeting, and every member of APPLE pledged $1 per parking space for something mysteriously called a "slush fund." It was never made clear exactly whose slush would be bought with these funds, but several months later a resolution was

If a utility like the telephone company was broken down into smaller producers, what might the effects on service be?

What might be some of the functions of the courts in a market economy? Are they needed? Why or why not?

adopted by the city council requiring licensing for anyone in the parking lot business.

The preamble to the new ordinance read like the speeches at the earlier meeting. It required that anyone parking cars for a fee must have a minimum capital devoted to the parking lot business of $25,000. They must have liability insurance in an amount not less than $500,000. Finally a special driving test for these parkers (which would be designed and run by APPLE) would be needed. The law also required that every lot charge a single posted price for parking and that any change in the posted price be approved in advance by the city council. Incidentally, most members were able to raise their fees by about 20 percent before the first posting.

Then a funny thing happened to drivers on their way to the stadium for the next big game. They saw city police in unusually large numbers, who told them that it was illegal to pay a non-licensed parking lot operator for the right to park a car. These policemen also reminded parents that it was against the law for their children to park cars. There were no driveway parking lots that day.

Back at the commercial parking lots, another funny thing occurred. Proceeding from the entrance of each of these parking lots within twelve blocks of the stadium were long lines of cars waiting to park. The lines got larger as the lots were closer to the stadium. Many drivers had to wait so long or walk so far that they missed the entire first quarter of the big game.

At the end of the game it was even worse. The confusion was massive. The lot attendants could not cope with the jam-up. Some cars were not retrieved until the next day. It was even rumored about town that some cars had been lost forever. Industry spokesmen denied this, however.

Naturally there was a lot of grumbling, but there was no agreement on what had caused the problem. At first, everyone said there were merely some "bugs" in the new system that would have to be ironed out. But the only "bug" ironed out was a Volkswagen which was flattened by a careless lot attendant in a Cadillac Eldorado.

The situation did not improve at later games. The members of APPLE did not hire more people to park cars. Operators near the stadium were not careful to follow their previous practice of parking cars in such a way as to have them easy to reach. Employees seemed to become more surly. And the number of dented-fender claims rose rapidly.

ACTIVITIES

This activity is designed to involve you in the kind of rough competition that takes place in the real business world.

1. Split the class into five groups. Four groups will represent the management of four separate and competing transport companies. The fifth group will represent the board of directors of a leading appliance manufacturer. Each group's goal is to make the most profits now and in the future.
2. The game is divided into days. The four transport companies compete against one another each day by bidding for the business of delivering appliances to a chain of suburban department stores.
3. Each transport company must bid high enough for the company to cover expenses and to make a profit but low enough to compete successfully with the other bidders. Each truck can make only one delivery per day.
4. The appliance manufacturer has a contract with the suburban store chain to deliver at least twenty shipments each week. The appliance factory can manufacture enough appliances to make only five shipments a day.

GAME RULES

a. The manufacturer states the number of trucks needed for the first day.
b. The manufacturer goes to all the transport companies to urge them to submit low bids. The final bid of each company is put on a separate bid sheet and given to the manufacturer.

Transportation Company:

_____(number)_____ trucks at $ _____ each

---

c. The manufacturer can now return to any or all of the transport companies to get them to lower their bids. The manufacturer may or may not give them truthful information about the other companies' bids. Each company then has the option to submit a new bid.

d.   The manufacturer decides and announces which company or companies will get how much business for that day. There need be no mention of the price of the bids.

e.   Each transport company must figure out how much cash it has on hand at the end of that day. All expenses must be subtracted from this figure. (These figures will be supplied to each group by the teacher.) Then, whatever profit there is for that day is added to that amount. If at any point a transport company cannot meet its expenses, it is considered bankrupt and must leave the game.

f.   At the end of each day, one person representing each transport company may, but does not have to, meet with the other representatives.

5.   At the end of each day, discuss the following questions:

   a.   How do the members of your company operate as a group?

   b.   How do the transport companies work as one group? How do they operate as separate groups?

   c.   How do you deal with the conflict in your goals?

6.   When the game is over, discuss as a class the following questions:

   a.   At what levels of competition was the game played?

   b.   What strategies were thought up to deal with the manufacturer? with the transport companies?

   c.   Which groups were successful as a group? Which groups were successful in the game? How did you measure success?

Who would pay for this kind of research in a purely competitive economy?

Monopoly, Oligopoly, and Imperfect Competition

Competition can be thought of as having two extremes. Perfect competition is at one extreme and monopoly is at the other. Under perfect competition, competition is unrestricted. Under *monopoly*, there is no competition at all. A monopoly exists when one seller supplies all of the demand for a particular product or service. It does not have to compete with any other sellers. In between perfect competition and monopoly are various forms of *imperfect competition*. Of these, the most common and most important is *oligopoly*. An oligopoly is a market dominated by just a few large producers.

Some of the best-known products in the United States are produced under conditions of oligopoly. There are three important kinds of oligopoly. In one kind, identical products are produced. The steel industry is an example of this type. Since the products made by the major steel companies are the same, buyers have no reason to prefer one brand to another—unless one brand sells for less than the others. None of the steel companies want to set off a "price war," however, so they all charge the same prices. When one company raises prices, the others quickly follow. In this kind of oligopoly, it is usually the high cost of starting production that keeps new competitors away.

Another kind of oligopoly occurs in the gasoline industry. Here products are basically the same. Advertising attempts to convince consumers that there are

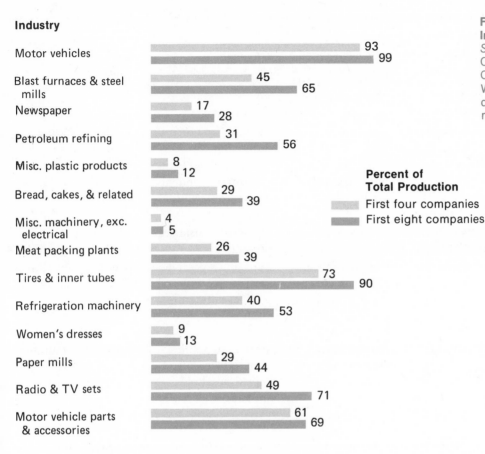

Industry

Motor vehicles — 93 / 99

Blast furnaces & steel mills — 45 / 65

Newspaper — 17 / 28

Petroleum refining — 31 / 56

Misc. plastic products — 8 / 12

Bread, cakes, & related — 29 / 39

Misc. machinery, exc. electrical — 4 / 5

Meat packing plants — 26 / 39

Tires & inner tubes — 73 / 90

Refrigeration machinery — 40 / 53

Women's dresses — 9 / 13

Paper mills — 29 / 44

Radio & TV sets — 49 / 71

Motor vehicle parts & accessories — 61 / 69

Percent of Total Production
First four companies
First eight companies

Figure 14-1   U.S. Industry Concentration
Source: Department of Commerce, Bureau of the Census
Which market model best describes conditions in most U.S. industries?

important differences between one brand and another. So, consumers will often stick with their favorite brand even if its price goes up and the others stay the same. But they will do this only up to a point. If the price of a favored brand of gas goes up *too* much, consumers will leave it for another brand. For this reason, the prices of the different brands of gas do not vary within a given region of the country by more than a few cents a gallon.

An example of imperfect competition with many sellers is the furniture industry. Here many firms produce many kinds of furniture designed to appeal to different tastes, needs, and incomes. In this kind of imperfect competition, prices will vary a great deal from one maker to another.

Monopolies, oligopolies, and imperfect competition all represent attempts to control markets and prices. Often these efforts are helped by the laws. By giving

CHARACTERISTIC	MARKET MODEL			
	Perfect competition	*Monopolistic competition*	*Oligopoly*	*Pure monopoly*
Number of firms	A very large number	Many	Few	One
Type of product	Standardized	Differentiated	Standardized or differentiated	Unique: no close substitutes
Control over price	None	Some, but within rather narrow limits	Circumscribed by mutual interdependence; considerable with collusion	Considerable
Conditions of entry	Very easy, no obstacles	Relatively easy	Significant obstacles present	Blocked
Nonprice competition	None	Considerable emphasis on advertising, brand names, trademarks, etc.	Typically a great deal, particularly with product differentiation	Mostly public relations advertising
Example	Agriculture	Retail trade, dresses, shoes	Steel, automobiles, farm implements, many household appliances	AT&T, local utilities

**Table 14-1
Characteristics of the
Four Basic Market
Models**

inventors the sole rights to their creations, government gives to one firm an advantage over others. In this way it tries to encourage new inventions. Government can also tax imported goods, thus giving home producers an advantage over foreign ones. When states require licenses of doctors, nurses, and lawyers, they are limiting the number of people who can offer these services. This is a big advantage to those who are in these professions. All of these practices restrict competition.

Labor unions are another source of imperfect competition. Where closed shops exist, they can restrict the number of people who compete for certain jobs. That tends to increase the wages paid to workers who belong to unions. Firms, too, can restrict competition in hiring when they set arbitrary standards for certain jobs. They can require a college degree or past experience, even though the job could be done as well by a person without them. This practice tends to give those who are socially advantaged a monopoly over the best jobs.

A *natural monopoly* exists whenever the nature of a market is such that one producer can best supply all of its needs. Many public utilities, such as electric

(1) Price	(2) Demand	(3) Total revenue	(4) Changes in total revenue	(5) Changes in demand	(6) Marginal revenue [col. (4) ÷ col. (5)]
$10.00	100	$1,000			
9.00	200	1,800	$800	100	$8
8.00	300	2,400	600	100	6
7.00	400	2,800	400	100	4
6.00	500	3,000	200	100	2
5.00	600	3,000	0	100	0
4.00	700	2,800	−200	100	−2
3.00	800	2,400	−400	100	−4
2.00	900	1,800	−600	100	−6
1.00	1000	1,000	−800	100	−8

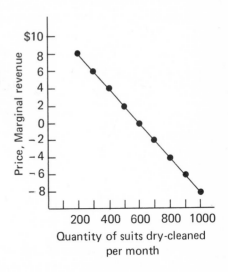

companies and telephone companies, are examples of this. It would be wasteful to have several telephone companies in the same town. In the case of natural monopolies, therefore, the economic question is not whether there should be more competition. Rather, it is how much of the monopoly's policies (for example, its prices) should be set by the government.

The effects of monopoly and oligopoly are many. To begin with, prices under all forms of imperfect competition are apt to be higher than they would be under perfect competition. Profits, too, will be higher. After all, in the absence of competition, a producer can set prices almost anywhere. Resources are likely to be used less efficiently under imperfect competition. There is no incentive to find the lowest production costs. Also, resources under imperfect competition do not get used for the products that are most in demand. They are used instead for the products commanding the highest prices—in other words, for those made by oligopolies and monopolies.

How important is monopoly power? Even back in 1776, Adam Smith was complaining in *The Wealth of Nations*: "People of the same trade seldom meet together, even for merriment and diversion, but the conversation ends in a conspiracy against the public, or in some contrivance to raise prices."

Sometimes you may feel like a victim of a monopoly. For instance, if one person has too much power or prestige, everyone may feel pressured to do what he says. But usually groups have more power than individuals do. By acting as part of a group, you can stand up to your opponents and make your own choices. Oligopolists can set outrageous prices or conditions if everyone in the group goes along. In the same way, with a group to back you up, you can say and do things that you'd be afraid to try alone. Oligopolists can control the practices of their industries. Groups too can create their own lifestyles.

Table 14-2 (left)
Demand, Total Revenue, and Marginal Revenue for Dry Cleaning Suits

Figure 14-2 (right)
Demand and Marginal Revenue Curves
How would you define marginal revenue?

☐ The reading for this lesson describes the creation and operation of an oligopoly. As you read it, ask yourself the following questions:
1. What effect does the Philip Morris acquisition have on beer consumers?
2. What power might Philip Morris gain by buying up companies in different industries?
3. What power might Philip Morris gain by helping its small competitors? by buying them?
4. What power do you get from the groups you belong to?

── THE BATTLE OF THE BEERS ──

There was a time when it seemed as if every large town or small city had its own brewery. Certainly every large city had three or four, and sometimes more. Immediately after Prohibition ended in the 1930's, there were in fact over 700 breweries in the United States. By 1965, this number had dwindled to 120. By 1975, there were fewer than 60. Many people now feel there may only be 15 by the 1980's.

What happened to all the local breweries? They have been eaten alive by the big giants. The graph below shows dramatically what has been happening just recently.

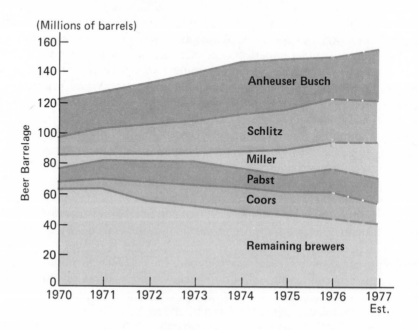

(Millions of barrels)

One of the newest entries into the Battle of the Beers is the Philip Morris Company. What prompted a cigarette company to buy out a beer company?

"We'd already been dealing with farm products," one of their executives said. "We were used to making packages that would be thrown out after their use. The beer business isn't that different. There are the same kinds of markets. You have to advertise in the same kinds of ways.

"You have to understand," the woman continued, "the day of the small business is gone. It has been replaced by the large corporation. But a corporation like Philip Morris isn't just a larger business than Miller Brewing Company, which we bought. Our corporation is really a group of corporations.

"We bought Miller because it makes us stronger. On the one hand, you could say we get more powerful as we get bigger. But it isn't as simple as that. We get more powerful because we become a larger group. There are more corporations acting together. We benefit from having more products to sell. We can afford to hire better managers. And when we bought Miller, we got a company that was already known by the public. It was much better than starting our own brewery. That is what makes the Philip Morris Company such a competitive corporation. As a large group, all our corporations are stronger than they could be if they were each acting alone."

The new management's breakthrough was in the way it packaged its product. It began with a new 7-ounce bottle, instead of the standard 12-ounce size. This did for Miller's sales what the flip-top box did for the sales of Philip Morris's Marlboro cigarettes.

What type of corporation produces these products? Why aren't there more producers?

After introducing several new brands without success, the company came up with a big winner: the low-calorie Lite beer. It has been one of the most successful beers in history. Now Miller is playing with other ideas: an 8-ounce can and a premium beer to challenge Michelob.

All of this costs money, big money. Philip Morris has spent close to $500 million on buying and revitalizing Miller. Already Miller is beginning to show big profits; 1976 brought the company over $75,000,000 in profits, 1977, even more. And the Philip Morris people expect an even brighter future.

Not surprisingly, this has prompted the giant in the industry— Anheuser-Busch—to respond. Busch is now spending record amounts on its own advertising. That company is coming out with smaller bottles and smaller cans. And it has begun a price war by reducing prices on most of its products.

Both these companies are increasing their production capacity. Busch has just opened up a new factory in California. All its plants are working at or near full capacity. Each year it increases the amount of beer it makes and the amount it is capable of making.

Who are the victims in this battle of the giants? Many observers of the industry feel it is the small regional breweries. They simply don't have the resources to build huge plants. They can't match the huge advertising campaigns that Miller and Schlitz and Budweiser mount.

Do unions contribute to monopolistic growth? In what ways?

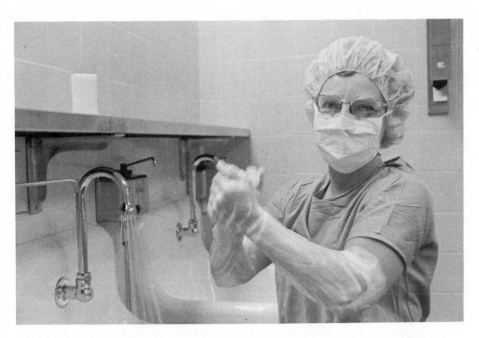

Does licensing of this profession create, in any way, a type of monopoly? Is this necessary?

When asked about this trend and what it will mean for the regional companies, a Busch executive explains: "Just because numbers one, two, and three are being aggressive doesn't mean the smaller companies will have to close down. It's a competitive world. And it's good for the consumer.

"Of course," he continues, "if they need our help, we are more than willing to help. We have bought up many of these small companies. We can provide them with the money they need to expand or even to keep alive. We can provide them with the know-how and distribution outlets. We will do everything we must to keep competition alive, even if it means buying out our competitors. Competition is the spice of life."

After all, we all know that what is good for Bud is good for the country.

ACTIVITIES

I. In this activity, the game of Monopoly has been restructured to let you try various degrees of imperfect competition. Think of the nonmaterial as well as the material benefits of the way your team plays the game.

1. Three variations of the game of Monopoly are listed. The basic rules of the game should still be followed.
2. The class divides into teams of two or three students each who will play together against no more than four other teams.
3. Choose one of the following ways of playing:
   a. Each team rolls the dice. The team rolling the highest number gets $4,000 more than the other teams.
   b. After all teams have gone around the board once, deal out the remaining property cards.
   c. Group the property cards according to color. Each team then writes down a secret bid for the color or colors it wants most. Teams can bid for as much property as they want, given the money they have. After all the teams have written their bids, all the bids are opened. The property is bought by the highest bidder.
4. Discussion questions
   a. What were the effects of the various types of power given to the teams playing each of the games?
   b. How was competition discouraged and encouraged in your game?
   c. What were the advantages and disadvantages of playing on a team?

II. This activity is about the power you can gain from being part of a group. It may help you to understand how corporations become more powerful by grouping together.

1. Split up into groups of six to eight students. Each group chooses a role play situation from the list below or makes up another one.
   a. You have been invited to spend the weekend with friends. You must convince your parents to let you go.
   b. You are trying to convince your best friend to run for class president.
   c. Your family has just moved to a new apartment building. The superintendent does not know you and becomes angry when he finds you exploring the hallways. He threatens to call the police.

    d. You are trying to get the best deal you can on sports equipment. You try to talk the store manager into giving you a discount.

2. As a group, discuss the situation. How could a person effectively persuade the people he must convince? Would it be more effective to argue alone, with one person to back you up, or with a larger group behind you?

3. Take turns role playing the different strategies to see which one is most effective. Start alone; then role play with one or two others. Finally, role play with three or four others.

4. Discussion questions

    a. When was the size of the group important?

    b. In which situations did you benefit from group membership? In which situations was it a hindrance? Why?

    c. When have you gotten power from group membership?

What monopoly did this industry replace? Is this industry becoming monopolistic? How?

Factor Markets

In a market economy, each of the three kinds of resources (human, natural, and capital) is bought and sold in a market. The resources are called factors of production. The markets are called *factor markets*. Those for the three basic resources can be thought of in the same way as the market for goods and services. Producers shop in factor markets for the resources they need. The prices of resources are subject to the same laws of supply and demand that affect goods and services.

Firms decide what to make based on the prices they have to pay for resources. If the price of resources needed for one product goes too high, they may switch to making a different product. For example, leather seat covers were once standard equipment in cars. Leather was cheap compared to substitutes such as cloth. But when plastic was invented, it gradually came to be cheaper than either leather or cloth. As a result, auto makers began installing plastic seat covers in cars. Leather seat covers then became a "luxury."

The price of resources also determines how things are produced. For example, firms will decide to use machines instead of human labor if machines are cheaper. Suppose a worker is hired to sand a floor by hand. It takes 40 hours to complete the task, and the worker is paid $4 an hour, or $160 for the entire job. Now, if the same worker can do the job with an electric sander in only 8 hours, the machine will be making a contribution equal to 32 hours of hand labor. The machine, in other words, will be "earning" $128—the amount of money the worker could earn by hand in 32 hours (at $4 an hour). If the owner of the machine charges less than $128 for its use, it will be cheaper to use the machine than to pay the worker to do the job by hand. But if the owner charges more than $128 for the machine, it will be cheaper to let the worker do the entire job by hand.

The demand for these productive factors is called a *derived demand.* This is because the demand for the factors depends on (is derived from) the demand for the goods and services the factors can make. If the demand for a good or service increases, then the demand for the factors used to make it will also increase. But if the demand for a good or service decreases, the demand for those factors will decrease too.

The price of a good or service is at least equal to the sum of all the payments for factors used to produce it. In the example given, $160 was the price for sanding the floor. At first, it all went to the worker. Later, $32 went to the worker and

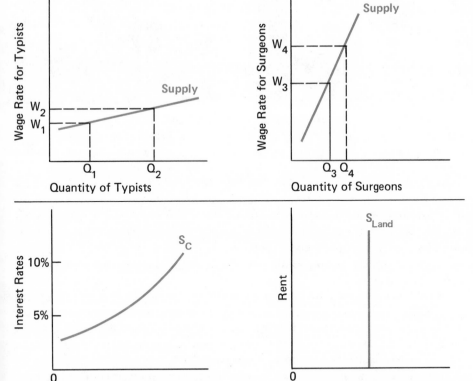

Figure 15-1 (left)
Figure 15-2 (right)
Why is the quantity of typists affected more by wage increases than the quantity of surgeons?

Figure 15-3 (left)
Figure 15-4 (right)
How is the supply of capital different from the supply of land?

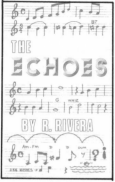

up to $128 to the owner of the sander. In theory, each factor receives a payment that is equal to its contribution to production. In practice, it may be hard to measure the exact contribution of each factor. Factors whose contributions are easier to measure tend to earn more than less measurable factors.

In a market economy, therefore, the "for whom" question is answered in factor markets. The owners of resources receive income that is equal to the prices of the goods and services made with those resources. For example, the owners of oil deposits will continue to earn income as long as oil is needed to make industrial products. The owners of valuable skills such as carpentry, plumbing, or dentistry will continue to earn income as long as people require the services of carpenters, plumbers, and dentists.

The market, however, does not provide income for people who do not own resources. That is, it will not support those who have no labor skills, or who own no natural or capital resources. That is a social problem, not an economic one. As such, it must be solved outside the market, by social policies that transfer income from those who can earn it to those who cannot.

A product, then, is the sum of the contributions of its factors of production. The worth of each factor can be bargained over in the market. You can also look at yourself as a product. The groups you belong to are factors that help make you who you are. Your sense of who you are and what you are worth comes from who your groups are and what they think you are worth. You might see yourself, for example, as a member of some of the following groups:

    family
    age group
    sex group
    religion
    ethnic group

Some of these groups are worth more to you than others, just as one resource may be more valuable than others for making a specific product.

☐ The reading for this lesson is taken from an article by Louise Kapp Howe. In it, two women talk about their lives and their work. You can see that who they are reflects the groups they belong to. You can also see how the value of their labor is determined both by their place in the factor market and by their group memberships. Their employer keeps their wages low in order to keep his prices low. At the same time, he is able to keep his prices low because his workers have to accept their low wages. As you read the article, ask yourself the following questions:

1. What influences the price of labor in the factor market for hairstyling?
2. How do Avis and Marianne see themselves as workers? as members of other groups?
3. How do your groups memberships define you?

PINK COLLAR WORKERS

Once in a while in the midst of a tint or a set or a bleach, a customer would trot out that old only-my-hairdresser-knows line, and then whoever heard would usually laugh in return. But aside from those moments, the women who worked in the California beauty shop stuck to the plainer term beautician. The sign on the window, in bold black letters, announced the shop's chief selling points. The prices, all apparently low for most areas of the country, were even lower than the prices of the other beauty shops in that community, which was located about 15 miles from San Francisco.

The shop looks tiny from the outside, surprisingly spacious when you enter. In the softly lighted rectangular room, everything is pink and lilac and gold and white.

Suzy, the manager of the shop, was tall, blond, and, above all, happy-looking. When she welcomed you with that rusty old standby, "What can we do for you today?" she *welcomed* you. The shop had three full-time all-purpose beauticians: Marianne, six feet tall and the only black woman there, was the most animated; Jackie, maybe 40 pounds overweight, seemed to carry herself with the hauteur of a *Vogue* model; Avis, in contrast, appeared skinny and shy.

Because the women still need their jobs, I can't tell you the name of the shop's owner (who comes by once a week to check on his investment), but it won't hurt to pass on the nickname the workers gave him: Bumblebrain.

AVIS   When she was 15, Avis worked every night serving cocktails at a neighborhood bar—precisely as her mother had done when she was the same age. Hating school, Avis cut classes until she was 16 and could officially drop out. Two months later her dream came true. Marriage. To John, an older man of 17 who was working at the local gas station.

What are some of the factors to consider in the production of this "product"?

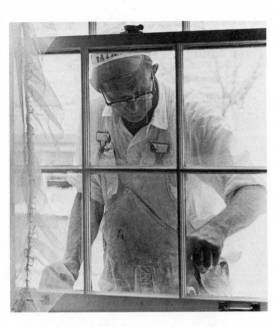

What kinds of things affect the cost of this factor?

After three years of marriage and one child they broke up. At which point Avis decided to be a beautician.

"I guess I didn't know what else to do. I didn't want to babysit, couldn't type, hated the thought of staying home all the time. I was on the county then—on welfare—and I'd have done almost anything to get off.

"The beauty school let me go on a special program they call 'Workway.' That means you don't have to pay tuition, but you do have to do extra work for the owner, like cleaning up the place. And you still have to pay for uniforms, brushes, and supplies. In my case, if it hadn't been for one girlfriend who watched Johnny for practically nothing, I wouldn't have made it."

But she really enjoyed the work. "I loved styling hair and trying new things out. Once I even won a trophy in a contest they had. It was only third place, but it meant a lot to me."

After graduating, Avis found a job but quit in six months.

"The girls were all snotty, and the boss was always switching my days around, and then she would swear at me because I wasn't building a clientele, which is pretty hard to do if nobody knows when you are going to be there."

That was seven months ago and since then, she says, she's felt a million times better.

How might the derived demand for this factor be determined?

"I like it at the shop. And I really like the girls. We have pretty good times together.

"We get paid an hourly rate. The minimum wage. Plus we get a commission on what our customers spend.

"On the average I guess I am taking home about three hundred dollars a month. And then on top of that figure about a hundred dollars a month in tips. So that's four hundred dollars a month. And now at last my ex-husband has started to chip in with child support, so that's another seventy-five dollars."

MARIANNE Of the five women who work in the shop, she is the only one who always wanted to be a beautician. To be now the only black woman in an all-white shop is like a trip back into her childhood, for she grew up in the only black family on an all-white block in San Francisco. "I learned then," she says, "that the only way to handle yourself is to know you are as good if not better than anyone else."

But there are difficult moments at work. If a customer realizes she has been assigned to a black woman, she may jump up and take a seat at the next table, fast. Marianne has a way of handling this.

"I'll walk up to them and then very quietly ask: 'You're not prejudiced, are you? You're not going to deprive yourself of the best haircut or hair set of your life, are you?' I laugh with them and most of the time it works.

"I really do think I give great haircuts, and I want everyone to think so, too. If a woman walks out and she doesn't like what I've done, then I really feel bad. Because, you see, that's my good name she's going to be spreading bad tales about."

AT THE SHOP   It seems Bumblebrain had been on one of his periodic tight-ship periods. Get the ladies out fast, get the workers on point, stop all that schmoozing around when the place isn't busy. The final straw came when Jackie supposedly "sat around" on a quiet day when Mrs. Bumblebrain was in for a frosting. He fired Jackie the next day. No severance. No notice. No union, no grievance procedure. She got the minimum unemployment: $40 a week.

And meanwhile the tight ship got tighter. "After the blowup with Jackie, the good atmosphere we were all trying to create blew up, too," Suzy told me.

Marianne decided that if Bumblebrain could do it like that to Jackie, he could do it like that to her, and when she heard from a friend about another job in the area, she grabbed it and quit. Suzy has applied for a job selling cosmetics. Linda and Avis, both needing the money and having no other place to go, are staying on for the time being. "But the morale," Avis said, "the thing that made it fun, is completely gone."

Select from any source—magazines, books, etc.—at least three images of the *same kind* of retail store (such as service stations, supermarkets, jewelers, auto dealers, etc.). Based on what you see in each picture discuss some of the factors that influence costs for the products in these stores. If you interchange products among the pictures would prices be the same? Why? What kinds of competition exists among sellers of these products? Is this indicated in the pictures? How?

VISUAL
ACTIVITY

ACTIVITIES

I. In this activity, you will look at the factors that go into making a pair of jeans. You will need to assess the importance of each factor and decide what a suitable profit would be for each step of production. This is similar to how you might assess the importance of the factors that influence you and help shape your identity.

1. On the following page is a list of the costs of the goods and services that are necessary in the production of a pair of jeans.
2. A factor analysis chart in the Workbook illustrates the production process. If you don't have a Workbook, copy the chart in the text. Place each of the costs referred to in Step 1 in the appropriate boxes on the chart. Estimate a fair percentage of profit for each factor. Add the profit to the cost at each step to compute the final retail price of a pair of jeans.
3. Go to a retail store and find what the actual price of a pair of jeans is.
4. If necessary, decide on a more appropriate percentage of profit. Compute profit and cost again to reach a more realistic price for a pair of jeans.
5. Discussion questions
    a. What seemed a fair percentage of profit for each step of production? How did you arrive at this figure?
    b. What are some reasons the prices of two pairs of jeans might differ? Consider the amount of labor that went into each pair and the costs of labor in different parts of the country.
    c. What would you do if you found that the price of a pair of jeans in one retail shop was double the price of an identical pair in another shop?

JEANS GOODS AND SERVICES LIST

Cotton field machinery—40¢   Cotton pickers and planters—43¢
Sales tax—35¢   Retail store rent—60¢
Buttons, rivets, zippers—42¢   Packing and shipping of jeans—$1.95
Rent on cotton fields—40¢   Denim factory rent and machinery—70¢
Advertising—40¢   Retail selling costs (incl. salaries)—$2.90
Seamstress workers—$1.96   Weavers—62¢

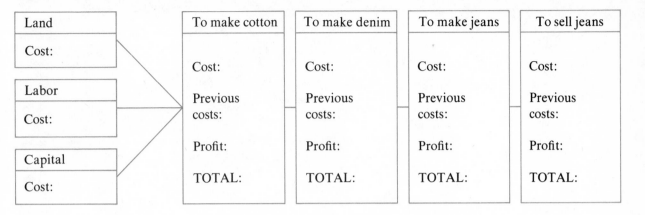

Land		To make cotton	To make denim	To make jeans	To sell jeans
Cost:		Cost:	Cost:	Cost:	Cost:
Labor					
Cost:		Previous costs:	Previous costs:	Previous costs:	Previous costs:
Capital		Profit:	Profit:	Profit:	Profit:
Cost:		TOTAL:	TOTAL:	TOTAL:	TOTAL:

II. Just as an economist looks at the various factors that go into the making of a product, in this activity you will look at the factors that have shaped your special identity.

1. The class brainstorms all the possible group memberships of the students in the class. List the groups on the board.
2. Pick the four groups you belong to that are most important to you personally.
3. Make a chart to show how your group memberships have helped make you the person you are. Find several visuals for each of the four memberships you have chosen. You may cut out or create pictures, quotes, drawings—as long as you feel that in some way they represent your group membership. Select one visual for each of the four groups you belong to that will be most typical of that particular group. Tape them onto a large piece of paper to make a chart that will look like the one at the right.
4. Now find one visual that you feel shows the sum total of who you are. Tape this picture in the large circle. (You may want to use a "factor" photo again.)
5. Display the charts in the room for everyone to see.
6. Discussion questions
   a. What influence does each factor have on your total self? Do any of them dominate?
   b. What are the relationships among your various memberships? Do any of them conflict?
   c. What groups brainstormed by the class were not included? Why?
   d. Do any memberships represent more than the group?

Note: When you are finished with your charts, paste each of the four photos onto the four sides of a paper lunch bag. Give them to the teacher to save for Lesson 18.

CHAPTER 6 LIMITATIONS OF THE MARKET MODEL

Unrealistic Assumptions

The American economy is far from being a model of perfect competition. Perfect competition requires many equal buyers and sellers, each operating alone. In fact, monopolies and oligopolies account for a large share of the country's economy. Perfect competition requires the production of identical goods and services. For example, if all brands of soap were just the same, consumers could make a choice on the basis of price alone. In fact, products and services differ from one seller to the next. Even where competition does exist, the perfect knowledge and mobility needed to take advantage of it are often absent.

Lack of information about prices has grave effects on a market economy. How does a consumer shopping in one store learn of the prices charged elsewhere? It is possible, of course, to find out by going from one store to the next or by reading the ads in the papers. But this takes time and in the end may not be worth the effort. Finding out about prices or wages throughout the country takes even more time. Getting perfect information about market conditions, in short, is costly. If it costs more than the money saved, it is not worth doing.

Mobility is another unreal assumption of the perfect competition model. Resources just cannot be shifted around at will. Economists call this problem *resource immobility*. It can be severe when people are first adjusting to new conditions. Unemployed workers, for example, cannot always afford the cost of

Table 16-1   After-tax Profits in the United States, 1976
Source: Economic Report of the President, 1978
If you were in business, which way of measuring profit would you use when reporting to your stockholders? To the general public?

	As a % of stockholder's equity	As a % of sales
All manufacturing corporations	13.9	5.4
Durable goods industries	13.7	5.2
Iron and steel	9.0	4.1
Machinery except electrical	15.5	7.5
Electrical and electronic equipment	12.5	4.4
Motor vehicles and equipment	17.0	5.3
Nondurable goods industries	15.3	6.1
Food and kindred products	14.9	3.5
Tobacco manufactures	15.9	8.5
Paper and allied products	13.8	5.8
Petroleum and coal products	14.3	8.4

moving to where the jobs are. Or they may not want to leave their homes, even for better jobs. Resources such as machines are expensive to move from one part of the country to another. And some natural resources, such as land, can't be moved.

The perfect competition model also assumes that all of the costs of a product will be reflected in its price. But *third-party costs,* such as air and water pollution, are not covered by the price of a product or service. These third-party costs are paid by the public at large. There are also *third-party benefits* to production that are not covered by prices. When you paint your house, for example, you are improving your neighborhood. This benefits your neighbors—even though they did not help pay for the job.

How do third-party costs and benefits affect what is produced under imperfect competition? The answer lies in what profits are to be gained from different types of goods and services. For instance, if the maker of a product with third-party costs, like cars, had to pay all the costs of pollution, cars would cost a lot more to produce than they do now. Consumers would therefore buy fewer cars, and profits would go down. So fewer cars would be made in the first place. The reverse is also true. If the users of goods and services with third-party benefits, like public schools, had to pay the full price of the benefits they received, many more such goods and services could be produced. They would then not be a drain on state or local governments.

It is thus easy to see why more goods with third-party costs than those with third-party benefits are produced by the U.S. economy. There might be a better

balance if the government taxed the companies that created third-party costs or forced them to compensate those hurt by them. The government could also simply outlaw them. In the same way, the government could encourage the production of goods with third-party benefits by subsidizing their producers. In these ways, the government can make the market fairer, but it can rarely eliminate imperfect competition.

How do these consumers find out about the prices charged in other stores? How do this store's employees find out about wages paid by similar employers?

The perfectly competitive model developed for human affairs breaks down in the same ways as the economic model does. People can never only be free and equal individuals who act on their own. They also belong to groups. Your groups give you power, a feeling of belonging, and a sense of who you are, but they also limit you.

Each of your groups has its own way of seeing the world, its own secrets and code words. In other words, your groups provide you with certain information and make other information harder for you to get. They thus create one kind of "market failure."

Groups also increase resource immobility. Because of your feelings for your group, you try not to do things that would cut you off from it. You therefore live within its rules. In this way, other group members become third parties for you. Much of what you do, both in and out of the group, affects other group members. They may feel proud, disappointed, betrayed, loved, included, or left out. When you make choices, you consider their effects on your relationships.

☐ The reading for this lesson is from a book by Richard Balzer. In it, a
father (Bill) and son (Mike) tell how they feel about their work and
about each other. Both are limited in their job choices because of
their groups and relationships. The following questions will help you
think about their lack of information and resource immobility:
1.   What kinds of information would have given Mike more job
     choices? Why was this information hard for him to get?
2.   How did group membership limit Mike's and Bill's job mobility?
     How could they overcome these limits?
3.   How do your groups limit you?

CLOCKWORK: FATHER AND SON

Michael Beal was just out of the service. His father had helped him get
his job at Western. The first few weeks Mike and his father had lunch
together almost every day. Mike talked a lot about his father. He was
worried about how hard he was working, holding down two jobs.

"You know," Mike said, "before I went in the service my father
could do just about anything. But he's really kind of tired these days.
Working two jobs takes a lot out of him. He doesn't have as much
energy. I tell him that he should stop the second job, but he won't
listen. He tells me we need the money for the camp, and the boat. I tell
him what good is the money, he's going to run himself down and he
won't be able to enjoy it."

During a smoking break, one afternoon, Mike introduced me to his
father. Bill mentioned that he had four children. I casually remarked
that I hoped the others were better than Mike. He took my joking
seriously and, putting his arm on Mike's shoulder, said, "I'll be glad if
they turn out as well as Mike."

Mike worked very hard the first week, harder than I did. But after a
month had passed his attitude toward the job had soured, and his
disposition with it. He found the work we were asked to do boring and
monotonous. One day he told me that he burned his finger because
he wasn't paying attention to his work. He kept saying he couldn't
stand being cooped up, that he wasn't suited for the work. As the
weeks of the summer went by, he became more and more short-
tempered, more anxious to get out.

One day in sheer frustration, he asked Tom, an older worker, "Do
you think I should take the 33 grade coil wrapper job in Lawrence?"

Tom said, "No."

Then he asked, "How do you think I can get ahead?"

"Quit, go to school."

"I can't, I need the money."

Tom shrugged his shoulders and said, as he walked away, "Well, then you'll just have to keep on doing what you're doing now."

Mike was still working when I left Western, but he was complaining about it more often. Three months later, he quit and took a job delivering milk. He held the new job for only four months. His temper got the best of him one day at work and caused him to be fired.

Michael is unemployed now, but is thinking about going back to Western for another try. He doesn't see how he can work things out on the job until he clears up his personal relationship with his father.

"My father and I were real close," Mike says, "but not any more. It really changed since I got out of the service. See, I didn't come back the way he thought I would. He wanted me to come home like Joe. Man. You know, I'm still twenty years old. There's a helluva lot that I don't know. The Army doesn't teach you everything about life. He seemed to think I was going to come back like him; just settle right down, grab myself a woman, marry her, have a few kids, buy a house, the whole thing. But I'm not like that. I want to be free for a while.

"I'll tell you one of the big reasons I went into the Army was because I thought my father would like it. He was always talking about the Navy, so I figured I'd go into the Army when I got out of high

What might be some of the "third party benefits" from this type of neighborhood improvement?

school. It made him happy, I guess, but he never really told me exactly what he thought about it.

"So I joined the reserves. I was only seventeen years old. They sent me to Fort Jackson, South Carolina, for basic training. They made me a squad leader; that meant a lot to me. From basic I went to A.I.T.— Advanced Infantry Training. I became a squad leader down there too. I graduated fifteenth in a class of almost seventy, and decided to extend my reserve active duty.

"When I came out of the service I found my father was lecturing me all the time. I guess I never really noticed it before but being away made it really noticeable. When I came back from the Army, after being the man for a while, I realized my father is pushing me around. Maybe he doesn't realize it, but that's the way he acts toward me. I do something in the house, he says, 'Don't do that again.' I'm twenty years old, I've been in the Army. I was the man. I was a drill sergeant, a leader and he still lectures me as if I were ten years old.

"My father is a terrific guy. I mean everyone likes him, but we can't get along. Things are getting worse and worse between us. He forgets I'm an individual and need to decide things for myself. I don't think he even knows but he's holding on too tight. He's holding on so tight that I've got to yell, 'Let go of me.' He's squeezing me so tight I have to get out. If I don't I'll get crushed. Me and my mother talked the whole thing over and we came to the same conclusion, that I should leave home. She doesn't want to throw me out but she says it would be best. It's tearing her apart seeing me and my father arguing all the time.

"When I quit Western I didn't tell my father because I knew he wouldn't like it. He would have started on me, how it was such a steady job, and how I should stick it out. I didn't want to hear all that. I

What might groups like these have to do with "market failures" and "resource immobility"?

hated the job. I was just sitting around putting on weight. I couldn't stand being inside, and the job was so boring and monotonous. I wasn't going anywhere. I would've been stuck on that bench for a long time. It was driving me crazy.

"He says he understands that, he knows how boring bench work is, but still I know he'd want me to stay. He'd tell me you can't always have a job you like. He'd tell me how it was boring for him when he first started. Maybe it was boring for him when he started, but he's doing what he likes now. He likes working on those machines. He's got friends at work. He goes into work, stands around tending those machines, goes into the men's room and has a couple of smokes. He's got a little pull at Western, so it isn't so hard for him.

"I didn't want him lecturing me, so I quit and didn't tell him. I guess I was afraid of disappointing him. I've always tried pleasing him, and it gets in the way. When I was in high school I wanted to wear my hair long but I didn't because I knew my father wouldn't like it. I got a job working six hours a day after school not only for the money but because I thought my old man would think more of me.

"This whole thing has given me a wicked temper. My temper got to me while I was delivering milk and got me fired. I'm beginning to wonder if maybe I should see a psychiatrist, because I know I've got a problem, an authority type thing. I can't stand anyone telling me what I should do, or ordering me around. It's not actually the being told, it's the way it's done. If someone tells me the way my father does, that's when I fly off the handle. I've got to learn to control my temper. I've got to start making my own life and my own decisions. If I want to grow my hair, or play in a band, I'm going to do it because I want to, no matter what my father thinks. I don't know, maybe we can get back together and be close the way we were, but it's got to be man to man."

In what ways might this image demonstrate "resource immobility"?

ACTIVITIES

This activity will help you to see how lack of information, resource immobility, and third-party costs affect people's choices. It will help you to understand how your group memberships limit you both in the market and in other areas of your life.

1.   The following situation explains an issue to be debated:
     A new and highly popular magnet school—intended to attract students from all areas of the city—on the other side of town has an opening for one student from your school. Your friend Carlotta has been recommended by her teachers. Although no one she knows from her neighborhood goes to the school, it is large, with many different kinds of students. As a sophomore, she would spend two and a half years in the school in a program of her choice. Should Carlotta transfer to the magnet school?
2.   Form six groups. Three of them are primary groups, which will take the negative point of view in the debate. They will consider the following problems:
     a.   resource immobility
     b.   lack of information
     c.   third-party costs
3.   Each primary group will face a corresponding rebuttal group. The three rebuttal groups will take the positive point of view in the debate and think of ways of overcoming the problems set forth by the primary group.
4.   Each group meets alone to consider all aspects of the position it will present. Try to think out ahead of time what the opposing group might say and have a strong argument ready to defend your position.
5.   Set up the groups as illustrated. A general question has been given to each group to start you off. In the debate, each of the six groups has two minutes in which to speak.
     a.   One of the primary groups presents its position on Carlotta's decision.
     b.   The corresponding rebuttal group answers, and other groups take their turns in similar fashion.
     c.   One person from each opposing side then makes a final statement to sum up the debate.
6.   All groups should discuss the following questions:
     a.   What did you decide Carlotta should do?
     b.   What limitations can Carlotta overcome? What limitations can't she overcome?
     c.   How can Carlotta deal with these limits?

7. Discussion questions
   a. What impact did the different rebuttal groups have on the final decision?
   b. How can you make use of this activity to deal with the limits imposed on you by your group memberships?
   c. In what ways are consumers', workers', and producers' choices similar to Carlotta's? In what ways are they different?

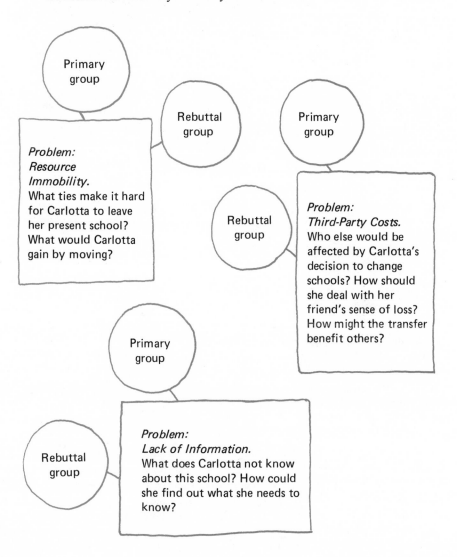

Discrimination

In the market model, the basic questions of what, how, for whom, and how much are answered by competition. Competition among producers is for the highest profits. Competition among consumers is for the best goods and services at the lowest prices. These motives are the only ones the model considers, because they are the only ones that are, strictly speaking, economic. In the real world, things are more complex. Other motives enter. One of the most important of these non-economic motives is prejudice. It often results in *discrimination.*

Discrimination occurs when a person makes an economic decision for reasons that have nothing to do with economics. Perhaps the most familiar kind is racial discrimination. An employer can refuse to hire someone because of that person's race, regardless of her skills. The opposite also happens. An employer can hire a worker because of that worker's race, in order to make up for discrimination against that race. Economists call both acts discrimination because they make distinctions between people for noneconomic reasons. The same is true when employers refuse to hire people because of their sex, age, or religion, or when they pay certain kinds of workers less money than others who do the same work.

Discrimination also exists in the consumer market. People are sometimes denied apartments or credit because of their race, religion, sex, or age. Consumers discriminate when they refuse to buy from people of a different race, religion, or

What are some of the ways in our economy that this person might be discriminated against? Does this need to change? How?

Major occupational group	Median wage or salary income		Women's median wage or salary income as a percentage of men's
	Women	Men	
Professional and technical workers	$6691	$10,151	65.9
Nonfarm managers, officials, and proprietors	5635	10,340	54.5
Clerical workers	4789	7351	65.1
Sales workers	3461	8549	40.5
Operatives	3991	6738	59.2

Table 17-1 Median Wage or Salary Income of Full-time Year-round Workers, by Sex and Selected Major Occupational Group *Source:* Department of Commerce. What accounts for the differences in salaries earned by men and by women? What could be done to equalize those salaries?

political viewpoint, or when they deliberately buy from those whose beliefs they share.

Most forms of race and sex discrimination are now illegal in the United States. There are also laws preventing some kinds of discrimination because of age. But not all forms of discrimination are bad. By economic reasoning alone, anyone with enough money to buy a car should be allowed to own and drive one. But few of us would want ten-year-olds to get drivers' licenses. Age requirements of

Is discrimination likely to occur in places like this? Why?

admission to some movies are another form of discrimination most adults are in favor of. Perhaps your uncle owns a shoe store and you would rather buy shoes from him than from someone else. That, too, is a form of discrimination no one would want to pass a law against.

Another form of discrimination that has wide support in the United States allows people to work at certain jobs only when they have earned a license. You cannot become a doctor or a lawyer, for example, until you have passed exams given to you by other doctors and lawyers. The same is true of selling real estate and insurance, teaching school, or working as a plumber. Such discrimination is

Age, sex, race	Average annual unemployment %
Total, 16 years and over	7.7
Males, 20 years and over	5.9
Females, 20 years and over	7.4
Both sexes, 16–19 years	19.0
White, total	7.0
Males, 20 years and over	5.4
Females, 20 years and over	6.8
Both sexes, 16–19 years	16.9
Black and other, total	13.2
Males, 20 years and over	10.6
Females, 20 years and over	11.3
Both sexes, 16–19 years	37.0

**Table 17-2
Unemployment in the
United States, 1976**
What role does
discrimination play in the
unemployment problem
in the U.S.?

legal. It is believed necessary by many people to prevent unskilled people from entering these fields.

How does discrimination affect the workings of the market economy? The market model predicts that competition will produce the most efficient mix of resources and the greatest consumer satisfaction. If so, then discrimination of any kind reduces that efficiency and satisfaction. Resources are used differently and goods and services distributed differently. Race and sex discrimination, for example, keep qualified people from contributing to the country's resources. This results in waste and inefficiency. Hiring one's relatives to do work for which they are not qualified results in poor work. Refusing to buy in stores owned by members of a certain race or religion prevents the free movement of goods and services. This may result in higher prices or worse products.

What the market model shows is the difference between economic motives and noneconomic ones. It helps us to see that human behavior is the result of many different, and often conflicting, forces.

Discrimination means treating different people differently. Some people say that all discrimination is unfair and that everyone should be treated equally. Others argue that certain kinds of discrimination are good because people should help out their friends and relatives. Members of your own groups are like you; you can sympathize with each others' problems. You share certain goals, feelings, and ways of viewing the world. You should be able to count on each other. But what happens when helping a member of your group means that you must sacrifice something? What do you do when you cannot help a member of your group without unfairly hurting someone else?

☐ The reading for this lesson presents this kind of dilemma. It raises questions about what discrimination is, when it is good or bad, and what people owe to members of their own group. As you read it, ask yourself the following questions:

1. In what ways would hiring Dan be discrimination? How would not hiring him be discrimination?
2. What are Josephine's obligations to her fellow Indians? What are her obligations to her fellow workers at Hammond's?
3. How would you decide in a similar situation?

AFFIRMATIVE ACTION

It is a cool, crisp day in downtown Denver. The clouds wander slowly through the sky in this mile-high city. Dan Flying-By gets a morning paper. He has bought one every morning for the past three months. He breezes through the headlines on his way to the Help Wanted section.

How long will it be, Dan wonders to himself. There are fewer jobs in Denver than there were back in North Dakota. It has hardly been worth the bus fare.

Dan reads every ad carefully. Since coming to Denver, he has been to enough interviews to know what to look for and what to avoid. His eyes finally come to rest on one listing.

FULL-TIME CLERK

Hammond's, Denver's fastest-growing department store, has a full-time position for an experienced clerk. Apply to the Affirmative Action Office at the Downtown Store.

Hammond's is an Equal
Opportunity Employer

Maybe this is finally it, Dan thinks. I have the experience, and I don't have to start at the Personnel Office. Dan decided to apply.

Hammond's wasn't the biggest department store in Denver, but it was the newest and usually the most crowded. Dan had never been in the store before, but he had walked past it several times. The security guard showed him the way to the Affirmative Action Office.

"I'd like to talk to someone about this job," Dan said, showing the receptionist the newspaper clipping.

"Have a seat, please. One of our counselors will be with you in a minute."

It wasn't even a minute before a tall Indian woman came out of one of the inner offices to meet Dan. "Good morning," she said. "I'm Josephine Begay. Why don't you come into my office."

"Thanks," Dan answered. I can't believe it, he thought to himself. I'm going to get interviewed by one of my own. I think this really is it.

The office was small, but brightly decorated with a number of colorful rugs and wall posters. Josephine is from Nazlini, Arizona, and she is proud of the accomplishments of her people.

"So, you're answering the ad we had in this morning's paper?" she began. "What kind of experience have you had for this type of job?"

"I worked as a clerk," Dan said slowly, "for three years in a grocery store in Fort Yates. I had to stock the counters, work the cash register, even make out some of the weekly orders."

"That certainly is the kind of experience we're looking for," Josephine said smiling. "All too often, we get applicants who need a great deal of training. But that certainly doesn't seem to be the case with you."

Dan smiled too.

"Let's get to work on some of these forms," Josephine continued, "and see what we've got. When did you graduate from high school?"

"I never did," Dan answered. "I quit school to work in the store."

Are these people representative of those commonly discriminated against?

Why must this person be licensed in order to carry a gun? Is this a form of legal discrimination?

"That's going to be a problem," said Josephine. "One of the requirements for this job is a high school diploma."

"But I have the experience. How can a diploma be so important?"

"I can understand your feelings," Josephine said calmly, "but the Personnel Office wants all of Hammond's employees to have a high school diploma. It's going to be hard to make an exception. And even if the office does decide to make an exception, which is unlikely, you'll still have to pass the reading test. Can you read at an eighth-grade reading level?"

"I don't know," replied Dan. "But I can read well enough to do whatever the job requires. It can't be that different here from what it was at Fort Yates."

"I'm afraid there's not going to be much I can do for you."

"Look. You have a job here," Dan began slowly. "Your job is to help Hammond's hire Indians, among others. You are an Indian yourself."

"A Navajo."

"I'm an Indian, and I have the experience. What more do I need to do the job?"

"You need a high school diploma and an eighth-grade reading level."

"But I can do the job without them."

"I'd like to help you, Dan, you know that. You're right. That's my job. And I won't lie to you. It's a tough job. A lot of people like yourself come into my office and can't get a job because they don't have one or two of the qualifications. They have the experience but not the diploma. Or they have the diploma and then fail our reading test."

"But don't you see," Dan said, more angrily than before, "that, in the end, Hammond's *is* discriminating against us?"

"But they hired me to make sure that they would not discriminate against Indians or other minority groups," Josephine answered.

"They hired you to make sure they could discriminate and not get caught at it. They make up tests and crazy job requirements that let them discriminate."

"That's just not fair," Josephine said. "All Hammond's employees have to have a diploma, and the reading test is just to make sure you can do the paperwork that goes with the job."

"You're blind," Dan shouted, as he stomped out of the office.

"I wish there were something I could do," Josephine said to the empty doorway.

ACTIVITIES

There are two debate activities in this lesson. Both are based on the reading entitled *Affirmative Action.* They will help you to look at discrimination issues from the point of view of fairness and from the point of view of people's obligations to their groups.

I. In this debate, you will discuss hiring policy at Hammond's Department Store.

1. Divide the class into two groups representing the following positions:
    Group A: The basic requirement in hiring policy is that 30 percent of the store's employees should be American Indians or members of other minority groups.
    Group B: The basic requirement for hiring is that all employees must have a high school diploma.
2. Your discussion will take the form of a circle debate. Each side forms a circle. The members of each group should look at each other, not at the members of the other group. One person should sit between the two groups and act as recorder.
3. Group A should begin. The group has one and a half minutes to write a one-sentence statement of its position and the reason for it. One person from Group A then addresses the statement to Group B. The recorder writes the statement on a ditto master.
4. Group B has one and a half minutes to decide on a counter-statement. One person from the group addresses its statement to Group A. Again, the recorder should write the statement on a ditto master.
5. While Group B is deciding on its statement, Group A tries to guess what Group B's statement will be. Group A also is planning its own responses one or two turns ahead in the debate.
6. The debate continues, with each side offering additional reasons for its position and arguing against the position of the other group. The debate ends only when one side convinces the other or the time runs out.
7. When the debate is finished, run off what was written by the recorder on the ditto masters. Use it to help discuss the debate and the issues it raised.
8. Discussion questions
    a. Was your position based on economic or noneconomic motives?
    b. Which side was arguing in favor of discrimination?
    c. Was your attitude changed by the debate?

II. The second debate will focus on the issue faced by Josephine in the reading. Use the same format as in Activity I to discuss the question of group obligation.

1. Divide into two groups representing the following positions:
   Group A: As one of the store's employees, Josephine is obliged to support its hiring policy.
   Group B: As an American Indian, Josephine should help members of her ethnic group.
2. Discussion questions
   a. Based on the arguments given in both debates, what do you think Josephine should have done?
   b. Was Dan discriminated against?
   c. Could a compromise plan have been worked out?
   d. Which argument was most convincing in the first debate? in the second debate? overall?
   e. What are your group obligations? How do you deal with conflicts?

Equity and Efficiency

A nation pursues many goals, both economic and otherwise. Some of the goals pursued in the United States, for example, have been freedom, efficiency, equity, stability, and growth. Economists study how countries use their resources to pursue such goals. One of the things they have learned is that there are bound to be conflicts.

Take, for example, two of the goals just mentioned, *equity* and *efficiency*. Equity means fairness. An action is equitable when it conforms to a group's ideas about what is fair. If two boys spend their summer mowing lawns, and if each does as much work as the other, they will think it fair to split their earnings 50/50. But if one of the partners provided the power mower and paid for the gas, the two will probably agree that in a fair division of what was earned, the first boy would get more money than the second.

Efficiency means at least two things. What economists call *technical efficiency* means using the least amount of resources to produce a product. Put another way, it means getting the largest production out of a given amount of resources. For example, the boys in the mowing business might decide that their power mower burns up too much gas. They decide to trade it in for a mower with a more efficient engine. (Assume it's an even trade.) That way they would be using a smaller amount of resources—in this case, gas money—to produce the same

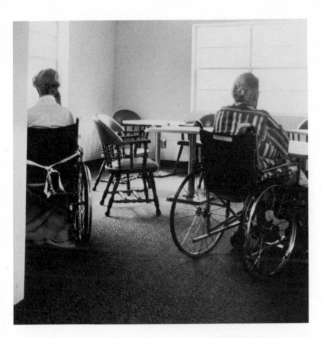

How would these people survive in a purely competitive economy? How do they survive in our economy?

amount of work. Economists also talk about *economic efficiency*. This means that, over the long run, the benefits of an economic activity are greater than its costs. A lawn mowing business is efficient in this sense if, at the end of the summer, the total amount of money earned is greater than the costs of buying the mower, paying for gas, cleaning and repairing tools, and so on.

How do the two goals of equity and efficiency conflict? Suppose that one of the boys in the lawn mowing business was hurt in an accident and couldn't work. How should the profits be divided up at the end of the summer? Should the boy who was injured get any of the money? He helped set up the business. He was ready to work, and would have worked hard, if he had not been injured. On the other hand, he did none of the mowing. If he were to be given some of the profits, that would mean that the boy who did the actual work would have less money to use for other things. He could not, for example, buy shovels to set up a winter snow shoveling business. The money produced by the lawn mowing business would thus not be used efficiently. But to deny the injured boy *any* of the money would go against many people's ideas of *fairness*.

This problem could be multiplied many times over when we look at the whole country. There are many people (the old, the sick, those without job skills or education) who cannot make much of a contribution to the nation's economy. If the real economy were exactly like the market model, those who couldn't contribute would not receive anything. In other words, in the model economy, people who

could not support themselves might not survive. But in the real economy, considerations of equity and fairness have led the government to provide support for such people. These may take the form of welfare payments, food stamps, or social security. Most Americans have solved the conflict between equity and efficiency by deciding that they would rather not live in a totally competitive economic system. In other words, they just don't think it is fair or humane.

Of course, not everyone agrees about what equity and efficiency mean. For example, some people do not think that it is fair for those who do not contribute to be supported by those who do. Furthermore, not everyone agrees about what is the most efficient way to use resources.

Countries must always make tradeoffs. They have to decide how much of one goal they are willing to give up in order to achieve some part of another goal. For example, fairness might mean raising taxes to provide money for those who are out of work. Yet higher taxes could stop firms from expanding their operations. This could lead to fewer and fewer jobs. At some point, therefore, the country would be forced to reach a compromise between total fairness and total efficiency. Such decisions are never easy. They always mean that some people will be better off and some people worse off than they were before the decision.

One of the problems with groups is that they make it hard for others to see you as a person. Outsiders often deal with you simply as a member of your group. You are like other group members in many ways. But the differences make you

you. You need to be given credit for your strengths. You need help in overcoming your weaknesses. In many ways this special treatment seems only fair. Yet it is sometimes too inefficient, and perhaps in some ways unfair, for others to deal with you in this way.

☐ The reading for this lesson is by Carolyn Shaw Bell, an economist. It presents one side of the "what is fair" argument on a larger scale. Many government programs, taxes, and benefits are geared to families instead of to individuals. This is quite efficient. Because households usually pool their resources, it is families, not individuals, who are rich or poor. It seems unfair for one family to have or get more than another. In this article, however, an economist argues that all families are not alike. No matter how efficient it is, dealing with families instead of with individuals is to her unfair and thus wrong. As you read her argument, think about the following questions:

1. Look at the income tax or another of the policies Bell mentions that deal with families, not individuals. Would Bell's policy be fairer? Would it be better?
2. Think of three types of families that are different from the "typical" American family. What special considerations would each need?
3. How are you different from other members of your group?

── LET'S GET RID OF FAMILIES! ──

The Census defines a family as a group of two or more people related by blood, marriage or adoption who live together: families exist, obviously, because people want them to. For some reason, however, we think and talk about the family as if it existed all by itself, apart from its members. We describe the "family life cycle," and worry about the "death of the family." Business and government view policy decisions in terms of "the average family." President Carter has even promised a "family impact" statement to accompany new legislation.

Most of us accept without question the repeated use of that "typical" American family—the married man supporting a wife and two children—when we talk about social and economic policies. The Census Bureau has just revealed, however, that this familiar type has practically vanished. There are 56 million families in this country and only 3.3 million of them fit this pattern—a mere 6 percent of the total.

Why don't we stop having families as the focus of our concerns, and concentrate on individuals instead? If we stopped pretending there was such a thing as "the typical American family," we might be more sensitive to the actual problems posed by the many different ways we live—both in and out of families.

TAXES AND CHOICES

Start with income taxes. Most income in the country is earned at work and consists of wages and salaries. But families don't work and earn wages, family members do. "The worker" is an individual—the worker's income belongs to the earner. How those of us who earn wages choose to share our income is our business, not that of the tax authorities. If you want to spend your income supporting a wife and I want to spend mine supporting a child and somebody else wants to spend his supporting a hobby of collecting antique automobiles or a crusade for preserving the wilderness, let us respect each of our individual choices. Why involve "the family"?

Of course, if we Americans decide that having children is a good

Are these families treated equally in our economy? Are they treated equitably? In what ways?

thing, and if we want to help parents support their children, then we can provide cash payments, or subsidies to parents. Such children's allowances exist in most European countries and in Canada to express society's interest in its future citizens.

Move on to national health insurance. *If* we want good medical care, we want it for individuals. Families don't get measles, or heart attacks, or die of cancer. If we want to *pay* for medical care by taxing payrolls, that doesn't mean medical benefits have to be provided via the people on payrolls—"the worker and the worker's family." Most workers are married to other workers so they'll both pay taxes to provide medical benefits.

THE COST OF LIVING
Why tie health care to "the worker's family" when people move in and out of families? Babies are born, children go off to college, young adults leave to form their own families or live alone. Death or separation breaks up a family unit and some adults become new

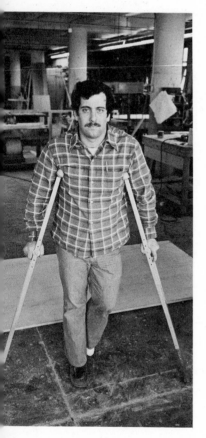

What might be some of the "equitable" ways in which an employer could deal with this employee?

dependents for their relations. Once we recognize that "the family" is a dynamic concept, and that families incessantly change, then we can agree that caring for individuals is what's essential.

Consider the high cost of living, and the battle (if there's to be one) against inflation. Our basic measure of living costs, the Consumer Price Index, doesn't pretend to measure every price change that affects us. Although a new, more representative index will shortly appear, the current figure includes only those commodities purchased by a fairly small group of families—urban wage earners and clerical workers.

Furthermore, the cost of living figures most frequently quoted refer to that same familiar group—John Doe supporting his wife Mary and their two kids Dick and Jane—that makes up such a tiny minority of all families. We need cost-of-living data for childless couples—who outnumber the "typical" family eight to one. We need to know how inflation hits the single mother supporting her children—there are twice as many of them as of the mythical average family.

Think about minimum wages. George Meany protests that $2.50 an hour (proposed by the White House) is below the poverty level. But he's referring to the poverty-level income for a *family,* not for an individual worker.

When minimum wages were first enacted during the Depression of the '30's, the "typical" American family was a lot more prevalent. Most children lived in homes where the father was the breadwinner and most women were supported by their husbands. One man's wages probably did represent one family's income, and the link between minimum earnings and poverty did make sense.

Today the one-earner family is in the minority. Fourteen million husbands support their wives, with or without children. One and a half million wives are the sole earners for their husbands and families, and there are five million other women without husbands, whose earnings provide family income. But all told that's less than one out of three families. Most wage earners live in families with other wage earners. And families come in all sizes—it's impossible to calculate a minimum wage for one person that would keep all kinds of families above the poverty level.

Of course, we may wish to provide additional income for poor families. But let's keep wages a matter of the individual worker and the individual job.

ISSUES AND INDIVIDUALS
You can try thinking about other social issues in terms of individuals. It would help the city welfare administrator struggling with three

definitions of the family to determine eligibility for housing, for medical care, and for public assistance. It would help the elderly widow and widower who won't marry because they'll lose social security benefits.

I think we should start thinking about individuals because we exist. More of us are being separate persons rather than family members these days. Between 1970 and 1975 the number of people living by themselves increased by about 40 percent. We live individually as young adults escaping from our parents, as older adults choosing not to marry, as people of any age whose marriages have dissolved through death or separation.

Thinking about individuals doesn't mean that families don't count, or that the family way of life is obsolete. It does mean that we live and grow as human beings, we move in and out of different families as family members, but each of us is a person from birth to death.

Select at least three illustrations from this text that deal with or demonstrate a limitation in the market model. What is it about each picture that indicates the limitation? Are there people in these images? Describe them. What could you change in these images to indicate improvements in the situations they represent?

ACTIVITIES

I. This activity is designed to help you examine the equity/efficiency issue within your class and within yourself. You will need to devise a set of standards that can be used to measure you and your classmates.

1. Pretend an experimental program is going to start in your school. A few students in your class will be chosen to receive the minimum wage for attending classes. You should decide the requirements for acceptance into the program.
2. Divide into six groups. Each group makes a list of the five most important criteria for acceptance into the program.
3. Each group in turn announces its five qualifications and lists them on the board. Place a check mark next to a requirement every time it is announced/duplicated. (Criteria that are nearly alike should be combined.)
4. The eight most commonly mentioned requirements are chosen and written down on separate cards. Each group makes its own set of cards.
5. Working in groups of six, sort the cards into categories according to whether they are
    a. equitable
    b. efficient
    c. both equitable and efficient
    d. neither equitable nor efficient
6. The entire class should now make a final selection of the criteria to be used for acceptance into the program.
7. Discussion questions
    a. Was the method your group used in choosing its five criteria fair? Was it efficient?
    b. Was the method the class used for selecting eight criteria to be considered fair? Was it efficient?
    c. Were the criteria finally chosen fair? Were they efficient?
    d. Which is more important to you, being fair or being efficient? Why?
    e. What real-life situations are like this? How is this sort of analysis useful to you?

II. The conflict between equity and efficiency arises because people are different from each other. Some have "unfair" advantages or disadvantages. In this activity you will have a chance to reexamine your group memberships and to find ways in which you differ from other members of your groups.

1. Get the bag with photos attached that you made during Lesson 15. The outside faces of the bag symbolize your definition of yourself based on your group memberships. You may add photos, slogans, quotes, drawings, etc. to each of the four group memberships that are represented on each of the four sides of the bag.
2. Collect pictures that symbolize the ways in which you differ from other people in your groups. Place these inside the bag. You may choose parts of yourself that are personal and unknown to your classmates. Everything you put in the bag will remain confidential unless you decide to share it.
3. When the bags are complete, everyone in the class may walk around and look at the outsides of others' bags. You may share your reasons for choosing the symbols on your own bag.
4. Answer these questions for yourself:
   a. With which group did you decide to meet? Why?
   b. How different from others did you expect to be? How different were you?
   c. What advantages do you have compared with other members of your group? What special treatment do you need?
5. Discussion questions for the whole class
   a. Even when it is efficient, is it always fair for people to treat you just the same as others?
   b. What implications does this have for economic policies like affirmative action, tax deduction, and unemployment compensation?
   c. When should efficiency be more important than fairness?

CHAPTER 7 GOVERNMENT INTER-VENTION AND REGULATION

Enforcing the "Rules of the Game"

The "rules of the game" are those basic laws that set limits on the way the economy runs. These are the ground rules everyone must observe. They determine much of what goes on in economic life. For example, a person who signs a contract is then bound to live up to that contract. Another basic rule is that a person can't take somebody else's property. A person also can't engage in unfair business practices, such as putting out false statements about a competitor's product. There are many such rules. Enforcing them is one of the most important ways in which the government affects economic life.

Why does the government establish "rules of the game"? One thing any society wants is for disputes to be settled as peacefully as possible. In industry, conflicts often occur between those who want more money and power and those who want to keep the wealth and power they already have. Disputes between firms and their employees are one example. In the 1930's, the United States set the basic rule that workers have the right to join unions and to bargain collectively with their employers. This rule allows most fights about wages and working conditions to be settled at a conference table instead of by strikes or violence.

Another important "rule of the game" has to with money. In order for the economy to operate smoothly, everyone in a country must use the same system of money. People have to know what their money is worth. They have to believe that it will not become worthless overnight. It is the federal government's duty to establish a single system of currency for the United States. This has led to its chartering national banks and to its regulating the operations of all banks.

The same is true for the system of weights and measures that industry uses. The government decides how much, for example, a one-pound can holds. It then guarantees that a one-pound can of coffee in New York contains the same amount of coffee as a one-pound can in California.

Another rule enforced by the government states that if you invent something, you can earn a profit on that invention for a certain period of time. During that time nobody can copy it without your permission. This is done to encourage people to come up with new products and new ways of doing things.

Economic activity can sometimes get very complex. In order to operate, firms must have a great deal of information. For example, they may need to know how much is paid for a certain product in Florida and how much is paid in Maine. The government helps move things along by publishing a lot of facts on topics such as this. That way, people who buy and sell can have accurate information on

What is the function of this group? How did it come about? For what purpose?

which to base their decisions. All of this government activity is designed mainly to make the economy run smoothly. In this respect, the government is a little bit like an umpire in a baseball game.

Enforcing the "rules of the game" is just the beginning of government's role in the economy. Government, which represents the public, can also change the rules of the game. One of the rules is that workers and employers should bargain together over wages. Until the 1930's there was no such rule. This is an example of how the government can step out of its role as "umpire." It can become a maker of rules as well as an enforcer of rules.

Buyers and sellers are bound not only by their own interests and their interests as group members. They are bound also by the rules of society. They must answer to the government as well as to themselves and their fellow workers.

You too are an individual, a group member, and a member of society. When you see yourself as part of society, you recognize your ties to a larger group. You take some responsibility for people you do not know. You see the need for order and law and for everyone to follow the same rules. You can judge what is right by the rules of the game. Or if the rules seem outdated or unfair, you can work to change them.

How does currency "work"? Why is it valuable? Is it always worth the same? Why?

How does this group make or change the "rules of the game"? How do they get the authority to do so?

☐ The reading for this lesson is from an article by Kenneth Boulding. It compares the market economy to a basketball game. It shows the likeness between an economy, or society, and the game as a whole. The competing teams can be compared to firms or groups within the economy or society. The reading will help you to understand what a society is and what it means to be a part of one. As you read the essay and study the diagram that goes with it, ask yourself the following questions:

1. What are the most important rules of the game in a society with a market economy?
2. Why is government necessary in a society with a market economy?
3. How is a society (or economic system) different from a group?

THIS SPORTING LIFE

Throughout my life I have avoided sports the way some people avoid religion. I went to one football game some thirty years ago and decided it was both boring and beyond me. I have not been to another since. I am in favor of gentle exercise: swimming around in an empty pool, or climbing a 14,000 foot mountain. But anything which involves dressing up in crazy clothes and running around on a field or court is not my thing.

One of our sons is a great sports fan and something of a basketball star at his college. Out of a sense of family duty, I let my wife take me to watch him play, in a place that could pass for a large church. I was surprised at what I got out of the game. The game was nip and tuck. First one team was ahead, then the other. Towards the end, the second team began to pull ahead to a large lead. I almost felt a twinge.

I was watching a tribal rite, but of a certain sort. It was not what I would have expected: asking the gods for their support. Rather, it was like a mini-social conflict, limited by rules and subjected to order. I saw two men on the court, obviously elders of the tribe in mufti. They carried whistles and made strange gestures which the players clearly obeyed. They had no police officers to back them up. This could only mean that the game was run by a social contract. Like all social contracts, it was subject to a little fudging.

So, the game was a sort of mock-up for society. More to the point, the game was like a market economy, with the teams playing the roles of rival companies. Each was a group with a common goal, in this case to score points. Competing companies are also groups, each with a common goal, in their case to make a profit. The players on the team are bound together by loyalty to the group, team spirit, and personal relationships. The same is often true of the people who work for a company.

The success of each team seems to rest on a subtle and shifting division of labor. Everyone is allowed to score, but the secret to scoring lies in passing the ball from one player to another until the closest puts it in the basket. It is easy to see a similar division of labor in the business firm.

In comparing this game to a market economy, I was struck by many likenesses. In each case, people's roles are more important than their real identities. For instance, you don't care what a person eats for supper if he is a good center. A manager can be whoever she wants to be if she can balance the accounts. Of course, a team is different from a game. On the team, it does matter who a person is, while in the game itself it doesn't matter.

The rules of the game provide order both in basketball and business. And yet both sets of rules can be changed. Fair enforcement of the rules is key in both situations. And the rules apply to everybody. Anyone can be called for a personal foul, and contracts must always be honored. There are even rules for each role. Forwards play close to the basket, while guards must get back on defense. In

How might these measures have been created? standardized? Are they everywhere?

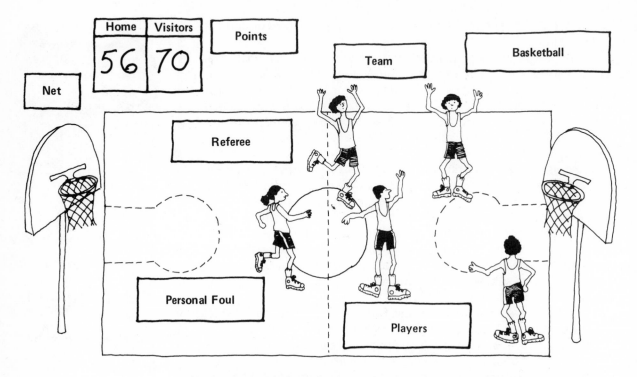

the market, there are certain collective bargaining rights for labor that are different from those for management.

Each situation has its own institutions. In the basketball game there is the net, or "hoop," the ball, and the court itself. In the market economy, the institutions include private property, money, and so forth. It would be interesting to see which institutions in the market were like which institutions in the game. Is money more like the net or the ball? What in the game is private property most like?

Looking at a basketball game as a mock-up for society, one is struck by the fact that it combines cooperation and competition, as almost all social operations do. The rules of the game control the behavior of two complex organizations—the teams—each made up of five independent decision-makers. There is a relatively simple object, the score, which is the equivalent of accounting profit.

The parallel of profit is quite exact. The prime interest is in the relative score of the two teams, just as the firm's survival rests on its rate of profit *relative* to other firms and industries. The mock-up is not perfect, however. It could be improved if the high-scoring team were allowed to have more players. If the high-scoring team were allowed to take players from the other team, of course, this might lead to a

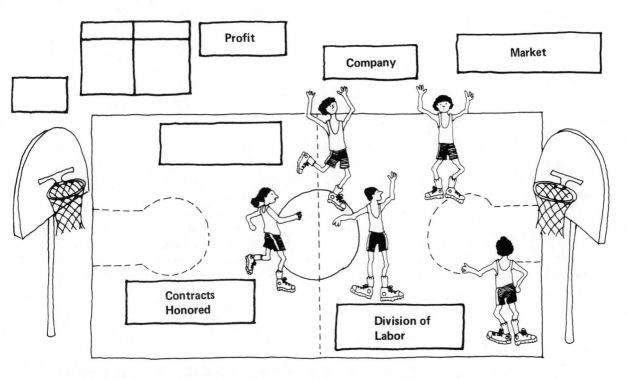

monopoly. Then the losing team would be reduced to zero, and the game ended.

The odd thing about basketball is that it is peace: it is regulated conflict, justice imposed by impartial referees (we hope). The competition is real—somebody wins and somebody loses—but still a ritual, so that gain and loss are bearable. The ball passes from one team to the other according to reasonably well-defined rules, designed originally to create excitement without damage.

One always worries, of course, about the stability of such a system. Even in basketball, injuries increase. The game gets rougher and more serious. The task of the referee becomes harder. Rule-breakers meet with punishment less and less often. Perhaps, horror of horrors, it will one day come to the mutual poisoning of beer. Then there will be war. But this seems improbable and, if we can have stable basketball, we should have stable peace.

ACTIVITIES

Points

Team

Basketball

Referee

Personal Foul

Net

I. This activity will give you the chance to compare American society to a basketball game.

1.   The reading included a drawing of a basketball game, with some of its features labeled. Imagine that American society is like a basketball game. What in society would be like the score in a basketball game? Fill in the boxes in the Workbook drawing with your answer. What in American society is like the team in basketball? Fill in the appropriate box. Fill in the rest of the boxes. If you do not have a Workbook, copy the boxes on a piece of paper.
2.   When you are finished, share your answers with others in the class. Did other students come up with different answers? What were their reasons? Did hearing their answers lead you to change your mind about any of yours? Why?
3.   When you are finished, discuss these questions:
     a.   In what ways is American society like a basketball game?
     b.   In what ways is American society different from a basketball game?
     c.   An analogy is a comparison between two things that are similar in some important way. Are there other games that would provide a better analogy to American society than a basketball game? Why do you think they would be better?
     d.   What does it mean to be a member of a team? a player in a game? a member of society?

II. This activity is designed to help you compare American society to the market economy. It is a more complex version of Activity I.

1.   Following are two drawings of a basketball court, with empty boxes to be labeled. You will need a partner for this activity.
2.   First, fill in the net box in the American society drawing in the Workbook. If you don't have a Workbook, write your answers on a separate sheet of paper. Have your partner fill in the same box in the American society drawing. Ask yourself what in American society is like the net in a basketball game. Now have your partner fill in the same box in the market economy drawing. Ask yourself what in a market economy is like the net.
3.   Trade papers with your partner. You must now ask yourself what in the market economy is like whatever your partner wrote in the "net" box. Your partner must do the same for your answer. When you are finished, compare and discuss your answers with each other.

4. Now do the same for the "team" box. Ask yourself what in American society is like a team in basketball. Your partner does the same. Then trade papers.
5. Each of you must decide what in the market economy is like what your partner wrote in the "team" box. When you are finished, compare and discuss your answers.
6. Do the same for the rest of the boxes.
7. When everyone is finished, discuss as a class these questions:
    a. Which is more like a basketball game, American society or the market economy? Why?
    b. Which of the analogies in this lesson is most useful to you? Explain.
    c. How do you use analogies in your own life?

Regulation and Controls

The government acts as the author and enforcer of rules. It also *participates* in the economy when it acts as a regulator. When the government *regulates* the economy, it does more than just insure a smooth operation of economic activity. It intervenes in the economy to promote goals the nation has decided on.

Government usually tries to control the effects of a *natural monopoly*. A natural monopoly exists when a company sells a product or service that is impractical or impossible for another company to reproduce. It would be a waste of resources if more than one utility company provided a town with electricity. In areas like these, whichever company starts operating first gains a natural monopoly in that business. Government then steps in to keep the company from taking advantage of its monopoly position. It regulates the price of phone calls, for example, as well as the price of gas and electricity. It also may act if customers find that the monopoly's services or products are not as good as they should be.

When companies try to put each other out of business, the effects on a community can be quite serious. Government then steps in to regulate such *destructive competition*. Pricing one's goods so low as to force all other companies in the same line out of business is one such practice. As a result, pricing has come under regulation by the government. The federal government regulates which routes

Does government affect competition between these businesses? How is competition restricted or encouraged?

airlines can fly and the fares the airlines charge. This restricts competition, resulting in a lower output of services and higher prices for consumers.

At the other extreme are cases where competition is too weak. For example, when firms get together and agree on what prices they will charge for similar products, then there is too little competition. Such agreements, called "price-fixing," are illegal in the United States. Company executives have sometimes been fined or even jailed for making them. Laws against price-fixing are designed to *strengthen competition*. The government may also use the antitrust laws to break up combinations of business firms in order to increase competition.

The government is also involved in regulating *property rights*. For example, at the start of the radio era, several stations would sometimes try to broadcast over the airwaves on the same frequency. This meant that none of their programs could be heard very clearly. Since nobody can claim to own the air, the government decided to regulate its use. It assigned frequencies to each station and forbade any other station to broadcast on that frequency. Because radio and TV stations now earn huge profits, government also requires them to show they are serving the public interest.

Government regulation is also used to protect the *rights of consumers*. The government tries to insure that products sold in the market are fresh, safe, and honestly labeled. Truth-in-lending laws require lenders to provide information about the actual costs of a loan. Safety devices in cars, the testing of new drugs, and the inspection of restaurant kitchens are other examples of government efforts to protect consumers.

Regulating the economy is done by many government agencies. Keeping track of what all these *regulatory agencies* are doing is not an easy task. Sometimes the agencies are taken over by the very businesses or professions they are supposed to regulate. At other times the need for regulation passes but the agency continues to operate in the same old way.

The basic rules of the game for the economy are supposed to be fair. Yet, in spite of the rules, powerful groups and people emerge. Sometimes the government must step in to prevent the powerful from taking advantage of the weak.

Sometimes you can feel dominated by a group you belong to. You may want to do something that the group won't let you do. Or you may get caught between groups. Two groups that are important to you may ask you to take opposite stands. In such situations you tend to feel powerless. You need help from a higher authority. Industries, consumers, and small businesses look to the government to protect them from overly powerful firms and groups. You can appeal to law, religion, or moral principles to justify your independent actions.

Year	Particulates	Sulfur oxides	Nitrogen oxides	Hydrocarbons	Carbon monoxide
1970	26.8	34.2	22.7	33.9	113.7
1971	24.9	32.3	23.4	33.3	113.7
1972	23.4	36.7	24.6	34.1	115.8
1973	21.9	35.6	25.7	34.0	111.5
1974	20.3	34.1	25.0	32.9	103.3
1975	18.0	32.9	24.2	30.9	96.2

Table 20-1   Summary of National Emission Estimates in the United States (millions of tons a year)
Have third party costs been increasing? decreasing? How can you tell?

☐ There are two readings for this lesson. The first presents the dilemma of a steel company executive, Robert Chamberlain. His steel plant is polluting his city. His neighbors urge him to solve this problem. However, the solution is costly. Other steel companies have turned it down. Chamberlain could risk going against this group, but the expense may force him out of competition. He must also think of his obligations to his stockholders and fellow workers. Torn between the conflicting demands of these groups, Chamberlain looks to the government to solve his problem. As you read his story, ask yourself the following questions:

1. How would a government regulation that required scrubbers free Chamberlain from his bind?
2. Would this regulation be in the interests of all the steel companies?
3. How can an appeal to higher authority help you when you are torn by conflicting group demands?

STEELTOWN'S CRISIS

Steeltown's crisis began early on a Monday in November as an unusual amount of smog settled over the city. By Tuesday morning the pollution level was dangerously high. Children and adults with breathing problems or heart disease were warned to stay inside and to avoid physical effort. County health officials telegrammed the city's twenty-three companies asking them to cut smoke emissions by 60 percent. Some firms acted promptly. Yet emissions were down by only 20 percent as of Wednesday.

At that point federal officials from the Environmental Protection Agency decided to act. Claiming emergency powers under the Clean Air Act of 1970, the EPA obtained a court order halting the operation of all twenty-three of Steeltown's plants. When the companies banked their furnaces on Thursday, there was a clear improvement in the level of emissions. A saving rain scattered the smog, and the immediate crisis was over.

Steeltown had known emergencies before. Pollution had reached the danger point sixty-five times before this crisis. There had been serious trouble in March. Intervention by the EPA, however, brought a new element. Several of the companies thought of suing the federal government for damages incurred when production was halted. Labor union leaders were also mindful of the layoff of 5,000 workers and the loss of $400,000 in wages. They prepared to demand that the companies agree to protect workers against wage losses when plants were shut down during such crises.

The worst part of the crisis was that it need never have occurred. The technology for removing the tons of soot that each day poured out of Steeltown's stacks had been available for years. Some of the larger companies might now take the necessary steps to modernize their operations over the next two to three years. Several of the smaller firms would not be able to absorb the added costs, however, and some Steeltown workers could face permanent loss of their jobs.

What might the function of this place be? What might the government do with the information it provides?

What are the penalties for violating this rule? Who determines this? Why is this rule needed?

Robert Chamberlain, manager of the American Steel Corporation plant in Steeltown, had been one of the first to comply with the request of county health officials. Like other plant managers, he acknowledged Steeltown's pollution problem. But he had not been able to do much toward solving them. Until the parent corporation gave the environment top priority, he could not justify a request for the $12,000,000 that would be needed for pollution control.

Chamberlain believed that the EPA action might work to the benefit of the American Steel Corporation. They could afford the extra expense and might well make up the costs through the use of byproducts recovered. He also believed it would be but a short time before outraged Steeltown citizens would sue American Steel for damage to the environment.

He also knew there were company executives who disagreed with him. Not all stockholders would support spending millions to lessen pollution. And the prospect of falling profits might jeopardize his career with the company.

Should Robert Chamberlain recommend a $12,000,000 expenditure for pollution-control devices?

ACTIVITIES

I. Just as small businesses and consumers can seek backing from the courts and regulatory agencies, there are higher authorities you can turn to when you need support or advice. This activity is about looking for help when you feel dominated or pressured by a group to which you belong.

Read the following situations as if you were the person faced with the dilemma. Then write down the authoritative source(s) (other than parents and friends) you could turn to for help in choosing a course of action. You can seek help from persons, organizations, books, science, religion, law, or moral principles. But whether your authority is a point of view or a person, you must justify the position you adopt by a specific argument supporting it.

A.   Your town has organized an after-school job market for the young people who live there. You want a job, and several are still available. Your parents strongly urge you to apply for the most complex job because it commands the highest pay. They want you to earn money to help pay for your college education. You are anxious because you fear that you will not do well at such a difficult job and that it will take too much time away from homework and friends.

B.   You have finally been accepted into the Wilderness Club and your friends want to celebrate with a week-long camping and hiking trip in the state park. You have never gone on such a long trip, and now the forecast is for rainy, cold weather. Though you have all had some camping experience, you really don't feel that the group should take this trip.

C.   A desirable training program is accepting a limited number of candidates. Acceptance depends on the grade you receive on the entrance exams. You know that several of the students are going to cheat on the test. You don't think it's fair for them to take this advantage.

D.   The elevator in your apartment building has not been working right for over a month. You know that it's a terrible safety hazard, endangering the lives of everyone in the building. Your landlord lives in another part of town and is not cooperative. He doesn't even speak your language. Your parents and neighbors don't want to complain because they are afraid of being evicted. You have the same worries as your parents but don't want to be taken advantage of by the owner, whose responsibility it is to fix the elevator.

☐ The second reading for this lesson shows that the government can influence the actions of buyers and sellers through formal regulations. These regulations are often hard to enact and enforce. Because of this, government officials sometimes make use of *informal controls.* The following speech, made by President John F. Kennedy in 1962, is an example. In it, the President tries to persuade a company to reverse a decision that he considers against the national interest. He uses the authority of his office to appeal to the company executives' moral responsibilities as citizens. He is also appealing to public opinion. As you read the speech, ask yourself the following questions:

1. How did Kennedy use his authority as president to protect people from a powerful group?
2. How might the executives of U.S. Steel have defended their action as responsible?
3. How can a similar appeal to law, religion, or moral principles protect you at times from control by your parents or friends?

KENNEDY VS. U.S. STEEL

The simultaneous and identical actions of United States Steel and other leading steel corporations increasing steel prices by some $6 a ton constitute a wholly unjustifiable and irresponsible defiance of the public interest.

In this serious hour in our nation's history, when we are confronted with grave crises in Berlin and Southeast Asia, when we are devoting our energies to economic recovery and stability, when we are asking reservists to leave their homes and families for months on end, and servicemen to risk their lives—and four were killed in the last two days in Vietnam—and asking union members to hold down their wage requests, at a time when restraint and sacrifice are being asked of every citizen, the American people will find it hard, as I do, to accept a situation in which a tiny handful of steel executives whose pursuit of private power and profit exceeds their sense of public responsibility can show such utter contempt for the interest of 185 million Americans.

If this rise in the cost of steel is imitated by the rest of the industry, instead of rescinded, it would increase the cost of homes, autos, appliances and most other items for every American family. It would increase the cost of machinery and tools to every American businessman and farmer. It would seriously handicap our efforts to prevent an inflationary spiral from eating up the pensions of our older citizens, and our new gains in purchasing power. It would add, Secretary McNamara informed me this morning, an estimated one billion dollars to the cost of our defenses, at a time when every dollar is needed for national security and other purposes.

It will make it more difficult for American goods to compete in foreign markets, more difficult to withstand competition from foreign imports, and, thus, more difficult to improve our balance-of-payments position and stem the flow of gold. And it is necessary to stem it, for our national security, if we are going to pay for our security commitments abroad.

And it would surely handicap our efforts to induce other industries and unions to adopt responsible price and wage policies.

The facts of the matter are that there is no justification for an increase in steel prices.

The recent settlement between the industry and the union, which does not even take place until July 1, was widely acknowledged to be noninflationary, and the whole purpose and effect of this Administration's role, which both parties understood, was to achieve an agreement which would make unnecessary any increases in prices.

Steel output per man is rising so fast that labor costs per ton of steel can actually be expected to decline in the next 12 months. And, in fact, the acting Commissioner of the Bureau of Labor Statistics informed me this morning that, and I quote: "employment costs per unit of steel output in 1961 were essentially the same as they were in 1958." The cost of major raw materials—steel scrap and coal—has also been declining.

And, for an industry which has been generally operating at less than two thirds of capacity, its profit rate has been normal, and can be expected to rise sharply this year in view of the reduction in idle capacity. Their lot has been easier than that of 100,000 steelworkers thrown out of work in the last three years.

The industry's cash dividends have exceeded 600 million dollars in each of the last five years, and earnings in the first quarter of this year were estimated in the February 28 "Wall Street Journal" to be among the highest in history.

In short, at a time when they could be exploring how more efficiency and better prices could be obtained, reducing prices in this industry in recognition of lower costs, their unusually good labor contract, their foreign competition and their increase in production and profits which are coming this year, a few gigantic corporations have decided to increase prices in ruthless disregard of their public responsibilities.

Why does government regulate these products? Why might people need this kind of protection? What might happen without it?

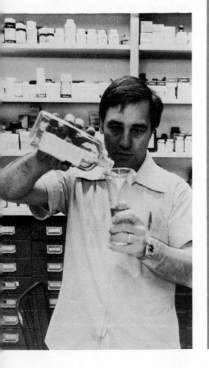

The Steelworkers Union can be proud that it abided by its responsibilities in this agreement, and this Government also has responsibilities which we intend to meet. The Department of Justice and the Federal Trade Commission are examining the significance of this action in a free, competitive economy.

The Department of Defense and other agencies are reviewing its impact on their policies of procurement.

And I am informed that steps are under way by those members of the Congress who plan appropriate inquiries into how these price decisions are so quickly made and reached, and what legislative safeguards may be needed to protect the public interest.

Price and wage decisions in this country, except for very limited restriction in the case of monopolies and national-emergency strikes, are and ought to be freely and privately made. But the American people have a right to expect, in return for that freedom, a higher sense of business responsibility for the welfare of their country than has been shown in the last two days.

Some time ago I asked each American to consider what he would do for his country, and I asked the steel companies. In the last twenty-four hours we had their answer.

ACTIVITIES

II.   The Kennedy statement is an unusual example of an administration's successful use of informal controls to resolve a conflict. There are also many everyday situations in which settlements are reached informally. In this activity, you will use an organized format to analyze a problem and to decide what alternatives, both formal and informal, are available to you.

1.   For each of the following situations, there are several boxes containing space for some vital information. Divide into small groups to discuss the situations and then answer the questions in each box in the Workbook. If you do not have a Workbook, copy the boxes onto a separate piece of paper. Read the situation and decide the following:
   a.   What is being sought by the person issuing the complaint?
   b.   Who is affected by the situation? Is this a problem that concerns just two individuals, or will it affect many others? Who would be touched by third-party benefits and/or costs?
   c.   What formal authority or authorities could deal with the problem? What rules and regulations are in their power? What are the pros and cons of how they would handle it?
   d.   How could you settle this informally? What gives this method its power or authority? What are the pros and cons of how it would be handled?

Situation A: A rock music group needs its amplifier repaired or replaced before an important concert that is scheduled to take place in one month. The guarantee is still in effect, but the manufacturer refuses to take responsibility for the amplifier because he feels the musicians have abused it.

a. What is being sought?

b. Who is affected?

c. Formal settlement	or	d. Informal settlement

Situation B: A small bicycle repair shop has been waiting three months for a popular type of hand brake it ordered and paid for. The shop's customers are complaining and threaten to take their business elsewhere.

a. What is being sought?

b. Who is affected?

c. Formal settlement	or	d. Informal settlement

Situation C: Your younger brother comes to you every day to borrow lunch money. He never has any of his own because the bigger kids at school threaten him and take it away from him.

a. What is being sought?

b. Who is affected?

c. Formal settlement	or	d. Informal settlement

2. Discussion questions for the whole class
    a. Which type of control, formal or informal, seemed to offer the best solution for each problem?
    b. What sources of authority were available? How did they compare in terms of cost? time? effectiveness?
    c. When have informal controls worked best for you?
    d. How has the existence of formal authority helped you?

Public Goods

Most of the goods and services the economy produces are paid for by those who use them. The price of a loaf of bread, for instance, covers the cost of the wheat and the cost of baking it, packaging it, and sending it to the stores. Whether the bread is bought or not depends on whether its benefits seem equal to or greater than the money the buyer pays for it. But there are some kinds of goods and services that people enjoy without paying the full price. Economists call these *public goods.*

A public good is one that can benefit many people at once, even those who do not pay for it. In other words, it has third-party benefits. The loaf of bread a person buys can only be used by that person. Once it is consumed, no one else can eat it. Economists say such goods are *rival in consumption.* But a person can use the local park without preventing others from using it. All can swim at a public beach. Everyone can benefit from the country's system of national defense. These things are not rival in consumption.

The market system can only produce goods whose full cost is paid by the user. It therefore produces few public goods. It would not be practical for a private company to build a park, for instance, because hardly anyone would be willing to pay for using it. In cases like this, the government steps in and becomes the major producer of public goods.

Who pays the salaries of these people?
Why?

The fact that the market underproduces public goods is a major reason for government taxes and spending. National defense and space programs, parks, roads, public health programs, and police and fire service are examples of things the market would not be able to produce. They all involve third-party benefits. That is, their costs are not fully paid by those who benefit directly from them.

Fire protection is a good example of why the government has become the major producer of public goods. In the early nineteenth century, fire protection was provided by private companies that competed with one another. A homeowner would sign a contract with a particular fire company. If there were a fire, that company would come and put out the fire. But if a neighbor had a contract with another firm, that company would not come unless the fire spread to the neighbor's house. Under this system, fires tended to spread rather quickly. People without enough money to pay for a fire protection contract simply watched their homes burn. Dissatisfaction with this system led to the creation of public fire departments, which would put out fires anywhere as soon as they started.

There are people who think that some kinds of public goods could be provided as well or better by private companies in the market system. Public education is a public good in the United States, provided by the government. Some people have recently proposed a plan whereby education would be provided by market competition. Under this plan, students would be given *vouchers* (coupons). These could be used like money to pay for education offered by private schools competing for their business. Many different voucher plans have been suggested. All of them claim that students would get a better education if they could simply go out and buy whatever kind of education they wanted. Of course, these plans do not provide for citizenship education, which was a major reason for adopting public schooling.

Other people think that some private goods that are now provided by the market system could be better provided by the government. One such example is health care. They claim that more people would have access to better medical care if it were offered and paid for largely by the government. This could be done through some system of taxation that put aside a certain amount of money just for that purpose. The rationale for making this private good a public one is that it is so important that everyone should have it, regardless of how much money they have. This is one reason why education is a public good. The same logic could also be applied to other goods, like housing.

From these examples, it can be seen that the line between "public" goods and

"Where's the fire?"

"private" goods is not always easy to draw. In order to decide where the line should be drawn, it is helpful to ask several questions. Are there third-party benefits involved? Is the good or service one that benefits many people at once, even those who do not use it directly? Can the good be provided by the free market? Can the government do a better job of providing that good or service?

There are two issues involved in any private vs. public debate—choice and responsibility. Should people who don't want a particular good or service have to pay for it with their taxes? Does the government have the right to make this choice for people? On the other hand, should a good or service be only for those who can afford it? Or would society as a whole be better off if it were available to everyone? Does the government have the responsibility to provide it?

☐ The reading for this lesson is from a paper by Peter Singer. It presents part of the debate over health care. It argues for a system of government care similar to the one Great Britain has. As you read the article, ask yourself the following questions:
1. Should health care be a public responsibility or a matter of individual choice in the market?
2. Which arguments for each position are the strongest?
3. What choices should your society make for all its members?

BLOOD, MARKETS, AND MEDICAL CARE

Should the goods and services necessary to preserve and restore our health be bought and sold in the marketplace, like television sets and haircuts? This question underlies much of the current debate about how health care should be provided and paid for. A national health service, national health insurance, health maintenance organizations, and traditional fee-for-service medicine are all variations on a spectrum that ranges from "socialized medicine" to a pure free market.

The marketplace, it is said, extends and preserves freedom, in that it allows consumers and producers alike to choose what they buy and sell. The case of health care allows us to examine the argument that market-based distribution of goods and services increases people's freedom.

Could private companies provide this service? At what cost? At what level of efficiency?

The medical care market in this country, for example, differs from conventional markets in several ways. First, the demand for medical care is irregular and unpredictable, unlike practically every other significant item in the average household budget. The need for the service may come suddenly, and the consumer may be in no position to shop around. Nor can the cost of care be predicted in advance.

Next, the ethics of the medical profession make medical care unlike other businesses. Physicians neither advertise nor carry on open price competition. When physicians advise further treatment, they are supposed to be entirely unaffected by considerations of self-interest. Then too, the very existence of a licensed medical profession severely limits the supply of medical care. Acceptances to medical school determine the number of doctors that can be licensed in future years. Thus the supply of medical care is not directly affected by the profitability of providing it, as would be the case in a normal market. A further consequence of this situation is that the range of care (quality and price) available is sharply curtailed.

Many of the features that distinguish medical care from other commodities are the work of professional bodies such as the American Medical Association. Although the AMA strongly opposes any move away from the status quo toward some sort of national health service, the organization is equally firm in its opposition to measures that would move toward more open competition and more effective consumer choice.

There can be no freedom without adequate information on which to make a choice. Clearly, consumers would have more freedom if they were better informed about items like fees. Open competition would also lead to some fee reduction. But before we conclude that such a move is desirable because it increases freedom, we need to consider its effect on medical practice.

In an open market, the individual doctor would be less secure economically than he or she is at present. Economic considerations would therefore become more prominent in doctors' relationships to their patients. This could undermine the relationship.

Should we then take medical care out of the marketplace altogether?

Any national health service must be financed by taxation. It does, therefore, limit the freedom of taxpayers to decide how much they will spend on health and how much on other items. What can be said in defense of limiting freedom in this way?

First, it may be that society as a whole can obtain goods that the individual could never obtain. Cheap, uncontaminated blood is one example, and medical services that have not been distorted by the threat of malpractice suits may be another. The special nature of medical care may make it unsuited to market control for other reasons too. For instance, the market's answer to the uncertainty of an individual's need for extensive medical care is private insurance. Private insurance, however, seldom covers ordinary visits to the doctor. Most people are insured for hospitalization and not for office visits. Yet much medical care that now takes place in hospitals could be done much more economically in the patient's home or the

Does everyone pay for this service? Does everyone use it? How might a "voucher" system work?

doctor's office. As a result, consumers pay more for their medical insurance than they otherwise might.

This difficulty is not one that can be eliminated simply by a system of national health insurance like those envisaged in recent congressional bills. These proposals would retain the principle of paying the doctor for each treatment. If office visits were covered, the system would still be wide open to abuse unless a large and expensive army of inspectors were employed. If office visits were not covered, the proposals would accelerate the trend toward unnecessary hospitalization.

A national health service that pays doctors on some basis other than the cost of the treatments they prescribe can avoid this problem. In Britain, for example, doctors are paid according to the number of patients they treat. Patients may, of course, see their doctors as often as they like under such an arrangement. This fact has led critics of a national health service to fear that doctors will be burdened with unnecessary visits. But British statistics do not show any rise in demand per patient since the inauguration of the National Health Service.

Whatever the reason, Britain spends a smaller percentage of its gross national product on health care than the United States, despite the fact that health care is free to all in Britain. Quite apart from the question of expense, though, it should be asked how many cases of overutilization are needed to offset one case of a patient who dies because he or she postponed treatment in order to save money. The security and peace of mind that arise from knowing that one will never be in this situation is one of the greatest benefits that a society can bestow on its citizens.

Select from this book, outside of this chapter, at least three images, either drawings or photos, that demonstrate some form of business. For each picture you select, you should imagine, or create in your own mind, a second picture that shows one way in which government interacts with this business. Describe this imaginary image in as much detail as possible. Are there people in it? What are they doing? What government rules are evident in these pictures? How can you tell?

VISUAL ACTIVITY

ACTIVITIES

One goal of government is to provide services to society. You as an individual must decide which of these services you want to use and support. This card sorting activity is designed to help you think about and discuss the implications that public goods and services have for you and for society.

1. The cards in this lesson describe things that the government either does or could do for society at the local, state, and national levels. Think of at least ten other examples of government services or goods and write them on blank cards. Use the cards in the Workbook or make your own.
2. Split up into groups of three or four students each and sort the cards into these three categories:
    a. things the government must provide
    b. things the government should never provide
    c. things you might want the government to provide
3. Now combine piles *a* and *c*. Add eight or ten cards representing other services that you think government should provide. Try to think of some things that your governments do not provide now. Take all the cards in this pile and sort them into the following categories:
    a. services and goods that are only of interest to people like you
    b. services and goods that are good for society as a whole but that you don't care about personally
    c. services and goods that are good for you (or your group) and for the society as a whole
4. Discussion questions
    a. Why should people have to pay for goods and services that they feel don't help them?
    b. Should any goods or services in the *a* category under #3 be provided by the government? Why or why not?

national defense	regulation of drugs
censorship of media	disaster relief
building codes	public jobs programs
rent subsidies	public transportation
national health care	gun registration
national pollution standards	foster care of children
air traffic control	street vendor licensing
immunization of children	public education
national forests	game for hunters to shoot
subsidies for business firms	youth centers

CHAPTER 8 INCOME DISTRIBUTION AND REDISTRIBUTION

Sources of Income

People's incomes in large part determine their shares of the economy's goods and services. Where does income come from? In a market economy, people get income in several ways. They work and earn wages. They make money by renting out their property to others. They earn interest on money they deposit in banks or lend to others. They earn profits by selling goods and services. People also receive income called *transfer payments*. These payments give money to people who have not earned it in the ways explained above. Important government transfer payments include welfare, food stamps, and unemployment compensation, as well as social security and veterans' benefits. Pensions, gifts, and inheritances are important private transfer payments.

The shares of the nation's income that go to various groups of resource owners is called a *functional distribution of income*. The circle below (Figure 22-1) is called a "pie graph"—each share of income is pictured as a "slice" of the "pie." Employee compensation includes wages and fringe benefits like health insurance and pensions. Proprietors are people who own their own businesses.

As Table 22-1 shows, many of the slices have remained the same size for a long time. During a depression, when business profits decline (see 1930–1939), the wages slice of the pie gets bigger. During a period of great prosperity (see 1939–1970), the profits slice of the pie gets bigger.

	EMPLOYEE COMPENSATION	PROPRIETORS' INCOME	CORPORATE PROFITS	INTEREST	RENT	TOTAL
1900–1909	55.0	23.7	6.8	5.5	9.0	100
1910–1919	53.6	23.8	9.1	5.4	8.1	100
1920–1929	60.0	17.5	7.8	6.2	7.7	100
1930–1939	67.5	14.8	4.0	8.7	5.6	100
1940–1948	64.6	17.2	11.9	3.1	3.3	100
1949–1958	67.3	13.9	12.5	2.9	3.4	100
1959–1963	69.9	11.9	11.2	4.0	3.0	100
1964–1970	71.7	9.6	12.1	3.5	3.2	100
1974	77.1	7.6	7.3	6.1	1.9	100
1975	76.4	7.1	8.2	6.5	1.8	100
1976	76.0	6.7	9.4	6.5	1.7	100
1977	76.0	6.4	9.2	6.6	1.7	100

Note: Because figures in each row have been rounded off, they do not always add up to 100.

Table 22-1 Percentage Shares of U.S. National Income, 1900–1977 *Source:* Economic Report of the President, 1977 and 1978.

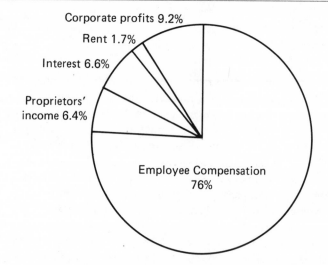

Figure 22-1 National Income, 1976 *Source:* Economic Report of the President, 1977.

Another way of looking at income is to look at the *personal distribution of income.* This measures the way income is shared among the individuals and households who make up the economy. It is a way of measuring "who gets how much." Thus, Table 22-2 shows what percent of families in the United States falls into each of several income brackets.

TOTAL MONEY INCOME	NUMBER OF FAMILIES	PERCENT
Total	56,245,000	100
Under $1,000	} 1,209,000	} 2
$ 1,000 to $ 1,999		
$ 2,000 to $ 2,999	1,356,000	2
$ 3,000 to $ 3,999	1,908,000	3
$ 4,000 to $ 4,999	2,293,000	4
$ 5,000 to $ 5,999	2,310,000	4
$ 6,000 to $ 6,999	2,351,000	4
$ 7,000 to $ 7,999	2,444,000	4
$ 8,000 to $ 8,999	2,495,000	4
$ 9,000 to $ 9,999	2,320,000	4
$10,000 to $10,999	2,597,000	5
$11,000 to $11,999	2,415,000	4
$12,000 to $12,999	2,716,000	5
$13,000 to $13,999	2,373,000	4
$14,000 to $14,999	2,460,000	4
$15,000 to $19,999	10,548,000	18
$20,000 to $24,999	6,518,000	12
$25,000 to $49,999	7,148,000	13
$50,000 and over	783,000	1
Median Income	$13,719	
Mean Income	$15,546	

Table 22-2   Income Level, 1975
Source: Department of Commerce, Bureau of the Census, 1977.

Note: Because figures in the percent column have been rounded off, they add up to slightly less than 100.

Income distribution can also be shown by dividing the number of families into fifths. It can then be seen what percent of the total income goes to each fifth, that is, each 20 percent.

Table 22-3 shows that the personal distribution of income has changed very little over the past twenty-five years or so. There has been a slight decrease in the proportion that goes to families at the very top of the economy. There has been a slight increase in the proportion that goes to families at the very bottom. The proportion that goes to families in the middle has stayed just about the same.

YEAR	LOWEST FIFTH	SECOND FIFTH	MIDDLE FIFTH	FOURTH FIFTH	HIGHEST FIFTH	TOP FIVE PERCENT
1947	5	12	17	23	43	18
1950	4	12	17	23	43	17
1955	5	12	18	24	42	17
1960	5	12	18	24	42	16
1965	5	12	18	24	41	16
1970	6	12	17	23	42	16
1973	6	12	18	24	41	16
1975	5	12	18	24	41	16

Note: Because figures in each row have been rounded off, they do not always add up to 100.

Table 22-3   Percentage of Mean Family Income Received by Each Fifth of Families and Top Five Percent for Selected Years
Source: Office of Management and Budget, 1973, Department of Commerce, 1977.

What this kind of table does not show is whether the gap between rich and poor is increasing or decreasing. It also does not tell whether the relative standards of living have changed over time. In recent years, the richest fifth has received more and more income in the forms of expense accounts, fringe benefits, and more enjoyable work roles. At the same time, the poorest fifth has received more and more transfer income from the government. This makes it harder to tell if the income distribution is getting more or less balanced.

What percent of the population do you think earns approximately the same income as this person? What percent earns more? less?

Both the source and the size of your income determine where you fit into society. They place you in a certain economic group or social class. Where you fit does not depend on your personal traits alone. For instance, people of the same sex, age, and race often find themselves in the same social or economic slots.

None of the groups you belong to defines itself purely in economic terms. Your group may make contributions to the society as a whole that are not reflected in the amount of income its members receive. They may be underpaid or not paid at all for the work they do. Or they may own resources that allow them to earn more money for less work than others do. Your groups can also contribute in noneconomic ways. They may make their community a better place to live in. They may have new ideas or force you to deal with hard questions. These and other important contributions are ignored in an economic view of society. To understand how you and your groups fit into society, you must look at the whole picture from more than one point of view.

☐ The reading for this lesson presents an economic picture of our society. People are ordered and seen only in terms of their incomes. As you read this description, ask yourself the following questions:
1. Why must three-fourths of society pass by before a person of average income reaches you?
2. Where do young people fit in? What happens as they get older?
3. Where do your other groups fit into this picture? How do they fit into society as a whole?

A PARADE OF DWARFS (AND A FEW GIANTS)

Imagine that you have just been told that yours is an "average" income. This is the money that comes to you before you pay any taxes. You are curious about who makes how much in America and want to see where you stand in relation to others on the income ladder. You assume you must be in the middle. The best way of finding out how income is distributed would be if you were to organize an hour-long parade in which the marchers all represented various levels of income and the different occupations or social roles associated with those incomes.

So, you put your imagination, backed up by some government

statistics, to work. For fun, and so as to make the size of each marcher's income clearer, you decide that the height of people marching in the parade will be proportionate to their incomes. For this purpose, a host of midgets and giants appears as if by miracle. The midgets, with their midget-sized wallets and pocket books to match, are scheduled to begin the procession; the giants will bring up the rear. You will have a clear view of these strange and ill-assorted folk from your perch in the reviewing stand. You, of course, being of average income, are also of average height.

At first, in the few seconds after the parade has come your way, you hear the sound of the band but you don't see a thing. Then you suddenly spot a number of people who seem to be upside down. They are in fact hanging by their toenails and walking on their hands in a trench below street level. These are not the shorties you expected. They are simply the financial basket cases, the farmers or business people who have filed for bankruptcy or suffered serious losses. Being in the red, they are minus income. Sometimes they even stand quite tall, but in the wrong direction.

They are followed by tiny people less than a finger high who take

How much training is necessary before one can earn an adequate income? What is an adequate income?

What percent of minorities earn less than this person? Why?

some five minutes to pass. Watching them makes you feel like Gulliver in Lilliput. Included in their ranks are young people just starting their careers late in the year, housewives and students who by choice have worked only part-time, and small business people who can hardly make ends meet and therefore fear they will go under. There is also a handful of basically unemployed people who have managed to find only a little work.

Then come the true midgets, people all of three feet tall. Here you see old people living on social security, mothers of small children whose husbands have deserted them, unemployed workers who collect a low amount of compensation, divorced women who do not receive alimony, and divorced men who each month must pay out both alimony and child support. Their faces are noticeably pinched. In their ranks are also men and women with physical or mental handicaps, people who do not work steadily, and artists and writers who work hard but seldom sell the paintings or novels they create. They take some six minutes to pass you.

Then, for the next fifteen minutes, you watch a mass of slightly taller midgets, people between three and four feet high. You are surprised at what a large proportion of them are women, also by how many are black or brown. Most of them are ordinary workers, many of them manual, who hold down low-paying jobs—part-time store clerks, dishwashers and busboys in restaurants, building janitors, migrant farm laborers, telephone sales people working for the minimum wage, and apprentices in trades.

In their wake come a bunch of people who are taller than midgets but still very short; they would barely reach your neck. These are the mass of ordinary workers who have some technical skills but not a great many. They represent a large part of the population and take some ten minutes to pass the reviewing stand.

At last you begin to spot people who look more familiar to you. But you have had to wait thirty-six minutes to see anyone even approaching your height. For thirteen minutes you watch as more highly trained people sail by. Some are skilled workers in factories; others are office workers or government bureaucrats. Those in front tend to be younger; they are probably in the last stages of their training.

When you finally see people who are exactly your height, your watch tells you that 48 minutes have already gone by. You are

What kind of contribution do these volunteers make to society? Is it important that they don't get paid? Why?

astonished, because this means that four-fifths of the people in the income parade are less well-off than you. And you thought you were "average"! Now you see skilled workers like yourself (you are a carpenter) as well as factory supervisors, insurance salespeople, shopkeepers, and teachers. But they are gone in six minutes.

Now the height of the marchers starts to shoot up fast. They're all way over six feet, and you begin to feel that *you* may be shrinking. For here come the top 10 percent of income receivers in the country. They start with the successful farmers, small contractors, people staffing the federal government, middle-management executives, engineers, run-of-the-mill lawyers, and senior college professors. Most of these people, you realize, are college-educated. Many, in fact, have advanced or professional degrees.

The giants only appear in the last few minutes of the parade. Here you see an amazing number of doctors—not your ordinary G.P.'s, but specialists like surgeons with big reputations. With them you will also find corporation lawyers or lawyers who are partners in big-city firms, certified public accountants, managers of large companies, well-known professional athletes, and famous actors. They all loom large, about seven to nine feet tall, and they tend to be older than average. The stilts that many of them walk on so nimbly symbolize the dividends and bank interest they receive above and beyond their salaries or fees.

Only at the close of the parade, in the last thirty seconds, do you see the mile-high people who reduce almost everyone else to midgets. These are the super-rich, many of them heirs to inherited wealth. But also among them are stars from the worlds of art or entertainment and the owners or senior executives of large and prosperous businesses.

So now you know what average means. You are ahead of 80 percent of the marchers in the parade. But the top 10 percent has so much more income than anyone else that when theirs is counted in, yours seems only average. In the course of just an hour, you have learned something about the meaning of the word "relative." Relative to most people, you feel like a giant. But relative to the really rich, you are just a pygmy.

ACTIVITIES

In this activity you will predict the source of income, and judge its impact on the quality of life, in three very different neighborhoods.

1. Three neighborhoods, representing lower-, middle-, and upper-income levels, are described below.

Neighborhood A.   This crowded neighborhood of 10,000 residents was once a busy and thriving factory district. Then modern technology greatly reduced the need for unskilled labor. Ever since, over 50 percent of the residents who normally work to support their families have been unemployed. Though housing is substandard here, poor families and the elderly are still attracted to the area because of its low rents. The area also appeals to people who like the privacy to be found in its many apartment buildings. A small shopping district consists mainly of small, private businesses. They struggle to compete with the new shopping malls on the other side of town. There are small public parks every few streets, but they are not well-maintained. They are usually used only by young people, who have no other place to meet.

  Though the community is poor and run-down, many of the residents still take pride in the different ethnic groups and cultural richness to be found there. They can also recall the days when their factories made a big contribution to the economic development of the region as a whole. The dropout rate in the old neighborhood school is high. Yet there is hope today that the modern school just completed with federal funds will have a good effect on the attitudes of the young.

Neighborhood B.   This is a fairly new community of about 5,000 residents. People here take pride in their neat and tidy single-family dwellings. A few modern townhouse units have also been built. They have proved popular with single people and young families. A good 80 percent of the potential labor force is employed, mainly in skilled and semiskilled positions. There are also some owners of small businesses. The new shopping mall nearby has offered a variety of jobs to the people of the area, and access to the inner city is made easy by public transport. Neighbors often meet for backyard barbecues or at the local recreation center. The local schools in Neighborhood B are not modern. Yet residents respect the teachers and administrators who run them and rely on them to make the best decisions for their children.

Neighborhood C.   This neighborhood is very much as it was a hundred years ago. Even descendants of some of the original settlers still live here. The homes are very large and are spaced far apart on large wooded lots. The population is only about 1,000. Because of the long distances between homes, neighbors tend to rely on the phone, private weekend parties, or gatherings at the local country club to keep in touch. Many of the families live here for only a part of the year. They spend the rest of their time at vacation homes or aboard their yachts. There is a private day school that most of the younger children attend. For the most part, the older children go to private boarding schools, though a nearby public school is available. Some members of the community own small businesses, but most either have executive positions or are independently wealthy. They can commute by car to their jobs and businesses by way of a new highway bordering a large park. The residents here are proud of their neighborhood, and especially of the contributions—bike trails, solar heating, and land conservation—it has made to the town.

2.   As a class, compile a list of all the possible sources of income for the residents of each of the three neighborhoods. List them on the board.
3.   Estimate the percentage of income for each neighborhood that comes from the different sources you have listed.
4.   Divide into groups of five or six students each. Create a redistribution plan for all three neighborhoods, using source of income as the means. Your goal here is to devise a plan that will enable Neighborhoods A and B to raise themselves economically. Try to create a plan that is both fair and legal. Your plan should answer the following questions:
   a.   What contributions do these neighborhoods make to the society?
   b.   How can their residents get a fairer share of income in return for their contributions?
   c.   What new sources of income would be worthwhile for these neighborhoods to develop?
   d.   What kinds of help would the neighborhoods need in order to develop these sources of income?
   e.   What should the government do? What should Neighborhood A do? Neighborhood B? Neighborhood C?
6.   Discussion questions
   a.   What share of the economy's goods and services did each neighborhood have before you redistributed incomes? after?
   b.   What are the best features of each plan?
   c.   How realistic are your plans?
   d.   Why would Neighborhood A go along with the plan? Neighborhood B? Neighborhood C? How could each be convinced?
   e.   Do your redistribution plans benefit society as a whole?

Private Groups and Income Distribution

Distribution of income is not at all equal. Often the government will step in to reduce the worst effects of this inequality. Private groups also interfere with the workings of a pure market economy to change income distribution. Business organizations, labor unions, farmers, bankers, and professionals, for example, all act to win for themselves a larger share of the economic pie. Sometimes they put pressure on Congress. Sometimes they just set up rules that will favor them.

A business increases its share of the economic pie by increasing its profits. It can do this in many ways. One way—if the public goes along—is simply to raise its prices. Another is to expand its markets by driving out competitors or by starting operations in areas where there is little or no competition. The Volkswagen company of Germany, for instance, began selling small cars in the United States when there were no other small cars for sale. A business can increase profits by decreasing the costs of its operations. That is, it can use cheaper materials, cheaper labor, and so on. It can also persuade government officials to limit competition from abroad that undersells American-made goods.

Labor unions increase their share of the economic pie by increasing wages. This they accomplish in three basic ways: (1) by restricting the supply of labor; (2) by increasing the demand for labor; and (3) by using their power to bargain for higher wages.

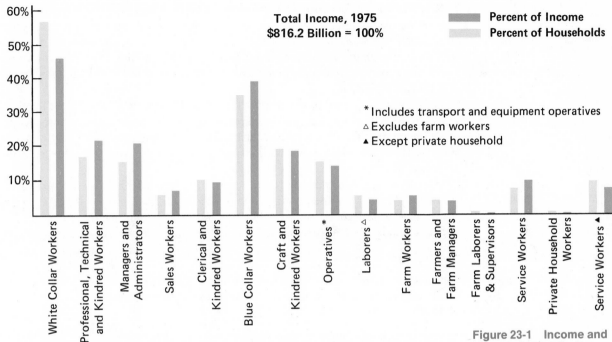

60%

50%

40%

30%

20%

10%

Total Income, 1975
$816.2 Billion = 100%

■ Percent of Income
□ Percent of Households

* Includes transport and equipment operatives
△ Excludes farm workers
▲ Except private household

White Collar Workers

Professional, Technical and Kindred Workers

Managers and Administrators

Sales Workers

Clerical and Kindred Workers

Blue Collar Workers

Craft and Kindred Workers

Operatives *

Laborers △

Farm Workers

Farmers and Farm Managers

Farm Laborers & Supervisors

Service Workers

Private Household Workers

Service Workers ▲

Figure 23-1   Income and Household Distribution by Occupation of Head, 1975
Which groups received the largest income shares? The smallest?

First, the most common way of restricting the supply of labor is to require everyone who works below the management level in a particular place to join the union. (This is called a "union shop.") By also limiting the number of people in the union, the union can control the supply of labor and thus make the labor of each individual worker more valuable. However, all unions are not limited in membership. Professional groups like doctors can keep their ranks small by limiting the number of accredited medical schools. As a result, they receive high prices for their services.

Second, if workers become more productive, business activity will expand. The demand for labor will then increase, creating more jobs. Unions also increase the demand for labor by trying to get consumers to buy only union-made goods. They can also try to restrict imports of foreign-made goods that compete with goods made by American workers.

Finally, unions use collective bargaining. This power is backed up by the right to strike if union demands are not met. By bargaining collectively with employers, workers are able to get higher wages than any individual worker would be able to get alone. Economists estimate that in two-thirds of the union jobs in the United States, workers earn from five to twenty percent more than they would earn without unions.

When any group succeeds in increasing its share of the economic pie, the percent of the pie going to other groups declines. When businesses raise prices, consumers can buy less. Of course, if the economic pie keeps getting larger, people may not notice that their percent of the total is getting smaller. But when the economic pie stays the same size, or when it shrinks, the people with smaller shares feel a definite pinch.

Every group is trying to get what it thinks best for itself. What is best for the group, however, is not necessarily what is best for the society as a whole. As a group member and as a member of society, then, your interests and loyalties may sometimes conflict. In some situations, this would force you to make a hard choice.

For instance, if your outlook is, "My friend, right or wrong"—even when your friend may have committed a crime—you may be tempted to help that friend at the expense of everyone else. But when you look at the total picture, you see that society's needs must also be met. You realize that if everyone put friendship ahead of the law, the rules of the game could easily become meaningless. Then everyone would lose. When you see situations in this way, you gain a broader view. However, you may also lose something if you act on this insight. Someone you care for a lot may not understand your moral principles and may even feel betrayed.

What kind of private group might this be? What might be some of the possible topics of conversation?

☐ The reading for this lesson is a debate. One side argues for laws that strengthen labor unions. This will give them more power to affect the distribution of income. The other side argues that these laws are unfair because they interfere with people's right to choose. As you read their arguments, ask yourself the following questions:

1. Which arguments on each side are based on the needs of the whole society? Which arguments are based on the needs of a particular group?
2. What are the strongest arguments for each side in the debate?
3. What do you gain by seeing yourself as a member of society? What do you lose?

WHOSE "RIGHT" TO WORK?

Should the requirement of membership in a labor organization as a condition of employment be illegal?

The debate thus becomes basically concerned with so-called "right to work" laws. These are laws, passed by 19 states, which say in effect: No person shall be deprived of the right to work at his chosen occupation because he is a member of a union *or* because he refuses to join a union.

A *closed shop* is one in which only union members can get and hold jobs. A *union shop* is one in which anyone can get a job provided he joins the union within a specified time after getting the job. Any business which employs both union and non-union help is generally called an *open shop.*

FOR!
1. *"Right to work" laws protect the freedom of every individual in America.* Throughout the world, America is proudly recognized as "the land of the free." But what is free about being *forced* to join or pay dues to a union in order to hold a job? Yet this is the situation that exists in many of America's industrial communities today.

"Right to work" laws would do away with this lack of freedom. They would protect the right of every individual in America to work for a living regardless of whether or not he is a member of a labor organization.

These laws do not say "Don't Join Unions" nor do they say "Join Them." They leave the choice up to each worker.

Labor leaders fought hard for many long years to win laws which make it illegal for an employer to *deny* a job to a person because of union membership. But these laws should not be allowed to become a weapon by which workers are denied the right to a job unless they first join a union (as in a "union shop").

2. *"Right to work" laws are needed to check abuses by some unions.* Union leaders are forever trying to justify their policies by pointing out how "oppressive" employers would be if there weren't unions. However, the fact is that when unions become large and powerful they, too, can be as oppressive to the individual worker as was the "slave-driving boss" of the last century.

To compel a man to join a union as a condition of holding his job puts irresponsible power in the hands of union bosses. "Right to work" laws, therefore, will help check abuses which arise when labor bosses get too powerful. As Lord Acton said many years ago: "Power tends to corrupt, and absolute power corrupts absolutely." A union shop—in which all workers must join the union or lose their jobs—gives the union bosses such absolute power.

What group could be associated with this product? How does this group influence the laws that regulate sales of this product?

3. *"Right to work" laws are not anti-labor laws.* Some opponents of "right to work" laws say these laws are anti-labor. Yet, from 1934 to 1951, the Railway Labor Act specifically forbade all attempts to compel workers to belong to unions. During those years, unions in the railroad industry increased their membership threefold! Can "right to work" laws thus fairly be called anti-labor?

Laws which give the worker complete freedom of choice are not "anti-labor" laws. They are, instead, an expression of America's sense of fair play and dislike of coercion.

Besides, Federal law provides safeguards for unions which no state law can interfere with. For example, employers can't *prevent* employees from selecting a union to bargain for them. Also, employers are required to bargain with the union. Employees cannot be dismissed for choosing to join and support the union. All that "right to work" laws do is say that employees, likewise, cannot be fired for failure to join or pay dues to a union.'

4. *"Right to work" laws are good for the nation's prosperity.* Good jobs and good wages depend on a prosperous economy. "Right to work" laws encourage industry to expand. This creates more jobs at good wages than does the union shop or other agreements that *restrict* the right to work and discourage industrial expansion.

Many of those who now favor compulsory unionism admit that it violates individual freedom. But they try to make excuses for this violation—justifying it on various economic, social, or moral grounds. If we let our freedoms be nibbled away today by such excuses, somebody will take a bigger bite out of them tomorrow with some other excuse.

The basic strength of a union—as with any organization—comes from the *free choice* of its members. "Right to work" laws affirm the principle that a man has the right to join or not to join a union, as he freely chooses.

AGAINST!

1. *The real purpose of "right to work" laws is union-busting.* The term "right to work" is misleading. Any "right" to work is, at best, a *conditional* right.

This means that workers at any plant or office have to accept certain conditions of employment. They must, first of all, be qualified for a job. They must report at a specified time, and work a specified number of hours. They must accept certain deductions from their wages for social security, etc.

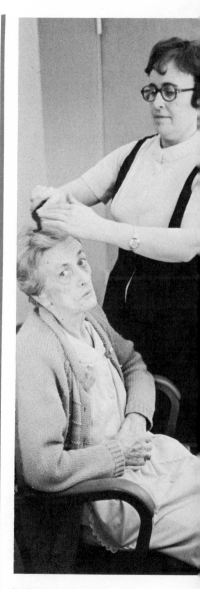

Is there a private or "special interest" group that might represent this elderly person? What kinds of things might be important to this group?

It is understood that if a worker accepts a job he also accepts these *conditions of employment.* So why shouldn't the conditions also include union membership? Yet so-called "right to work" laws would, in effect, outlaw this legitimate condition.

Unless a union is strong, it has little bargaining power with management. And without strong bargaining power, it could not achieve favorable working conditions.

2. *"Right to work" laws undermine the right of collective bargaining.* Federal laws require unions to represent *all* the workers in a company—not just those who are members of the union. And any benefits won by a union at a collective bargaining table are shared by *all* the workers.

Yet the cost of supporting a union is borne only by union members—from their dues. Isn't it only fair, then, for unions to seek agreements preventing "free loaders" from cashing in on the benefits of membership without sharing its burdens? The "union shop" is such an agreement.

3. *"Right to work" laws will destroy labor stability in many communities.* Without "union shop" agreements many businesses could not enjoy stable labor relations. And it is this stability which permits businesses to prosper and expand.

What many supporters of "right to work" laws fail to realize is this: a strong union can be a help to management as well as to the workers.

4. *"Right to work" laws flout the tradition of majority rule.* "Right to work" laws give a nonunion member an unfair advantage over his fellow-workers who want a union shop. They let him profit from the labor, efforts, time, and sacrifice of the majority who want the union. They make a mockery of the democratic ideal of "the majority rules."

Union shops are no more unfair or undemocratic than state legislatures or the U.S. Congress. Representatives of a majority of voters pass laws which the minority party may not like. Yet minority party members obey such laws.

This is the democratic way. Unions are based on the democratic right of representation. "Right to work" laws try to interfere with that real right by arguing about a phony "right."

ACTIVITIES

STRIKE is a board game in which you will be forced to make choices between your loyalty to a group and your obligations to society.

1. You have been a hardworking firefighter for several years. You are proud of your profession. You feel it is both challenging work and a service to your community. Though you have never been an officer of your local firefighters' union, you have always been a faithful and supportive member. Recently, negotiations between union officials and the city council have been at a standstill. You have been working without a contract for two months. The main issues are a 10 percent wage hike retroactive to the time contracts expired, replacement of all trucks and equipment lacking modern safety features, on-the-job training programs, and increased pension benefits.

    There have been rumors of a strike and you are very concerned about the effects of such a decision. To cut down or eliminate fire protection for the city would be a drastic and dangerous measure. Besides, strikes by city employees are against the law. On the other hand, you wonder how long you can work without the protection of a contract. You also know that the quality of fire protection is not what it should be with inferior equipment and poorly trained firefighters. Further, qualified people will only be attracted to the field when there are decent wages and a solid pension program. Clearly, there are good arguments on both sides.

2. Discussion questions
    a. Which of your decisions were based on loyalty to your group? Which were based on your obligations to society?
    b. How did you decide when there was a conflict between two groups you belong to?
    c. Have you had to make any personal decisions where you were forced to choose between your group and society? How do you decide in these cases? What do you lose and gain when you decide in favor of society?

| Your spouse is running for school committee and is loosing support because of your position. What do you do? | An emergency fire breaks out at a local hospital. What do you do? | Judge rules that all strikers must go to jail. What do you do? | City council agrees to all items except increased pension benefits and only 8% salary increase. What do you do? | | START → |

STRIKE

An emergency meeting has been called for all union members. Will you support a strike?

GAME RULES

a. Five or six can play. Moves are determined by the roll of dice.

b. As you move around the board, you must answer each question based on your obligation to society. Give the reason for your decision. There are no decisions to be made on empty squares.

c. It's the job of other players to tell you what you might lose as the result of your decision.

d. You must then convince the other players that your decision is the best one for you because you will gain more from it than you will lose.

e. If you are unable to convince the other players, you lose one turn.

f. The game continues until at least one person reaches the final square.

Your union strike pay is ¼ of your usual salary. You have a new car and are having trouble making the payments. What do you do?

Are you going to argue actively in support of your position?

City council agrees to provide a training program, but won't budge on other items. What do you do?

You're in violation of a court order and will be fined $100 a day. What do you do?

How do you choose to vote at the union meeting?

Sparky, the fire dog, is in the station without food or water. Do you cross the picket line?

A court issues a return-to-work order. What do you do?

Your fire station is staffed with volunteers. The emergency whistle signals a fire in your neighborhood. What do you do?

A majority of members have voted to strike. Are you going to participate?

Government Tax and Transfer Policy

The way income is distributed affects everyone because income determines what goods and services people can buy. The government does a number of things that bear on the distribution of wealth. Some of its tax measures serve to *redistribute income.* For instance, the government can take money from one part of the population and give it to another part. It can provide services directly to those who cannot pay for them. Or it can spend tax money on projects such as roads and schools that tend to help everyone.

Taxes are probably the best-known way in which government influences the distribution of income. The *progressive income tax* is designed to take a larger percentage of a rich person's income than of a poorer person's income. For example, a family that makes $75,000 a year might have to pay thirty percent of its income in taxes, while a family making $15,000 a year might be required to pay only fifteen percent of its income. The richer family would pay $22,500, the poorer farmily only $2,250. If both families had to pay the same percentage of their incomes in taxes (say, 20 percent), the family with the larger income would end up paying $15,000 and the family with the smaller income $3,000. In the first case, the richer family would be left with $52,500. In the second case it would be left with $60,000. In the first case, the poorer family would be left with $12,750.

In the second case it would be left with $12,000, or barely enough for a modest standard of living in an American city.

A progressive income tax is designed to insure that the projects undertaken by the government will be paid for mostly by those with a greater ability to pay. This is an indirect form of income redistribution. It uses money from wealthier people to provide services to everyone, regardless of income.

There are other kinds of taxation, however, that are not progressive in intent. These are called *regressive taxes* because they take a larger share out of the incomes of poorer people. *Sales tax* rates, for example, are the same for everyone, regardless of ability to pay. So are *use taxes,* such as tolls on highways and bridges. *Excise taxes* on alcohol and cigarettes have the same effect.

Another indirect form of income redistribution occurs when the government provides services to people for which they would otherwise have to pay or do without. Public schools are a good example of this kind of service. A city might spend $2,000 a year on every student in its school system. This would in effect provide a *subsidy* to parents who cannot afford or do not wish to spend $2,000 of their own money on educating their children.

A direct form of income redistribution comes from *transfer payments.* These are payments made directly to persons in need or to persons who can qualify for such payments for other reasons. The most important transfer payments in the American economy are social security benefits, welfare payments, food stamps, unemployment compensation, and veterans' benefits. Not all transfer payments go to people with low incomes, however. Veterans' benefits and social security benefits, for example, are paid to anyone who has served in the armed forces or who has worked enough years before retirement.

What is the total effect of all this government action? It is not easy to say. The

Table 24-1 Federal Government Transfers in the United States (estimates in billions of dollars)
Source: Office of Management and Budget, 1977.
Which transfers are given for reasons other than need? Are these reasons valid?

	1978	1979	1980	1981	1982
Social security & railroad retirement	97.7	108.4	119.7	131.4	143.0
Military retired pay	9.1	9.8	10.7	11.4	12.2
Other Federal employees retirement & insurance	11.2	12.7	14.2	15.7	17.1
Unemployment assistance	12.7	12.1	11.5	11.1	10.2
Veterans benefits	12.8	12.6	12.1	11.6	11.2
Medicare & medicaid	37.7	43.9	50.9	58.6	67.2
Housing payments	3.7	4.7	5.9	7.3	8.7
Public assistance & related programs	21.9	22.8	23.7	24.5	25.2
Subtotal, payments for individuals	206.9	227.0	248.6	271.6	294.8

usual way of figuring income does not take into account the value of goods and services provided by the government. But if we measure only such things as wages, rent, interest, and profits, then the distribution of income in the United States has not changed much over the last thirty years. The poorest 20 percent of all families today gets 5 percent of the income; the richest 20 percent of families gets 40 percent. This is about the same as it was at the end of World War II.

Some people believe that the present distribution of income is unfair and that the government should take strong measures to correct it. Others believe this would be undue interference in people's lives. The government bases its right to affect people's lives on more than naked power or personal loyalty. Leaders are elected according to the rules of the game. Also in keeping with the rules, laws are enacted by these same representatives. We consent to government because it represents us all. We feel morally bound to obey its laws.

But what happens when government fails to represent us all? What if it becomes just another group, out to advance its own interests? Then it can no longer claim that everyone has a moral duty to obey its commands. It is therefore important for you to be able to separate the interests of society from what the government says they are. You need a set of principles that can tell you what is right for everyone. These principles can help you decide whether the government has a right to ask you to act in certain ways. They can also help you decide how to act.

☐ The reading for this lesson, a science fiction story by Robert Silverberg, is about government tax and transfer policy. However, it is not money that is being redistributed. Healthy people are required by law to donate spare kidneys and other bodily organs to save lives. In other words, organs are being taxed from the "haves" and transferred to the "have-nots." The characters in the story must decide whether or not to pay their "taxes." Is this policy really designed for the whole society, or only for a certain group? Does the government have the right to ask this of its citizens? Do they have a right to resist? As you read the story, ask yourself the following questions:

1. Does the organ draft law benefit society as a whole, or does it benefit only particular groups? Can an argument be made in defense of it?
2. What laws and policies in your country are like the organ draft?
3. What does your society have a right to ask of you?

CAUGHT IN THE ORGAN DRAFT

Look there, Kate, down by the promenade. Two splendid seniors walking side by side near the water's edge. They radiate power, authority, wealth, assurance. He's a judge, a senator, a corporation president, no doubt, and she's—what?—a professor emeritus of international law, let's say. There they go toward the plaza, moving serenely, smiling, nodding graciously to passersby. How the sunlight gleams in their white hair! I can barely stand the brilliance of that reflected aura; it blinds me, it stings my eyes. What are they, eighty, ninety, a hundred years old? At this distance they seem much younger—they hold themselves upright, their backs are straight, they might pass for being only fifty or sixty.

Today my draft notice, a small crisp document, very official-looking, came shooting out of the data slot when I punched for my morning mail. I've been expecting it all spring: no surprise, no shock, actually rather an anti-climax now that it's finally here. In six weeks I am to report to Transplant House for my final physical exam—only a formality. They wouldn't have drafted me if I didn't already rate top marks as organ-reservoir potential—and then I go on call. The average call time is about two months. By autumn they'll be carving me up. Eat, drink, and be merry, for soon comes the surgeon to my door.

A straggly band of senior citizens is picketing the central

headquarters of the League for Bodily Sanctity. It's a counterdemonstration, an anti-anti-transplant protest, the worst kind of political statement, feeding on the ugliest of negative emotions. The demonstrators carry glowing signs that say:

BODILY SANCTITY—OR

BODILY SELFISHNESS?

and:

YOU OWE YOUR

LEADERS YOUR

VERY LIVES

and:

LISTEN TO THE VOICE

OF EXPERIENCE

The picketers are low-echelon seniors, barely across the qualifying line, the ones who can't really be sure of getting transplants. No wonder they're edgy about the League.

I know people my age or older who have taken asylum in Belgium or Sweden or Paraguay or one of the other countries where Bodily

Where does money for this purpose come from? Who else might receive "transfer payments"?

Does everyone pay the same amount for this service? Why?

Sanctity laws have been passed. There are about twenty such countries, half of them the most progressive nations in the world and half of them the most reactionary. But what's the sense of running away? I don't want to live in exile. I'll stay here and fight.

Naturally they don't ask a draftee to give up his heart or his liver or some other organ essential to life, say his medulla oblongata. Kidneys and lungs, the paired organs, the dispensable organs, are the chief targets so far. In another fifty years they'll be drafting hearts and stomachs and maybe even brains, mark my words; let them get the technology of brain transplants together and nobody's skull will be safe. It'll be human sacrifice all over again.

The law was put through by an administration of old men. The problem was this: not enough healthy young people were dying of highway accidents, successful suicide attempts, diving-board miscalculations, electrocutions, and football injuries; therefore there was a shortage of transplantable organs. Meanwhile there was an urgent and mounting need for organs; a lot of important seniors might in fact die if something didn't get done fast. So a coalition of senators from all four parties rammed the organ-draft measure through the upper chamber in the face of a filibuster threat from a few youth-oriented members. It had a much easier time in the House of

Do the people in these two pictures pay the same percent of their income in taxes? Why?

Representatives, since nobody in the House ever pays much attention to the text of a bill up for a vote, and word had been circulated on this one that if it passed, everybody over sixty-five who had any political pull at all could count on living twenty or thirty extra years which to a representative means a crack at ten to fifteen extra terms of office.

For a year and a half I was the chairman of the anti-draft campaign on our campus. Mainly we would march up and down in front of the draft board offices carrying signs proclaiming things like:

KIDNEY POWER

and:

A MAN'S BODY IS
HIS CASTLE

and:

THE POWER TO
CONSCRIPT ORGANS
IS THE POWER TO
DESTROY LIVES

    We never went in for the rough stuff, though, like bombing organ-transplant centers or hijacking refrigeration trucks. Peaceful agitation, that was our motto. Naturally, I was drafted the moment I became eligible.

    My call notice came today. They'll need one of my kidneys. The usual request. "You're lucky," somebody said at lunchtime. "They might have wanted a lung."

    Kate and I walk into the green glistening hills and stand among the blossoming oleanders and corianders and frangipani and whatever. How good it is to be alive, to breathe this fragrance, to show our bodies to the bright sun! Her skin is tawny and glowing. Her beauty makes me weep. She will not be spared. None of us will be spared. I go first, then she, or is it she ahead of me? Where will they make the incision? Here on her smooth rounded back? Here, on the flat taut belly? I can see the high priest standing over the altar. At the first blaze of dawn his shadow falls across her. The obsidian knife that is clutched in his upraised hand has a terrible fiery sparkle. The choir offers up a discordant hymn to the god of blood. The knife descends.

My last chance to escape across the border. I've been up all night, weighing the options. There's no hope of appeal. Running away leaves a bad taste in my mouth. Father, friends, even Kate, all say stay, stay, stay, face the music. The hour of decision. Do I really have a choice? I have no choice. When the time comes, I'll surrender peacefully.

I report to Transplant House for conscriptive donative surgery in three hours.

"After all," he said coolly, "what's a kidney?" I'll still have another one, you know. And if that one malfunctions, I can always get a replacement. I'll have Preferred Recipient status, 6-A, for what that's worth. But I won't settle for my automatic 6-A. I know what's going to happen to the priority system; I'd better protect myself. I'll go into politics. I'll climb. I'll attain upward mobility out of enlightened self-interest, right? Right. I'll become so important that society will owe me a thousand transplants. And one of these years I'll get that kidney back. Three or four kidneys, fifty kidneys, as many as I need. A heart or two. A few lungs. A pancreas, a spleen, a liver. They won't be able to refuse me anything. I'll show them. I'll show them. I'll out-senior the seniors. There's your Bodily Sanctity activist for you, eh? I suppose I'll have to resign from the League. Good-bye, idealism. Good-bye, moral superiority. Good-bye, kidney. Good-bye, good-bye, good-bye.

VISUAL ACTIVITY

Select from any source at least five images—photos or drawings—that show people who belong to a specific group. Based on what you see in these images discuss what each group might want from the economy. What might these people want as members of society? Does this present a conflict? How could you demonstrate this conflict in visual terms?

ACTIVITIES

I. The issue of taxation is often controversial, depending on whose interests you represent. In this activity, you will analyze the costs and benefits of four situations in terms of their benefits to society and to individuals within society.

1. Divide into groups of five or six students each. Read each dilemma situation and as a group think up all possible arguments on both sides of the question. This is not the time to take a position on the rights or wrongs of the situation; it is a time to express ideas and opinions.
2. On your own, decide how you would resolve each dilemma.
3. Use the grid in the Workbook to analyze each dilemma. If you don't have a Workbook, copy the grid in the text onto a piece of paper.

Dilemma #____ Resolution:	How will society benefit?	lose?	How will individuals or groups benefit?	lose?
Yes				
No				
Other				
Other				

Dilemma A. A retired husband and wife are living on social security benefits and personal savings. In upcoming elections they will be asked to vote on a school bond issue. If passed, this will raise their property taxes. They realize that the present high school is grossly inadequate but do not see how they can pay any more taxes. Should they vote for the bond issue?

Dilemma B. A liberal-minded engineer recognizes and enjoys the material benefits of his middle-class status. A more progressive income tax would help those less fortunate than he is but would demand certain sacrifices in his standard of living. He doesn't want to be a hypocrite but he also doesn't want to alter his current lifestyle. Should he support a more progressive income tax?

Dilemma C. Ramps and elevators are required in all public buildings so that the handicapped and the elderly can have equal access to services that were formerly denied them. The installation and renovation of ramps and elevators are very expensive. The tradeoff is that the prices of goods and services located in these public buildings will be raised to cover the costs of the ramps and elevators. Are they worth it?

Dilemma D. A city needs additional funds to cover its school budget. Some of its funds are now being used to provide testing and reading tutoring for students in parochial schools. Some people have suggested that these services be withdrawn to help meet the city's fiscal crisis. The parochial schools cannot afford these services for themselves. Parochial school parents feel that they are entitled to these services because they pay taxes. However, some city councilors argue that it would be cheaper to provide these services in public schools. This would mean that many parochial students would have to enroll in the public schools. Should the city continue to support the parochial schools?

4. Discussion questions
   a. How did you decide on the real benefits and costs of each situation?
   b. Did the initial group discussion affect your opinion? How?
   c. What new, untried alternatives might solve each dilemma?

II. In this activity, look at two examples of advertising and decide whose interests are represented by them.

1. Use the chart in the Workbook to analyze and compare advertising samples from newspapers or magazines. If you don't have a Workbook, copy the chart on a piece of paper.

	Ad #1	Ad #2
A. What is the argument or position of the group that sponsored the ad?		
B. What arguments might you make against this ad?		
C. How will the group sponsoring the ad be affected by the policy that it supports?		
D. How will society be affected?		
E. How will you (and your group) be affected?		
F. Who will benefit the most from the policy promoted in this ad?		
G. Do you support this policy? What do you base your position on?		

2. Discussion questions
   a. Did you consider third-party or long-term costs and benefits in your analysis?
   b. How would each policy benefit the group that promoted it? the society as a whole? you and your group? What do you do when these conflict?
   c. How can you judge a group's claim that what it proposes is good for society? Is there a way of telling when the claim is made to hide a group's self-interest?

THREE

MACRO-ECONOMICS

CHAPTER 9 NATIONAL INCOME ACCOUNTING

Gross National Product

The study of a country's whole system of making and using goods and services is called *macroeconomics*. The "how much" question is its central focus.

It is hard to begin such a huge task. All of the goods and services that are made each year have to be counted. Every new car and truck, every egg laid by every hen, every carrot, pea, and celery stalk, every tree, tomato, and taco has to be included. Services must be counted, too, such as haircutting and nursing.

Suppose all of these things and many more besides were stacked up in one big pile. It would still be hard to know the value of all the goods and services produced by the economy. Yet this is what the *Gross National Product* (GNP) tries to measure. It works something like this:

First, instead of counting the actual things made and sold and all of the services performed, economists add up what these things sold for in dollars and cents. In other words, they are using money as a *unit of account*. So, if people buy 2,000,000 bushels of apples at $1 per bushel, and 2,000,000 books at $1 per book, they add $4,000,000 to the Gross National Product.

Second, economists do not count everything in the country. They count only those things produced during a given period of time—say, one year. Then they know what the Gross National Product was for that particular year. Anything made before or after that year does not get added in.

What are some of the
ways these people might
influence the Gross
National Product?

Third, not everything made and sold during the year can be counted. For example, the paper in this book was once part of a giant roll of paper in a paper mill. Some people worked hard to make that roll of paper, and others worked hard to make this book. Both of them are products. But if the money paid for both the roll of paper and the book were counted, the value of the same paper would be counted twice. This will give a wrong idea of what the Gross National Product is. So to avoid this problem (which is called "double counting"), economists only count a product in its final form. They count the paper, for example, in its final product form as a book, a newspaper, a magazine, or a shopping bag. They refer to these as *final goods and services.*

There are two different ways of counting the value of goods and services, but they both give the same answer. The first way, the *flow of product* approach, is by counting all the money spent on goods and services (see Figure 25-1). The second way, the *earnings and cost* approach, is by counting all the money received for producing goods and services (see Figure 25-1). Each of these ways looks at a different side of an economic activity—spending or earning. In other words, if a person makes a chair and sells it for $50, both seller and buyer have helped increase the Gross National Product by $50. In figuring out what the Gross National Product is, an economist might count the $50 the buyer spent for the chair. He might also count the $20 that went to the lumber yard owner, the $5 that went to

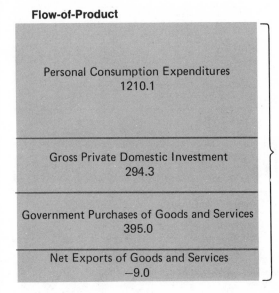

Flow-of-Product

Personal Consumption Expenditures 1210.1
Gross Private Domestic Investment 294.3
Government Purchases of Goods and Services 395.0
Net Exports of Goods and Services −9.0

Gross National Product (GNP) 1890.4

Earnings-and-Cost

Depreciation 197.0
Indirect Taxes 172.1
Compensation of Employees 1078.1
Rental Income of Persons 25.3
Net Interest 147.9
Incomes of Unincorporated Enterprises 97.9
Corporate Profits Taxes 69.2
Undistributed Corporate Profits 61.7
Dividends 41.2

the paint store owner, the $5 for wear and tear on tools used in making the chair, and the $20 for the cost of labor. They would also add up to $50.

If the Gross National Product is counted by counting what people spend, four different kinds of spending must be taken into account. These are 1) spending by ordinary consumers; 2) spending by the government; 3) spending by businesses on new equipment; and 4) spending by foreigners who buy American goods.

If Gross National Product is counted by counting what people receive, things such as business profits, wages and salaries paid to workers, taxes received by the government for the services it performs, interest on bank deposits, money received as rent, and other forms of income must be counted. Figuring the Gross National Product in this way is a little bit like figuring out what the entire country earns for the things it makes and the things it does.

Of course, no way of adding up the Gross National Product can be entirely accurate. But the two ways discussed here give a rough estimate of the total value of what the economy produces in a given year. Better still, measuring the Gross National Product each year can show if the economy is growing or shrinking, healthy or sick. It is a standard by which the economy as a whole can be judged. It can be used to compare one economy with another. It can also be used to compare an economy with itself over time.

You use standards in similar ways to judge your own success. You measure yourself and others by grades, physical fitness scores, moral codes, social standing, and many other standards. Your feelings about how well you are doing depend on which standards you choose.

Figure 25-1 Two Ways of Looking at Gross National Product (1978 figures in billions of dollars)
Source: Department of Commerce
Why must the flow-of-product method of measuring GNP produce the same answer as the earnings and cost method?

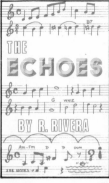   

☐ The reading for this lesson comes from interviews by Peter Cohen. In this selection, several business school students discuss their career plans. They all have somewhat different goals because they all define success differently. As you read their comments, ask yourself the following questions:

1. How does each student define success for himself?
2. What standards might each one use to measure his personal success?
3. What standards do you use to judge yourself?

STRATEGIES FOR SUCCESS

Sidney O'Mara, twenty-nine, married, B.S., M.S.E.E., University of Kansas, previous job: sales, Mersham Alloys, Inc. (four years).

"The kind of life style I like is one in which there isn't too much structure, formality, status. You know, I don't have an eight-ply rug on the floor and all sorts of things on the wall, and I don't have mahogany furniture, and I don't dress in a Brooks Brothers suit. That's not the style of the company I'm going to work for; it's not my style.

"If I wanted to be rich, I wouldn't do some of the things I'm going to be doing. Like living in Manhattan. I most certainly don't spend money foolishly, but there is a certain strategy a person follows if he wants to accumulate money. And that's too big a price to pay. I really don't feel I can be bothered with that right now. I'm sure if I would want to get rich, I would save money and would start investing and be worried about that. I think you know, I'm *not* oriented in that direction."

Dave Kearney, twenty-seven, married (two children), B.S., Carnegie Institute of Technology, M.S., Pennsylvania State, previous job: plant engineer, Willard Elevator Corp. (two years).

"Like the typical Business School student, I want to start at the top.

"It has to be something where I am out there, at the line. I want to get a chance of running people. And it has to be something that is exceptionally challenging. I don't want to be just another nice guy. I want something I can work hard at, something that makes a lot of sense to me. But I guess I also want something where you can get some money back. You know, really win it, money-wise. Roughly twenty K plus a stock option.

"I guess I want to make it quick. I want to be able to be the head of a company at a young age. You know, working long, long hours in a

How do economists measure this woman's work in calculating the GNP?

big company, working up the corporate ladder slowly—I guess no Business School student really wants to do that. I don't want to wait around for five years and then take a chance. Where, when the stakes are there, the guy above me grabs them and runs.

"I don't think I have any long-range objectives beyond what I've already said. I know that sounds strange, but I think the biggest thing is flexibility. I want to be able to do what I want in fifteen years. I don't know what that'll be, but it's always been very important to me to be able to pick up at a moment's notice."

Frank Charvis, twenty-nine, married (one child), B.S., mechanical engineering, University of Pennsylvania, previous job: marketing-executive, North American Steel Inc. (five years).

"Quite frankly, and maybe this sounds kind of dismal or black in a way, but how do you exploit situations that you run into? Some people are going to block your way like crazy. How are you gonna get around them? How are you gonna capitalize on opportunities without walking all over everybody else?

"You know, what are the ethics? Operationally speaking, what do you do? You are gonna make bucks—*that's* what you will do. Because that's what everyone else does. Because that's what the people you're trying to impress do. No matter how long you talk about it, you're always gonna get down to the nitty-gritty reality of making bucks.

"Now whether making bucks is correct or not, it's—let's put it this way, if you're not the head of the operation, you've got to face the reality that there is little else you can do.

"Minority employment, social responsibility—it's not bad to talk about these things. But you've got to respond to the system, otherwise you just run into a blank wall."

Allan McGrady, twenty-eight, bachelor, B.S., mathematics, Yale, previous job: systems analyst, Datamesh, Inc. (three years).

"At some point, I would like to take over the operation of a small, technically oriented company. I don't care whether it's electronics or machine tools or whatever. A typical small company, started by a bunch of engineers; that, because business was successful, got to a certain plateau and now has all kinds of trouble getting somebody to run it.

"One of the reasons why I want to run my own company is that, like most of us at the school, I'm not really a nine-to-fiver. And working for

Which is counted in calculating the GNP, the products this man is shopping for, or the materials that go into making them? Why?

someone else, with certain exceptions, you almost have to be, because other people are counting on you. You got to be there. You know, your phone is ringing and you've got to pick it up and answer.

"Running your own show, particularly a smaller company, gives you the latitude to expand yourself as a person.

"I am looking for an environment where I think I can be used, where I can make a contribution, and where I am needed. And when I say needed, that means on a personal as well as on a technical basis. You know, it's where I kind of enjoy the people I'm around. Now if I go into a place and, clearly, the interpersonal relationship with them is bad; if I can see that I just don't mesh with anybody, then that isn't even a candidate. All right?

"Well, once I've lined up my candidates, then money is the key factor. My strategy is to accept the highest paying offer I get, unless we're talking about just a small difference. Number one because, when the time comes for a raise, raises are normally a percentage of your base. Number two because, if you leave that company in a couple of years, you'll leave it at a higher base. And three, which I think is most important, because the more a company pays you, the less chance there is that you get a crummy job. If they are paying you twelve thousand, they can afford to let you sit in a corner for a while. If they are paying you twenty, now they start to worry about: 'What is this guy doing for us? How is he justifying that salary we're paying him?'

"The guys who try to buy me off cheap with promises, they are just going to stick me into a very routine, dirty job. And that's fine, but, you know, that's not what I want coming out of the Business School. I'm not interested in promises."

Keith Kurowski, twenty-five, bachelor, B.S., M.S., chemical engineering, Massachusetts Institute of Technology, previous job: research engineer, Lenox Pharmaceutical Corp. (one year).

"I look at my father, I look at my mother, I look at some of my friends, and what I want out of life is a happy relationship with my wife and good children. And health and . . . you know, that's about it.

"Now you can say, well sure, do you want a house? You want three cars? But I can't answer that. I really don't know if I want a house and three cars. You can say, do you want power? I want to work hard and working hard leads to power. But I don't know if I want power in and of itself.

"I think the way I see it now, the next couple of years, working for somebody else, I'll play the businessman's game. I'll play: maximize personal wealth, maximize earnings per share because that's the measure to use. If and when I am in business for myself, I may play that game or I may play a slightly different game, where I'll be willing to suffer a penalty because of my values, where I won't insist on earnings per share.

"I went through this same thing, you know, about what I want out of life with this friend of mine: 'Just a good wife and a family and enough money to have a little wine and cheese on the table.'

"And he says: 'What vintage wine?'"

What are some of the things you see in this photo that go into calculating the GNP?

ACTIVITIES

I. The GNP is a standard that many economists use to measure the U.S. economy. This activity is about finding a standard for measuring yourself.

1. Several examples of standards you might use to measure yourself are given below. As a class, add at least fifteen more standards to the list and write them all on the board.
   - how much money your parents make
   - how well you make decisions
   - how quickly you pay a debt
   - the number of inches around your waist
   - your Lovability Quotient (L.Q.)
   - the length of your hair
2. Choose those standards that seem most useful in measuring yourself.
3. Now use the standards you chose to measure yourself. Put together a confidential personal profile chart. Use the chart in the Workbook or copy this one on a separate piece of paper.

Standards	Measure									
	1	2	3	4	5	6	7	8	9	10

4. Discussion questions
    a. Which standards were chosen by the members of the class? Which not?
    b. What does your choice of standards tell you about yourself?
    c. What was not measured by the standards you chose?
    d. How might you create a single standard to measure yourself?

II. Economists use two perspectives in the study of economics. Micro means looking at parts or units of the economy. Macro means looking at the big picture. This activity will help you to see the advantages and disadvantages of both these angles. Work in groups of three or four students each.

1. With a partner, find pairs of cards that show the two economic approaches, micro and macro. Use the cards in the Workbook, or make your own cards.

tree	your grade-point average	an office	
floor plan of a house	your town's unemployment	society	
forest	bee		
hive	national unemployment		
your grade in economics	aerial photograph		

2. If you find cards that do not match, use the blank cards to write matches for these cards. Eight blank cards are left for you to create your own four pairs.
3. Choose two or three pairs. Think up situations that will show how and when a particular perspective might be useful. The first chart contains an example that can be followed in completing the other charts. As you complete each chart in the Workbook, discuss the advantages and disadvantages of using a particular perspective. If you don't have a Workbook, copy the charts onto a piece of paper.

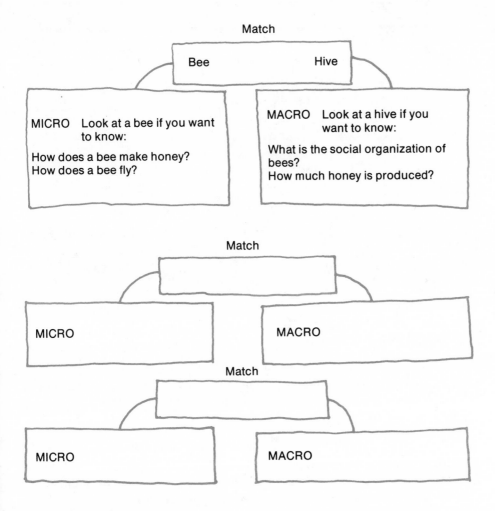

Match

Bee   Hive

MICRO   Look at a bee if you want
to know:

How does a bee make honey?
How does a bee fly?

MACRO   Look at a hive if you
want to know:

What is the social organization of
bees?
How much honey is produced?

Match

MICRO   MACRO

Match

MICRO   MACRO

4. Discussion questions
    a. When is it useful to use a macro perspective? a micro perspective?
    b. What are the pros and cons of each?
    c. Which of the economist's four basic questions (what? how? for whom?
        how much?) are micro? Which are macro?

Adjusting Gross National Product

There are two major problems with the method economists use to measure the Gross National Product. These are due to the effects of changing prices and population growth. Because of these problems, economists have had to devise ways of adjusting their figures.

Remember that the GNP is a measure of production. Its purpose is to show if the economy is healthy—that is, if production is increasing. But prices tend to increase over time. Since the Gross National Product is measured by adding prices things sell for, GNP can increase even if actual production does not.

To avoid this problem, economists use a *price index* called the *GNP deflator.* The government devises this index by comparing the prices of goods and services for the year being studied with the prices of goods and services from a base year chosen for purposes of comparison. If 1972 is chosen as a base year, for example, prices are expressed as being more or less than those of 1972. Economists give a value of 100 to the prices in 1972. If prices in another year are half what they were in 1972, then that year's price index is 50. If prices are twice what they were in 1972, then the price index is 200.

Once this has been done, it is then easy to divide the Gross National Product by the price index. To make sure the decimals come out right, economists must also divide by 100. The results will give a more realistic basis for comparing two

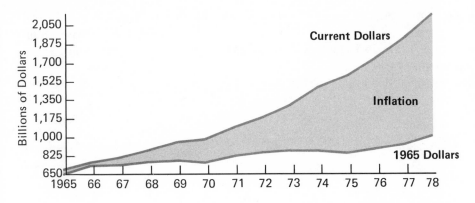

Figure 26-1   A Growing Economy
Source: Department of Commerce
How much of the increase in GNP since 1965 is the result of increasing prices? How much real growth has occurred?

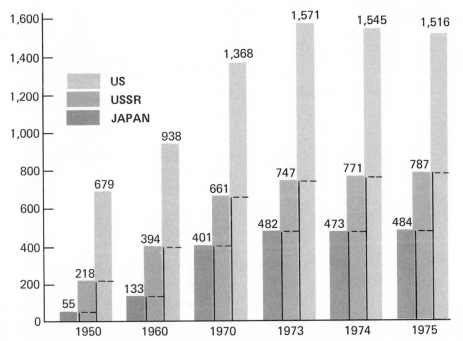

Figure 26-2   U.S., Soviet, and Japanese Gross National Product (in billions of 1975 dollars)
Source: Department of State, 1977
Which of the three nations has grown the fastest? the slowest?

years in which prices differed. Economists call this adjusted figure a real GNP or *constant dollar GNP.*

The other problem with the Gross National Product is the effect of population increases. Remember that the Gross National Product measures production. If the population increases, production will probably increase too. To know if production is really increasing, people will want to know if it is increasing per person, or *per capita.* To find this answer, simply divide the constant dollar Gross

National Product by the number of people in the country. This will give the GNP per person. This is a much truer way of measuring increases or decreases in production. Table 26-1 displays adjusted and unadjusted GNP figures for various years since 1929.

Using an unadjusted GNP as a standard can be misleading. To be useful, the

Figure 26-3   United States Population, 1950–2000
What factors will determine which of the three possible growth rates will be realized? How will this choice affect the economy?

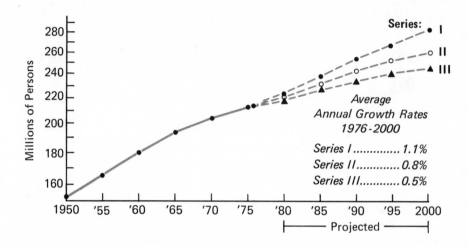

Table 26-1   Growth of the GNP in the United States, 1929–1977
Source: Economic Report of the President, 1978

YEAR	CURRENT $ GNP (IN BILLIONS)	GNP DEFLATOR	CONSTANT $ GNP (1972 = 100) (IN BILLIONS)	POPULATION	CONSTANT $ GNP PER CAPITA
1929	103.4	32.87	314.7	121,767,000	2,584
1939	90.8	28.40	319.7	130,880,000	2,443
1949	258.0	52.59	490.7	149,188,000	3,289
1959	486.5	67.52	720.4	177,830,000	4,051
1969	935.5	86.72	1078.8	202,677,000	5,323
1970	982.4	91.36	1075.3	204,878,000	5,248
1971	1063.4	96.12	1107.5	207,053,000	5,349
1972	1171.1	100.00	1171.1	208,846,000	5,607
1973	1306.6	105.80	1235.0	210,410,000	5,869
1974	1412.9	116.02	1217.8	211,901,000	5,747
1975	1528.8	127.18	1202.1	213,540,000	5,629
1976	1706.5	133.88	1274.7	215,118,000	5,926
1977	1890.4	141.32	1337.6	216,817,000	6,169

GNP must be adjusted under certain conditions. The same is true for any standard. Suppose, for example, that you expect to get at least a B in each of your courses. Should you be disappointed with a $C+$ in a very hard college-level course? Should you be satisfied with a B in a very easy course? If you are talented in Music but poor in Math, do you expect to get the same grade in both courses?

Some people value grades for their own sake. Their standard is fixed. A B is a B in any course. Others use grades to measure what they have accomplished. They have different goals for different courses.

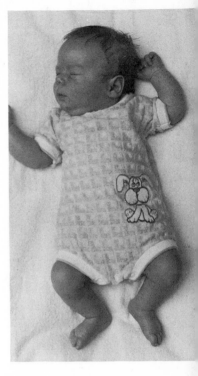

☐ The reading for this lesson comes from a novel by Mark Twain. In this excerpt, the hero argues with a blacksmith named Dowley. Each man thinks people are better off in the country he knows best. Dowley judges according to a fixed standard—how many dollars a worker earns. (In both countries, 1 dollar = 100 cents, and 1 cent = 10 mils = 100 milrays.) The hero uses an adjusted standard. As you read their debate, ask yourself the following questions:

1. What would a similar argument about the size of GNP in a country at two different times be like?
2. When do you adjust your standards for judging yourself?
3. When do you use fixed standards and make no excuses?

How does a population change affect the GNP? How is it compensated for?

A CONNECTICUT YANKEE IN KING ARTHUR'S COURT

At first glance, things appeared to be exceeding prosperous in this little tributary kingdom—whose lord was King Bagdemagus—as compared with the state of things in my own region. They had the "protection" system in full force here, whereas we were working along down toward free trade, by easy stages, and were now about half-way. Before long, Dowley and I were doing all the talking, the others hungrily listening. Dowley warmed to his work, sniffed an advantage in the air, and began to put questions which he considered pretty awkward ones for me, and they did have something of that look:

"In your country, brother, what is the wage of a master bailiff, master hind, carter, shepherd, swineherd?"

"Twenty-five milrays a day; that is to say, a quarter of a cent."

The smith's face beamed with joy. He said:

"With us they are allowed the double of it! And what may a mechanic get—carpenter, dauber, mason, painter, blacksmith, wheelwright, and the like?"

"On the average, fifty milrays; half a cent a day."

"Ho-ho! With us they are allowed a hundred! With us any good mechanic is allowed a cent a day! I count out the tailor, but not the others—they are all allowed a cent a day, and in driving times they get more—yes, up to a hundred and ten and even fifteen milrays a day. I've paid a hundred and fifteen myself, within the week. 'Rah for protection—to Sheol with free trade!"

And his face shone upon the company like a sunburst. But I didn't scare at all. I rigged up my pile-driver, and allowed myself fifteen minutes to drive him into the earth—drive him *all* in—drive him in till not even the curve of his skull should show above-ground. Here is the way I started in on him. I asked:

"What do you pay a pound for salt?"

"A hundred milrays."

"We pay forty. What do you pay for beef and mutton—when you buy it?" That was a neat hit; it made the color come.

"It varieth somewhat, but not much; one may say seventy-five milrays the pound."

"*We* pay thirty-three. What do you pay for eggs?"

"Fifty milrays the dozen."

"We pay twenty. What do you pay for beer?"

"It costeth us eight and one-half milrays the pint."

"We get it for four; twenty-five bottles for a cent. What do you pay for wheat?"

"At the rate of nine hundred milrays the bushel."

"We pay four hundred. What do you pay for a man's tow-linen suit?"

"Thirteen cents."

"We pay six. What do you pay for a stuff gown for the wife of the laborer or the mechanic?"

"We pay eight cents, four mills."

"Well, observe the difference: you pay eight cents and four mills, we pay only four cents." I prepared now to sock it to him. I said: "Look here, dear friend, *what's become of your high wages you were bragging so about a few minutes ago?*"—and I looked around on the company with placid satisfaction, for I had slipped up on him gradually and tied him hand and foot, you see, without his ever noticing that he was being tied at all. "What's become of those noble high wages of yours?—I seem to have knocked the stuffing all out of them, it appears to me.''

But if you will believe me, he merely looked surprised, that is all! He didn't grasp the situation at all, didn't know he had walked into a trap, didn't discover that he was *in* a trap. I could have shot him, from sheer vexation. With cloudy eye and a struggling intellect he fetched this out:

''Marry, I seem not to understand. It is *proved* that our wages be double thine; how then may it be that thou'st knocked therefrom the stuffing?—and I miscall not the wonderly word, this being the first time under grace and providence of God it hath been granted me to hear it.''

Well, I was stunned; partly with this unlooked-for stupidity on his part, and partly because his fellows so manifestly sided with him and were of his mind—if you might call it mind. My position was simple enough, plain enough; how could it ever be simplified more? However, I must try:

''Why, look here, brother Dowley, don't you see? Your wages are merely higher than ours in *name,* not in *fact.*''

''Hear him! They are the *double*—ye have confessed it yourself.''

''Yes-yes, I don't deny that at all. But that's got nothing to do with it; the *amount* of the wages in mere coins, with meaningless names attached to them to know them by, has got nothing to do with it. The thing is, how much can you *buy* with your wages?—that's the idea. While it is true that with you a good mechanic is allowed about three

How might increasing costs of these products affect the GNP? How is this compensated for?

dollars and a half a year, and with us only about a dollar and seventy-five—''

''There—ye're confessing it again, ye're confessing it again!''

''Confound it, I've never denied it, I tell you! What I say is this. With us *half* a dollar buys more than a *dollar* buys with you—and *therefore* it stands to reason and the commonest kind of common sense, that our wages are *higher* than yours.''

He looked dazed, and said, despairingly:

''Verily, I cannot make it out. Ye've just *said* ours are the higher, and with the same breath ye take it back.''

''Oh, great Scott, isn't it possible to get such a simple thing through your head? Now look here—let me illustrate. We pay four cents for a woman's stuff gown, you pay eight cents four mills, which is four mills more than *double.* What do you allow a laboring-woman who works on a farm?''

''Two mills a day.''

''Very good; we allow but half as much; we pay her only a tenth of a cent a day; and—''

''Again ye're conf—''

''Wait! Now, you see, the thing is very simple; this time you'll understand it. For instance, it takes your woman forty-two days to earn her gown, at two mills a day—seven weeks' work; but ours earns hers in forty days—two days *short* of seven weeks. Your woman has a gown, and her whole seven weeks' wages are gone; ours has a gown, and two days' wages left, to buy something else with. There—*now* you understand it!''

He looked—well, he merely looked dubious, it's the most I can say;

How might technical advances that result in industrial growth require an adjustment to the GNP?

so did the others. I waited—to let the thing work. Dowley spoke at last—and betrayed the fact that he actually hadn't gotten away from his rooted and grounded superstitions yet. He said, with a trifle of hesitancy:

"But—but—ye cannot fail to grant that two mills a day is better than one."

Shucks! Well, of course, I hated to give it up. So I chanced another flyer:

"Let us suppose a case. Suppose one of your journeymen goes out and buys the following articles:

"1 pound of salt;

1 dozen eggs;

1 dozen pints of beer;

1 bushel of wheat;

1 tow-linen suit;

5 pounds of beef;

5 pounds of mutton.

"The lot will cost him thirty-two cents. It takes him thirty-two working days to earn the money—five weeks and two days. Let him come to us and work thirty-two days at *half* the wages; he can buy all those things for a shade under fourteen and a half cents; they will cost him a shade under twenty-nine days' work, and he will have about half a week's wages over. Carry it through the year; he would save nearly a week's wages every two months, *your* man nothing; thus saving five or six weeks' wages in a year, your man not a cent. *Now* I reckon you understand that 'high wages' and 'low wages' are phrases that don't mean anything in the world until you find out which of them will *buy* the most!"

It was a crusher.

But, alas! it didn't crush. No, I had to give it up. What those people valued was *high wages;* it didn't seem to be a matter of any consequence to them whether the high wages would buy anything or not. They stood for "protection," and swore by it, which was reasonable enough, because interested parties had gulled them into the notion that it was protection which had created their high wages. I proved to them that in a quarter of a century their wages had advanced but thirty per cent, while the cost of living had gone up one hundred; and that with us, in a shorter time, wages had advanced forty per cent, while the cost of living had gone steadily down. But it didn't do any good. Nothing could unseat their strange beliefs.

ACTIVITIES

I. This activity is about adjusting old standards and creating new ones.

1. Choose one of the standards by which you measure yourself from Lesson 25, Activity I.
2. Think of a situation that would require you to make an adjustment in that standard. The following questions should help you think of a situation.
   a. What does the standard measure?
   b. When or where would you use the standard?
   c. What might occur that would change the usefulness of the standard?
3. Adjust the standard so that it can effectively measure just what you want it to measure.
4. Discussion questions
   a. Is it dishonest to adjust a standard?
   b. What do you gain and lose from an adjusted standard?

II. This activity is based on Table 26-1.

1. Using GNP measured in current dollars as a standard, what happened to the U.S. economy
   a. between 1929 and 1939?
   b. between 1969 and 1970?
   c. between 1974 and 1975?
2. How would your answers change if you used GNP in constant dollars as your standard?
3. How would your answers change if you used constant dollar GNP per capita as your standard?
4. Constant dollar GNP per capita is a measure of what has been produced. What would you need to know in order to judge whether the people are better off when that measure increases?

III. Like GNP, any standard must be adjusted at certain times. This activity is designed to let you think up solutions to the problems a college admissions board is having with its standard.

1. A small, private coeducational college has developed a set of admission standards that represent the educational goals and outlook of that institution. Traditionally, there have been 3,000 applications per year. Present staff and facilities can handle only 1,000 new students. The main standard for judging applicants has been their college SAT scores. For the most part, only students with scores of 600 or better have been accepted.

2. A student's SAT score is considered a useful standard because it allows the college board to select the number and type of student the college wants. There have been times in the college's history, however, when the 600 standard was not useful. Five situations are listed below in which the college had to adjust its 600 standard.

3. After you read each situation, decide how the college might have adjusted its standard to meet the demands of that situation. Use the chart in the Workbook or copy this one on a piece of paper.

Situation	How might you *adjust the standard?*
A. 6,000 applicants meet the standard of 600+ SAT scores	
B. The average score of applicants has dropped 100 points. 3,000 students have applied.	
C. There is room for 500 more applicants and the number of applicants with scores of 600 or more has not changed.	
D. Many strong candidates apply with scores of 580–599.	
E. The athletic department has 30 scholarships still available. The 30 most qualified students applying for these scholarships have scores between 550 and 579.	

4. Discussion questions
   a. What was the adjusted standard for each situation? How did it work?
   b. What was gained by the adjusted standard? What was lost?
   c. Which factors were measured by the new standard? Which were not?

What GNP Does Not Measure

We have seen how the GNP can be adjusted to take into account such things as rising prices and population growth. These adjustments make the GNP a better measure of total economic production. But even after making these changes, some serious problems remain. These make the GNP a less than ideal measure of the way the economy works. What are some of these problems?

First, GNP counts only those goods and services that are sold. It does not count goods and services given away free. For example, people do a lot of work at home for which they do not get paid salaries. Since GNP can only measure things that have price tags on them, a great deal of productive work does not get counted. Nor can the GNP count other forms of nonpaid labor, such as volunteer work in hospitals or daycare centers. Nearly everyone performs some kind of work without getting paid for it. For instance, if you mow your own lawn, that work is not included in the GNP. But if you mow someone else's lawn, and get paid for it, then it does get counted as part of the GNP.

Second, the GNP does not take into account the fact that Americans work fewer hours than they once did. They produce more goods and services while working forty hours a week than their grandparents did working sixty hours a week. This means that their work is more efficient. Yet there is no way in which the GNP can measure that increased efficiency.

This woman fixes her own car. Are her efforts included in the Gross National Product? Why?

Third, the GNP cannot measure changes in the quality of the goods and services produced. It only measures quantity. Television sets, for example, are much better today than they were in 1955. In general, they also cost less. But the GNP does not take that fact into account. It can only show that more television sets are made now than in 1955.

Finally, perhaps the most serious problem with using GNP as an economic standard is that it cannot show whether the economy is making people's lives better or worse. For example, industry creates a lot of air and water pollution. The GNP measures the output of industry, but it does not measure the pollution that goes along with that output. GNP does, however, measure the money that has to be spent to clean up the air and the water.

Some economists have proposed a different way of measuring the economy. The new method would try to measure the quality of life as well as the quantity of production. They call this measure the NEW, which stands for *Net Economic Welfare.* "Net welfare" means the welfare (that is, the good things) left after money has been spent to get rid of the bad effects of the economy, such as air and water pollution. The Net Economic Welfare standard would also include labor

and production that are not now paid for, such as work at home or volunteer work. This would give a better idea of how much work is being done by the whole society. It would show how many goods and services are actually being provided by the society.

It would be hard to establish a standard such as the NEW. This is because in order to measure goods and services with this standard, there would still have to be a dollar value for everything. It would not be easy to assign a dollar value to work that is now being done for free. It would be even harder to assign a dollar value to the quality of life around us. After all, how much money is it worth to have clean air and water?

Many people feel that GNP is not a good enough standard because it leaves out too much of what is important. They try to devise new standards that will be more useful.

The standards by which you and others judge your performance are often misleading too. They may gloss over important things and play up less important ones. Suppose, for example, that your grade in this course is based on tests and class participation. Yet you feel that you have learned much about yourself and the world that you could not express in class or on tests. How then should you be judged?

☐ The reading for this lesson comes from an article by an economist, A. A. Berle, Jr. Berle claims that GNP is not an adequate standard because it doesn't consider the whole picture. He therefore proposes a new standard. As you read the essay, ask yourself the following questions:

1. What are the advantages and disadvantages of GNP? of NEW? of Berle's standard?
2. Are Berle's "disproducts" the same as third-party costs?
3. What "products" and "disproducts" do your own standards measure? What important ones do they ignore?

WHAT GNP DOESN'T TELL US

It is nice to know that at current estimate the Gross National Product of the United States in 1968 will be above 850 billions of dollars. It would be still nicer to know if the United States will be better or worse off as a result. If better, in what respects? If worse, could not some of this production and effort be steered into providing more useful "goods and services"?

Individuals, corporations, or government want, buy and pay for stuff and work—so it is "product." The labor of the Boston Symphony Orchestra is "product" along with that of the band in a honky-tonk. The compensated services of a quack fortune teller are "product" just as much as the work of developing Salk vaccine. Restyling automobiles or ice chests by adding tail fins or pink handles adds to "product" just as much as money paid for slum clearance or medical care. They are all "goods" or "services"—the only test is whether someone wanted them badly enough to pay the shot.

This blanket tabulation raises specific complaints against economists and their uncritical aggregated figures and their acceptance of production as "progress." The economists bridle, "We," they reply, "are economists, not priests. Economics deals with satisfaction of human wants by things or services. The want is sufficiently evidenced by the fact that human beings, individually or collectively, paid for them. It is not for us to pass on what people ought to have wanted—that question is for St. Peter. A famous statistic in *America's Needs and Resources*—published by the Twentieth Century Fund in 1955—was that Americans in 1950 paid $8.1 billion for liquor and $10.5 billion for education. Maybe they ought to have cut out liquor and paid for more education instead—but

This kind of product has been improved to a great degree over the past twenty years. Is this improvement reflected in the GNP? Why?

they didn't, and value judgments are not our job. Get yourself a philosopher for that. We will go on recording what did happen.''

Any system of social indicators requires solving two sets of problems. First, with all this Gross National Product reflecting payment to satisfy wants, did America get what it paid for? In getting it, did it not also bring into being a flock of unrecorded but offsetting frustrations it did not want? Essentially, this is economic critique. Second—and far more difficult—can a set of values be put forward, roughly expressing the essentials most Americans would agree their society ought to be, and be doing, against which the actual record of what it was and did can be checked? This second critique, as economists rightly contend, is basically philosophical.

As for the economic critique, let us take the existing economic record at face value. Work was done, things were created, and both were paid for. The total price paid this year will be around $850 billion. But, unrecorded, not included, and rarely mentioned are some companion results. Undisposed-of junk piles, garbage, waste, air and water pollution come into being. God help us, we can see that all over the country. Unremedied decay of parts of the vast property we call ''the United States'' is evident in and around most American cities. No one paid for this rot and waste—they are not ''product.'' Factually, these and other undesirable results are clear deductions from or offset items to the alleged Gross National Product we like so well.

The total of these may be called ''disproduct.'' It will be a hard figure to calculate in dollar figures. Recorded as ''product'' is the amount Americans spent for television sets, stations, and broadcasts. Unrecorded is their companion disproductive effects in the form of violence, vandalism, and crime. Proudly reported as ''product'' are sums spent for medical care, public health, and disease prevention; unheralded is the counter-item, the ''disproduct'' of loss and misery

These people work fewer hours than they used to, and earn more money. How is this considered in formulating the GNP?

as remediable malnutrition and preventable disease ravage poverty areas. Besides our annual calculation of "gross" national product, it is time we had some idea of Gross National Disproduct. Deducting it, we could know what the true, instead of the illusory, annual "net national product" might be. (Economists use "Net National Product" to mean Gross National Product less consumption of capital—but it is not a true picture.)

There is a difference, it will be noted, between "disproduct" and "cost." Everything made or manufactured, every service rendered by human beings, involves using up materials, if only the food and living necessities of labor. These are "costs." They need not enter into this calculation. Conventional statistics already set up a figure for "capital consumption," and we deduct this from "Gross National Product." That is not what we have in mind here. We are trying to discover whether creation of "Gross National Product" does not also involve frustration of wants as well as their satisfaction. Pollution of air and water are obvious illustrations but there are "disproducts" more difficult to discern, let alone measure.

Scientists are increasing our knowledge of these right along. For example, cigarettes (to which I am addicted) satisfy a widespread want. They also, we are learning, engender a great deal of cancer. We know at the end of any year how many more automobiles have been manufactured. We also know that each new car on the road means added injury and accident overall. Carry this process through our whole product list, and the aggregate of "disproduct" items set against the aggregate of production will tell us an immense amount about our progress toward (or retrogression from) social welfare.

Once we learn to calculate disproduct along with product and discover a true "net," as well as a "gross," we shall have our first great "social" indicator. We shall know what the country achieved.

Find at least five photographs or drawings of products and services. Exactly what in each image affects the gross national product? How are these things recorded? Are there any things in these pictures that the GNP does not measure? Which of these should be measured? What kinds of adjustments must be made in the GNP to accurately reflect what you see in these images?

VISUAL
ACTIVITY

ACTIVITIES

I. The object of both NEW and Berle's "Net National Product" is to include the important things that GNP does not measure. In this activity, you will try to improve on a personal standard so that it can include the important things you really want to measure.

Section A

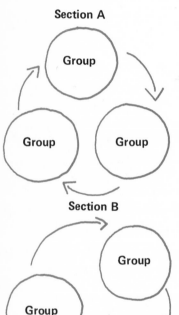

Section B

1. Divide the class into two sections. Each section will do the same activity. Within each section, divide into three groups.
2. Each small group chooses a standard that it feels would be useful in measuring success with peers in school. You may use a standard thought up in a previous activity or think of a new one. Divide a piece of paper into three parts. Write the standard you have chosen on Part 1 of the paper.
3. Pass the paper to another group in your section. Your group will receive a standard from another group. The activity should look like the drawing at left. Then consider those things that this new standard does not include. Ask yourselves how it could be improved. On Part 2 of the paper that has been passed to you, rewrite the standard so that it takes into account all the important things the previous standard did not cover.
4. Repeat the previous step and rewrite the improved standard on Part 3 of the paper.

   The paper should look like this:

Part 1: standard you chose to measure success with peers in school
Part 2: revised and improved standard
Part 3: revised and improved standard

5. Discussion questions
   a. What standards were chosen? How were they improved?
   b. What did you gain by improving each standard? What did you lose?
   c. How do you know when a standard should be improved?
   d. What personal standards would you like to improve?

II. This activity is about your Net Economic Welfare.

1. Each student should make a list of the ten most important purchases they made over the past year and the prices paid for them.
2. Divide into small groups and compile a master list for each group.
3. For each item on the group's list, decide if there is a disproduct item.
4. Each group should decide on a dollar cost for each disproduct item.
5. Each group then computes its own Gross National Product and Net Economic Welfare.
6. Finally, the class reunites and shares each group's results.
7. Discussion questions
   a. What disproducts were identified by more than one group?
   b. What costs were decided on for these disproducts? How did the groups reach their decisions?
   c. What does this activity show about the problem of devising a new standard to replace the GNP?

Is damage to the environment accounted for in the GNP? Why?

CHAPTER 10 AGGREGATE DEMAND AND AGGREGATE SUPPLY

Total Economic Performance

The last chapter discussed output, spending, and income. This lesson looks at the relationships among these three things. No change can occur in any of them without causing an almost immediate change in the others. For example, if people start spending more money, output will increase. It is easy to see why. If people are buying more goods and services, businesses will be encouraged to produce more to keep up with demand. Increased output, in turn, means that more people are working. More people earning income means there will be even more spending. It works the other way too. If for any reason a factory slows down production, that means people working there will be earning less money. They will then be spending less, which will result in decreased production by other firms.

The relationship among these three things, then, is circular—each affects the other. A change in one will induce (that is, encourage) a change in the others. For this reason such changes are called *induced changes.*

Changes from outside this circle of output, spending, and income can also affect these three things. A strike, for example, will slow down or stop production in a particular industry. It will also stop the flow of income to workers. If it is a big industry (such as the automobile industry) and a long strike, the strike could affect other businesses as well. An energy shortage can have a similar effect on production. Natural disasters such as floods, earthquakes, or severe winters all slow down production. This then results in decreased earnings, decreased spending, and further decreases in production. Changes such as these are called *autonomous changes* because they come from outside the economy and act independently of it.

Autonomous changes, of course, do not always slow down production. They can also increase it. If a country's population increases rapidly, there will be a greater demand for goods and services. This will then lead to increased production, increased earnings, and increased spending.

Induced and autonomous changes both affect the ability of the economy to operate at its full potential. Full potential means the output that would result if all the economy's human, capital, and natural resources were used as much as possible. This rarely happens. There is always a gap between the potential output of the economy and the actual output. There is always some unemployment. There are always some idle factories. There are always some firms with less business than they could handle.

The government's economic policies are designed to help the economy reach its full potential. If the government pushes too fast (for example, by suddenly spending lots of money on goods and services), production will rise very quickly. Then earnings will rise, and then spending. And very quickly, prices are likely to rise too—perhaps too fast and too high. This is one way *inflation* can occur. Or the government might do the opposite. It might spend less money on goods and services, which would decrease production, decrease earnings, and decrease spending. All of this might decrease production so much that there would be a period known as a *recession,* in which unemployment would rise.

Guiding the economy toward its full potential, while avoiding the dangers of inflation and recession, is one of the biggest economic problems facing the country today. The problem is made harder by the fact that inflation and recession hurt different groups of people. Workers who do not belong to unions and who cannot bargain with their employers to get higher wages are one group of people

What are some of the induced changes that accompany increased output? decreased output?

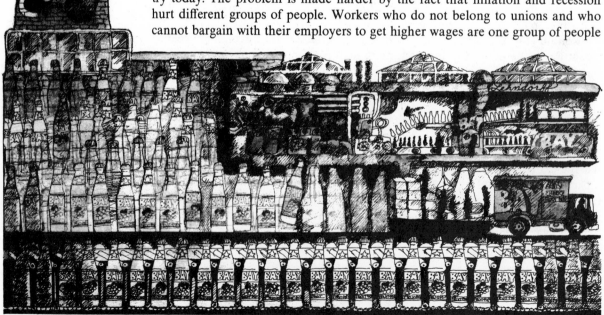

hurt by inflation. Old people living on pensions or Social Security are another. People who work in factories, on the other hand, are hurt by recession. There, even a small decrease in production can mean layoffs or less work (and less income) for millions of workers.

There are, then, two basic ways of judging the economy. It can be scored by means of an objective standard, like GNP, adjusted GNP, or NEW. It can also be judged by how well it is achieving its potential. Is the economy doing as well as it could?

You too can be judged in these two ways. Standards are useful for comparing yourself to others or to ideals. It is also useful to compare how well you are doing with how well you might be able to do.

But who defines what you can do? Society may tell you one thing—for instance, that you can make so much money if you try hard, or that you can become a leader in your community if you care enough. Your parents or teachers might think of your potential differently. You have a high IQ, a talent for music, sports ability, a head for business, a gift for making people laugh. You may define your potential in still another way. You believe that if you get the chance to try, and if you want it enough, you can achieve the goals you set for yourself.

☐ The reading for this lesson is a short story by Zona Gale. The main character struggles throughout his life with different ideas as to what he can and should do. By some definitions he is a success; by others he is a failure. As you read the story, ask yourself the following questions:

1. How is Bellard at the end of the story like an economy with low GNP that is achieving its full potential without inflation?
2. When is it useful to define an economy's success by GNP?
3. How does society define success for you? How do you define it?

THE WOMAN

Walking one day in a suburb, Bellard, wearing clothes in the extreme of the fashion, was torn by the look of a house on whose mean little porch near the street sat a shabby man of sixty, without a coat, and reading a newspaper. The man's fate seemed terrible: the unpainted house, the disordered hall, the glimpse of a woman in an apron. But the man looked up, and smiled at Bellard as brightly as if he himself had been young.

Bellard meant to be a financier. Instead, he shortly endured his father's bankruptcy, left college, found uncongenial employment, observed the trick of a girl's eyes, married her and lived in a little flat.

But this girl had the quality of a flower. Bellard could not explain it, but she was silent and fragrant, and hopeful like a flower. Once in April when he saw a pot of lilies of the valley blooming on the pavement, he thought: "They're like Lucile. They're all doing their utmost." In her presence it was impossible to be discouraged. He would go home from work hating his office, his routine, his fellows, his street; but as soon as he entered the flat, there would be some breath of that air for which he saw other men dying. Her welcome, her abstraction, her silence, her confidences were all really heavenly. Bellard wondered at her, did not comprehend her, adored her. He worked hard, and went home on the subway with a sense of happiness.

He longed to give her beautiful things, but she said: "How do people get like that, my dear—to want expensive things and to have people look up to them? Isn't it foolish?" He wondered how she knew that, and he wished that he knew it himself.

Their two children were like all agreeable children, and Bellard and Lucile went through the reverence, anxiety, and joy of their upbringing. And whether the moment yielded a torn frock or a hurt knee, croup or a moral crisis, Lucile seemed to put the event in its place and not to be overwhelmed by it. "She has a genius for being alive," Bellard thought.

As she grew older, she was not so beautiful, and he saw many women both beautiful and young. But when they chattered, pouted

What might happen to a business like this when nearby workers are out on strike? What else happens?

What are some of the economic
consequences of this kind of weather?
What are some other examples of
autonomous changes?

and coquetted, when they were cynical, bored, critical, or hilarious, he
thought about Lucile and her silences, her fragrance, her hope. Hope
of what? She knew that they would in all probability never have any
more than they had now. When he asked her wistfully what kept her
so happy she replied with an air of wonder: "You."

One day he overheard her talking about him with a friend. Lucile
was saying: "Other men live in things and events and emotions and
the future. But he seems to know that living is something else. . . ."
"What else?" this friend interrupted curiously. And he heard Lucile
say: "Well, of course every one knows, really. But he lives it too." "I'm
not good enough for her," Bellard thought, and tried his best to prove
that he was.

They went on like this for years; the children grew up, married,
came home and patronized them. Then Bellard, who had established
a little business, failed. His son tried to straighten things out, found it
impossible, and assumed control, frankly berating his father. His

How does inflation affect those who live in this kind of environment? How does it affect others? What about recession?

daughter came home with her three children, and filled the flat with clamor and turbulence. This woman said: "Mother, sometimes I think it's your fault. You're so *patient* with him." "I'm glad he's out of that business," said Lucile absently. "He never liked it." Her exasperated daughter cried: "But what are you going to live on?" Bellard heard her say: "Your father was responsible for three of us for a quarter of a century, you know, dear." At this Bellard rose on strong wings and felt himself still able to breast the morning and the night.

Lucile and Bellard moved to a suburb. There they rented a little house and Bellard went into a real estate office. All day he showed land and houses to men who wanted something better for less money. At night he went home and there was Lucile—less like a flower, but still silent, fragrant, hopeful. He said to her: "You'll never have anything more than you have now, Lucile, do you realize that?" She replied: "I don't want anything more to dust and take care of!" Once he said: "When you were a girl you dreamed that you'd have things different, didn't you, Lucile?" She said: "My dear, all that poor girl knew how to dream was just about having things!" He cried: "What do you want most of anything in this world?" She considered and answered: "I want you to be as happy as I am."

He thought of his own early dream of being a great financier, and said: "I'm the happy one, you know." He thought: "This is what the world is dying for."

One day, when he was sixty, he was sitting on his mean little porch near the street. The house was small and unpainted, the hall was disordered with house cleaning, Lucile in an apron was in the doorway. Bellard, without a coat and reading a newspaper, lifted his eyes, and saw walking by the house, and wearing clothes in the extreme of the fashion, a youth who looked up at him with an excess of visible compassion.

On this youth Bellard looked down and smiled, a luminous smile, a smile as bright as if he himself had been young.

ACTIVITIES

I. This activity will help you think about the values that are reflected in the way Americans spend their money.

1. As a class, add five to ten values to this list that you feel are representative of American society. Then check the five values you think would be tops for most Americans. Use the lines in the Workbook. If you don't have a Workbook, use a separate sheet of paper.

☐ power	☐ good health	☐ _____
☐ equality	☐ _____	☐ _____
☐ progress	☐ _____	☐ _____
☐ fun	☐ _____	☐ _____
☐ generosity	☐ _____	☐ _____

2. Work in small groups. Look closely at the national spending chart on pages 292–293. Decide what values from your list are reflected in each category. Write those values in the spaces provided on the chart in the Workbook or copy this one on a separate piece of paper.
3. You will now have a chance to alter the categories and figures on the spending chart so that they reflect the values selected in step 1 of this activity. Remember that you are trying to create a budget with the potential of achieving the goals desired by the American people. Use the blank budget chart included in the Workbook or copy the one from this activity.
4. The following are rules you must abide by in reordering the budget:
   a. The total money spent must stay the same.
   b. You may put dollars from one category into another.
5. Compare your revised budget with the original one. What values does the new budget reflect? Write the values on the chart.
6. Discussion questions
   a. How realistic was your budget? Explain.
   b. How would you judge the American economy as it is today?
   c. What values are reflected in the way you spend your money?

II.   This activity is designed to help you decide what you must do to achieve your full potential both in terms of the values you yourself hold and the values society subscribes to.

1.   Working in small groups, complete the chart in the Workbook of how a 25-year-old person would spend one week of his time. If you don't have a Workbook, copy the following chart onto a piece of paper. You should include specific examples of what that person does to achieve society's values. In making your choices you may want to think about some of the following ways a person could spend time:

leisure-time activities   family ties   job or career
education   spiritual growth   volunteer work
peer relationships   developing physical skills

2.   Still working in small groups, think of all the ways you might spend your time over one week. Share these ways with the whole class.
3.   On your own, make a list of the five values most important to you personally. Then complete a confidential chart of how your behavior in one week reflects (or does not reflect) your values and society's values. You can use the chart in the Workbook or copy this one.

BEHAVIOR OVER ONE WEEK	Is this person achieving his full potential in society's terms?	Which behaviors are generally considered good? Which seem to be a waste of time?	How could this person spend one week to achieve his full potential?
MORNING			
AFTERNOON			
EVENING			

Your five values	Your behavior over one week	What other values are reflected? Whose are they?

TOTAL SPENDING $1,606,300,000	Value represented
INVESTMENTS $241.2 billion	....
NET EXPORTS $6.9 billion	....
GOVERNMENT Defense $88.2 billion	....
Federal (non-defense) $45.2 billion Cancer research	....

State and local $232.3 billion
  Welfare
  Roads and schools
	....

PERSONAL CONSUMPTION
Food $233.9 billion
  Diet aids
  Fresh fruit
  Frozen foods
	(Example: good health, fun)
	....

Clothing $124.1 billion
  Unisex fashions
  Jogging outfits
  Work uniforms
  Disposable diapers
	....

Transportation $148.9 billion
  Mopeds
  Air shuttle service
  Subcompacts
  Subway renovation
	....

Recreation $70.9 billion
  Rock concerts
  Parks
  Skydiving
  Hunting
  Family camping
	....

Education $17.7 billion
  Books
  Adult education
  Museum trips
  Violin lessons
  Tutors
	....

TOTAL SPENDING (cont.)	$1,606,300,000	Value represented

Medical $85.1 billion ....
   Immunization
   Hair transplants
   Life-sustaining machinery
   Office visits to doctors
   Drugs
Housing $311.9 billion ....
   Vacation homes
   Camper trailers
   Renovation
   Aluminum siding
   Solar panels

Source: Economic Report of the President, 1977.

TOTAL SPENDING	Value represented

INVESTMENTS ....

NET EXPORTS ....

GOVERNMENT ....
....
....
....

PERSONAL CONSUMPTION ....
....
....
....
....
....
....
....
....

Economic Problems: Unemployment and Inflation

Ever since World War II, the United States has been trying to achieve two economic goals, *full employment* and *stable prices.* It has not always been successful at either goal. Unemployment had become a serious problem in the 1970's. This can be seen in Table 29-1.

Unemployment is hard to live with. Besides the loss of income, unemployment brings other hardships. People without work often blame themselves for their problems. They think they have failed in some way because they can't find work. But in fact, it may not be their fault at all. They may simply be victims of economic forces beyond their control. For example, they may have been laid off because of a slowdown in their industry. Or the entire country may be suffering from a *recession.*

No matter what its cause, unemployment brings suffering to those out of work. It also affects those who still have jobs. Society loses the production of the unemployed person. What is more, unemployed workers no longer have incomes to spend. This means a decline in the demand for goods and services in many different businesses. This in turn leads to reduced production in those firms, and that means even more unemployment.

It is for these reasons that the U.S. government has made full employment one of its major economic goals. The term "full employment" does not mean 100 per-

YEAR	PERCENT OF WORK FORCE
1967	3.8
1968	3.6
1969	3.5
1970	4.9
1971	5.9
1972	5.6
1973	4.9
1974	5.6
1975	8.5
1976	7.7
1977	7.0

Table 29-1   Selected Unemployment Rate, 1967–1977
Source: Economic Report of the President, 1978

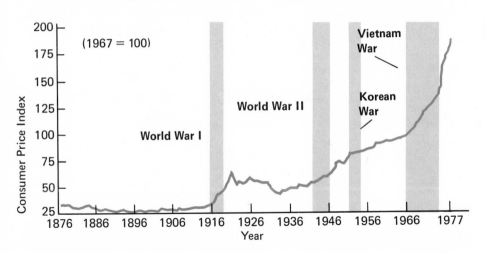

Figure 29-1   Changes in Consumer Price Index
What does war do to prices? Why?

cent employment. It does not mean that everyone is working, but rather that nearly everyone is. The reason for this is that it is not possible to get rid of all unemployment. For example, some workers quit their jobs to look for better ones. They are unemployed for a short time between one job and the next. New workers enter the labor force every day, and they are usually unemployed for a short time before they get their first jobs. Some people move from one part of the country to another, and it usually takes them some time to find work in their new homes. For these reasons, in the 1960's economists defined "full" employment as 3 to 4 percent unemployment. Recently, some economists have claimed that at the present time the country cannot get the unemployment rate below 5 percent.

The government has not been very successful at keeping prices stable either. Prices have gone up steadily for the past thirty years. *Inflation,* like unemployment, is a hard thing to live with. When prices go up faster than wages, the effect is the same as a decrease in income. For example, a person earning $5 an hour would have to work five hours to earn enough money to buy a $25 pair of shoes. But if the price of shoes goes up to $36 and the person's income goes up only to $6 an hour, it would take six hours of work to buy the same pair of shoes. Real income has been reduced even though money income has gone up.

Inflation is especially hard on people whose incomes do not go up at all—for example, old people living on pensions or savings. It is hard on workers who do not belong to unions and who therefore cannot bargain for wage increases. And it is hard on unionized workers whose wage increases do not match the increase in prices.

Economists measure inflation by two scales, the *Wholesale Price Index* and the *Consumer Price Index.* Using 1967 as a comparison, or base, year, the Wholesale Price Index measures the cost of raw materials used by industry. If, for example,

Table 29-2 Price Indexes for Some Consumer Items
Source: Department of Labor, 1977
Compared to 1967, which of these products is now the best buy?

YEAR	TELEVISION SETS	WASHING MACHINES	REFRIGER- ATORS	AUTOMOBILES NEW	USED	CPI ALL ITEMS
1960	127.1	110.7	116.8	90.6	104.5	88.7
1965	107.3	100.2	104.2	96.3	100.9	94.5
1967	100.0	100.0	100.0	100.0	100.0	100.0
1970	99.8	107.3	105.8	107.6	104.3	116.3
1977	137.1	148.0	141.0	146.0	188.0	183.0

Figure 29-2 Unemployment in the United States, 1947–1976
If you wanted to reduce unemployment, what would be a reasonable goal?

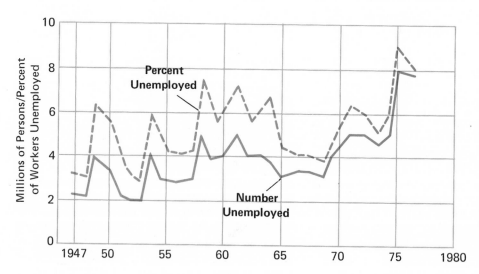

the raw materials cost $100 in 1967, compared with a cost of only $87.40 in 1953, then the Wholesale Price Index for 1953 is counted as 87.4. If the same raw materials cost $119.10 in 1972, the Wholesale Price Index for that year is 119.1. The Consumer Price Index does the same thing for a list of items (such as groceries, health care, transportation, housing, and so on) bought by the family of an average urban wage earner.

Table 29-2 shows that prices went up slowly in the 1950's and early 1960's. Then they began to rise more steeply. The Consumer Price Index, for example, increased from 72.1 in 1950 to 91.7 in 1963. This was an increase of 27 percent in 13 years. But in the next 13 years, from 1963 to 1976, the Consumer Price Index increased from 91.7 to 170.1—an increase of 85 percent.

Unemployment and inflation are problems that occur when government does not meet its economic goals. They can be looked at on a macro level, as problems for the whole society. They can also be looked at on a micro, or personal, level.

What happens to people when social goals are not met? Often this means that they cannot fulfill their personal dreams. The jobs they want don't exist. The money they saved has lost some of its value. The directions they chose are not thought important.

What can you do when the reality you face doesn't allow for your dreams? How can you meet your needs and keep your self-respect? Do you give up your dream and find something else? Must you settle for less? Can you change society? Can you find a way to fulfill your dream in spite of society?

YEAR	CONSUMER PRICE INDEX	WHOLESALE PRICE INDEX
1933	38.8	34.0
1941	44.1	45.1
1945	53.9	54.6
1950	72.1	81.8
1953	80.1	87.4
1957	84.3	93.3
1963	91.7	94.5
1967	100.0	100.0
1970	116.3	110.4
1972	125.3	119.1
1974	147.7	160.1
1976	170.1	182.9
1977	181.5	194.2

Table 29-3 **Wholesale Price Indexes and Consumer Price Indexes for Selected Years, (1967 = 100)** *Source:* Economic Report of the President, 1978

☐ The reading for this lesson by Elliot Liebow describes a group of unemployed and underemployed people. The jobs they can get do not satisfy their needs. This reading was written in 1967. The salary figures it quotes are therefore out-of-date—$1 then would be worth more than $2 in 1980. As you read it, ask yourself the following questions:

1. Why are Tally and the other men often unemployed?
2. How have Tally's dreams been affected by society's values and commitments?
3. In practice, what could Tally do to achieve his dreams or increase his self-respect?

MEN AND JOBS

A pickup truck drives slowly down the street. The truck stops as it comes abreast of a man sitting on a cast-iron porch and the white driver calls out, asking if the man wants a day's work. The man shakes his head and the truck moves on up the block, stopping again whenever idling men come within calling distance of the driver. At the Carry-out corner, five men debate the question briefly and shake their heads no to the truck. The truck turns the corner and repeats the same performance up the next street. In the distance, one can see one man, then another, climb into the back of the truck and sit down. In starts and stops, the truck finally disappears.

What is it we have witnessed here? A labor scavenger rebuffed by his would-be prey? Lazy, irresponsible men turning down an honest day's pay for an honest day's work? Or a more complex phenomenon marking the intersection of economic forces, social values and individual states of mind and body?

Objective economic considerations are frequently a controlling factor in a man's refusal to take a job. How much the job pays is a crucial question but seldom asked. He knows how much it pays. Working as a stock clerk, a delivery boy, or even behind the counter of liquor stores, drug stores and other retail businesses pays one dollar an hour. So, too, do most busboy, car-wash, janitorial and other jobs available to him.

The most important fact is that a man who is able and willing to work cannot earn enough money to support himself, his wife, and one or more children. A man's chances for working regularly are good only if he is willing to work for less than he can live on, and sometimes

What percentage of these people are likely to be working? Who might not be? How do you tell?

not even then. On some jobs, the wage rate is deceptively higher than on others, but the higher the wage rate, the more difficult it is to get the job, and the less the job security. Higher-paying construction work tends to be seasonal and, during the season, the amount of work available is highly sensitive to business and weather conditions and to the changing requirements of individual projects.

A crucial factor in the streetcorner man's lack of job commitment is the overall value he places on the job. *For his part, the streetcorner man puts no lower value on the job than does the larger society around him.* He knows the social value of the job by the amount of money the employer is willing to pay him for doing it. In a real sense, every pay day, he counts in dollars and cents the value placed on the job by society at large. He is no more (and frequently less) ready to quit and look for another job than his employer is ready to fire him and look for another man. Neither the streetcorner man who performs these jobs nor the society which requires him to perform them assesses the job as one "worth doing and worth doing well." Nor does the low-wage job offer prestige, respect, interesting work, opportunity for learning or advancement, or any other compensation.

Job assessments typically consist of nothing more than a noncommittal shrug and "It's O.K." or "It's a job."

One reason for the relative absence of talk about one's job is, as suggested earlier, that the sameness of job experiences does not bear reiteration. Another and more important reason is the emptiness of the job experience itself. The man sees middle-class occupations as a primary source of prestige, pride and self-respect; his own job affords him none of these. To think about his job is to see himself as others see him, to remind him of just where he stands in this society. And because society's criteria for placement are generally the same as his own, to talk about his job can trigger a flush of shame and a deep, almost physical ache to change places with someone, almost anyone, else. The desire to be a person in his own right, to be noticed by the world he lives in, is shared by each of the men on the streetcorner.

Tally and I were in the Carryout. It was summer, Tally's peak earning season as a cement finisher, a semiskilled job a cut or so above that of the unskilled laborer. His take-home pay during these weeks was well over a hundred dollars—"a lot of bread." But for Tally, who no longer had a family to support, bread was not enough.

"You know that boy came in last night? That Black Moozlem? That's what I ought to be doing. I ought to be in his place."

"What do you mean?"

Why might it be difficult for this person to find work? What are some of the consequences of his being unemployed?

"Dressed nice, going to [night] school, got a good job."

"He's no better off than you, Tally. You make more than he does."

"It's not the money. [Pause] It's position, I guess. He's got position. When he finish school he gonna be a supervisor. People respect him. . . . Thinking about people with position and education gives me a feeling right here [pressing his fingers into the pit of his stomach]."

"You're educated, too. You have a skill, a trade. You're a cement finisher. You can make a building, pour a sidewalk."

"That's different. Look, can anybody do what you're doing? Can anybody just come up and do your job? Well, in one week I can teach you cement finishing. You won't be as good as me 'cause you won't have the experience but you'll be a cement finisher. That's what I mean. Anybody can do what I'm doing and that's what gives me this feeling. [Long pause] Suppose I like this girl. I go over to her house and I meet her father. He starts talking about what he done today. He talks about operating on somebody and sewing them up and about surgery. I know he's a doctor 'cause of the way he talks. Then she starts talking about what she did. Maybe she's a boss or a supervisor. Maybe she's a lawyer and her father says to me, 'And what do you do,

What are some more realistic examples of inflation, and how might they affect you?

Mr. Jackson?' [Pause] You remember at the courthouse, Lonny's trial? You and the lawyer was talking in the hall? You remember? I just stood there listening. I didn't say a word. You know why? 'Cause I didn't even know what you was talking about. That's happened to me a lot.''

''Hell, you're nothing special. That happens to everybody. Nobody knows everything. One man is a doctor, so he talks about surgery. Another man is a teacher, so he talks about books. But doctors and teachers don't know anything about concrete. You're a cement finisher and that's your specialty.''

''Maybe so, but when was the last time you saw anybody standing around talking about concrete?''

The streetcorner man wants to be a person in his own right, to be noticed, to be taken account of, but in this respect, as well as in meeting his money needs, his job fails him. The job and the man are even. The job fails the man and the man fails the job.

What might you find if you compared the present Consumer Price Index and Wholesale Price Index with what they were when this picture was taken? What does this mean?

ACTIVITIES

I.   This activity is about what happens when your own goals or standards differ from society's.

Body language can be a telling aspect of your personality. Use it in this activity to let society know who you are and what you believe. Pretend you are part of a sculpture group and that you must place your body so as to express your ideas and feelings. Think of ways to hold your head, facial expressions you can make, and where to put your arms and legs. Where you locate yourself in relation to the other students in the sculpture will be important too.

1.   Divide into two groups. The members of one group will represent SOCIETY, while the members of the other will act as themselves, as INDIVIDUALS. For this activity, it will probably be helpful if the desks and chairs can be moved to the outer edge of the room.
2.   SOCIETY should meet separately to decide just how it feels the INDIVIDUALS should behave. The members of SOCIETY will have a chance later in the activity to dictate to the INDIVIDUALS according to the standards they choose. This will mean changing and adjusting the scuplture in any way they see fit.
3.   One INDIVIDUAL will begin by placing herself in the center of the room and assuming a body position that shows who she is and how she wants society to view her.
4.   One by one, the other INDIVIDUALS take turns joining the sculpture as it forms in the center of the room. If possible, someone outside the sculpture should take an instant photo of the group. Individuals can take turns stepping outside the sculpture to see what they have shaped.
5.   When all INDIVIDUALS have joined the sculpture and feel they have placed themselves in ways that express who they are as individuals, it is SOCIETY's turn to dictate to them. SOCIETY will tell the INDIVIDUALS what is expected of them based on the standards chosen in step 2 of this activity.
6.   INDIVIDUALS may respond to SOCIETY in three ways. They can
   a.   change to what SOCIETY dictates;
   b.   collapse on the floor if they can't change;
   c.   drop out of society and form a counterculture.
7.   Discussion questions
   a.   How different were society's goals from individuals' goals?
   b.   How different were each individual's goals from one another?
   c.   How did individuals respond when society tried to mold them?
   d.   How do you respond when society tries to shape you?

II. This activity gives INDIVIDUALS a chance to try to mold SOCIETY.

1. SOCIETY creates a sculpture following the same procedures outlined in steps 4 and 5 of Activity I. This sculpture, however, will depict an important social or economic issue chosen from the list below or thought up by a classmate.

   citizen participation in government   ethnic integrity
   Equal Rights Amendment   full employment
   the American dream   inflation

   SOCIETY's goal in this sculpture is to place itself in such a way that American society's attitude toward the issue is shown.

2. Now INDIVIDUALS will have a turn to mold the kind of society in which they would feel most comfortable. INDIVIDUALS should do this one by one or in groups. INDIVIDUALS have the option to comment on how society is molded.

3. Switch roles and try sculpting another issue.

4. Discussion questions
   a. How did SOCIETY sculpt the issues? What goals were portrayed?
   b. How did INDIVIDUALS choose to change society?
   c. How might people really change society when it doesn't allow them to fulfill their dreams?

III. This activity is based on Table 29-3.

1. Working in small groups, complete the following chart. Use the one in the Workbook or copy it on a separate sheet of paper.

	Most affected by unemployment	Least affected by unemployment
Groups of persons		
Occupations		
Industries		

2. Discussion questions
   a. What are some possible reasons for the high rates of unemployment?
   b. What are some possible effects of these high rates of unemployment?
   c. What changes might be possible for dealing with the problem of unemployment?

SELECTED CATEGORIES	AVERAGE ANNUAL UNEMPLOYMENT %
AGE, SEX, RACE	
Total, 16 years and over	7.7
Males, 20 years and over	5.9
Females, 20 years and over	7.4
Both sexes, 16–19 years	19.0
White, total	7.0
Males, 20 years and over	5.4
Females, 20 years and over	6.8
Both sexes, 16–19 years	16.9
Black and other, total	13.2
Males, 20 years and over	10.6
Females, 20 years and over	11.3
Both sexes, 16–19 years	37.0
OCCUPATION	
White-collar workers	4.6
Professional and technical	3.2
Managers and administrators, except farm	3.1
Salesworkers	5.4
Clerical workers	6.4
Blue-collar workers	9.5
Craft and kindred workers	6.9
Operatives	10.1
Nonfarm laborers	13.7
Service workers	8.5
Farmworkers	4.5
INDUSTRY	
Nonagricultural private wage and salary workers	8.0
Construction	15.7
Manufacturing	7.9
Durable goods	7.7
Nondurable goods	8.2
Transportation and public utilities	5.0
Wholesale and retail trade	8.6
Finance and service industries	6.5
Government workers	4.4
Agricultural wage and salary workers	11.8

Table 29-4 Profile of Unemployment in the United States, 1976
Source: Department of Labor

Economic Goals: Full Employment and Stable Prices

Why has the government had so little success in achieving full employment and stable prices? One reason is that the government does not have full control over the decisions of business firms. If a business firm installs a computer, it may fire a dozen bookkeepers. The government is powerless to stop it. If a company decides to move its factory to another part of the country or to a foreign country, the government cannot stop that either. Both actions will increase *structural unemployment.* This is unemployment that results from a change in the structure, or organization, of an industry.

The government does not have full control over the ups and downs of the business cycle either. A *business cycle* is a pattern of growth and decline in a particular business. By spending more or less money, the government can increase or decrease the demand for goods and services in a particular industry. But other factors besides government spending affect demand. If the price of gasoline goes too high, for instance, people will buy fewer new cars. That would lead to a decline in production in the auto industry, which could spread to other industries as well. This would lead to an increase in *cyclical unemployment,* or unemployment that is caused by the cycle of growth and decline.

Seasonal unemployment occurs in industries that are seriously affected by the weather—farming, for example. When crops are harvested, the demand for workers is high. But when winter sets in, the demand is reduced almost to zero. The same is true of the construction industry, where employment goes down during the winter.

There is another kind of unemployment that is hard for the government to fight, because it is hidden. *Hidden unemployment* includes those workers (and nobody knows for sure how many there are) who have become discouraged by their failure to find work, and who have stopped looking. These workers are not counted in the official unemployment statistics. Neither are those workers whose skills are higher than the skills called for in the jobs they do. These workers are *underemployed* because they are not able to work at their full potential. Some part-time workers, who would rather work as full-timers, can also be counted as underemployed.

The fight against unemployment may be hindered by the fight against inflation. This is because some of the things that decrease unemployment increase inflation. And some of the things that decrease inflation increase unemployment.

For example, one way to decrease inflation is to get people to spend less money. If they spend less, demand for products will go down, and prices will not rise too quickly. Tax increases are one method used by the government to decrease spending. However, when total spending and demand go down, production has to go down too. And that means layoffs and unemployment.

On the other hand, unemployment can be reduced by increasing the amount of money spent by consumers, businesses, and government. The government can

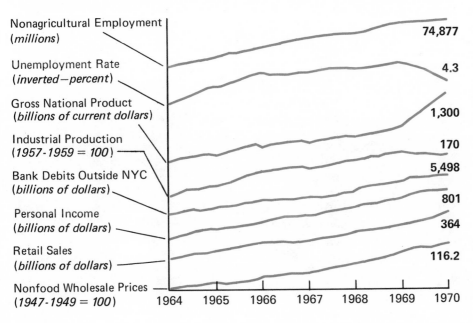

Nonagricultural Employment (*millions*) — 74,877

Unemployment Rate (*inverted—percent*) — 4.3

Gross National Product (*billions of current dollars*) — 1,300

Industrial Production (*1957-1959 = 100*) — 170

Bank Debits Outside NYC (*billions of dollars*) — 5,498

Personal Income (*billions of dollars*) — 801

Retail Sales (*billions of dollars*) — 364

Nonfood Wholesale Prices (*1947-1949 = 100*) — 116.2

1964   1965   1966   1967   1968   1969   1970

Figure 30-1 Economic Indicators
Source: Department of Commerce
How are these economic indicators related? How do you explain the sharp increase in GNP between 1969 and 1970?

encourage spending by reducing taxes and raising the amount of money it spends on various programs. But increased spending means that prices will go up—that is, more inflation.

Finding the right mixture of government policies is not easy. It means trying to increase spending by just the right amount, and in just the right areas of the economy. Too much spending, and prices will go up too quickly. Too little spending, and unemployment will continue to rise.

The goals we stress for our economy reflect our beliefs about what is important. When we push for full employment, we are not only trying to use our resources fully. We are also acting on our belief that work is good for people. We feel that those who want to work should be able to. When we push for stable prices, we are asking for security. We want to know that money will be worth tomorrow what it is worth today.

Our basic economic goals affect our approach to social goals. As we plan programs to clean up rivers, improve cities, or fight disease, we look at their impact on the economy. Sometimes social programs fulfill economic goals and economic programs fulfill social goals. When the two conflict, we must look at the tradeoff.

The country's social and economic goals affect you in two ways. First, they help to shape your values. When the government makes a major commitment to human needs, for instance, people look for ways to help others. Second, society's goals affect your opportunities. You try to choose goals for yourself that you will be able to reach.

How might the decisions made here affect spending? inflation? recession?

The reading for this lesson argues that full employment should be a national priority. The author, Coretta King, first looks at the effects of employment and unemployment on individuals. She then looks at how full employment would affect the economy as a whole. Finally, she looks at full employment as a moral issue that affects the whole society. As you read her plea, ask yourself the following questions:

1. What are the strongest arguments for full employment?
2. How would a national commitment to full employment affect people's goals and sense of themselves?
3. How do national goals affect your goals and sense of yourself?

WHY WE STILL CAN'T WAIT

Twelve years ago, when my husband, Martin Luther King Jr., sat in the Birmingham jail during the civil-rights campaign in that city, he received a letter from a group of concerned white clergymen. While they recognized the clear justice of his cause, they wondered would it not be better to ask for less and accept that one must wait for progress.

My husband's answer, written on scraps of paper and smuggled out of his cell, was one of the great documents of the civil-rights movement. The "letter from a Birmingham jail" laid out for all Americans the moral and social reasons why we can't "wait."

I was reminded of Martin and the letter from a Birmingham jail recently when I went to Washington to testify in favor of the "Humphrey-Hawkins Full Employment and Balanced Growth Act of 1976"—a measure that would commit the government to take all practical steps to lower unemployment to 3 per cent for adults by 1980. Although the issue was different, full employment rather than civil rights, and involved both black and white Americans, once again the less fortunate were being told that practical men had decided for them that it would be better to "wait."

My husband can no longer raise his voice in reply, but there is no question what his answer would be. There are three burning reasons why America's jobless cannot wait for some far-off day before we have full employment.

The first reason is that our current high unemployment is nothing less than a guarantee that America's future will hold deterioration rather than progress. The men and women breadwinners of America are not isolated individuals but a pivot on which the whole health of

What do the people who work here do in the summer? What are some examples of other types of unemployment?

our community depends. A man with a decent job is a provider for his children and a model for their behavior. He is the support of his aging parents and a force for stability in his neighborhood and city. Clean and safe streets, decent housing, adequate medical care and even racial peace are all goals that can only come from a base of stable jobs. Without decent jobs, neither the "special programs" of the cautious nor the pious lectures of the uncaring can do anything but add the insult of indifference to the injury of unemployment.

Nothing less than the future of America is at stake. Right now a new generation is growing up, all too many in homes where the parents are without work. Tolerating high unemployment in 1980 will be nothing less than a guarantee that we shall walk down dirty streets, past bitter youths and sad-eyed old men, on into the 21st century. High unemployment is nothing less than a vile investment in continuing decay.

The second reason why America's unemployed cannot wait is that the last 30 years have offered compelling proof that waiting is no solution at all. Do we really need to be reminded that the many postwar cycles of prosperity and recession have always left millions of Americans behind? Have we forgotten that in 1968, when the deceptive unemployment rate was below 4 per cent, the ghettos of America were in flames? Millions of people involuntarily work part-time or shuffle from one poverty-level job to another, all of them excluded from the unemployment rate we watch so closely.

Genuine full employment requires a major improvement of our educational system and expanded job training to prepare the unemployed for good jobs. It requires tax and regulatory policies to ensure that jobs are located where people can reach them, and not policies that encourage the "export" of jobs to foreign countries. It requires not "leaf raking" but major investment in mass transit, in energy and a host of projects that will benefit all America. And not a single one of these things will be achieved by waiting. Full employment will be achieved by forceful government action or it will not be achieved. The proposal that we wait is in reality the proposal that we do nothing.

The final and most compelling reason why America's unemployed cannot be told to wait is that full employment is at base a moral issue, and questions of justice cannot be solved by waiting. We who support full employment know full well that there are realistic limits to our economic capacity and we do not ask for miracles. All we seek is an America where every person is given the chance to productively contribute to his country and where he can receive a fair and equitable share of the wealth that production creates. There is no

Why might this person be under-employed?

economic mystery in this; only a simple demand for justice. The current government policy, on the other hand, is deeply unfair. Accepting unemployment to control inflation amounts to choosing the people at the very bottom of the economic pyramid to bear the entire economic burden. In the so-called war against inflation, America's 10 million unemployed have been made the Administration's conscript army.

Yet, there are those who try to avoid this moral issue. Full employment is indeed a just and decent goal, they say, but it is just too complex to be solved with a clear and direct government commitment to its elimination.

To be frank, I cannot but consider this the most reprehensible evasion of all. Since when have we begun to decide our ethics on the basis of how difficult they are to fulfill? In 1963 we did not decide our view of the Civil Rights Act on the basis of whether it would create complex problems of litigation. What we asked was whether God created all men equal. In 1965 we did not ask how much the Voting Rights Act would cost in terms of Federal inspections. We asked if America was indeed to be a land of justice and a country of free men.

And so today what we must ask is not whether full employment will be simple or convenient or cheap, but whether tolerating unemployment is morally right or wrong.

For myself, if the alternative to full employment is simply to wait, to tolerate in silence the shattered dreams of jobless youth and the broken hearts of laid-off old men, then my choice is clear.

America's jobless cannot "wait," not only because waiting is no solution and not only because waiting has social consequences that are frightening to contemplate, but because to do nothing when we have the capacity to act is morally and socially wrong.

Go back over the photos and drawings in this chapter. Select at least five of them. Picture for yourself another image to fit each caption. What does your "picture" look like? Try to imagine the image in as much detail as possible. What is the point of your picture? Are there people in it? What do they look like? What are they doing? How do they feel? Try to describe your picture to your classmates in as much detail as possible. What pictures do others think of?

VISUAL
ACTIVITY

ACTIVITIES

This activity will help you think about the way economic goals influence social goals. Consider the following hypothetical situations:

1. Congress has $15,000,000,000 to spend on a program that will aid the American people. Because present unemployment is 11.1 percent, it is important that the program chosen be able to create new jobs. There has been a decline in the constant dollar GNP during the past two quarters, and the Consumer Price Index has been increasing at a yearly rate of 7 percent. A research committee has come up with two suggestions, both of which, it feels, will benefit society.

PROGRAM A: SPACE SHUTTLE
The National Aeronautics and Space Administration (NASA) needs money to continue its plans for a space shuttle. New technology creates new jobs for both the present and the future. Scientific research in one area often leads to new discoveries in other areas such as medicine and engineering. With a growing world population, it may also soon be necessary to transport people from the earth to the moon or other planets.

PROGRAM B: CLEAN AIR
More and more cities across the country are requesting funds for their clean air programs. Pollution levels are reaching the danger point for humans, not to mention plants and animals. Research indicates that the problem is growing fast, and it is predicted that one day we will all have to wear face masks just to breathe. Because of the factories and transportation systems that contribute to the problem, this is a very complex issue with far-reaching effects.

2. The class takes a simple hand vote to show individual preferences for either the space shuttle program or the clean air program.
3. Divide into two groups. Each group will argue in favor of one of the programs. The groups should spend about 20 minutes forming a presentation that will describe why they feel their program would be good for society. Each group should consider the economic benefits that their social program will bring.

4. The following outline is designed to help you organize your presentation:
   a. What resources will be used? natural? capital? human?
   b. Are the necessary resources presently overutilized or underutilized?
   c. How will use of these resources for your program affect the rest of the economy? What will the economic results be?
   d. What will the human consequences be? What jobs will be created (directly and indirectly)?
   e. Who will be eligible for the jobs? How might the members of your class be affected?
   f. How will society's future be influenced? How will the program affect policies and investments?
5. Each group takes a turn presenting its position to the rest of the class.
6. Discussion questions
   a. What does each program produce?
   b. Which program did you choose before the presentation? Which after? How did the presentations influence your decision?
   c. How does society help you choose your own goals?

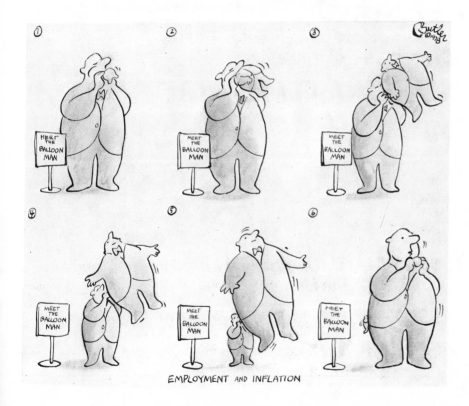

EMPLOYMENT AND INFLATION

CHAPTER 11 MONEY AND MONETARY POLICY

The Forms and Functions of Money in the United States

Money is the best known economic institution. It is something people see and use almost every day. No modern economy could get along without it. But what is money? What forms does it take? What functions does it perform?

The familiar green paper bills and metal coins used in the United States are only two of the forms money can take. In the past, many things have served as money—beads, shells, dogs' teeth, cattle, stones, tobacco, fish hooks, and even slaves. Precious metals, especially gold and silver, have been a favorite form of money. Some of the things used as money, like fish hooks or cattle, have also had value as consumer goods. But most of the things used as money have had value only because people agreed that they could be exchanged for goods and services. In other words, what makes something valuable as money is not what it can be used for, but what it can be exchanged for.

In most modern economies, money serves several functions. First, it is a *means of exchange*. When people take $5 to a grocery store and buy food with it, they are using the money as a means of exchange. Less complex societies often do not use money at all. They simply barter one good for another—a bushel of wheat for a jar of milk, for example. The more complex a country's economy is, the harder it would be to use a system of trading one good for another. Money is the answer to that problem.

Money can also be used as a way of *storing value*. That is, people can save their money for use later on. Storing goods is not as easy as storing money. Many goods, such as food, spoil quickly. Others, such as cars, take up a lot of space. But money can be kept in a bank, or a safe, or a pocketbook until it is needed.

Money is also a *standard of value*. It can be used to compare the value of one thing with the value of another. Everyone knows about how much a dollar will buy. People can therefore compare the worth of one $100 item with other items worth the same amount of money. The value of all the goods and services produced by the economy can be added up by adding up their prices. This, of course, is how the GNP is figured.

The total money supply of the United States is not limited to paper bills and metal coins, which are called *currency*. Eighty percent consists of money in the form of checking accounts. When $100 is deposited in a bank checking account, the sum the depositor can draw on is increased by that amount. From then on, the depositor will not have to have $100 in paper bills or coins in order to buy something worth $100. She can simply write out a check to cover its costs. Almost all firms use checks to pay their bills, and most people also get paid by check.

There are several other things used like money. Economists call things that are used for some but not all of the functions of money *near money*. Credit cards, for

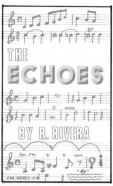

example, are an ever more common way to pay bills and purchase goods and services. If the card is used to buy gasoline, the gas station will record the name and number and send it along with the bill for the gasoline to the credit card company. The credit card company will then pay the gas station and send the buyer a bill for the amount of the gasoline. The advantage of credit cards is that people who own them can pay many of their bills at one time each month.

Food stamps can be exchanged for food just as money can. They are not money, however, since they can be traded only for food. Money can be exchanged for anything.

A savings account is a store of value. When people place their money in a savings account, they are choosing to use it in the future instead of in the present. The bank book has a record of people's deposits and the interest paid by the bank for the use of the money. Insurance policies, stocks, and bonds are stores of value and can easily be exchanged for money.

Because money is a store and standard of value, as well as a means of exchange, it is very important in our society. We can judge the worth of such diverse things as pets, paintings, medical care, and car washes. We can then compare their value by what they cost. The society at large decides how much money everything is worth. People whose jobs are thought to be more important get higher salaries than those whose jobs are considered less important. Thus people are often judged by how much money they make.

You have your own beliefs about the value of goods, services, jobs, and people. The value you place on an item will often be different from its monetary value. You may feel that some things are priceless and that others are not worth as much as they cost. Your own values dictate what you are willing to do for pay. You judge yourself and others by your own standards and act accordingly.

How is money used as a means of exchange? What is money really worth? How is this decided?

☐ The reading for this lesson, a short story by O. Henry, is about what money can and can't buy. As you read it, ask yourself the following questions:
1. What can't money buy?
2. What forms and functions of money are shown in the story?
3. How does the way you use money reflect your values?

MAMMON AND THE ARCHER

Old Anthony Rockwall, retired manufacturer and proprietor of Rockwall's Eureka Soap, looked out the library window of his Fifth Avenue mansion.

And then Anthony Rockwall, who never cared for bells, went to the door of his library and shouted "Mike!"

"Tell my son," said Anthony to the answering menial, "to come in here before he leaves the house."

When young Rockwall entered the library the old man laid aside his newspaper, looked at him with a kindly grimness on his big, smooth, ruddy countenance, rumpled his mop of white hair with one hand and rattled the keys in his pocket with the other.

"You're a gentleman," said Anthony, decidedly. "They say it takes three generations to make one. They're off. Money'll do it as slick as soap grease. It's made you one. By hokey! it's almost made one of me."

"There are some things that money can't accomplish," remarked young Rockwall, rather gloomily.

"That's why I asked you to come in. There's something going wrong with you, boy. I've been noticing it for two weeks. Out with it. If it's your liver, there's the *Rambler* down in the bay, coaled, and ready to steam down to the Bahamas in two days."

"Not a bad guess, dad; you haven't missed it far."

"Ah," said Anthony, keenly; "what's her name?"

Richard began to walk up and down the library floor. There was enough comradeship and sympathy in this crude old father of his to draw his confidence.

"Why don't you ask her?" demanded old Anthony. "She'll jump at you. You've got the money and the looks, and you're a decent boy. Your hands are clean. You've got no Eureka soap on 'em. You've been to college, but she'll overlook that."

"I haven't had a chance," said Richard. "Every hour and minute of her time is arranged for days in advance. I must have that girl, dad, or this town is a blackjack swamp forevermore. And I can't write it—I can't do that.

"I'm allowed to meet her with a cab at the Grand Central Station tomorrow evening at the 8:30 train. We drive down Broadway to Wallack's at a gallop, where her mother and a box party will be waiting for us in the lobby. Do you think she would listen to a declaration from me during that six or eight minutes under those circumstances? No, dad, this is one tangle that your money can't unravel. We can't buy one minute of time with cash; if we could, rich people would live longer."

"You say money won't buy time? Well, of course, you can't order eternity wrapped up and delivered at your residence for a price, but I've seen Father Time get pretty bad stone bruises on his heels when he walked through the gold diggings."

That night came Aunt Ellen to brother Anthony at his evening paper, and began discourse on the subject of lovers' woes.

"He told me all about it," said brother Anthony, yawning. "I told him my bank account was at his service.

"Oh, Anthony," sighed Aunt Ellen, "I wish you would not think so much of money. Wealth is nothing where a true affection is concerned. Love is all-powerful."

The following three pictures demonstrate things of approximately equal monetary value. Are these things really worth the same? How valuable is the service illustrated at the left?

How valuable would these clothes be if you didn't have any? if you had lots of clothes?

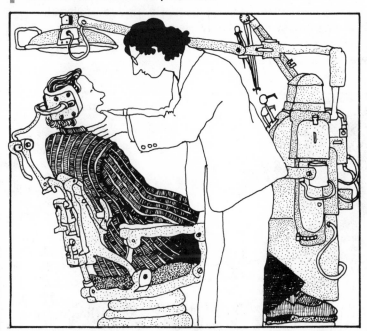

At eight o'clock the next evening Aunt Ellen took a quaint old gold ring from a moth-eaten case and gave it to Richard.

"Wear it to-night, nephew," she begged. "Your mother gave it to me. Good luck in love she said it brought. She asked me to give it to you when you had found the one you loved."

Young Rockwall took the ring reverently and tried it on his smallest finger. It slipped as far as the second joint and stopped. He took it off and stuffed it into his vest pocket.

At the station he captured Miss Lantry out of the gadding mob at eight thirty-two.

"To Wallack's Theatre as fast as you can drive!" said Richard loyally.

At Thirty-fourth Street young Richard quickly thrust up the trap and ordered the cabman to stop.

"I've dropped a ring," he apologised, as he climbed out. "It was my mother's, and I'd hate to lose it. I won't detain you a minute—I saw where it fell."

In less than a minute he was back in the cab with the ring.

But within that minute a crosstown car had stopped directly in front of the cab. The cabman tried to pass to the left, but a heavy express wagon cut him off. He tried the right, and had to back away from a furniture van that had no business to be there. He tried to back out, but dropped his reins and swore dutifully. He was blockaded in a tangled mess of vehicles and horses. The entire traffic of Manhattan seemed to have jammed itself around them.

How valuable would this meal be if you were starving? if you had just finished a big meal?

"I'm very sorry," said Richard, as he resumed his seat, "but it looks as if we are stuck. They won't get this jumble loosened up in an hour. It was my fault. If I hadn't dropped the ring we—"

At 11 o'clock that night somebody tapped lightly on Anthony Rockwall's door.

"Come in," shouted Anthony, who was in a red dressing-gown, reading a book of piratical adventures.

Somebody was Aunt Ellen.

"They're engaged, Anthony," she said, softly. "She has promised to marry our Richard. On their way to the theatre there was a street blockade, and it was two hours before their cab could get out of it.

"And, oh, brother Anthony, don't ever boast of the power of money again. A little emblem of true love—a little ring that symbolised unending and unmercenary affection—was the cause of our Richard finding his happiness. He dropped it in the street, and got out to recover it. And before they could continue the blockade occurred. He spoke to his love and won her there while the cab was hemmed in. Money is dross compared with true love, Anthony."

The story should end here. I wish it would as heartily as you who read it wish it did. But we must go to the bottom of the well for the truth.

The next day a person with red hands and a blue polka-dot necktie, who called himself Kelly, called at Anthony Rockwall's house, and was at once received in the library.

"Well," said Anthony, reaching for his cheque-book, "it was a good bilin' of soap. Let's see—you had $5,000 in cash."

"I paid out $300 more of my own," said Kelly. "I had to go a little above the estimate. I got the express wagons and cabs mostly for $5; but the trucks and two-horse teams mostly raised me to $10. The motormen wanted $10, and some of the loaded teams $20. The cops struck me hardest—$50 I paid two, and the rest $20 and $25. But didn't it work beautful, Mr. Rockwall? And never a rehearsal, either! The boys was on time to the fraction of a second. It was two hours before a snake could get below Greeley's statue.

"You didn't notice," said he, "anywhere in the tie-up, a kind of a fat boy without any clothes shooting arrows around with a bow, did you?"

ACTIVITIES

I. This activity will help you to think about the American attitude toward money and how it relates to your values and to the ways you spend money.

1. Make a large class mural illustrating "Value in America." You may use magazines, photographs, original drawings, titles of articles, or anything else you feel reflects the American attitude toward money.
2. Complete the chart included in the Workbook. It is designed to help you analyze the mural for the social and personal values it reflects. If you don't have a Workbook, copy the chart in the text.
3. In the first part of the chart, you must pick the three items from the mural that are most popular with Americans.
4. In the second part of the chart, list the three items in the mural that are the most expensive.
5. In the third part of the chart, list three things that *you* consider highly valuable. (They do not have to be taken from the mural.)
6. The following is a description of what to do with the items you listed:
   Column A: Enter three items from the mural.
   Column B: Write down the group or person who uses or desires the item.
   Column C: Identify the value the item has for the person or group using or desiring it.
   Column D: Pinpoint what this item and the value attached to it say about society.

	A. Item	B. Who desires it?	C. Group or individual values	D. Influence on society
Part 1. Popular items	1. 2. 3.			
Part 2. Expensive items	1. 2. 3.			
Part 3. Items you value	1. 2. 3.			

7. Discussion questions
    a. What is the difference between price and true value?
    b. How did the price of an item affect its value for the group who uses it? for you? for society?
    c. How does your notion of value relate to the American notion of value?
    d. How do the things that you value influence your values?
    e. How do your values affect how you spend your money?
    f. Why might some people buy certain items because they are expensive? How does this behavior relate to the market model?

II. Anything that people will accept as payment can be used as money. A great many different things have been used as money in the past. In this activity, you will develop standards for judging how useful different kinds of money are.

1. Divide into small groups. Each group should develop a list of standards for "good" money. (Good money must be _____.)
2. Complete the chart included in the Workbook. It is designed to help you judge different kinds of money by the standards you have developed. If you don't have a Workbook, copy the following chart.
3. Discussion questions
    a. Were your standards adequate for judging all the kinds of money?
    b. Were there any kinds of money that met all your standards? none?
    c. What might cause you to change your standards?

Kinds of money	Standard: portable	Standard: durable	Standard:	Standard:	Standard:	Standard: ....
Salt	light					
Tobacco		crumbles				
Dogs' teeth						
Cattle						
Ice cubes						
Olive oil						
Gold						
U.S. currency						
Other						

How Money Expands and Contracts

The money supply of the United States consists of two kinds of money, *currency* and *checking accounts*. Checking accounts are also called demand deposits because their owners have the right to demand them from the bank whenever they wish. The total money supply is constantly changing. Sometimes it expands (grows larger) and sometimes it contracts (gets smaller). The government prints new bills and mints new coins every year to replace those that are worn. It also changes the supply to meet people's needs.

The supply of checking account money, or demand deposits, also changes. And it is largely the banks that decide whether the supply of checking account money will expand or contract. How do the banks do this? Let's follow some ordinary bank activities and see where they lead us.

Suppose that a local lawyer named John Winslow deposits $10,000 of his earnings in his checking account. What does the bank do with this $10,000? It puts that money to use by lending it to people and charging interest. *Interest* is the fee a borrower pays the bank for the use of money.

Banking laws in the United States require a bank to set aside a certain percent of its deposits. This is called the bank's *reserves*. In this case it is 10 percent of total deposits. So the bank keeps $1,000 of Mr. Winslow's money in reserve. The other $9,000 it lends to anyone it thinks will be able to pay it back, with interest.

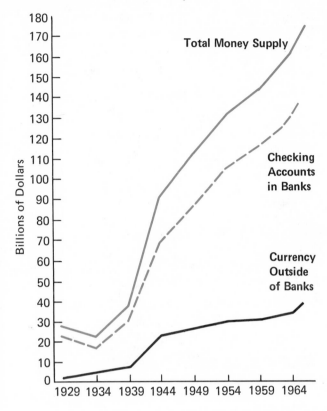

Figure 32-1   United States Money Supply, 1929–1965
What has happened to the composition of the money supply since 1929?

Next, Jane Diaz comes along and asks to borrow $9,000 for her tuition at Harrington Medical School. She signs an agreement to pay back the $9,000 with interest. The bank then gives her a check for $9,000, which she gives to the medical school. The school puts the money in its account at its own bank. That bank holds 10 percent ($900) in reserve and lends the rest, $8,100, to George Graham, who wants to buy a computer from the ABC Computer Company. When the company deposits Mr. Graham's $8,100 in its bank, that bank keeps 10 percent ($810) in reserve and lends the rest, $7,290, to Justine Craig, so she can buy a new car. The E-Z Terms Auto Agency deposits Ms. Craig's $7,290 in its account, and the process continues.

What has happened to the money supply? First of all, none of these transactions involved currency. They were all done through checking accounts. Second, the total supply of checking account money has been expanded. Here's how it happened. John Winslow still has $10,000 in his checking account. The Harrington Medical School has $9,000 in its account. The ABC Computer Company has $8,100 in its account. And the E-Z Terms Auto Agency has $7,290 in its account.

STAGE	DEPOSITS	RESERVES	LOANS
1. John Winslow	$ 10,000	$ 1,000	$ 9,000 to Jane Diaz
2. Harrington Medical School	9,000	900	8,100 to George Graham
3. ABC Computer Company	8,100	810	7,290 to Justine Craig
4. E-Z Terms Auto Agency	7,290	729	
All other stages together	65,610	6,561	59,049
TOTAL	$100,000	$10,000	$90,000

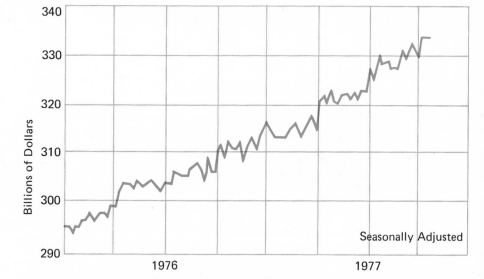

Figure 32-2   Money Supply, 1976 and 1977
Source: Federal Reserve System, 1978
Why has the money supply continued to increase?

So how much money is there in all the checking accounts? Adding $10,000, $9,000, $8,100, and $7,290 gives $34,390. In other words, the original $10,000 in checking account money has grown, because of loans, to a total of $34,390. Table 32-1 summarizes this activity.

Can this expansion go on forever? There are several things that stop the process of expansion or even reverse it. One is the law requiring the bank to keep 10 percent of its deposits in reserve. Thus, that original $10,000 deposited by Winslow is enough reserve to cover $100,000 in deposits. Therefore, when the banks have lent a total of about $90,000, they will not be able to lend any more money. When that happens, the bank will have to increase its reserves by collecting the loans it has made in the past.

Then, too, if the bank stops making loans because it cannot find any more people who are "good risks," expansion will stop. If people stop putting their money into checking accounts, the bank will not be able to make loans. Finally, if a lot of people suddenly withdraw their money all at once, the bank will have to stop making loans. Instead, it will start calling for payment of its loans so that it can increase its reserves.

In a way, the money supply seems to be based on magic. You put some money in a bank and, suddenly, there is more money. The magic, of course, is people's credit. The money you put in the bank is yours because you can count on the bank to pay it back. The bank in turn can count on being able to pay you back because it can count on its borrowers to pay it back.

Thus borrowing from a bank is different from borrowing from a friend. If you don't repay your friends, they may be hurt or angry. But if you can't pay them back, they will probably understand. If you don't pay the bank back, you lose more than your good name, or credit. If everyone acted as you did, the whole banking system would collapse.

☐ The reading for this lesson is taken from a novel by John Steinbeck. It presents a tough dilemma—all the farmers in one area have borrowed money from the bank but are unable to pay it back. They guaranteed the loans with their land. Because they cannot repay their loans, the bank now owns their land. The bankers must sell the land to get the bank's money. But this course of action could be cruel. Should the bankers take the land? Should the farmers refuse to repay the loans with their land? Think about what you believe is right. Read the story and see if you change your mind. As you read, ask yourself the following:
1. Who owns the land? Why?
2. How did collecting loans for the bank change the "owners'" views of how people should be treated?
3. How have your actions affected your beliefs?

THE GRAPES OF WRATH

The owners of the land came onto the land, or more often a spokesman for the owners came. They came in closed cars, and they felt the dry earth with their fingers, and sometimes they drove big earth augers into the ground for soil tests. The tenants, from their sun-beaten dooryards, watched uneasily when the closed cars drove along the fields. And at last the owner men drove into the dooryards and sat in their cars to talk out of the windows. The tenant men stood beside the cars for a while, and then squatted on their hams and found sticks with which to mark the dust.

In the open doors the women stood looking out, and behind them the children—corn-headed children, with wide eyes, one bare foot on top of the other bare foot, and the toes working. The women and the children watched their men talking to the owner men. They were silent.

Some of the owner men were kind because they hated what they had to do, and some of them were angry because they hated to be cruel, and some of them were cold because they had long ago found that one could not be an owner unless one were cold. And all of them were caught in something larger than themselves. Some of them hated the mathematics that drove them, and some were afraid, and some worshiped the mathematics because it provided a refuge from thought and from feeling. If a bank or a finance company owned the land, the owner man said, The Bank—or the Company—needs—wants—insists—must have—as though the Bank or the Company were a monster, with thought and feeling, which had ensnared them. These last would take no responsibility for the banks or the companies because they were men and slaves, while the banks were machines and masters all at the same time. Some of the owner men were a little proud to be slaves to such cold and powerful masters. The owner men sat in the cars and explained. You know the land is poor. You've scrabbled at it long enough, God knows.

The squatting tenant men nodded and wondered and drew figures in the dust, and yes, they knew, God knows. If the dust only wouldn't fly. If the top would only stay on the soil, it might not be so bad.

The owner men went on leading to their point: You know the land's

Why are the checks this person is filing called demand deposits? Why does the supply of checking account money change?

How might a predetermined amount of money "grow" into more money over time?

getting poorer. You know what cotton does to the land; robs it, sucks all the blood out of it.

The squatters nodded—they knew, God knew. If they could only rotate the crops they might pump blood back into the land.

Well, it's too late. And the owner men explained the workings and the thinkings of the monster that was stronger than they were. A man can hold land if he can just eat and pay taxes; he can do that.

Yes, he can do that until his crops fail one day and he has to borrow money from the bank.

But—you see, a bank or a company can't do that, because those creatures don't breathe air, don't eat side-meat. They breathe profits; they eat the interest on money. If they don't get it, they die the way you die without air, without side-meat. It is a sad thing, but it is so. It is just so.

The squatting men raised their eyes to understand. Can't we just hang on? Maybe the next year will be a good year. God knows how much cotton next year. And with all the wars—God knows what price cotton will bring. Don't they make explosives out of cotton? And uniforms? Get enough wars and cotton'll hit the ceiling. Next year, maybe. They looked up questioningly.

Why do banks keep money in reserve? What happens to this money?

We can't depend on it. The bank—the monster has to have profits all the time. It can't wait. It'll die. No, taxes go on. When the monster stops growing, it dies. It can't stay one size.

Soft fingers began to tap the sill of the car window, and hard fingers tightened on the restless drawing sticks. In the doorways of the sun-beaten tenant houses, women sighed and then shifted feet so that the one that had been down was now on top, and the toes working. Dogs came sniffing near the owner cars and wetted on all four tires one after another.

Sure, cried the tenant men, but it's our land. We measured it and broke it up. We were born on it, and we got killed on it, died on it. Even if it's no good, it's still ours. That's what makes it ours—being born on it, working it, dying on it. That makes ownership, not a paper with numbers on it.

We're sorry. It's not us. It's the monster. The bank isn't like a man.

Yes, but the bank is only made of men.

No, you're wrong there—quite wrong there. The bank is something else than men. It happens that every man in a bank hates what the bank does, and yet the bank does it. The bank is something more than men, I tell you. It's the monster. Men made it, but they can't control it.

The tenants cried, Grampa killed Indians, Pa killed snakes for the land. Maybe we can kill banks—they're worse than Indians and snakes. Maybe we got to fight to keep our land, like Pa and Grampa did.

And now the owner men grew angry. You'll have to go.

But it's ours, the tenant men cried. We—

No. The bank, the monster owns it. You'll have to go.

We'll get our guns, like Grampa when the Indians came. What then?

Well—first the sheriff, and then the troops. You'll be stealing if you try to stay, you'll be murderers if you kill to stay. The monster isn't men, but it can make men do what it wants.

But if we go, where'll we go? How'll we go? We got no money.

We're sorry, said the owner men. The bank, the fifty-thousand-acre owner can't be responsible. You're on land that isn't yours. Once over the line maybe you can pick cotton in the fall. Maybe you can go on relief. Why don't you go on west to California? There's work there, and it never gets cold. Why, you can reach out anywhere and pick an orange. Why, there's always some kind of crop to work in. Why don't you go there? And the owner men started their cars and rolled away.

The tenant men squatted down on their hams again to mark the dust with a stick, to figure, to wonder. Their sunburned faces were dark, and their sunwhipped eyes were light. The women moved cautiously out of the doorways toward their men, and the children crept behind the women, cautiously, ready to run. The bigger boys squatted beside their fathers, because that made them men. After a time the women asked, What did he want?

And the men looked up for a second, and the smolder of pain was in their eyes. We got to get off. A tractor and a superintendent. Like factories.

Where'll we go? the women asked.

We don't know. We don't know.

And the women went quickly, quietly back into the houses and herded the children ahead of them. They knew that a man so hurt and so perplexed may turn in anger, even on people he loves. They left the men alone to figure and to wonder in the dust.

After a time perhaps the tenant man looked about—at the pump put in ten years ago, with a goose-neck handle and iron flowers on the spout, at the chopping block where a thousand chickens had been killed, at the hand plow lying in the shed, and the patent crib hanging in the rafters over it.

The children crowded about the women in the houses. What we going to do, Ma? Where we going to go?

The women said, We don't know, yet. Go out and play. But don't go near your father. He might whale you if you go near him. And the women went on with the work, but all the time they watched the men squatting in the dust—perplexed and figuring.

Look through all of the visual material in this chapter again. How many are photographs? How many are drawn art? How do they work differently? What photos can you think of to replace the drawings? What drawings can replace the photos? What do your new images say about the forms of money, how money expands and contracts, and the Federal Reserve? Which of these new images do you think work best with photos and which work best with drawings?

VISUAL ACTIVITY

ACTIVITIES

I. This activity will help you to look at some of the ways in which your actions influence your standards and values.

1. Separate into four groups—A, B, C, and D. Groups A and B will present CASE #1, which will be organized like this:
    - Group A will represent the prosecution (the bank).
    - Group B will represent the defense (the farmer).
    - Groups C and D will be the jury.

    Groups C and D will present CASE #2, which will be organized like this:
    - Group C will represent the prosecution (Hemlock, the moneylender).
    - Group D will represent the defense (Sal).
    - Groups A and B will be the jury.

2. Each group meets separately to read and talk about its case and about the person or institution in the case it will represent. You have fifteen minutes in which to discuss the issues and to develop strategies for the presentation you will make in front of the jury.

CASE #1 For the people in the reading from *The Grapes of Wrath,* it must seem as if the world as they know it is doomed. How can they travel without any money or any place to go? The land was theirs just as it had been their parents' and their grandparents' before them. There must be some unwritten law that binds a man and woman to the plot of earth that has been their whole life.

Another type of survival is discussed in the narrative of this lesson. The survival of the banking system depends on the integrity of both borrowers and depositors. It only works because of the commitment made by you and the bank. The implications of what happens when the bank needs to collect the money it is owed are serious and affect everyone who has relied on the system. The farmer has not made his mortgage payment and the money he borrowed could be yours!

CASE #2 Even on her deathbed, Sal's wife had warned him never to go to Hemlock no matter how desperate his finances might be. But he had no choice. With only his meager income and no assets, what bank would give him, a penniless man with three small children, credit? He was a hard worker and some day he would make it in his company. But his bills were for the present, not the future, and Hemlock, the moneylender, represented his only chance to pay them. If he was ever going to build up credit anywhere, he had to pay his bills. This meant his youngest could get the medical care he needed, his wife's funeral would be paid for, and the family's food and rent would be covered until he got the raise he had been promised.

From the time the child next door tagged her Hemlock, Hemlock could not kick the name. She had never been popular, even with her own family. And her present occupation did not endear her to anyone. She provided an ugly but needed service to the community. How could she explain that her survival meant their survival? Eighteen hundred dollars might seem a petty amount to some, but her survival depended on it. What would happen to her credibility if word got around that Hemlock was getting soft? She brought Sal to court because he hadn't paid her the $1,800 he owed her. Was it her fault he didn't get his raise? She was just a woman doing her job.

3. You may want to arrange your seats as shown in the diagram at right so that it will be easier to organize your presentation.
4. CASE #1 will be tried first.
   a. The prosecution has five minutes to present its case.
   b. The defense has five minutes to respond.
   c. The prosecution may make one final statement.
   d. The defense may make one final statement.
   e. Members of the jury decide in favor of the defense (by putting their thumbs up) or against (by putting thumbs down).
   f. To the jury: If you decide in favor of the defense and therefore agree to extend the time payment is due, how will you judge the defendant (thumbs up or thumbs down) after 3 months? 6 months? 1 year? 2 years? 5 years?
   (Continue extending the time until the jury shows thumbs down, or until it becomes clear that it will always be in favor of the defense.)
5. CASE #2 should be tried, just as CASE #1 was, following steps a through e. Step f. To the jury: If you decide in favor of the defense, then you must decide how much money it would be acceptable for Sal to owe Hemlock: $75? $100? $350? $700? $1,000? $2,500? $5,000?
   When would you allow the moneylender to use force to get her money?
6. Discussion questions
   a. How did your opinions change as the situation changed?
   b. What is the difference between CASE #1 and CASE #2?
   c. Have your beliefs about how people should act changed in any way as a result of this activity?
   d. Can you think of other situations in which your actions have affected your beliefs?

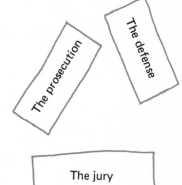

II. The purpose of this activity is to show how the actions of the banking system can expand the supply of money. The role of reserve requirements in limiting the amount of expansion will be demonstrated.

1. Divide the class into two groups. Each group should select a banker and a Federal Reserve Bank clerk. The rest of the group will function as depositors, borrowers, and consumers.
2. a. One person in each group will be given $10 in cash (including $1 in change, down to pennies).
    b. That person will deposit the $10 in the bank, and the banker will enter the deposit on the bank's statement of accounts. Use the charts in the Workbook or copy the ones in the text.
    c. One group will have a reserve requirement of 10 percent; the other group will have a reserve requirement of 50 percent. The Federal Reserve Bank clerk will collect the required reserve from the banker and enter the amount in the bank's account with the Fed.
    d. The banker will lend the amount of the deposit left (after the required reserves have been deposited in the Fed) to a member of the group and enter the loan on the bank's statement of accounts.
    e. The borrower will use the money borrowed to purchase something from a member of the group (a book, a watch, a pen, etc.).
    f. The seller of the good will then deposit the money received in the bank.
    g. Repeat Steps b–f for a total of ten rounds.
3. Discussion questions
    a. Each group should report total deposits, reserves, and loans.
    b. How did the money supply expand in your group?
    c. How did the reserve requirement affect expansion of the money supply?

BANK STATEMENT OF ACCOUNTS

Depositor	Demand Deposits	Reserves (10%)	Borrower	Amount of Loan
1. Jackie	$10.00	$1.00	Peter	$9.00
2. Ben	9.00			
3.				
4.				
5.				
6.				
7.				
8.				
9.				
10.	_____	_____		_____
TOTALS				

FEDERAL RESERVE BANK STATEMENT OF ACCOUNTS

Reserve Requirement (circle appropriate one) = 10%, 50%

Reserve Deposits
1.
2.
3.
4.
5.
6.
7.
8.
9.
10. _____
TOTAL

The Federal Reserve System and Monetary Policy

Above the banks stands a government superbank, a "bank for bankers," called the Federal Reserve System—or "the Fed," for short. It is the Fed's duty to keep an eye on the supply of money and to take steps to expand or contract it.

Why does the U.S. government worry about the money supply?

When the money supply contracts, banks are not lending as much as they did when money was expanding. And if banks don't lend money, people can't buy the houses or cars or any of the other expensive products for which they need to borrow money. Thus, the demand for these products goes down. Production goes down and workers get laid off. The result is rising unemployment.

On the other hand, if the money supply expands too rapidly, production goes up quickly in response to increased spending. As the spending for goods and services goes up, prices tend to go up as well. If prices go up too rapidly, inflation is the result.

How does the Fed control the supply of money? The laws setting up the Federal Reserve System give it three important tools.

1. The Fed can determine what percent of its deposits a bank must keep *in reserve*. If the reserve requirement is 10 percent, a bank must keep $1 in reserves out of every $10 in deposits. It can loan $9 out of every $10. If the requirement is raised to 20 percent, $2 must be kept in reserve and $8 can be

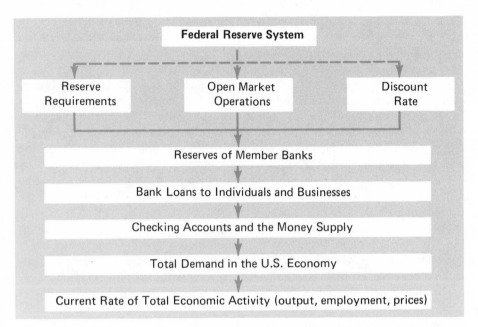

loaned out. By raising the reserve requirement, therefore, the Fed is contracting the money supply. By lowering the reserve requirement, it is expanding the money supply.

2. The Federal Reserve System lends money to banks and, like any other bank, charges interest on its loans. The *discount rate* is the interest banks must pay to borrow money from the Fed. By raising the discount rate, the Fed discourages banks from borrowing. This means they then have less money to lend to customers. By lowering the discount rate, the Fed encourages bankers to borrow from it. This means they then have more money to lend to customers. Raising the discount rate contracts the money supply. Lowering the discount rate expands the money supply.

3. The Fed is permitted by law to buy and sell government bonds. A government bond promises that the government will pay the owner the cost of the bond, plus interest, once a certain time limit is up. When the Fed sells a bond and receives a check, money is transferred to the Fed out of the bank that issued the check. This reduces the amount of money the bank has on hand for loans. When the Fed buys bonds from banks, money flows in the opposite direction. The Fed's selling bonds contracts the banks' money supplies. Buying bonds expands the banks' money supplies.

When the Fed expands the money supply, it is called an *easy money policy*. Money, in other words, is easy to borrow because there is lots of it in the banks.

When the Fed contracts the money supply, it is called a *tight money policy*. In short, money is scarce and hard to borrow. Easy money means increased demand and production, lower unemployment, and higher prices. Tight money means lower demand and production, increased unemployment, and lower prices.

Since there are pros and cons to both easy money and tight money policies, what the Fed does is always controversial. When unemployment is high, people demand easy money. When prices are too high, people demand tight money. Striking a balance between these two extremes is not an easy task. It is made harder because it is difficult to get accurate information about the economy quickly enough to make the right choice.

The Fed, through its monetary policies, attempts to adjust the economy to achieve certain goals. How can it judge its own actions? How can society judge the Fed's actions?

There are two main ways in which you judge your own and others' actions. The first is by intention. What was the action meant to do? What values did it seek to promote? Do you agree with these values? Wrecking a car to avoid an animal, for example, is not the same as wrecking a car while speeding for fun.

The second way of judging an action is by its results. How did it affect others? What did it accomplish? What did it prevent? What values did it in fact promote? People who volunteer just because it makes them look good may still end up helping others.

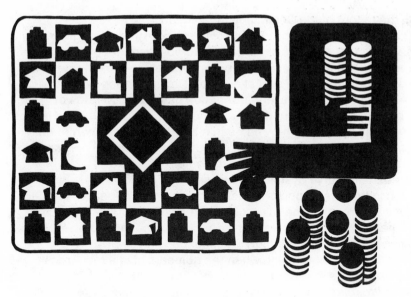

How might the Fed determine how much money a bank must keep in reserve? How does the reserve requirement affect the money supply?

☐ In the reading for this lesson, some senators question the chairperson of the Fed. The senators are trying to get information that will help them to judge the Fed's actions. As you read their discussion, ask yourself the following questions:

1. What do Burns's intentions seem to be? What does Proxmire think they should be?
2. What does Burns think the results of his actions will be? What does Proxmire think?
3. How would you judge Burns's actions?

"WE FORGET WE HAVE A PRIVATE-ENTERPRISE SYSTEM"

Who should control money and credit? The President and Secretary of the Treasury? Or—as now—the independent Federal Reserve Board?

This issue boils up in every recession as demands grow for cheap money to stimulate the economy. So, in March 1975, Congress passed a resolution requiring Federal Reserve Chairman Arthur Burns to tell it more about "Fed" plans and policies. Dr. Burns agreed to at least reveal the goal for the money supply's expansion in the year ahead. Then he and members of the Senate Banking Committee debated some basic points about the U.S. economy.

From the record of the Committee meeting on May 1—

Dr. Burns: Of late, there has been some concern in the Congress and elsewhere that supplies of money and credit were not growing fast enough. We in the Federal Reserve know that the growth rates of money and credit that are fitting at any point in time depend on basic economic conditions. At present, our nation has very high rates of unemployment and idle industrial capacity. Thus, even though an upturn in business activity may be near at hand, the restoration of full employment of our labor and capital resources will remain a central aim of public policy for many months to come.

The Federal Reserve System is now seeking a moderate rate of expansion in the total supplies of money and credit. We believe that the course we are following will promote an increase of five to seven and one-half percent in currency and checking account supplies over the next year. This is a rather high rate of expansion by past standards. But it is not too high when the numbers of idle resources are great and prices are rising.

Senator Proxmire of Wisconsin, Committee Chairman: By telling us the Federal Reserve Board's present views as to the right ranges of growth in the total supply of money and credit for the next year, you have aided the cause of informed, intelligent government.

As to your specific plans, the Joint Economic Committee heard other testimony last week. This was that we need an eight to ten percent growth in money supply over the next year if economic recovery is not to be nipped in the bud and if unemployment is to be reduced to six percent by the end of 1977. Why are these others wrong?

Dr. Burns: I am not going to say they are wrong. Their views differ from mine. I have found, Senator, that most economists move from platform to platform these days and from one hearing room to another. They pay very little heed to the business cycle. They have never even studied it thoroughly. Or, if they have, they have forgotten

How might the Federal Reserve buy and sell bonds? How does each of these affect the money supply? Why?

what they once knew. In particular, they give very little attention to the turnover of money.

Members of the economics profession put a great deal of emphasis on the stock of money. In my judgment, they are stressing the wrong thing. Far more important than the stock of money is the willingness to use the existing stocks.

The important factor in the business cycle is not the stock of money but the rate of turnover of money. This depends on the state of confidence. If you look at the record, you will find that in the first year of recovery, it is the rate of turnover of money that shoots up dramatically in contrast to the change in the existing stock. This is the main source of our difference with other economists.

Senator Proxmire: Can you tell us what your proposal will do for unemployment and prices in the next year?

Dr. Burns: The monetary path we are on is quite enough in our judgment to assure a strong economic recovery. With recovery, unemployment will, of course, come down.

Senator Proxmire: How much will it go down by the end of the year? Will it go down one percent—one-half of one percent?

Dr. Burns: I don't know, Senator, any more than you do or anybody else.

Senator Proxmire: Will it be below nine percent?

Dr. Burns: I would hope so.

Senator Proxmire: What do you assume as to the inflation rate at the end of the year?

Dr. Burns: I remain an optimist. If we act responsibly in the budget and monetary areas, the rate of inflation may come down to five percent.

Senator Packwood of Oregon: If we go ahead with a 70-billion dollar deficit next year and the tax cut we passed, will we have a good enough recovery without increased inflation? Or is 70 billion dollars too much?

Dr. Burns: It may well be too much. If so, you ought to undo some of the actions you have taken before. If you find that it is too much, then you ought to welcome a bill from the President deferring it or rescinding it. And if he is slow in doing that, you ought to get the jump on him.

Senator Biden of Delaware: Congress is faced with the question as to what effect our actions will have on interest rates. If the Fed can't or shouldn't concentrate on that, who should? How should we handle interest rates?

Dr. Burns: You know, you could leave interest rates alone. After all, we have highly competitive money and capital markets. If you are going to engage in price-control exercises, you ought to turn to those sectors of the economy where you have pockets of monopoly. Wages is one of them. We don't talk about wages. And yet we have pockets of monopoly in the field of labor.

Senator Proxmire: Are you telling us that if you had an eight or nine percent growth in the money supply, and with unemployment at an eight percent level, even with that kind of stimulus, you wouldn't be able to slow down in time to stop?

Dr. Burns: Senator, economists have a very poor record in forecasting recoveries. If they can't see where the recovery will come from, they conclude it won't come at all or will be a mild one. It's not given to us to see. We have millions of decision-making units in this country. Let's give them a chance to do their part.

You know, we kind of forget we have a dynamic, private-enterprise system. So many economists and so many others in private or political life talk as if the government pushes the economy, as if the economy is a purely passive thing. The economy contains recovery forces of its own just as it contains recession forces of its own. And now, I think, in the private economy the recovery forces are under way.

ACTIVITIES

The purpose of this activity is to investigate examples of the Federal Reserve's decisions and to judge their effects on the American economy.

1. Find and analyze a specific decision made by the Fed. Here is a list of sources from which you might find the information you need. The class should look for additional sources.

   Reader's Guide to Periodical Literature
   New York Times Index
   Congressional Record
   Federal Reserve Office in your district
   A local banker (you may want to invite a bank officer to speak to the class)

2. Use the following questions to complete your analysis:
   a. Which decision did you choose?
   b. To what economic situation was it in response?
   c. What was the Fed's course of action?
   d. What was its goal in this action?
   e. How long did it take for the results to be felt?
   f. What was the overall economic result of the action?
   g. What other actions could have been taken, and why weren't they?
3. Share your work with the class.
4. Discussion questions
   a. How did the Federal Reserve judge its actions in the example you chose?
   b. How do you judge it?
   c. How easy was it to find the information for this activity? What does this say about the Fed?

This is the Federal Reserve. What might all this activity be about? What are some of the responsibilities of the Fed?

CHAPTER 12 FISCAL POLICY

The Uses of Fiscal Policy

The U.S. government tries to control the money supply to fight unemployment and inflation. By increasing the money supply (an "easy money" policy) the government increases spending. This leads to lower unemployment and higher prices. By decreasing the money supply (a "tight money" policy) the government decreases spending. This leads to higher unemployment and lower prices. Regulating the supply of money is what economists call the government's *monetary policy.*

The government has another way of regulating economic activity. That is by using what economists call its *fiscal policy.* Fiscal policies increase or decrease the total amount of income consumers and businesses are able to spend. The more money they can spend, the more likely it will be for output, spending, and income to go up. This means that unemployment will fall and prices rise. The less money they spend, the more likely it will be for output, spending, and income to decrease. This means that unemployment will go up and prices will go down (or stay the same).

How can the government affect the amount of money spent by businesses and consumers? One obvious and important way is through its power to collect taxes. By raising taxes, the government decreases total spending. This tends to stop price increases by slowing down economic activity. Tax increases, therefore, are used to fight inflation. By lowering taxes, the government is increasing the amount of money that can be spent. This tends to make output go up. When output goes up, more people are working and earning income. Tax cuts, therefore, are used to fight unemployment.

The government has another way to affect the amount of money spent. That is by spending money itself. The government spends money between October 1 and September 30. This is called the *fiscal year.* By doing this, the government increases the demand for products. This raises output and puts more people to work. A large increase in spending tends to increase the production of goods and services dramatically. A small increase usually means that the number of jobs does not increase as fast as the number of workers looking for jobs. This means that the unemployment rate will continue to climb.

A good example of how these fiscal policies work is the tax cut voted by Congress in 1964. The first effects of this tax cut (which affected both consumers and firms) were a rise in production and a decline in unemployment. The unemployment rate was 5.2 percent in 1964. After the tax cut went into effect, the unemployment rate began to drop. It went down to 4.5 percent in 1965 and continued to go down until 1969, when it reached 3.5 percent. The Vietnam War also contributed to this decline.

Fiscal policy is controversial for a number of reasons. First of all, the government does not spend money and collect taxes just so that it can regulate unemployment and inflation. The main reason for taxes and spending is the need to provide the programs and services that citizens demand. Sometimes these programs cost so much that the government has to raise taxes even when that will have a bad effect on the economy. For example, a large tax increase to pay for a war will mean consumers have less money to spend. This will lead to unemployment in industries that are very sensitive to reduced consumer spending—the automobile industry, for instance.

What is more, when the government decides to reduce its spending, programs that are very important to some people may be cut back or even stopped. Since

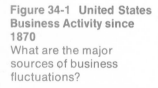

Figure 34-1 United States Business Activity since 1870
What are the major sources of business fluctuations?

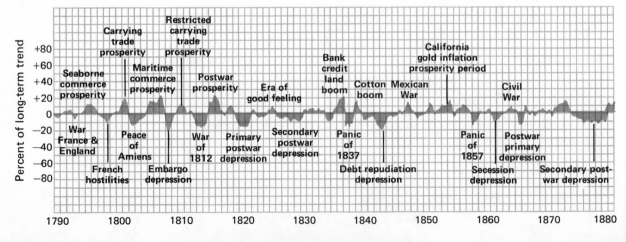

members of Congress have to face reelection every few years, they are reluctant to vote for cuts in government spending. This makes it harder for the government to use its level of spending as a way of regulating the economy.

For all these reasons, fiscal policy is a much more complicated way of controlling the economy than monetary policy is. But though it is complex, fiscal policy is very important.

Fiscal policy is also social policy. The ways in which a government collects and spends money reflect its values. The government can spend money directly to promote the values it favors. It can also use taxes to discourage certain kinds of behavior (like buying gasoline). It can encourage other actions (like giving to charity) by giving tax breaks. Both direct spending and tax breaks result in *subsidies* (extra money) for certain groups. Each subsidy reflects certain social values. Some subsidies are controversial. They reflect the values and interests of only special groups within the society. Others are accepted by nearly everyone. They reflect values that we all share, or at least never question.

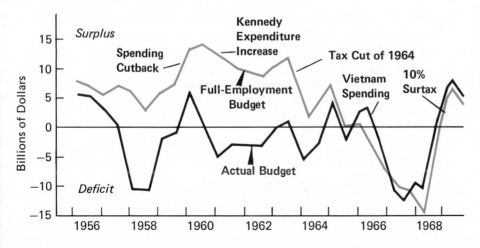

Figure 34-2   Full Employment and Actual Budget Deficits
Source: Federal Reserve System
During the years that the budget was in deficit, what would have happened if it had been possible to achieve full employment?

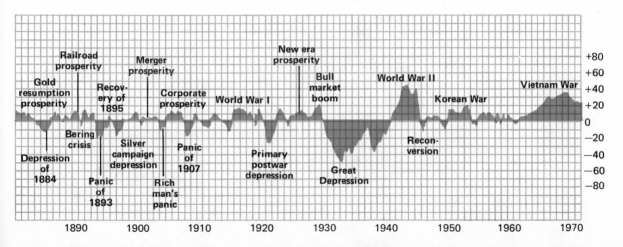

**Figure 34-3
Government Spending
and GNP, 1929–1971**
Source: Department of
Commerce
What seems to be the
long-term relationship
between government
spending and GNP? What
might change that
relationship?

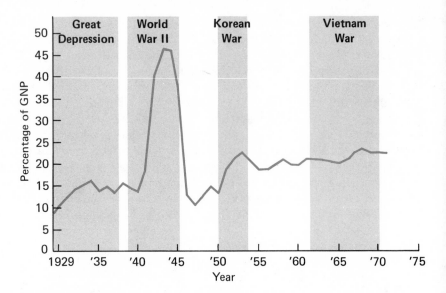

☐ The reading for this lesson describes several of these subsidies.
As you read it, ask yourself the following questions:
1. What values does each subsidy promote?
2. How does each subsidy benefit society as a whole? How does
    each subsidy benefit particular groups?
3. What important subsidies are left out of this article?

SOMETHING FOR ALMOST EVERYBODY

To many hard-hit taxpayers, the words "Government subsidy" mean
welfare handouts and massive loans to shaky corporations.

The fact is that most Americans get some sort of subsidy from the
Federal Government.

Sometimes the help comes in the form of direct handouts. More
often it is disguised in tax breaks or low-cost loans that people accept
without even knowing they're being subsidized.

Add them all together, and the Government's subsidy programs
cost taxpayers 111 billion dollars a year. This is without counting the
flood of checks being mailed out in direct cash assistance for the
needy.

That total means a 72 per cent increase in costs since 1970. And the fiscal year beginning July 1, 1975, is expected to show another jump to at least 116 billion dollars.

Although many major subsidies aren't listed in the budget, subsidies will be equal in size to one third of the total federal spending in 1976. This is according to estimates worked out by staff experts in Congress and at the White House.

Aid for the "average." Although many subsidies do go to aid businesses and low-income families, many billions are also spent to aid the average American. Some examples:

- Interest on mortgages and other loans that people routinely deduct from their incomes before figuring their taxes will cost the Treasury almost 10 billion dollars in 1976.
- 244 million dollars will go to help pay the interest costs of student loans that aid many Americans in financing their way through college.
- 179 million dollars will be granted to symphonies, theaters, operas and other cultural events to aid sponsors and performers. As this subsidy also helps keep ticket prices down, it is an indirect benefit to audiences.

Those are just three of the ways the Government assists selected groups of individuals and businesses through its subsidy programs.

More and more, subsidies come in for criticism. Opponents contend that many subsidies are too costly and hard to control. They argue that they often do not achieve the goals for which they were enacted.

Despite criticism, few subsidies are ever ended or reduced. In fact, pressure is constantly brought to bear on federal agencies and on Congress to expand them.

Big, but unnoticed. One reason is that so many Americans benefit from them. Another is that so few are aware of how extensive subsidies really are.

There's a 543-million-dollar subsidy, for instance, in Government payments to farmers. Under one program, the Government guarantees farmers a minimum price at harvest time. It also pays the difference whenever the market price falls below the guaranteed level.

There's a subsidy, too, in those loans by the Export-Import Bank to American exporters and foreign buyers at below-market interest rates. It will cost 403 million dollars to make up the difference between the

What are some of the ways individual income tax is used as a means of fiscal policy?

interest rate borrowers pay on the loans and the higher cost of money the Treasury pays to raise the money from banks and other lenders.

There's even a subsidy in many of those deductions and credits that confuse taxpayers each year. That's because each of those rules results in lower taxes. So far as the Treasury is concerned, this is the same as simply paying out cash.

None of these subsidies is as obvious as a direct handout. But all have major impact on the people they were designed to help.

Some examples. How do the subsidies work? Take a look at some of the biggest—

That deduction from taxable income for mortgage-interest payments shows just how complex a subsidy can be. Although home-owners benefit, the tax break is really a subsidy to the housing industry.

By making it easier for taxpayers to buy homes, the deduction boosts the demand for houses. It also ups demand for all the furniture, appliances, rugs and other items that go into them.

The subsidy will cost 6.5 billion dollars in 1976. Yet, because it's

Are corporate taxes also used as a means of fiscal policy? Explain.

What are some of the
things war does to
taxation? How does this
affect both businesses
and consumers?

granted to taxpayers instead of to producers, the huge size of the aid
program gets less attention.

The tax system will also give a whopping 16.1-billion-dollar subsidy
to states and localities. It will do this by letting taxpayers deduct the
cost of state and local sales, gasoline, property and income taxes
from their incomes. By absorbing some of the local tax bite through
the deduction, the Federal Government makes it easier for states and
cities to raise taxes.

The federal food-stamp program is another complex subsidy. In
fact, experts disagree over just who benefits and how much they
receive. What's clear is that about 4 billions will be spent this year to
help low-income people buy food. But since that means there's more
demand for food, some of the subsidy also goes to boosting incomes
for farmers, food producers and retailers.

Government agencies that make loans also offer many subsidies.
Loans to students and home buyers take up much of the loan-subsidy
budget. The farming industry is always one of the biggest recipients.
In fiscal 1975, low-interest loans to aid farmers are costing 2 billion
dollars.

A SAMPLING OF THE BREAKS PEOPLE GET

Direct Subsidies (in billions)		Indirect Subsidies (in billions)	
Medicaid payments	$5.7	Special treatment of individuals' capital gains	$7.0
Veterans' education benefits	3.1	Tax-free pension-plan payments	5.0
Medicare benefits	3.0	Interest deduction on home mortgages	4.9
Farm price supports, acreage payments	2.9	Investment tax credit	4.6
Food stamps	2.8	Deduction for charitable contributions	4.6
Postal Service subsidy	2.0	Lower tax rate for small corporations	3.3
Revenue sharing for manpower programs	1.9	Exclusion of employer contributions for medical insurance	2.9
Public-housing assistance	1.3	Depletion allowance for natural resources	2.1
School-lunch program	1.2	Tax-exempt interest for individuals on State, local securities	1.1
Mass-transit grants	0.9	Excess depreciation on buildings	1.0
Merchant-marine subsidies	0.5		

What are some of the ways taxes are used to discourage certain kinds of behavior?

ACTIVITIES

I. In this activity you will decide what values are reflected in the subsidies voted by Congress and which groups are benefited by them.

1. Select two or three items from the lists of direct subsidies and indirect subsidies included in the reading for this lesson.
2. You will need to decide three things about the subsidies you choose.
   a. What was the value that society intended to promote at the time the subsidy was created?
   b. Who at first was intended to benefit from the subsidy?
   c. What other group or groups have benefited indirectly?
3. Following the example, enter the subsidies you chose to analyze and your answers to the three questions on the chart in the Workbook. If you don't have a Workbook, copy the one in the text on a separate sheet of paper.
4. Discussion questions
   a. Does your notion of value change after you see what and how other groups benefit?
   b. What differences are there between direct subsidies and tax subsidies in terms of values? in terms of direct beneficiaries? in terms of indirect beneficiaries?
   c. What subsidies has your family ever qualified for? What values are reflected in them? Who else benefits from them?

Subsidy	A. Value(s)	B. Intended beneficiary	C. Other beneficiary
interest deductions on mortgage payments	stable neighborhoods	homeowners	housing industry

II. In this activity you will decide what fiscal and monetary policies are necessary to regulate economic activity.

1. Divide the class into small groups.
2. Carefully study the Economic Indicators for the situation shown at right. As a group, discuss the problems that you feel are present.
3. Following your discussion, decide which of the various monetary and fiscal policies should be used and complete the chart in the Workbook. If you don't have a Workbook, copy the chart in the text on a separate sheet of paper.
4. Discussion questions
    a. Was the economy in a state of depression, inflation, or stability in the situation?
    b. As a result of the actions that you proposed, would the economy expand or contract? Would the budget deficit increase or decrease? Would GNP increase or decrease?
    c. Who would benefit from the policies that you chose? What values are reflected in your choices?

Policy Alternative	Why Selected
1. Raise or lower corporate taxes	
2. Raise or lower personal taxes	
3. Increase or decrease government spending	
4. Lower or raise discount rate	
5. Raise or lower reserve requirements	
6. Sell or buy securities	
7. No action necessary	
8. Direct controls necessary	

Economic Indicators

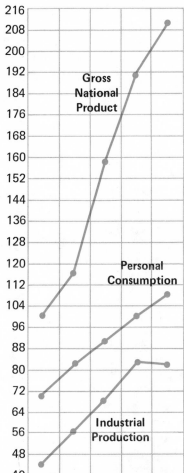

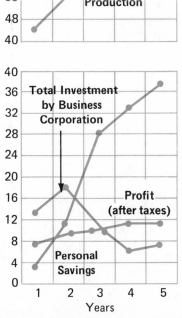

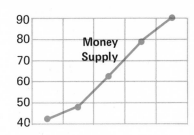

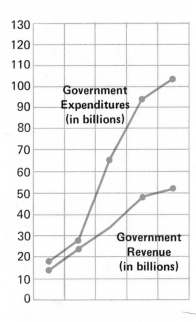

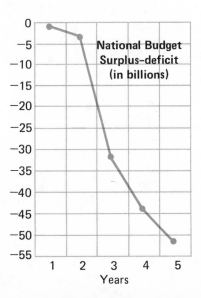

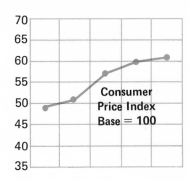

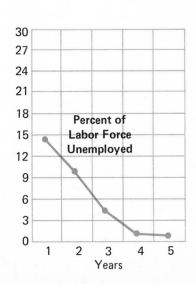

The Multiplier Effect and the Acceleration Principle

Nothing in the economy can change without causing changes throughout the system. This is easy to see in the case of the government's fiscal policies, where the effects can be widespread and startling.

Think of what happens when the government decides to spend a lot more this year than last year, or when it decides to cut taxes. In each case the first effect is to put more money in the hands of consumers and businesses, who turn right around and spend that money. Consumers spend it on consumer goods. Businesses spend it on wages, on investment in new machines or buildings, or to hire more workers. Each time a dollar is spent, it goes into the hands of someone else who spends it again. The process goes on in this way in what is called the *multiplier effect*. Each original dollar spent in effect multiplies itself by causing more spending.

The multiplier effect works like this. Suppose a manufacturer of motorcycles spends $10,000,000 on a new factory. That $10,000,000 is received by various people and firms. People affected include the workers who build the factory, the contractors who supply the materials for its construction, the architects who design it, the plumbers who put in the pipes, and many more. The money received is then spent, or at least part of it is spent. Some of it gets saved and some of it goes to the government in the form of taxes.

Assume that most people spend about two-thirds of what they receive. What then happens to the $10,000,000? Two-thirds of it ($6,666,666) will be spent by the plumbers, architects, and workers on consumers goods, wages, new equipment, extra employees, and other things. Two-thirds of that $6,666,666 ($4,444,444) is then respent by other consumers and businesses. Two-thirds of the $4,444,444 ($2,962,962) is respent, and so on, until the end of the process is reached. By that time, about $20,000,000 will have been spent. When added to the original $10,000,000, this gives $30,000,000—or three times what was started with. This means that if people spend two-thirds of their income, the multiplier effect is 3. Each original dollar spent will cause a total of $3 in extra spending. The chart below shows how this process works with a smaller sum.

Economists who have studied the spending habits of American consumers and businesses report that most people spend from one-half to two-thirds of their income. This means that the multiplier is usually somewhere between 2 and 3.

A similar principle affects businesses when they spend more on capital goods. This is called *investment spending*. For example, a shoe manufacturer has ten machines, each one of which makes 10,000 pairs of shoes yearly. This gives a total of

How is the money spent by this individual consumer spent again by others?

How $10 of original spending results eventually in $30 of total spending:
Original $10.00 received by Al, who spends 2/3,
　　or $6.66, which is received by Betty, who spends 2/3,
　　or $4.44, which is received by Cynthia, who spends 2/3,
　　or $2.96, which is received by David, who spends 2/3,
　　or $1.97, which is received by Ed, who spends 2/3,
　　or $1.32, which is received by Frank, who spends 2/3,
　　or $ .87, which is received by Ginny, who spends 2/3,
　　or $ .58, which is received by Hank, who spends 2/3,
　　or $ .39, which is received by Isabel, who spends 2/3,
　　or $ .26, which is received by Jack, who spends 2/3,
　　or $ .17, which is received by Ken, who spends 2/3,
　　or $ .11, which is received by Luke, who spends 2/3,
　　or $ .07, which is received by Mary, who spends 2/3,
　　or $ .05, which is received by Nancy, who spends 2/3,
　　or $ .03, which is received by Oscar, who spends 2/3,
　　or $ .02, which is received by Paula, who spends 2/3,
　　or $ .01　(actually a little more than 1¢, which is as far as the process can
　　　　　　　go, since 1¢ cannot be divided).
　　　　　All this spending and respending gives a total of

$19.91　(approximately $20) for a total of nearly $30 (the original $10
　　　　plus the extra $20)—3 times the original spending.

**Table 35-1
The Magic Multiplier**

100,000 pairs a year. The company has to replace one machine each year as it wears out. Its total investment spending is therefore one machine per year.

Assume that the government increases its spending or lowers taxes. Consumers now have more money to spend and so they buy 110,000 pairs of shoes each year—10 percent more than the year before. To meet this new demand, the company will have to buy an extra machine in addition to the replacement machine. This makes a total investment spending of two machines. Thus, investment spending has increased 100 percent as the result of a 10 percent increase in consumer spending. This is known as the *acceleration principle*. Table 35-1 illustrates this principle.

But notice what happens if, in the third year, consumers buy 120,000 pairs of shoes. Demand has increased again. The total investment spending is still two machines, the same as in the second year. In other words, consumer spending has increased another 10 percent but investment spending has stayed the same. If in the fourth year consumers buy the same number of shoes as in the third year

Table 35-2 The Acceleration Principle

YEAR	SALES	NUMBER OF MACHINES	NEW MACHINES	NEW MACHINES PLUS REPLACEMENT MACHINES
1	100,000	10	0	1
2	110,000	11	1	2
3	120,000	12	1	2
4	120,000	12	0	1

Figure 35-1 The Multiplier Effect

Why do increases in government spending or taxes have multiplied effects?

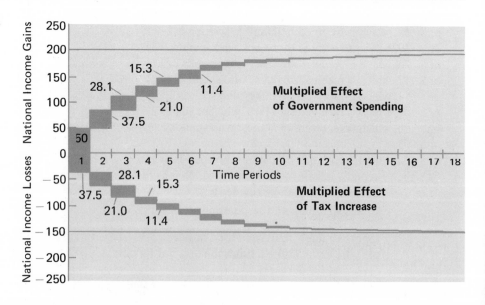

(120,000), the company will only have to buy one new machine—a replacement for an old one. Total investment spending is now one machine. Consumer spending has remained the same, but investment spending has declined by 50 percent.

The acceleration principle helps explain why the economy has to keep growing in order to stay in the same place. It is not enough for consumer spending to stay the same, or even to increase at the same rate each year. If consumer spending does not go up at a faster rate this year than last year, spending by businesses will start to go down. When it goes down fast enough, unemployment starts to climb.

The multiplier effect and the acceleration principle affect the carrying out of fiscal policies. Similar principles may operate when people or societies try to put their social values into practice.

An idea or program that starts small may grow rapidly as more people get on the bandwagon. People influenced by the program may go on to influence others. This is the multiplier effect.

Acceleration may also be at work when people put their social goals into practice. A program becomes a promise. People come to expect and demand it. They become dependent on the new social service, just as a company that invests in or produces a new machine becomes dependent on an increased level of demand. Then the program will no longer seem something special. It may even come to be seen as too little, so that some people feel they have slipped backward.

How is the money spent by this corporation on construction spent again by others?

☐ The reading for this lesson is by Lewis Carroll. It illustrates the acceleration principle. The acceleration principle helps explain why the economy has to keep growing in order to stay in the same place. As you read the selection, ask yourself the following questions:

1. Why does the acceleration principle affect producers of capital goods more than it does producers of consumer goods?
2. How would Alice judge the success of a social or economic program? How would the Red Queen judge its success?
3. What values are reflected in each way of judging?

┌─ THROUGH THE LOOKING-GLASS ─┐

For some minutes Alice stood without speaking, looking out in all directions over the country—and a most curious country it was. There were a number of tiny little brooks running straight across it from side to side, and the ground between was divided up into squares by a number of little green hedges, that reached from brook to brook.

"I declare it's marked out just like a large chess-board!" Alice said

at last. "There ought to be some men moving about somewhere—and so there are!" she added in a tone of delight, and her heart began to beat quick with excitement as she went on. "It's a great huge game of chess that's being played—all over the world—if this *is* the world at all, you know. Oh, what fun it is! How I *wish* I was one of them! I wouldn't mind being a Pawn, if only I might join—though of course I should *like* to be a Queen, best."

She glanced rather shyly at the real Queen as she said this, but her companion only smiled pleasantly, and said, "That's easily managed. You can be the White Queen's Pawn, if you like, as Lily's too young to play; and you're in the Second Square to begin with: when you get to the Eighth Square you'll be a Queen—" Just at this moment, somehow or other, they began to run.

Alice never could quite make out, in thinking it over afterwards, how it was that they began: all she remembers is, that they were running hand in hand, and the Queen went so fast that it was all she could do to keep up with her: and still the Queen kept crying "Faster! Faster!" but Alice felt she *could not* go faster, though she had no breath left to say so.

The most curious part of the thing was, that the trees and the other things round them never changed their places at all: however fast they went, they never seemed to pass anything. "I wonder if all the things move along with us?" thought poor puzzled Alice. And the Queen seemed to guess her thoughts, for she cried "Faster! Don't try to talk!"

Not that Alice had any idea of doing *that.* She felt as if she would never be able to talk again, she was getting so much out of breath: and still the Queen cried "Faster! Faster!" and dragged her along. "Are we nearly there?" Alice managed to pant out at last.

"Nearly there!" the Queen repeated. "Why, we passed it ten minutes ago! Faster!" And they ran on for a time in silence, with the wind whistling in Alice's ears, and almost blowing her hair off her head, she fancied.

"Now! Now!" cried the Queen. "Faster! Faster!" And they went so fast that at last they seemed to skim through the air, hardly touching the ground with their feet, till suddenly, just as Alice was getting quite exhausted, they stopped, and she found herself sitting on the ground, breathless and giddy.

The Queen propped her up against a tree, and said kindly, "You may rest a little, now."

Alice looked round her in great surprise. "Why, I do believe we've been under this tree the whole time! Everything's just as it was!"

"Of course it is," said the Queen. "What would you have it?"

"Well, in *our* country," said Alice, still panting a little, "you'd generally get somewhere else—if you ran very fast for a long time as we've been doing."

"A slow sort of country!" said the Queen. "Now, *here,* you see, it takes all the running *you* can do, to keep in the same place. If you want to get somewhere else, you must run at least twice as fast as that!"

 X  X  X

ACTIVITIES

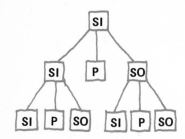

Day	Number of letters received by principal
1	1
2.	2

SI = student in the class
SO = student out of class
P = principal
X = break in the chain

I. This chain letter activity will show you how the multiplier effect can be used to help bring about changes important in your life.

1. As a class, choose an issue about which you will write to your school principal. The issue should deal with matters that are important and relevant to you. Try to select one that might receive support from your principal if a large number of students became involved and backed it. You may want to consider a community service issue, a student government concern, or a school environmental problem.

2. One person from the class begins the chain by writing letters to three people—one to the principal, one to a person in the class, and one to a person outside the class. The letter to the principal should request support for the issue the class has chosen in step #1 of this activity. The letters to the two other people should also request them to do the following:
   a. Write a letter to the principal asking support for the issue.
   b. Write to two students (the letter to the student in the class should include the direction to write to one person in the class just as you have done) asking them to continue the chain.
   c. Pass your letters on the day after you receive your letter.

3. Use the diagram in the Workbook, or copy the one in the text, to estimate how many letters the principal will receive in two weeks' time if the chain is not broken. Check with the principal each day to see how many have been received. In doing this, you can check your diagram to see if and when the chain has been broken.

4. Someone should volunteer to inform the principal of this project. Place a mailbox or envelope near the principal's office where letters can be dropped. Then check every day to count the number of letters that have been received.

5. Discussion questions
   a. How well did the multiplier effect work in this activity?
   b. In what ways is this activity similar to the way the multiplier effect works in business?
   c. The chain letter is a temporary phenomenon. How could it become a more permanent one?

II. This activity is designed to help you see what can happen when an idea is put into practice.

1. Divide into two groups both of which will do the same activity. Each group then forms three committees—a Values Committee, a Policy Committee, and a Consequences Committee.
2. The committees should follow this procedure:
    a. The Values Committee chooses a value that is not adequately represented in today's society. This begins round 1.
    b. The chosen value is then given to the Policy Committee. Its job is to create a policy or program that would support or reflect that value. The policy should not duplicate an existing policy.
    c. A brief description of the policy should then be given to the Consequences Committee. This committee must decide or predict how society would be affected if the policy were put into practice.
    d. A short explanation of the consequences must be given to the Values Committee, which decides what value or standard is reflected in the new situation. The Values Committee then picks another value that is not reflected in society and passes it on to the Policy Committee. This begins round 2.
3. There may be succeeding rounds until the committees have exhausted their creative abilities, until there is no more social need for them to exist, or until time runs out.
4. Below is a diagram of how the activity should be structured. Fill in the chart in the Workbook or copy this one on a piece of paper.

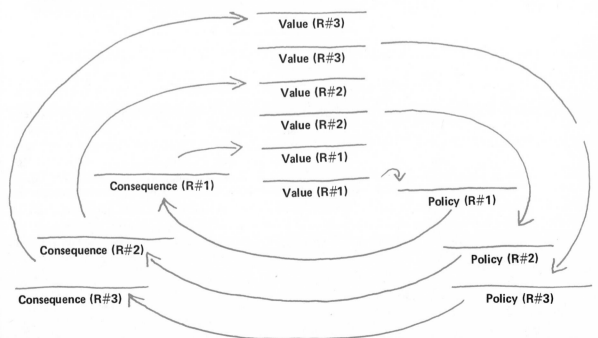

The National Debt

Government fiscal policy has one more important dimension. The government's decision to raise or lower taxes or to increase or decrease spending also has an effect on the size of the *national debt*. The national debt is the money that the federal government has borrowed to pay for expenses not covered by taxes.

Most of the current national debt was acquired as a result of wars. During wartime, the government is forced to spend huge amounts of money. Yet there is a limit to how high taxes can go. The shortage is made up by borrowing. The same thing occurs, though on a smaller scale, in peacetime, when government expenses often exceed tax revenues.

The national debt is owed to a variety of groups. About 25 percent of the debt is owed to workers as they become eligible to collect Social Security payments. Five percent is owed to foreign lenders. The rest is held by American banks, corporations, state and local governments, individual citizens, and the Federal Reserve. It is held mainly in the form of *government securities*. These are bonds promising to pay the owner the purchase price of the bond plus interest. They are sold in the market much like any other product or service. Some government securities, such as *Government Savings Bonds,* are payable after a fairly long period of time (7 years, 9 months). Others, such as *Treasury Bills,* are payable in only 3 to 6 months.

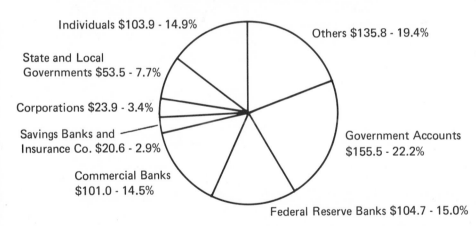

Individuals $103.9 - 14.9%

State and Local Governments $53.5 - 7.7%

Corporations $23.9 - 3.4%

Savings Banks and Insurance Co. $20.6 - 2.9%

Commercial Banks $101.0 - 14.5%

Others $135.8 - 19.4%

Government Accounts $155.5 - 22.2%

Federal Reserve Banks $104.7 - 15.0%

Why is a large portion of the national debt owed to those over 65?

Figure 36-3   Who Owns the National Debt? (in billions) *Source:* Economic Report of the President, 1978 How much of the national debt is held by government or the Federal Reserve banks? What would happen if the debt were paid off?

The national debt has always been a subject of controversy. When it was much smaller than it is today, many people thought that the nation would collapse if the debt got much bigger. The debt did get a lot bigger but the nation did not collapse. The debt grows because people are willing to lend the government money. And they are willing to lend money because they are fairly sure that the U.S. government will be able to pay off its loans as promised.

A lot of people worry about the size of the national debt. They argue that no household or business can afford to remain in debt forever, and neither can the government. Yet many economists feel that the size of the debt is not very important. They argue that so long as the economy is healthy and strong, the government will continue to "earn income." That is, it will collect taxes. So it will always be able to make its annual payments on the debt.

But the debt does have an important effect on the economy. Payments on the debt, like all government payments, must come from taxes. But the people who pay the taxes are not always the same people who own the government securities. Poor people and people with modest incomes do not normally own government savings bonds or treasury bills. So paying interest on the debt, or paying the debt itself, often results in a redistribution of income from the poor to the rich.

The most significant effect of the national debt, however, is its influence on consumer and business spending. After all, the government borrows money in order to spend it. Government spending tends to increase the demand for goods and services. This increases output, income, and employment. On the other hand, too much borrowing and too much government spending can be inflationary.

How can you judge a social or fiscal policy, such as the policy of increasing the national debt? You can look at it from the personal point of view. Should people go into debt? Are policy makers acting in good faith? Do you agree with their values? How does this policy affect people's lives? their values?

You can also look at a policy from a social point of view. Is it trying to promote the kind of society you would like to have? Is the policy good for society as a whole, or only for certain groups? What are the actual results of the policy?

Figure 36-1 (left) Size of National Debt

Figure 36-2 (right) National Debt as a Percentage of GNP
Source: Economic Report of the President, 1978
What has happened to the size of the national debt? to its relationship to GNP?

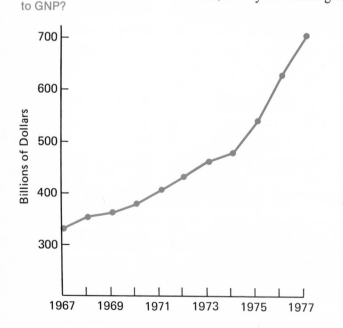

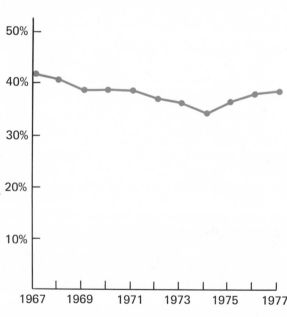

☐ The reading for this lesson was published by the Federal Reserve Bank of Philadelphia. It looks at the arguments people give for allowing the debt to rise and at the arguments for keeping the debt as low as possible. As you read the article, ask yourself the following:

1. Which arguments are in terms of people? Which are in terms of society?
2. What are the best arguments for allowing the debt to grow? What are the best arguments for keeping it as low as possible?
3. How would you judge the national debt?

NATIONAL DEBT OR NATIONAL ASSET?

Many people view the national debt in the same light as they might a museum painting that is hard to understand. Because it is strange, it strikes them as ugly. It suggests a mortgage on the future, rampant inflation, or even the nation's bankruptcy.

Clashes on the debt date back almost to the nation's start. Today, the dispute over the debt is even more common than it was then. One reason for this is that people tend to see the debt only from the borrower's side. They worry about the government's owing a lot of money. Because the effect of the debt depends in large part on who puts up the money and how they do it, it must also be looked at from the lender's side.

Opponents of the national debt believe that by having one, or by increasing it, "we are passing a burden to our grandchildren." They think that future generations will have to give up part of their income to reduce, or at least to pay interest on, the debt. But this doesn't have to be so.

Who the country's creditors are makes a lot of difference. If the

How does paying interest on the national debt, or paying the debt itself cause a redistribution of income?

U.S. Government borrowed from foreign lenders, for instance, it would have to send something of value abroad to reduce the principal and/or to pay the interest on its loans. But if it borrowed from lenders in this country, the debt would not be a burden on the country as a whole. For the most part, this is the case. The federal government has borrowed 95 percent of the money it needs from American lenders.

Yet even though the national debt may not be a burden for the United States as a whole, it can weigh more heavily on some Americans than on others. Of course, if each citizen and business paid taxes in exact proportion to the amount of government securities they held, the debt would be a very small burden. For they would get back in interest or principal repayments an amount nearly equal to the part of their taxes that was used for keeping the debt stable. It doesn't work out quite this way in practice.

The proportion of total taxes some people pay is greater than the proportion of federal securities they own, and vice versa. For instance, lower income groups in general do not own large amounts of government securities. Yet they pay many taxes besides the income tax. These taxes—on sales, food, gas—are not in proportion to income. So, because a part of all taxes are used for debt service, those with modest incomes are burdened to a greater degree.

On the plus side, it can be said that the existence of the debt makes the Federal Reserve Bank more effective. It works like this: The existence of many lenders who hold vast amounts of government securities makes it possible for the Federal Reserve to buy or sell on the open market. These open market dealings are one of the Federal Reserve's most important tools for influencing bank lending.

For example, when the Federal Reserve buys government securities, it pays out a special money that the commercial banks can use as reserves to increase their lending capacity. When the Federal Reserve sells securities, it gets this reserve money back; this in turn reduces the banks' lending ability. A huge supply of government securities gives the Federal Reserve a tool to help lift the economy out of serious recessions and depressions. If a recession should strike, and the demand for loans fade, the banks would be able to use their excess reserves to buy up some of the vast quantity of government securities on the market. These purchases would put spendable cash in the hands of former security holders and thus help to bring about recovery.

Is the debt leading us to national bankruptcy, as some people think? Bankruptcy is what occurs when lenders demand to be repaid and the borrower can't make it. The chances that a high proportion of the lenders of the national debt would demand repayment at once are

What is the function of government bonds?
How do they affect the national debt?

very slight. For one thing, only a small part of the total debt comes due at any one time. More important, most lenders would rather keep the securities than get their money back. Banks, trust and endowment funds, insurance companies, and individuals want safe investments. Government securities fit this bill well. Both the taxing power of the federal government and the economic strength of the United States are behind them.

"Is the national debt too big?" First, we have to ask, "Compared to what?" and "Compared to when?" For instance, in 1965 the national debt stood at $320 billion. But even this huge figure was only 50 percent of the GNP for that year. By comparison, the debt in 1946 was 124 percent of GNP. Other relative measures of the size of the national debt would be how much it amounted to for each person in the country, and what percentage of the GNP interest payments on the debt are. Are these figures going up or down over time? The most vital thing to find out is whether the debt has grown bigger or smaller in relation to the U.S. economy and the nation's ability to carry out its obligations.

Debt, or credit if you are looking at it from the lender's side, seems to be needed for economic growth. The lending-borrowing process transfers money from those who have saved it to those who wish to use it for productive purposes. In other words, it takes money out of mattresses and cookie jars—or savings accounts, with their low rates of interest—and puts it to work in the form of factories, machines, schools, and highways.

The importance of the debt to the nation can be shown by looking at what might happen if it were paid off or greatly reduced. The government would pay off the debt by collecting more in taxes than it spent. Reduced government spending, or higher taxes, or both would cause a drop in total spending—at least for a while. Purchasing power would be returned to those who had held the government securities. All these lenders would most likely search for other safe and profitable investments. But since the supply of government securities would then be very reduced, good investments would be harder to find. With borrowers in the driver's seat, interest rates on those investments still available would fall sharply. And this would have a bad effect on the many individuals and financial institutions who depend on interest for all or a part of their income. For these reasons, many modern economists believe that the national debt need not be reduced at all.

One real danger of the national debt is that we will come to view it as a sort of magic that can give us something for nothing. In this way we could lose our respect for sound financial principles. But spending tomorrow's income for today's goods and services is a valid and useful practice. The effective use of debt has done much to give America a high standard of living in the past generation. Has it now gotten a little out of hand? It is worth remembering that debt can be our servant if it is used wisely. But used recklessly, it has the power to make us its slave.

Select from any source, except this chapter, either drawings, paintings, or photos, two of which represent some aspect of the "multiplier effect" and two, the "acceleration principle." How are the images different? How are the concepts "multiplier effect" and "acceleration principle" different? Are these differences reflected in your images? Are there people in these images? How do they function in terms of the two concepts?

VISUAL
ACTIVITY

ACTIVITIES

Learning to judge the national debt can help teach you how to judge other social issues. This activity will show you how to judge policies both from a micro and a macro perspective.

1. Analyze the national debt by answering the questions on the following chart. Use the chart in the Workbook or copy the one in the text.

NATIONAL DEBT

Micro (personal)	Macro (societal)
A. What are the economic consequences for you as an individual?	A. What are the consequences of the national debt for the American economy as a whole?
B. Do you think people should go deeply into debt?	B. How does the national debt affect the relationship between the public and private sectors?
C. How does it affect the way you relate to others?	C. How does the national debt influence the country's values and actions?
D. Do you favor this policy?	D. Do you favor this policy?

2. Now select a social issue that is important to you. Place it at the top of the next chart and analyze it as you did the national debt.

SOCIAL ISSUE: _____

Micro (personal)	Macro (societal)
A. What are the consequences of this issue for you as an individual?	A. What are the consequences of this issue for the society as a whole?
B. Do you think people should act this way?	B. What kind of society does this produce?
C. How will this social issue affect your future?	C. How does the social issue affect the future of society?
D. Do you favor this policy?	D. Do you favor this policy?

3. Discussion questions
    a. Do your micro and macro judgments always agree? If not, how can you bring them together?
    b. How did this activity help you to judge the national debt? a social issue? How do you judge them?
    c. How is the national debt like your social concern? In what ways are they different?

FOUR

CHANGE

CHAPTER 13 ECONOMIC GROWTH

Increased Population, Investment, and Productivity

The growth of the U.S. economy is measured in constant dollar GNP. This means that the GNP is adjusted to take into account increases in prices. If the adjusted GNP is five percent larger this year than last, the economy has grown by five percent. Economic growth does not measure what is produced, only whether there is more of it this year than last.

Economic growth is influenced by many things. *Population growth* is one big factor. If production stays the same while the population increases, everyone's share of goods and services will be less. This is because the total has to be divided among more people. But at times population growth can by itself cause economic growth. An increase in the number of workers, for instance, means that production can increase. More people also means a larger demand.

What kind of population growth takes place is also important. If the population grows because of a higher birth rate, there will be an increased demand for certain kinds of goods and services—diapers and daycare, to name some early demands. Later on, there will be a higher demand for grade-school classrooms, children's clothing, and Christmas toys. If population growth is caused by immigration the effect will be different. New citizens will need to be trained in new jobs. Most will need to learn a new language. Housing for families will be required right away. If the population grows because people are living longer, then

**Figure 37-1   (left)
Distribution of
Population by Age and
Sex in the United States.**
Source: Bureau of the
Census.
What is the significance
of this distribution of
population?

an entirely different set of demands will arise. The country will need more medical care to take care of its old people. It will need nursing homes or old-age centers. Each kind of population growth produces its own set of demands for goods and services.

Another big factor in economic growth is the creation of new capital resources, such as machines, tools, and factories. This is called *investment.* Without new capital resources, production will not keep pace with population growth.

There are two kinds of investment, autonomous and induced. *Autonomous* investment is caused by influences from outside the economy. New inventions are a good example. When farmers first used machine-driven harvesters, the amount of land they could farm increased greatly. Other examples of outside forces that affect investment are wars, the discovery of new resources (such as oil or gold), and population growth.

Induced investment results from the host of decisions made by consumers, bankers, business leaders, and governments. Examples of such decisions include increased government spending, tax cuts, and wage increases. They all permit consumers to buy more goods and services than producers can make. When this happens, producers will invest in new plants and equipment so they can meet the higher demand.

The final important influence on economic growth is the rate of *productivity.* This is a measure of how much of a product each worker can make. Greater

**Figure 37-2   (right)
Components of
Population Change
in the United States
(millions of persons)**
Source: Bureau of the
Census.
How might the discovery
of a cure for cancer affect
the projection for the year
2000?

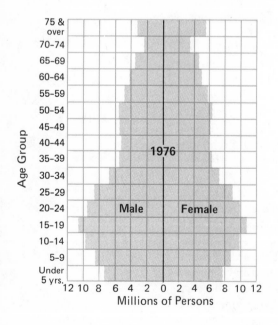

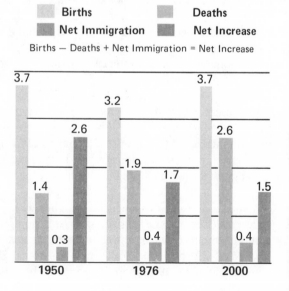

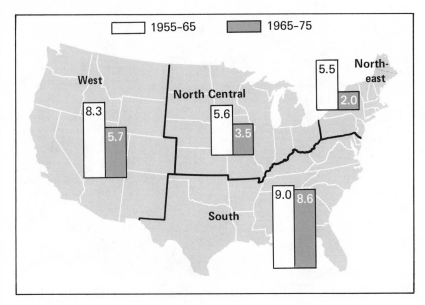

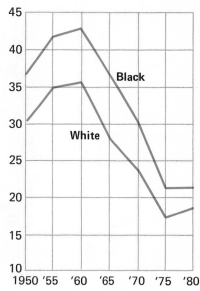

Figure 37-3 (left) Net Change in Population by Region (in millions) *Source:* Bureau of the Census. What factors might have produced these regional population changes?

Figure 37-4 (right) Fertility Rates (Live Births per 1,000 Women) *Source:* Bureau of the Census. What will happen to the racial composition of the population if present trends continue?

productivity means the economy can produce more as a whole. If each worker is producing more this year than last year, economic growth will occur even if population and investment stay the same. Increased productivity has been an important source of economic growth in the United States. Education increases workers' skills. They can produce more as a result of special training. Capital investment also raises productivity, since new equipment makes it possible for workers to do their jobs more quickly and skillfully.

Personal growth is in many ways like economic growth. It allows people to do more of what they have done before and also to try new things. It encourages people to do more for themselves and to be less dependent on others.

Your physical growth, for instance, can be compared to a country's population growth. Just as a larger population makes greater demands on a country, so your increasing age and size make new demands on you. More is expected of you now. You are given greater responsibility and judged by higher standards. As you stretch to meet them, you become more mature and confident.

You also grow by investment, just as an economy does. You make commitments to other people, to ideas, and to a chosen career. These commitments help you to define and extend yourself.

Another way in which you grow is to become more capable. You learn new skills and new ways of thinking. These help you to solve new problems and to solve old problems more easily. In other words, like a more productive economy, you develop new technologies that let you make better use of your resources.

What kinds of goods and services are needed when there is an increase in people of this age? What services will be needed 5, 10, or 20 years later?

☐ The reading for this lesson is a short story by William Brandon that deals with both personal and economic growth. As you read it, ask yourself the following questions:

1. What factors contributed to the growth of the farm's economy?
2. How did Jeremiah, his wife, and Lucy grow that summer?
3. How have you grown recently? What experiences helped you?

THE HIRED GIRL

"Yes, that girl," Jeremiah said. "Thank Providence, it's near September. That's when she goes back home. Good riddance of bad rubbish."

The county agent was surprised. "Why, your wife said—"

"I know what my wife says. The girl's worth her weight in gold, she says. Miracle how she gets things done, she says. Sure, sure. Well, a hired girl in the house is one thing, and a hired girl doing the barn work and the field work is another thing." Jeremiah turned from where he leaned with one foot on the running board of the county agent's car and looked glumly across the rolling fields to his house. "She's in the house now, her and Mother canning beet greens."

"I know," the county agent said. "They were just showing me what they'd been doing. Thirty pints of strawberry preserves, thirty quarts of cherries, thirty quarts of peas—"

"Yes, and twenty pints of asparagus, ten pints of dandelion greens, and heaven knows what all and what more yet to come. We'll have enough down cellar to feed a regiment. All that's Lucy's doing. Mother lets her lead her by the nose, turn and do whatever Lucy says. The place ain't been like home any time this summer. Something jumping every minute. I tell you, it's outrageous. I've thought so from the first. Why, you remember, Ben. I told you last May. I put my foot down the first mention of that girl coming here. A girl, I said, a schoolgirl from New York City, I said, for to be my hired man? Judas Priest, I thought the world was crazy. I still do. Well, what will you do for help? Mother says. Milking forty cows, and Jake in the Army and Justin gone to work in a factory, what will you do for help?"

Jeremiah got out his old pipe with the broken stem and a strip of tape wound around it for a bit and pared tobacco into it from his plug and turned to face the wind and strike a match, and so looked toward the house again. His eyes were getting old and dim but the bright red paint on the barn stood out and he thought he could make out the new top of the silo behind it, and he could see the sun flashing on the gleaming white hen houses.

"So," he said, puffing and turning again to the county agent, "up she come. Lucy. Seventeen years old. Just about big enough to swat a fly without help. Goes to high school in the winters. Signs up to work on farms during the summers to help out during the war. Help out, they say. Help out. Judas Priest! To get her we have to sign a contract to keep her till September, board her and pay her wages. Wages. Have to contract to pay her as much as we paid Justin. As much as we paid Justin, Ben!

"Well, she starts out telling how she's been trained. She's been trained, she says. She can milk. She can pitch hay. She's a first-class farmerette, she says, as if there's supposed to be something funny about it. Mother took to her right off.

"That first day coming home Lucy hears the peepers down in the pond. You'd think she'd heard the angel Gabriel. Why, they're wonderful. They're super, she says. Had to know all about 'em. Came home a couple of days later with a library book about 'em. Them and the birds. And the partridges and the foxes and the chipmunks and the skunks . . . I'm getting ahead of myself. Let me tell you.

What kinds of goods and services would be needed to accommodate an increase in immigration? What other kinds of population increases are there?

"The first morning she was here Mother woke me up at four o'clock. Four A.M.! Ju-das Priest! Why, Ben, I haven't got up at four o'clock in twenty years. Jake used to roll out early and Justin used to, but . . . well, Mother says, Lucy ain't Jake and she ain't Justin and she's set her alarm for four o'clock because somebody told her that's the time to get up and milk, and I'm to get up and get to work and let her help me. 'You don't want her knowing you sleep till seven, do you?' Mother says. 'You don't want to shame yourself in front of your own help, do you?'

"That was the beginning. Well, I thought, one or two mornings of this, young lady, and that will be all. Not so. The whole blessed summer, there she's been, up at four o'clock and ready to go, all smiles, all happy, just as if there wa'n't a thing to it. And I have to work harder than I've ever worked in my life. Every ten seconds she comes hiking along on the run and tells me something else to do. Is it any wonder the barn work gets done quicker than it ever got done before? Why, that girl is a wonder, my wife said. A miracle worker. I haven't been able to answer her all summer. I've been too tired.

"One day I found her mixing some barn paint. She and mother had sneaked into town and bought it. She's going to paint the barn, she says. It'll preserve the wood, she said. Judas Priest! As if I hadn't been trying to find the time to paint my barn again for five years! Well, no good to talk about it. There's the paint bought and it can't be wasted. So I painted my barn. Lucy said she'd do it, but she got nervous on a ladder."

These residents and city officials are arguing about taxation. What does this have to do with induced investment?

"It looks pretty good," the county agent remarked.

"Yes," Jeremiah said grudgingly. "I've always had the worst-looking barn and milked the most cows in the neighborhood. Always did want a nice red barn, too. But I never wanted it that bad. Ben, this summer has taken ten years off my life."

Ben laughed. "You don't look it. I'd have said you were getting younger, what with all these changes around your place this year. That new silo and those chicken houses and I've been seeing your new five-high fence all around, and a while ago your wife was telling me about your milk check—"

"Yes. Yes, more of Lucy's ideas. Weigh the milk from every cow, she says, so you'll know which ones to waste the grain on. Judas Priest! Telling a man that's sold milk for forty years how to run his business! Of course it's a good idea, but who's got the time to do it regularly? Well, I found time. Had to. Lucy tried to do it herself.

"Oh, that's no part of it. That silo I've been working on the last couple of years—she tried to finish it. So I found time for that. Then

How do new inventions result in autonomous investment? What else causes this kind of investment?

she brings home plans for those fancy hen houses and before I knew
it she had the lumber worked up and was starting in to build them. But
she couldn't drive a nail. She'd hit her thumb with the hammer and the
tears would come in her eyes and Mother would give me Hail
Columbia. So I put them up.

"Then there's the fences, that she started to fix and I had to
finish—and that garden! We haven't made much of a garden for ten
years. Been ten years since Mother's canned anything. Look at the
stuff they're putting up now. And I've got six acres of potatoes to dig.

"A miracle worker, Mother says that's what she is. 'Look at what
she's done to this farm,' she says, 'and now it's the finest.'" Jeremiah
knocked out his pipe and sighed. "But for me, I say it's crazy. I'll be
the happiest man in the town when she gets gone back home for the
winter. I'll have a few months of rest anyhow."

"For the winter?" Ben said. "You don't mean you're getting her
back next year?"

Jeremiah looked sourly at the ground. "Why, she seemed to take it
for granted that she was coming back. So blamed full of enthusiasm
about it I didn't have the heart to speak up. She says there's quite a
raft of stuff she wants to do next summer, that she didn't have time to
get around to this year." He cleared his throat and looked at the
house and the red barn. "Well, she does know how to load hay."

ACTIVITIES

I. In this activity, your group will have to make its economy grow. Your survival will depend on your cooperative and creative use of resources.

1. For this survival activity, half the class should group itself in one part of the classroom.
2. Imagine that while on a cruise of the South Pacific your group decides to go snorkeling off a large rubber raft a short distance from the ship. As you are swimming and diving, threatening clouds darken the sky. You try to paddle back but gusty winds separate your raft from the ship. After being tossed about and blown in every direction for what seems like hours, the wind finally settles and the sky becomes clear once again. As you scan the horizon, you find that your cruise ship is nowhere in sight. You realize that you must now depend on your own resources for survival. You find in the raft:

a bottle of suntan lotion	dental floss
a thermos of lemonade	a deck of cards
10 pairs of swim fins	an astrology chart
10 diving masks	a box of crackers
10 snorkels	4 tuna sandwiches
a pack of gum	5 ham and cheese sandwiches
12 life jackets	4 beach towels
Cosmopolitan magazine	rope

3. Your task is to determine how to survive your current predicament. Use the following questions to make a plan for your group:
   a. What resources are available? What is the best way to use them?
   b. What new resources can you discover or create to increase your chances of survival?
   c. How can you organize yourselves so that each person's skills are best utilized? What are each person's responsibilities?
4. Discussion questions
   a. How were existing resources used? What new resources were created? How did these influence your chances for survival?
   b. What were the most important human resources? How were they used?
   c. How did your group make decisions? What did you decide? How did your decisions and how you acted as a group influence your chances for survival?
   d. How did your economy grow? How did you grow personally?

II. In this activity, your survival will again depend on your cooperative and creative use of resources.

1. For this survival activity, the other half of the class should group itself in another part of the classroom.

2. You are flying to a resort island in the South Pacific. The plane's right engine sputters and then starts to burn fiercely. The pilot has to make a forced landing on a small deserted island. As the plane lands, it splits open—you barely manage to escape the spreading flames. Relieved that no one was hurt, you set about exploring the island. You find that it is about a half mile wide and has a small hill rising to the north. Vegetation consists mostly of palm trees and coconut trees as well as of exotic flowering plants you've never seen before. There is a pool of fresh water at the base of the hill. Though colorful birds and strange scaly reptiles are abundant, there is no sign of human life. Fortunately, the days are pleasantly warm, though the nights are a little chilly. As you search your pockets and the wreckage of the plane, you discover the following resources:

sunglasses	a fingernail file
a tin of matches	French perfume
a campaign button	6 chocolate bars
a miniature American flag	15 blankets
a harmonica	breath mints
a bag of elastic bands	a pocket calculator
a thimble	a spool of thread
a pair of dice	some Ray Bradbury short stories

3. Your task is to determine how to survive your current predicament. Use the following questions to make a plan for your group:
   a. What resources are available? What is the best way to use them?
   b. What new resources can you discover or create to increase your chances of survival?
   c. How can you organize yourselves so that each person's skills are best utilized? What are each person's responsibilities?

4. Discussion questions
   a. How were existing resources used? What new resources were created? How did these influence your chances for survival?
   b. What were the most important human resources? How were they used?
   c. How did your group make decisions? What did you decide? How did your decisions and your interactions as a group influence your chances for survival?
   d. How did your economy grow? How did you grow personally?

Advantages and Disadvantages of Economic Growth

In recent years, many people have argued that economic growth is a mixed blessing. Its advantages are fairly clear. By growing steadily, the economy provides more goods and services and raises the average standard of living. Growth also keeps people employed and earning income. Finally, it keeps the United States militarily powerful.

But what of the disadvantages? Critics of economic growth point out several.

1. *Use of Natural Resources*   By growing constantly, the economy uses up more and more natural resources each year. Many of these, such as oil and natural gas, cannot be replaced. It is expensive to look for new resources, and as the supplies are used up the price of resources goes up. As the price of resources goes up, the cost of the things made with them also rises. There will soon come a time, critics say, when the old sources of energy will run dry. And there will not be enough new forms of energy to take their place.

2. *Pollution*   Critics point out that there are "hidden costs" to economic growth. These are costs that are not reflected in the market price of goods and services. One hidden cost is the air and water pollution caused by most forms of industry. It is more expensive each year to clean up this pollution. And the damage it can cause to health alarms many people. What is more, as the population and the economy grow, the ordinary waste products of life

grow as well. Garbage disposal, for example, has become a serious problem for most major cities. Finding places to dump this waste is getting both harder and more costly.

3. *Destruction of the Environment*   Economic growth causes more than just air and water pollution. It also leads to the destruction of forests, wetlands, beaches, mountains, even the ocean beds. Controlling this destruction will cost money. This in turn will mean that the economy may not grow as fast as it would if people didn't have to worry about the destruction. For example, strip mining for coal—a popular and cheap way of getting coal out of the ground—involves stripping away the surface of the land. But this method leaves ugly, barren hills in the place of what was there before. If strip miners are required to restore the land, the cost of doing so will turn up in the price of coal. If coal is more expensive, industries that use it might cut back production or raise their prices to make up the difference. Either action could slow down economic growth.

4. *Uneven Growth*   Economic growth is a measure of the economy as a whole. But such a measure does not say much about those parts of the country that are growing more slowly than the rest. Some parts of the country may not be growing at all. Many older cities, for example, came to a standstill years ago. Critics of economic growth stress that balanced growth rather than mere growth itself should be aimed for. That way, all parts of the country and all groups of people could benefit equally.

What are some of the costs that go into this kind of service? What is happening to these costs? What are the alternatives?

Decisions about economic growth will not be easy to make. Slowing down growth may mean that some people will lose their jobs. On the other hand, continuing economic growth at the same pace may mean permanent damage to the air, water, forests, mountains, and oceans. In thinking about this question, it is useful to recall that natural resources are one of the three kinds of resources any economy needs to survive. If these resources are used in order to have more economic growth now, the results may be a sharp decrease in economic growth in the future. Yet new solutions to problems are sometimes to be found through growth.

Personal growth, like economic growth, has both benefits and costs. Growth brings increased privileges, greater ability, and deeper relationships. It means more independence, awareness, and power.

Privileges also bring more responsibility. Ability creates higher expectations. Independence can leave you on your own at a time when you need help. Your increased attachments to people, organizations, and beliefs can also create problems. Caring about someone or something is always a bit of a risk. You invest time, energy, and feelings in the relationship. Like any investor, you can be hurt if your trust turns out to be misplaced.

Even your new powers and awareness have some drawbacks. People can now ask more of you, and it is harder to turn them down. In addition, you become aware of the third-party costs of your growth. You find yourself growing away from people you were once close to. You don't want to hurt them, but you need to break away.

☐ The readings for this lesson are from a newspaper article by Ian Menzies and a piece of science fiction by Mack Reynolds. They present several points of view about how much economic growth is desirable. As you study them and the accompanying photographs, ask yourself the following questions:

1. How much growth do you feel is desirable?
2. Compare the advantages and disadvantages of economic and personal growth.
3. Which vision of the future do you believe in? How might this affect your personal growth?

A CAUTIOUS APPROACH TO DOOMSDAY

THE WOODLANDS, TEX.—A brainy collection of scientists, economists and futurologists who stirred the world five years ago with the notion that continued technical-industrial growth would lead to global chaos has softened its stand.

But the man who prepared the original alarming report has not.

"The world is closer to collapse, much closer to collapse than it was in 1972," Prof. Dennis Meadows of Dartmouth said at the annual gathering of the Club of Rome, which concluded here yesterday.

Meadows' 1972 report for the Club of Rome, called "Limits to Growth," was translated into 34 languages and has sold 3½ million copies worldwide to date. This book, and another by the German-born economist E. F. Schumacher, "Small is Beautiful," which was published in 1973, became the manifestos of a new movement.

The club, first founded in 1968, promotes its original beliefs that populations must be curbed, natural resources conserved, the environment protected, the world's processed goods shared more fairly and industry re-educated to a new social consciousness.

But 10 years later the club is showing signs of caution, too.

The subtle shift was evident at this week's gathering of 600 scientists and scholars from around the world:

—The meeting, which was billed last year as "Limits to Growth," was relabeled this year as "Alternatives to Growth."

—The club's founder and guiding light, the wealthy Italian industrialist Aurelio Peccei, stated to those assembled: "Some people think we want to dismantle industry. That is foolish. We'd like to change industry, not destroy it."

Does this area grow like others? Are there vital businesses and industries here? Why? What might public services be like here?

These signals were a red flag to Meadows.

"It's impossible for a wide variety of people to discuss the implications of limits to growth if they only have one image of the future, and that image is that growth is inevitable and essential.

"What we need is a Copernican revolution, and we don't have it. People don't know how set their minds really are."

At the first meeting in 1975, organized by Meadows, a powerful array of international speakers, including Schumacher, warned that without radical change the world will face many deaths from hunger, shortages of fresh water, an overload of poisonous wastes, and an escalating depletion of natural resources.

The conference was also told that unless the developed countries help the Third World countries to become self-sufficient there will be terror and nuclear blackmail by some poorer nations within 25 years.

Meadows feels that these warnings have now become fact, yet that people still believe that continuous growth is the only answer. He cited riots in Africa, growing water shortages across the world, increased famine and the growing depletion of raw materials.

Representing an opposing view, as he did two years ago, was outspoken Herman Kahn, director of the Hudson Institute and author of "The Next 200 Years." He again reassured his audience that the world's resources are adequate, that poverty can be kept under control and that "doomsday" predictions of limits to growth are nonsense.

Kahn's thesis also included a needling of "intellectuals." These people, he said, are out of touch with what the average American thinks and wants, such as big cars and whatever material goods are available and obtainable.

Kahn placed his faith in continued prosperity on continually improving technology. He sees oil costs, for instance, as being reduced from the present $12 a barrel to from $3 to $7 per barrel within 10 years.

Kahn was challenged by Mihajlo Mesarovic and Eduard Pestel from Case Institute in Cleveland who prepared an ambitious computer system based on a model of world resources, populations and appetites.

A group of 40 women who attended the meeting charged that the Club of Rome did not represent women, especially those from the Third World.

Through their representative, Elsa Chaney of the U.S. Agency for International Development, they demanded that this change by the next meeting in 1979.

This criticism of the meeting was not the only complaint, however. Before the sessions ended, a special meeting had been called to consider what went wrong—and why, as one organizer put it, "things fell apart."

It would seem that temporarily, at least, the alternatives to growth dialogue had reached its outer limits.

BARRY TEN EYCK

"Cotswold, let me tell you something. A big change took place in the United States about the middle of the Twentieth Century. For the first time in the history of the race we reached an era where man no longer had to work to secure subsistence. Technology had brought us to the point where we could produce an abundance with a minimum of labor. Your father and mine *had* to work for their daily bread, unless they were born into the ranks of the wealthy. No more. The average citizen today can simply go on what amounts to an endless dole, from cradle to the grave, if he so wishes."

Jim Cotswold said glumly, "And an increasing number so wish. A whole new generation has already grown up ignoring what we used to think were the basic virtues."

Willard Saxe nodded very seriously. "And under Meritocracy the trend will intensify."

Jim scowled at him. "How do you mean?"

"I mean that the highest ranking Meritcrats and the old rich who

Why has it become necessary to develop alternative energy sources such as solar power? How much might it cost?

As resources like coal grow increasingly scarce what will the effects be on industries like this?

own the cosmocorps do not wish changes in the status quo. Changes could jeopardize their privileges."

"Mr. Cotswold," Saxe said urgently, "man has reached one of the goals that has been before him since his infancy. We have the ability to make this world of ours a paradise now. Instead, what are we doing?" He made a gesture that encompassed the room, but was obviously meant to extend beyond. "We live like ants in demes [political units]. We eat mass-produced food and drink beverages that come out of laboratories and factories rather than from vineyards. We wear artificial textiles that have little real beauty and are deliberately manufactured to be disposed of after only a few days of wear. Ours is an artificial, unhappy society. Our adults as well as our children spend a disgusting percentage of the day staring at violence on their Tri-Di sets. And now the government is even ignoring, if not sponsoring, the use of trank, a happiness drug, to keep the rank and file content."

"Mr. Cotswold, now that we've solved the problem of producing abundance, we must return to the old things that used to bring man satisfaction. We should return to the arts, the handicrafts, the love of the countryside, the pleasures in nature. Here we are keeping ourselves cooped up in a few thousand demes scattered about the country. It's madness. Why, just take one thing, the forests. When the white man first landed in America, he promptly began cutting down some of the most beautiful forests on earth. He cut them down for lumber to build his homes, for firewood, for furniture. He cut them down to clear the land for his agriculture, later to manufacture paper. But now, Mr. Cotswold, we no longer use lumber for building materials, furniture, nor certainly for heat. Paper we use in moderation with the coming of modern media. We could embark upon a gigantic reforestation of our country which could make it one vast national park, save for those areas most suited to agriculture. All New England, for instance, could be a national park."

Jim said, "So, instead of taking in each other's washing, we'd take in each other's paintings, eh?"

The other chuckled ruefully, and began to come to his feet. "I'm being foolish. Obviously, I can't convert you to my way of thinking in half an hour. We might as well go. I suppose you'll want to turn me over to Roy Thomas's bully boys."

Cotswold didn't stir, as yet. He said, "Thomas told us that, given a dynamic organization such as the Futurists, the computers report Meritocracy could be overthrown within three years. But he's of the opinion that if the authorities can stave this off for ten years, they'll be so entrenched that no revolt would be possible."

Willard Saxe said bitterly, "And he's right. Past police states never had it so good. What spirit is left in our people will have been submerged in a sea of freeloading, Tri-Di shows, and trank. And the police will have their spy lenses and bugging down to the point where everything that anybody says or does will be computer monitored. But, as I say, I can't convert you in half an hour, Cotswold. Let's go."

ACTIVITIES

This activity will help you to look at the advantages and disadvantages of growth.

1. Write a paragraph describing an example of some form of growth (personal, economic, or psychological) that has taken place. Also, describe and predict the before and after aspects of that growth situation. To get the information for your paragraph, you may do one of the following:
    · recall a personal experience
    · observe a kindergarten class
    · use information from the reading in this lesson
    · observe friends
    · use a story you have read
    · use an episode from a familiar TV show

    Regardless of how you gather the information for this activity, it is important to remember that it must be a realistic example of growth taking place. Assume that you will have to invent some of the information.

2. Now take two large pieces of paper. On one, write "Advantages" and on the other, "Disadvantages." Under these headings, list the specific advantages and disadvantages of the growth situation you described in your paragraph.

3. Tape the advantages paper to your back and hold the disadvantages paper up front.

4. Walk around the room to share your paragraph with other students. At the same time, you should read out the advantages and disadvantages of your growth example. Students may write their comments on the two pieces of paper. Think up ways the disadvantages might be overcome. Write about what new or different problems might occur as a result of the advantages. The object of this part of the activity is not only to share your work with one another, but also to criticize the advantages and disadvantages of growth.

5. Discussion questions
    a. What types of growth were represented? What types were not? Why?
    b. What were the advantages of growth? How were these criticized?
    c. What were the disadvantages of growth? How was it suggested that these might be overcome?
    d. How do you deal with the conflicts caused by your growth?

Public Policy and Economic Growth

In the past, cultures were faced with a simple choice—grow or die. How they grew didn't matter much when the most important task was to produce the goods and services needed for survival. Any form or method of production that ensured this was good. Anything that got in its way was bad. In modern times, many developing countries still face this grim choice.

Many industrial countries have solved most of the basic scarcity problems. They now produce enough goods and services for all their people. If these were shared evenly, everyone would have enough to live a decent life. Modern industrial countries can now enjoy a degree of luxury that less developed ones only dream of. They can now think about things like clean air and oceans.

It helps to think of things like clean air and water as products because, like any other product, getting them involves a cost. It costs resources to keep the air and water clean, or to preserve a forest, or to make life more pleasant. Cleaning air, for example, requires natural resources (energy to run antipollution devices), capital resources (machinery to take chemicals out of the air), and human resources (labor to build the machines and operate them).

The resources used to produce a better environment or a more pleasant life are scarce resources. If they are used for one kind of production, they are not available for other kinds of production. It is the scarcity problem all over again.

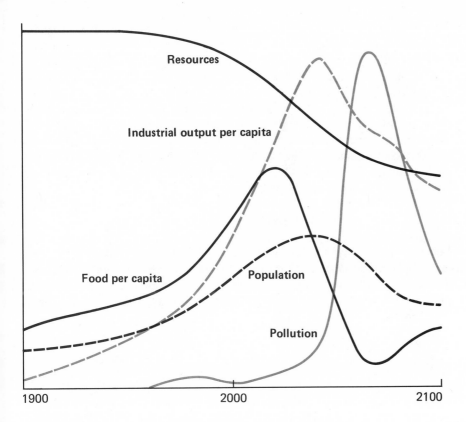

Figure 39-1   The Limits of Growth

What does it mean when food per capita drops off after the year 2000? What could change the shape of that curve?

Labels on figure: Resources, Industrial output per capita, Food per capita, Population, Pollution

Axis: 1900 — 2000 — 2100

If scarce resources are used to improve the environment, does this mean an end to economic growth? In theory, the answer is no. The goods and services produced by the economy could still increase. They would simply be different goods and services. Instead of producing cars that get only ten miles to the gallon, cars that get forty miles to the gallon could be produced. Instead of producing more cars each year, fewer cars and more buses and subways could be had. That way fewer people would have to pollute the air driving to work. In the same way, production methods that keep the rivers and oceans clean could be used.

Changing the kind of economic growth might result in a slowdown in economic growth. Any change would call for adjustments, and these might be hard to accept. Factories that have operated in one way for years would have to change their methods so as to pollute less. This might mean at least a temporary decrease in output. If the kind of growth is to be changed, therefore, it will take careful planning by both government and industry.

What will happen if the kinds of goods and services produced do not change?

Will this have any effect on economic growth? Possibly. With continued use of natural resources, their supply will keep getting smaller every year. As that happens, the price of resources will go up. As the price of resources climbs higher, the users of resources (like factories) may have to produce fewer goods and services. This will in itself lead to a reduction in economic growth.

In many ways, a society with a growing economy is like a growing person. Both want quality growth at the lowest possible cost. How can this be achieved?

There is no formula, of course, but there are some useful techniques. The person or society must make some hard value choices. What things are most important? What must be preserved? What are your goals? What kind of person do you want to be? What tradeoffs are you willing to make?

The answers to these questions can help a person or society decide which chances for growth to seize and which to reject. These answers can also be the basis for planning.

There are several ways to plan. You can make all the decisions yourself. You can turn to experts for advice. You can follow the examples of others. You can work things out with everyone who might be affected by the growth you are planning. People and societies use all of these techniques to manage their growth and the conflicts it creates.

The reading for this lesson is a song by Cat Stevens about growing up. Through a dialogue between a father and a son, Stevens points to some of the conflicts and questions involved in growth. The song shows how the son tries to deal with these problems. You can also read it as an analogy. Societies have similar doubts and debates about when growth is quality growth and when the price of growth (or no growth) is too high. They must also find ways to resolve their internal conflicts, to make plans, and to achieve their growth goals. As you read, ask yourself the following questions:

1. How might the son define quality growth? How does the father define it?
2. If your community were debating the kind of economic growth it should have, what would the son say? What would the father say?
3. What other techniques could the son use to manage the conflict his growth has created?

Why must things like saving the environment be thought of in terms of goods and services?

FATHER AND SON

FATHER: It's not time to make a change, just relax
take it easy, you're still young that's your
fault there's so much you have to know. Find
a girl, settle down, if you want you can marry,
look at me, I am old but I'm happy.

I was once like you are now, and I know that
it's not easy to be calm when you've found
something going on, but take your time, think
a lot, why think of everything you've got,
for you will still be here tomorrow but your dreams
may not.

SON: How can I try to explain, 'cause when I do
he turns away again. It's always been the same
same old story. From the moment I could talk
I was ordered to listen, now there's a way and
I know that I have to go. Away, I know, I have
to go.

FATHER: It's not time to make a change, just sit
down take it slowly, you're still young that's your
fault, there's so much you have to go
through. Find a girl, settle down, if you want you
can marry, look at me, I am old but I'm happy.

(right) Should we think of
things like clean water as
products? What might
this kind of thinking do?

(left) If we don't change
the kind of growth we
now have, what might
happen to clean city
areas like this?

SON: All the times that I've cried
keeping all the things I knew inside.
It's hard, but it's harder to ignore it. If they
were right I'd agree, but it's them they know, not me.
Now there's a way and I know that I have to go away.
I know I have to go.

Away, away, away, I know I have to make this
decision alone-no.

FATHER: Stay, stay, stay, why must you go and make this
decision alone?

Select from any source three photos that demonstrate the advantages of economic growth, and three that demonstrate the disadvantages. What do you see? What is similar and different in each picture? What do the people in each look like? How do they feel? What could be done to the "disadvantage" pictures to improve what you see? Could these changes be made in real life? If so, how? If not, why?

VISUAL
ACTIVITY

ACTIVITIES

The narrative in this lesson deals with ways of managing problems of economic growth. In this activity, you will apply some of those same methods to a personal growth concern you have. This will help you to see the advantages and disadvantages of these methods.

1. Several students volunteer to role play one of the situations listed below in front of the class. The role play should not try to resolve the conflict presented in the situation. That task will be tackled later in the activity. The purpose of the role play is simply to present the situation as realistically as possible so that it will be easier for students to think up ways of resolving or managing the problem.
   a. You've decided you are old enough to live on your own and you've moved out of your parents' house. But now you find you're having trouble making ends meet financially.
   b. Your recent interest in music has helped you to see many things in new and different ways. You try to explain this to your friends, but they don't seem to understand at all. You hate the feeling of being separated from them.
   c. You have gotten your driver's license recently. You had hoped it would allow you to become more independent. Now you find that you are constantly being asked to run errands for your parents and younger brothers and sisters.
2. The rest of the class forms four groups. These groups will represent four different ways of resolving or managing conflict.
   Group A: Let someone else solve the problem for you.
   Group B: Seek help from an expert.
   Group C: Work with others.
   Group D: Avoid the situation altogether.
3. The role play is presented to the four groups. Each group must then meet separately to discuss how the conflict could be resolved or managed by using its particular method of problem-solving.
4. The four groups briefly share their solutions with the class.
5. The role play situation together with the four possible solutions are recorded on a ditto sheet and run off so that each member of the class can have a copy. An example of what the ditto should look like is included with this activity.
6. Decide which method you would choose to deal with the role play problem. Record it under "Your Choice" on the ditto.

7. A space should be provided on the ditto for you to write in a personal problem. Record how you might deal with this problem using the four different methods. Then decide which would be the best method for you. You may want to use a method that is different from those the groups have used. (This part of the activity may remain confidential.)

8. There is also a space on the ditto for an economic growth problem to be included. The same procedure for deciding on a solution or way of managing the problem should be followed. You may decide on the economic situation as a class or choose one in which you are personally interested. The pictures and text in this chapter should give you some ideas.

9. Discussion questions
   a. Which methods did you choose for each situation? Why?
   b. What does your choice of methods say about your style of problem management?
   c. How do your methods of dealing with your personal growth problems compare with the methods society uses to manage its growth problems?
   d. What are the advantages and disadvantages of each method for managing your personal growth problems? for managing economic growth problems?

	Group A: Let someone else solve the problem for you.	Group B: Seek help from an expert.	Group C: Work with others.	Group D: Avoid the situation.	Your choice
Role play situation:					
Your personal problem:					
An economic problem:					

CHAPTER 14 THE PUBLIC SECTOR

Expenditures and Taxes

Few economic topics arouse as much feeling as taxes and government spending. Most people feel they have to pay more taxes than they should. Some people would also like to drop a few government programs to save money and reduce taxes. But each program picked for cutting is matched by a new program someone else would like to see started. One thing is clear. The federal government spends a great deal of money, and the only way to get it is through taxation.

After World War II, defense (along with the space program) and foreign affairs were one of the largest single items in the federal budget. They used up nearly a third of all the money spent by the U.S. government each year (see Table 40-1).

Social Security payments and veterans' benefits have become the biggest item in the budget in the past decade. Social Security payments are sent to workers who have retired. Veterans' benefits go to former members of the armed forces. They include pensions, medical payments, and education benefits.

The next largest budget item takes in various kinds of social welfare programs. The federal government, for example, pays most of the cost of food stamps, Medicaid (health care for the poor) and Medicare (health care for the elderly), and job training programs for unemployed workers. This category also includes loans to college students and other forms of aid to education.

The rest of the budget goes for many smaller expenses. Less than six percent is for water and irrigation projects, dams, highways, subways and railroads, and pollution control. About four percent is given to states and towns as part of the revenue-sharing program. They spend this money as they see fit. About three percent is used by the farm subsidy program, which gives money to farmers when crop prices fall too low. Almost nine percent is used to pay the interest on the national debt.

Where does all this money come from? By far the largest share comes from income taxes. In 1978, these personal income taxes made up nearly forty-five per-

Table 40-1 How the U.S. Government Spent Money in 1978 (Estimates from the Federal Budget for Fiscal Year 1979)

CATEGORY	AMOUNT (IN BILLIONS)	PERCENT OF TOTAL EXPENDITURES
1. Defense, space exploration, and foreign affairs, energy	$136.1	27.1
2. Social Security, veterans' benefits	157.8	31.4
3. Other social welfare programs (Medicare, Medicaid, food stamps, job training, housing subsidies, etc.)	75.3	15.0
4. Physical environment (irrigation, dams, transportation, air and water pollution control)	28.4	5.6
5. Revenue sharing and regional development (grants to states and local communities)	19.6	3.9
6. Producer subsidies (e.g., payments to farmers to keep up crop prices)	16.3	3.2
7. Interest on federal debt	43.8	8.7
8. Other	25.6	5.1
	$502.9	100.0

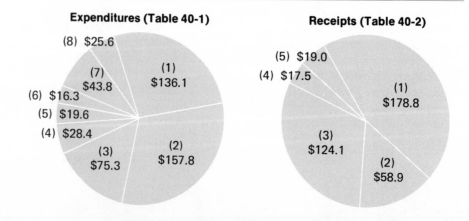

Expenditures (Table 40-1)

(8) $25.6
(7) $43.8
(6) $16.3
(5) $19.6
(4) $28.4
(3) $75.3
(2) $157.8
(1) $136.1

Receipts (Table 40-2)

(5) $19.0
(4) $17.5
(3) $124.1
(2) $58.9
(1) $178.8

cent of the money taken in by the government. Taxes on the income of corporations supplied almost fifteen percent of the total (see Table 40-2).

But corporate income taxes are only the third largest source of government income. The second largest source is from payroll taxes. This is money subtracted from workers' earnings by employers. They send it along with some of their own income to the government. It is then used to pay for Social Security benefits.

A much smaller percent of total government income comes from sales taxes. A sales tax (also called an excise tax) is either paid by the producer or added to the price of an item when it is sold. Important sources of the federal government's sales tax revenue are taxes on tobacco, liquor, and gasoline.

Of course, the federal government is not the only one that collects taxes and spends money. State and local governments do so too. In 1976 they collected 260.5 billion dollars in taxes, or about two-thirds the amount taken by federal taxes. Of this, 38.1 percent was spent on education, with 12.2 percent going for public welfare payments and 9.8 percent for highways.

Government spending pays for the goods and services that people get from the government. In turn, taxes are taken to pay for these things. This is what you or your parents give. Each person takes from the society and gives something in return.

This same kind of exchange works with things other than money. People volunteer their time, energy, and talents to improve their communities. They vote to elect people to political office. Young people give of their fresh outlooks and energies. They take existing values to define themselves and create new values from which others may gain. Older people contribute what they have learned from experience. Both take from each other.

The exchanges are not always fair. Some people may give more than their share; others may take more than they should. Some people may not be able to contribute; others may find that their contributions are not wanted. Some people will get more than they need from society; others may not be able to get enough.

SOURCE	AMOUNT (IN BILLIONS)	PERCENT OF TOTAL RAISED
1. Individual income taxes	$178.8	44.7
2. Corporate income taxes	58.9	14.7
3. Social Security and other payroll taxes	124.1	31.0
4. Sales taxes	17.5	4.4
5. Other taxes	19.0	4.7
	$400.4	100.0

Table 40-2   How the U.S. Government Raised Money in 1978 (Estimates from the Federal Budget for Fiscal Year 1979)

Note: Because figures in each column have been rounded off, they do not add up to the total in the column.

☐ There are two short readings for this lesson. The first, by Edward Fried and Charles Schultze, presents some standards for judging the federal budget. It gives you a way of deciding whether the government is giving what you want it to give. As you read the article, ask yourself the following questions:

1. How would you use these standards to judge your state's budget?
2. What standards would you add to or subtract from this list?
3. Society gives people opportunities and values as well as goods and services. How would you judge these "expenditures"?

THE FEDERAL BUDGET AND NATIONAL CHOICES

Any federal budget merits attention, whether it cuts programs, adds new ones, or merely continues along the lines of past years. Enormous resources are involved. National life is profoundly affected by decisions to spend more federal resources for health care and less for highways, or more for strategic submarines and less for day care centers. It is important whether we decide to shift tax burdens from corporations to individuals, or from the poor to the rich. Such decisions are reflected in the budget. It is the job of the President to propose a budget that embodies his priorities and judgments. It is the job of the Congress and the public to weigh it.

At least two factors inhibit informed debate on the budget. First, the budget is very hard to understand—even for those who work on it full time. Federal funds are spent for thousands of different purposes and programs, each with detailed rules and hidden results. Revenues are collected under equally complicated tax laws. Perhaps for these reasons, neither Congress nor the public ever really focuses on it as a whole or on the basic questions it raises. Citizens address themselves mainly to aspects of the budget that affect them most directly. Congressional committees concentrate on those parts for which they are responsible. Congress never votes on the budget as a whole.

Second, much of the budget reflects past decisions and commitments. Even if the Congress debated and voted on the budget as a whole, it would not be able to make drastic changes in any one year. This is because most of the budget is earmarked for the support of long-standing policies—social security benefits, for example, or troops for the defense of Europe or Asia.

The federal budget reflects choices of four different types. First, there are choices among *objectives.* What is the relative importance of the various things the federal government is trying to do? The budget implies judgments about the seriousness and urgency of the many problems facing the nation and about the relative weight to be given to more specific programs.

Second, there are choices about major *roles or strategies.* How should the government act in pursuit of its objectives? The defense budget not only reflects judgments about the importance of potential threats to national security. It reflects choices as to the international roles and military strategies to be used in response to them. For instance, should war be deterred by nuclear or conventional forces? What kind of commitments should the government make to other countries? When should it intervene abroad? Again, should the federal government freely turn over funds to state and local units, or should it specify how these funds are to be used? To what extent should it intervene to alter the private market's delivery of health care or housing?

Third, there are choices about *distribution.* Who should benefit from federal programs and who should pay for them? National defense and space programs may affect the whole nation. But others aid particular groups and represent public decisions about the relative importance or neediness of those groups. Particular taxes, moreover, fall more heavily on some groups than others.

Finally, there is the question of overall *size* of the budget. How big a share of national output should be devoted to the activities of the federal government? In the short run, the level of federal spending or receipts may reflect judgments about the present state of the economy. In the longer run, however, the size of the federal budget expresses a choice between public and private needs and between federal and state or local spending to meet public needs.

Why might such a large percentage of government spending go to the military? What does this money buy?

Why have veterans benefits increased over the last ten years? How much money is delegated for this use?

☐ The next reading, by Kenneth Boulding, explains why we pay taxes. It also suggests a way to make tax-paying more fun. As you read it, ask yourself the following questions:
1. Why should people pay taxes?
2. How might Boulding's proposal make people more willing to pay their taxes?
3. What would you like to give to society? What would you like to get in return?

TAXES CAN BE FUN

Nobody likes to pay taxes. If we financed government on a voluntary basis, most of us would contribute much less than we do. We pay taxes mainly because if we refuse we will get into more trouble than it would be worth. Nevertheless, we all accept some kind of tax system as legitimate. There are public goods which no market can provide, and we are willing to be coerced into financing them if everybody else is similarly coerced (this being the only way to avoid what economists call the "freeloader problem").

Nevertheless, taxes are something we have to agree about through some kind of political ritual. Our own society's ritual involves electing candidates to a legislature by a majority of the vote. We then accept the laws which are passed by a majority of the legislature. If the democratic process is not perceived to be legitimate, we're in for trouble. No amount of ritual can assure consent and conformity if the ritual is disbelieved. We saw this during the war in Vietnam, where rising resistance and diminishing popularity of the war eventually removed the people responsible for it from power.

Persuading people to pay higher taxes is crucial to the control of inflation. Taxes are essentially part of the "grants economy," as I have called it. To the individual, they represent a one-way transfer and a diminution in net worth, which is the ultimate definition of a grant. What we get for our taxes is merely a license to live in our society. It is absurd to suppose that we get anything more specific; it is the essential property of public goods to be unspecific.

Willingness to make voluntary grants, however, is closely related to our identification with the object of the grant. We make large grants within the family, something like 30 percent of GNP, because people identify with their children, their spouses, or even their parents and grandparents. We give smaller grants to causes with which we identify and to organizations that contribute to our identity, such as the church. We do not give grants voluntarily to people we know nothing about or for objects with which we do not identify. Even though we do not pay taxes voluntarily, our willingness to pay taxes—our perception of them as legitimate—depends on our identification with the object, just as it does in voluntary contributions. The more uncertain the object, the less will be our willingness to shell out for it.

Our willingness to pay taxes would be enhanced if we could help to direct how the money is spent. I suggest, therefore, that with every income tax return there should be a distribution form itemizing the government budget and the proportion of our taxes that we wish to allot to each. This would cheer some people enormously. It would probably not affect the government very much, for the ultimate decision on expenditure would still rest with government itself. Enough people would not bother to allocate their taxes so that over-all budgets would remain under the control of the legislature and President, as they are now. But there would be annual feedback which the government would be wise to note. Widespread differences between the allocations on the taxpayers' forms and the allocations on the budget would be a sure sign of trouble. A wise government would adjust accordingly.

A World Peace Tax Fund is being proposed by which a taxpayer

Who pays more in taxes, workers like those in the foreground, or corporations like the one in the background? Why?

How does Medicare
work? What might it cost?
Is it worth it? What are
some other examples of
social welfare programs?

would allocate a portion of his taxes to a special fund for world peace
and away from defense. That is a first step in the direction of personal
tax allocations, and seems to me sound. I hope it will mark the
beginning of a closer relationship between the preferences of the
taxpayer and the policies of government.

Voting should not be the only response of the citizen to
government policies. Personal tax allocation would challenge but not
undermine the essential authority of government; I suspect it would
even enhance the government's authority. It would certainly make
paying taxes a lot more fun.

ACTIVITIES

This activity will help you to look at your role in society and to decide how you give and how you take.

1. For this activity, you will need two small pieces of paper. On one piece, write what you can give to society, marking it GIVE. On the other piece, write what you want to take from society, marking it TAKE. You need not put your name on either paper. In deciding what you can give and what you want to take, you should consider some of the following categories:

a government service	a job opportunity
taxes	a certain standard of living
an idea or criticism	a value
your personal identity	your rights as a citizen
a skill or ability	

2. Someone volunteers to collect and list all the TAKES on the board.
3. The class makes up a list that will describe what would be needed if society were to provide the class with all those items listed in the TAKE column.
4. Someone volunteers to collect and list all the GIVES on the board.
5. Copy your own lists of gives and takes onto a single sheet of paper.
6. Randomly mix class members' papers. Then, divide into small groups and decide which papers show a fair balance between give and take. You will probably need to agree on a standard in order to measure the value and the costs of the two types of items.
7. Now, as a whole class, try to make the lists on the board balance. Create a fair tax system that will balance the budget.
8. Discussion questions
    a. Did what you could give balance against what you wanted to take? If yes, explain how. If no, explain why not.
    b. How did you measure the items so that they could be compared? Are they now equal in value?
    c. In what direction did you have to adjust your list? Did you expect too much or too little of society? Did you demand too much or too little of yourself?
    d. Why do people pay taxes willingly?
    e. Using the criteria described in "The Federal Budget and National Choices," judge the budget and tax system your class created.

Progressive, Proportional, and Regressive Taxes

The true burden of a tax does not always fall on those who pay it. The tax burden on businesses, for example, is often switched to employees (in the form of wage cuts) or to consumers (in the form of price hikes). Landlords may shift property taxes to those who pay rent. The total impact of a tax, therefore, can only be figured once its true burden is known. It can then be seen if the tax is progressive, proportional, or regressive.

A *progressive tax* takes a bigger percent of high incomes than of low incomes. Its impact therefore is to shift income from higher income groups to lower income groups. The income tax paid to the federal government is intended to be a progressive tax (see Figure 41-1). A *proportional tax* takes the same percent of all incomes. Its impact is to leave the spread of income unchanged. A *regressive tax* takes a bigger percent of a low income than of a high one. Its impact is to redistribute income from the poor to the rich. General sales taxes are regressive, because low income groups spend a greater part of their income on goods that have sales taxes.

Some taxes are proportional for one income group but regressive for another. For instance, the payroll tax used to finance the Social Security system has a built-in limit. Incomes are taxed only up to a certain limit. Above that limit, the

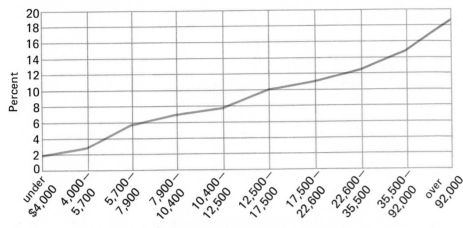

Figure 41-1 Estimated Distribution of Total U.S. Tax Burden by Income Brackets
Source: Richard A. Musgrave and Peggy Musgrave, *Public Finance in Theory and Practice* (New York: McGraw-Hill, 1973), p. 368.

tax is zero. Before the limit is reached, the tax tends to be proportional, taking the same percent of all incomes. But when the limit is reached, the tax then becomes regressive. The reason for this is that high incomes—those over the limit—are taxed only in part. Those incomes below the limit are taxed in full.

There are a great many kinds of taxes paid by Americans. The federal government taxes both personal and corporate incomes. These are also taxed by most states and even some cities. Local communities tax property. States and towns have sales taxes. The federal government places a sales tax on things like tobacco, liquor, and gas. Goods imported into the country are taxed. Figure 41-2 shows the different impacts of federal and state and local taxes. It also shows the burden of those taxes when they are added together.

Is the American tax system progressive, proportional, or regressive? Federal taxes tend to be progressive at both the high and the low end of the income scale. In the middle range, the percent paid does not change much from one income level to the next. State and local taxes tend to be regressive. They take a decreasing percent as income increases. Taken together, the impact of federal, state, and local taxes is much like the impact of federal taxes alone.

Americans often claim that they pay too much in taxes. Table 41-1 shows that there are many countries whose citizens pay even more taxes than Americans do.

We can look at any of the demands a society makes on its members as a kind of tax. We can ask whether these demands, too, are proportional, progressive, or regressive. For example, talented students in a school are often asked to give more than others. They are expected to help their teachers and other students and to be leaders. These expectations are like a progressive tax. At the same time, however, talented students may be given "tax breaks." Basketball stars may be

Table 41-1   Taxes in Selected Countries as Percentage of GNP

COUNTRIES	PERCENT OF GNP TAKEN AS TAXES
Sweden, France, West Germany, Austria, Norway, Netherlands, Great Britain	33% to 41%
Italy, Belgium, *United States,* Denmark, Canada, New Zealand	26% to 30%
Australia, Ireland, Algeria, Uruguay, Brazil, Greece, Japan, Iraq	18% to 24%
Kenya, Iran, Turkey, Costa Rica, Ghana, India, Mexico, Ethiopia	Less than 18%

given higher grades than they have earned if lower grades would force them off the team. Student council members may be excused for breaking rules when other students would be punished. These tax breaks may equal or exceed the extra tax burden, making the overall tax proportional or even regressive.

Some things are expected of all students in a school and of all members of a society. But different things are asked of different groups. As you grow, you must cope with the specific expectations that your society has of you.

☐ The readings for this lesson are taken from articles that appeared in popular American and foreign magazines and the *Congressional Record* shortly after Congress had passed a constitutional amendment in 1909 that would allow the federal government to tax incomes. The amendment then had to be approved by two-thirds of the state legislatures. The authors of these articles were trying to influence their legislators. They present a series of pro and con arguments. As you read their arguments, ask yourself the following questions:

1.   Which of these arguments are most valid today?
2.   How do the arguments for a progressive income tax relate to the different demands society makes of different groups of people?
3.   What expectations does society have of you?

THE INCOME TAX: PRO AND CON

PRO

I.   There is a kind of tax that the public is growing to favor. This is known as the graduated, or progressive, income tax. The tax would be placed chiefly on large incomes and would vary according to how much income a person received.

The principle behind such a tax is simple. Everyone contributes to the support of the government in proportion to their ability to do so. In other words, what people gave would be based on what they enjoyed.

The justice and fairness of this principle are clear. The burden of taxation would fall on those who are best able to bear it and on those who already benefit most from the state. The income tax would be imposed only on incomes above a certain level. And this level would be high

CON

I.   Of course, the plan for a progressive income tax appeals to the masses. Their argument in favor of it is simple: "Why should not a fellow with plenty of money give more to the state than a laborer? A few thousand francs more or less do not mean anything to him. He will not miss them, whereas every penny counts in the budget of the poor."

Yet it is easy to see that this theory holds good only if the benefits people get from the state increase according to the percent of taxes they pay. In reality, the reverse happens. It does not cost any more for the government to protect one man than another, or to look after large incomes than after small ones. The millionaire does not wear out the state roads any

Are taxes, on the average, regressive, proportional, or progressive, for people of this income level?

enough so as to exempt from taxation almost all other persons having only a small or moderate income.

II. All that government can hope to achieve is to treat all people of the same category in the same way. This does not mean that no distinctions can be made between classes. For instance, it would be clearly wrong for a state to tax A and to exempt B, when both were in just the same class or condition. But it is quite all right for the state to say that certain institutions should be tax-free—like churches, or schools, or specific industries or types of land. Again, it is quite all right for the state to exempt from taxes property below a certain amount. In this way, distinction is made between classes of people. All that is required by justice is that all persons in one class be treated the same.

more than the pauper. On the other hand, many public services, such as education, savings bonds, and public charities, are mainly organized to serve the interests of the poor.

II. Taxes should be based not on the ability of a person to pay the state but on the service the state gives to that person. And the cost of protecting persons does not vary much. It costs little or nothing more, for instance, to protect a banker who makes $20,000 a year than it does to protect a bookkeeper who makes only $1,000. But it costs a great deal more to protect the bank and the many corporations in which the banker has invested than it does to protect the small number of goods the bookkeeper has in his rented flat. A tax on income that came from investment would be fair, because such a tax would be placed on property; it would thus be proportional to the service given by the state to that person. A tax placed on income that came from industry is not fair; for such a tax would be proportional to the market value of the service given by that person to the state.

PRO

III. Opponents of the tax say that it asks too many questions and that it would make us a "nation of liars." But why should an income tax make us "a nation of liars" any more than our tariff or our present internal revenue taxes? There is nothing about an income which we *have* to hide. And such an income tax is not harder to pay, when it is never asked of a citizen unless his business shows a profit. It calls on none to pay except those who have had a good year. And surely those who have gained profits will not perjure themselves just to save the cost of a modest tax. I feel as sure as I do of any thing that the income tax will be paid as honestly and as promptly as other taxes are. I reject as a slander on Americans the statement that our prosperous people will lie so as to escape it.

CON

III. A strange feature of the country's past experience with this tax was that the returns were thrown open to the public. One commissioner of the IRS even instructed his officials to have them published in the pages of local papers. This was, so he said, to give the greatest chance for the detection of any false returns that might have been made. The idea did not find much favor with the public. In fact, during the later years of the tax, they were apt to look with great satisfaction on all successful attempts to evade it.

What kinds of taxes might a family like this pay? How do proportional taxes affect people of this income level as compared to others of different income levels?

PRO

IV. I believe that this measure is a wise step toward direct taxation and away from indirect taxation. A prime advantage of the direct method is that the people know when they are being taxed. As is, I am sure that the great mass of Americans don't have the slightest idea how many times in the day they are taxed for each comfort, commerce, or necessity of life. If they were aware of the scope of this taxation, they wouldn't stand for most of it beyond the next election. Little by little, we should work for direct taxation in place of indirect taxation in America. The result would be a huge reduction in taxes, to the great relief of our people. We would know when we were being taxed, how much we were being taxed, who was being taxed. The government would then get its money, and being held to stricter account, would administer both itself and the taxes with greater economy.

CON

IV. It is not for the sake of this class or that that we should condemn the income tax. It is as bad for those who are exempt from it as for those who are subject to it. To free the greater part of the people from this duty is not the way to make thrifty, hard-working, and patriotic citizens. To thrust a great burden upon a small class is not the way to produce cheerful, eager contributors to the national revenue. Worse still, a tax which depends on hired spies and eavesdroppers, and which combines the sly method of the Inquisition with the manners of the mugger, needs no speech to condemn it.

How do regressive taxes affect people of this income level?

ACTIVITIES

I. This activity will help you to think about what society expects of you. It will help you to look at the particular "taxes" that you will be asked to pay.

1. Write a paragraph describing yourself about ten years from now. It should combine a realistic prediction, based on who you are now, with your hopes or fantasies of what you might be. Try to write about yourself as a full-fledged member of society. Be sure to include such details as lifestyle, career, income, education, place and type of residence, family or relationship status, social life, debts, responsibilities, material possessions, and club memberships.
2. If possible, class members should move all the desks and chairs to the outer edge of the room. They should then lie on the floor in a circle with their heads toward the center, or sit in a circle facing outward, with eyes closed. Clear a small space in the center for the person who will begin the activity.
3. One person volunteers to begin and sits in the center of the circle. While everyone listens, this person should read the paragraph she has written.
4. As she reads, the class must think of what society will expect of her, given the way she describes her role in society. Each member of the class must think of one or two words that best describe what society's demands and expectations of the volunteer will be.
5. Now the class lets her know what they think society's demands will be. Members of the class may chant the word(s) they have chosen. It is not necessary for everyone to chant at once, but it is fitting to chant different words if new thoughts come to mind. Feelings and attitudes may be expressed through the tone and volume of your voice. The main goal is to bombard the person in the center with all the expectations that might be placed on her if she were to realize her chosen social role.
6. Let the chanting go on until it ends of its own accord. Continue with the same format until everyone who wants a turn has had one.
7. Write a second paragraph describing what society will expect of you, based on what you have heard the class chant. You will use this again in Lesson 42.
8. Discussion questions
    a. What will society expect of you?
    b. How realistic were the chanters? Explain.
    c. How did the chanting help you to think of new expectations?
    d. With which people did you share similar future roles? future societal expectations? How are these two factors related?

II. In this card sorting activity you will decide whether the demands made on people are similar to those made by a progressive, a proportional, or a regressive type of tax.

1. Use the cards in the Workbook, or copy the following general demands onto blank cards:

doing required school work	doing work required on a job
fulfilling sex roles	looking acceptable
voting as a good citizen	paying sales tax on cigarettes
living up to society's moral standards	coping with pressures to consume
amount of time team members must play in a basketball game	what people must do to prove they're adults

2. On additional blank cards, give fifteen to twenty specific examples of some of the pressures or demands made on you. You may want to include examples from some of the following categories:

   demands made by family members　　　demands made by government
   demands made by friends　　　　　　　demands made by society
   demands made by school　　　　　　　 demands made by community

3. Now sort the cards according to the type of tax each is most like:

   progressive　　　　proportional　　　　regressive

4. Complete the chart in the Workbook to help you decide how you feel about each demand (tax). If you don't have a Workbook, copy this chart onto a piece of paper. Use the chart as the basis for a class discussion.

5. Discussion questions
   a. Which tax is the easiest for you to live with?
   b. Which tax is the fairest?
   c. Who has control over your "taxes"?

What demand or "tax" is made on you?	Who demands this of you?	What tax system is it most like?	Is it fair?
1			
2			
3			
4			
5			
6			
7			
8			
9			
10			
11			
12			
13			
14			
15			
16			
17			
18			
19			
20			
21			
22			
23			
24			
25			
26			
27			
28			
29			
30			

What Is a Good Tax System?

For as long as there have been taxes, there have been disputes as to the merits of one kind of tax system versus another. The amount of money raised is only one of the things people have argued about. What are some of the issues that come up when people talk about whether a tax system is good or bad?

1. *Fairness* Who should pay the taxes the government needs in order to function? There are at least two standards that could be used. People could pay on the basis of the *benefits* they received from government programs. Or people could be taxed on the basis of their *ability to pay.* For example, truck and car owners have to pay gas taxes that are used to build highways. Super-highways are clearly a great boon to them. So, many people think it only fair for trucking firms to pay more to use these roads. Tolls on bridges or roads are based on the same principle. The federal income tax, on the other hand, is lower for low-income groups than for high-income groups. It is an example of an "ability to pay" tax.

2. *Efficiency* Two things can make a tax system inefficient. If it is very hard to understand, people will not know how much they should pay. Or if taxpayers think it is unfair, they may refuse to pay what they're supposed to. Either way, less money gets collected. But making a tax system more fair often makes it more complex. Probably the simplest tax system would be one that

said, "Everybody has to pay $1,000." No one would have any trouble figuring out what tax to pay, but a lot of people would think it an unfair system. Some taxes are easier to collect than others. Gasoline, sales, and payroll taxes are more efficient than property taxes for that reason.

3. *Fiscal and Monetary Policies*   Taxes have another purpose besides raising money. By raising or lowering taxes, the government can reduce or increase the amount of money consumers will spend. This can have important effects on the economy. More consumer spending means more jobs and higher incomes. Less spending means fewer jobs and lower incomes.

But fiscal and monetary policies might conflict with both fairness and efficiency. The government, for example, might decide that rich people were saving too much of their money. It would therefore raise taxes for higher income groups and increase government spending. This might help the economy, but high income groups would find such a tax unfair. Special breaks for some income groups might also make the tax system harder to operate.

4. *Administrative Costs*   The less the government spends on tax collection, the more it can spend on other things. The U.S. personal income tax system is rare in that it relies on taxpayers to fill out their forms, decide what their legal tax is, then send in the money freely. As a result, the United States spends less money to run its tax system than almost any other country.

5. *Using Taxes for Social Policies*   The government can use taxes to encourage or discourage certain kinds of behavior. If the government thinks that people should use less gasoline, it can raise the tax on gasoline. If it decides firms should stop pollution, it can levy taxes on them. If it thinks all people should have certain basic goods and services, it can tax those with high incomes and make payments to those with low incomes. People who want the government to have such power will think that a good tax system will permit it. People who oppose such government power will want a tax system that prevents it.

When we judge any tax or tax system, two kinds of questions arise. First, is the system fair? When all factors are weighed, is everyone asked to make an equal sacrifice? How you judge a particular tax or system rests in part on what meaning "fairness" has for you.

Second, is the tax legitimate? In other words, does the government have the right to impose it? To what extent can we permit the government to restrict our freedom? How much of our money will we allow it to tax?

These questions can be applied to any demands that a society makes on its people. Are the different expectations for men and women fair? Is it legitimate for others to demand that you live up to your sex role? Should you legally be required to work at a job you don't like when you can't find anything else? Is it fair to ask everyone to pay back the debts they have contracted? Is it legitimate to force them to? Is it right to expect people with special talents to use them to help their community? Is it fair for people to use their talents for themselves alone?

INCOME LEVEL	F.I.C.A. RISE	TAX CHANGE	NET CHANGE
$ 10,000	+$ 28	−$ 312	−$ 284
$ 15,000	+$ 42	−$ 258	−$ 216
$ 20,000	+$261	−$ 270	−$ 9
$ 25,000	+$439	−$ 320	+$ 119
$ 30,000	+$439	−$ 322	+$ 117
$ 40,000	+$439	−$ 218	+$ 221
$ 50,000	+$439	−$ 80	+$ 359
$100,000	+$439	+$ 590	+$1,029
$200,000	+$439	+$2,807	+$3,246

Table 42-1 (left) A Change in FICA
At what income level does FICA become a regressive tax?

Table 42-2 (right) The Carter Plan 1978
Who would benefit most from the proposed program? Is it fair?

Cut income-tax rates for individuals, grant $240 personal tax credit	−**$23.5 billion**
Reduce corporate income-tax rate	−**$6 billion**
Broaden 10 per cent investment tax credit	−**$2.4 billion**
Eliminate telephone excise tax, trim unemployment-insurance tax	−**$2 billion**
Limit some itemized deductions, including medical; end deductions for gasoline and state and local sales taxes	+**$5.8 billion**
Restrict individual tax shelters	+**$1 billion**
Limit business tax breaks, including foreign operations	+**$1.1 billion**
Limit travel and entertainment deductions by business, including meals	+**$1.5 billion**

NET TAX CUT: $24.5 billion

☐ The reading for this lesson is adapted from John Stuart Mill, a nineteenth-century philosopher. He presents his standards for a fair and legitimate tax system. As you read them, ask yourself the following questions:

1. Would you add to, subtract from, or change any of the standards Mill uses?
2. How do these standards apply to our present tax system and to other demands our society makes on its members?
3. What can your society legitimately ask of you? What should it not be able to ask?

ON TAXATION

The qualities most wanted in any system of taxation have been set down by Adam Smith in four maxims. These are as follows:

1. The citizens of every country ought to help support their government as best they can in proportion to their abilities. That is, they should give in proportion to the income they enjoy under the protection of the state.

Is this an example of a fair use of taxes? What kinds of taxes are used here? Who benefits?

2.   The tax each person is bound to pay ought to be certain, not arbitrary. The time, method, and amount of payment must be clear and plain. If not, all will be more or less at the mercy of the tax collector, who may then be emboldened to raise the tax or to threaten the same. An uncertain taxation can only give rein to corruption. Certainty, by contrast, is so vital that even some degree of inequality is to be preferred to a very small amount of uncertainty.

3.   Each tax ought to fall due at the time, or in the way, it is most fit for the subject to pay it. A tax on the rent of land or of houses can be paid at a regular term or when money is most apt to be at hand. Taxes on luxury goods can of course be paid at the time of sale.

4.   Every tax ought to be so managed that it will take out—and keep out—of the pockets of the people as little as possible beyond what it brings in to the public treasury. Waste is less to be feared when the number of officers in the tax service is kept down; it is less likely when the tax does not offer a temptation to smuggling; and it is less when the people are not subject to the frequent visits of tax gatherers, or to the restrictive trade practices that create them.

Of the four maxims, equality of taxation is least understood. Why should equality be the rule in tax matters? For the reason that it should be the rule in all state affairs. A government ought not to distinguish between persons or classes in the claims they have on it. What sacrifices the government requires from one of them should bear as heavily or as lightly on all. In this way, the least sacrifice will be felt by the whole.

If anyone bears less than his fair share of the burden, another must suffer more than his share; and the lightening of the one's share is not so great a good to him as the increased burden on the other is an evil to him. Equality of taxation, therefore, means equality of sacrifice. It means sharing what each person gives towards the costs of government so that no one will feel any more or less trouble than anyone else. This standard of perfection cannot, of course, be fully reached; but our first need is to know what perfection is.

Some people, it seems, are not content with mere justice as a basis on which to ground their rules of finance. They must have something more suited to the subject. What pleases them best is to look on the tax of each person as a sum paid for value, or services, received. In this view, those who have twice as much property to be protected receive twice as much protection. Therefore, they ought, on the principles of bargain and sale, to pay twice as much for it.

We find here a strange kind of reason. It cannot be agreed that to have the protection of ten times as much property is to be ten times as much protected. Nor can it be said that to protect £1,000 a year costs the state ten times as much as to protect £100 a year. The same judges, soldiers, and sailors who protect the one protect the other;

How are taxes collected in our society? Does this system work? Is it the same in other countries?

TAX COLLECTOR

and the larger income does not even always call for more policemen. Whether the labor and cost, or the feelings of the protected person, be made the standard, there is no such proportion as the one supposed.

Do we want to guess the degree of benefit that different persons derive from the protection of the state? Then we must think who would suffer most if that protection were withdrawn. And the answer to this question must be that those who are the weakest in mind or body, whether by birth or condition, would suffer the most. Indeed, it is slaves and children who best fit this description. If there were any value, therefore, in the notion advanced, then those who are least able to help or defend themselves would be those who most need the protection of the government; and, as such, these persons should pay the greatest share of its cost. Yet here we have the reverse of the true idea of justice. For this consists not in imitating the inequalities and wrongs of nature but in correcting them.

Government is so clearly a concern of all that to try to calculate those who are most interested in it is a barren chore. If a person or class receives so small a share of the benefits as to make the question necessary, then there is more than taxation amiss. The thing to do is to repair the defect, not recognize it.

As when money is offered willingly for a cause everyone can support, all are thought to have done their part when each has given according to his means. In the same way, this should be the principle of taxation. One can find no better ground for justice.

What are "benefits received" taxes? Are there problems associated with this kind of tax? Is this an example of one that is fair?

Pick one issue of a magazine that has a lot of pictures. (Some examples are *People, National Geographic, Time, Newsweek,* etc.) How many pictures can you find of things that are taxed? What kinds of things are these? Are there people in these pictures? What do they get from these things such that they are willing to pay the taxes? Is this indicated in the pictures? How? Where does the money from the taxes go? What percentage of the total number of pictures in that one magazine shows at least one taxable thing? Does this suggest anything about taxes?

VISUAL ACTIVITY

ACTIVITIES

I. This activity will help you to think about the possibility of creating an equitable tax system.

1. Split up into small groups of four to six students each. The task of each group is to create a fair tax system. Describe how the tax system would work.
    a.   How would you raise money for

parks	an animal protection service
national defense	medical research
the space program	the restoration of historical
highways	landmarks
funds for disaster victims	national seashore reserves
welfare programs	farm subsidies
urban renewal	.... (other)

    b.   Who would pay and how much would they pay?

rich people who don't work	people who consume excess
college students	amounts of energy
people on welfare	people with handicaps
high salary earners	prison inmates
senior citizens	workers with average incomes
war veterans	.... (other)

    c.   Describe the steps to be taken to set up the tax system you have devised.
2. Meet together as a class to share your tax systems with each other. As a class, try to show why each of the ideal systems described would be impossible to achieve or to maintain. What is it about people that makes a just tax system so hard to establish?
3. As a class, discuss both the work you did in small groups and your attempts to tear apart the various tax systems.
    a.   What common problems did all the tax systems share?
    b.   Why is it hard to imagine an equitable tax system?
    c.   Was it easier to create the tax system or to tear it down?
4. Pick the tax system that you feel has the best chance to survive. What would you contribute to this tax system? What would you receive from it? Would it be fair to you? Would it be right?

II. This activity is a continuation of Activity I, Lesson 41. In it you will have a chance to decide which of society's expectations you find acceptable and how you think they will affect your future life.

1. Read over the first paragraph you wrote describing what you thought you'd be doing about ten years from now.
2. Then read over the paragraph you wrote, based on what the class chanted, about what society would expect of you.
3. Now decide which of society's demands you could live with and which would be unacceptable. Sort the demands into these categories by filling in the chart in the Workbook. If you don't have a Workbook, copy the one in the text.

	Acceptable, because:	Unacceptable, because:
Too little is expected of me.		
It is unequal.		
It places too great a burden on me.		
They have no right to demand this.		
It reflects the wrong values.		
I'm not getting what I paid for.		

4. Discussion questions
   a. Which expectations did you consider totally unacceptable?
   b. How were you able to deal with those demands that were unacceptable but unavoidable?
   c. How are people's feelings about what is unacceptable reflected in the tax system?
   d. What are the best reasons for refusing a demand?
   e. How should society respond when people refuse demands for serious reasons?

CHAPTER 15 THE WORLD ECONOMY

Balance of Payments

Trade between different countries is not very different from trade between regions of the same country. The reasons why Maine ships potatoes to Florida and Florida ships oranges to Maine apply to world trade too. World trade, of course, is a lot more complex. Different countries use different kinds of money, have different political systems, and speak different languages. But the basic idea is the same.

The United States uses dollars for money. When people from other countries want to buy goods and services from American firms, they must pay in dollars. When Americans want to buy foreign products, they must pay in foreign money. People and businesses get the foreign money they need by buying it in foreign exchange markets.

Foreign exchange markets are just like other markets. Instead of buying and selling goods and services, people buy and sell money. Those Americans who want to buy goods from France provide the demand for francs. Those people in France who want to buy goods from the United States provide the supply of francs.

When the price of francs in dollars is determined by supply and demand, flexible or *floating exchange rates* are in use. This has been the case since the early 1970's.

During the 1950's and 1960's, a system of *fixed exchange rates* was in effect. Then the governments of the world decided on the rates of exchange. For this system to work, the fixed rates had to be supported. If there were a surplus of dollars at the fixed rate, for example, the United States government or the Federal Reserve Bank had to buy up that surplus. If they did not have enough foreign currency they used gold.

When the price of the dollar in francs falls in a flexible system, the value of the dollar is said to have *depreciated.* When the United States government increases the dollar price of francs in a fixed system, the dollar has been *devalued.* When either of these happens, American exports become better buys for foreigners and imports become more expensive for Americans.

Economists call the difference between exports and imports the *balance of trade.* For almost all the years since World War II the United States has had a surplus of exports over imports in its balance of trade.

The buying and selling of goods and services is only one kind of transaction among nations. Americans invest in other countries and foreigners invest in the United States. The United States government maintains military bases in other countries and makes grants to foreign governments. People who worked in the United States retire in other countries and have their pensions sent to them there.

The record of all these transactions of people, firms, and governments with the rest of the world is called the *balance of payments.* For almost all the years since World War II, the United States has had a deficit in its balance of payments. As a

Figure 43-1   United States Balance of Payment Deficits
Source: Council of Economic Advisors
How long can the U.S. continue to have a balance of payments deficit?

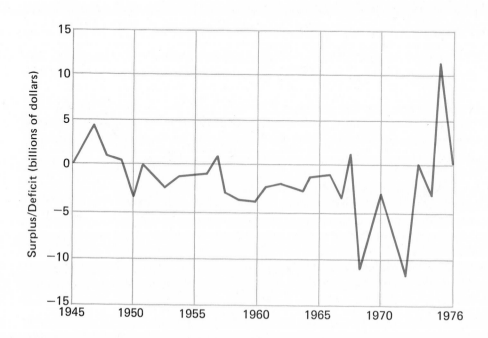

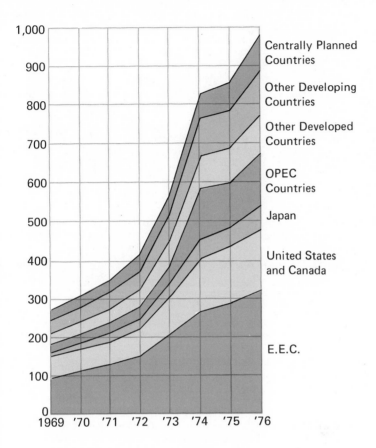

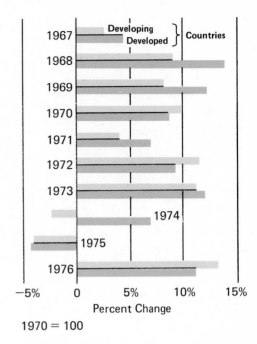

Figure 43-2 (left) World Exports (billions of dollars)
What accounts for the rapid increase in the value of exports by the OPEC countries?

Figure 43-3 (right) Volume of Trade
What are the implications of the growth of world trade since 1967?

result, foreigners own large amounts of dollars, many times more than the value of the United States gold supply.

The real value of the dollar is based on what it will buy in the United States. But many other nations use the dollar as an international currency. They see payments, deficits, and gold losses as signs of weakness. They fear that the United States will have to devalue the dollar. This makes them less happy about holding dollars as backing for their own money. This concern over the stability of the dollar led to a new form of international reserves in 1970 called Special Drawing Rights at the International Monetary Fund. The SDR's, sometimes called paper gold, are a kind of credit. Using a set of complicated rules, a country can borrow SDR's from the IMF and use them to buy back its own currency from other countries.

What economic institutions will be used to manage world trade in the future? Will flexible exchange rates and SDR's continue to grow in importance? The answers to these questions are not yet clear.

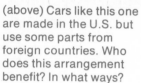

(above) Cars like this one are made in the U.S. but use some parts from foreign countries. Who does this arrangement benefit? In what ways?

(right) What are some of the reasons that ships of foreign registry bring products to the U.S.? What does this do for their countries of origin? For the U.S.?

☐ The reading for this lesson explains why nations trade with each other. Even when countries could produce what they need on their own, they often choose to specialize. They import some things and export others. The same principle that explains why countries specialize can also explain why people specialize. As you read this explanation, think about the following questions:

1. Why do countries choose to specialize and trade? When might they choose not to?
2. How does the principle of comparative advantage apply to you?
3. How can you choose a lifestyle that encourages you to do what you do best?

COMPARATIVE ADVANTAGE

Pretend for a moment that there are just two countries in the world, the United States and Mexico. Pretend also that they produce only two goods, shoes and shirts. Both countries make both products, spending half of their working hours on each. But the United States makes more shoes than shirts, and Mexico makes more shirts than shoes. This situation is shown in Table A.

TABLE A	Shoes	Shirts
United States	100	75
Mexico	80	100
TOTAL	180	175

Now, the sensible thing to do would be for each country to specialize in what it does best. The United States should make only shoes and Mexico should make only shirts. What will happen when each country spends twice as much time doing what it does best? It will make twice as much of its best product, as shown in Table B.

TABLE B	Shoes	Shirts
United States	200	0
Mexico	0	200
TOTAL	200	200

The world now has both more shoes and more shirts.

In this example, the United States was better at making shoes. Economists say that it had an *absolute advantage* at shoe-making. Mexico, on the other hand, had an absolute advantage at shirt-making.

Now suppose one country has an absolute advantage in both products. Is trade a good idea under these circumstances? Table C shows what production would be like if the United States had an absolute advantage at making both shoes and shirts.

TABLE C	Shoes	Shirts
United States	100	80
Mexico	80	75
TOTAL	180	155

In this case, the United States is better than Mexico at making both goods. But it is somewhat better at making shoes than it is at making shirts. Mexico is a little better at making shirts than at making shoes. It can make almost as many shirts as the United States can. Economists therefore say that the United States has a *comparative advantage* in shoe-making and Mexico has a comparative advantage in shirt-making. Table D shows what happens when each country specializes in the product in which it has a comparative advantage.

TABLE D	Shoes	Shirts
United States	200	0
Mexico	0	150
TOTAL	200	150

By specializing in this way, the United States and Mexico have increased the production of shoes by twenty units over what they produced before. But the world has lost five units of shirts. Production in Mexico could be adjusted to make up the difference. But specialization and trade pay off even if this is not done. The reason is that Mexico is now concentrating all of its resources in the industry at which it is most efficient. In this way, the total production of both countries has increased.

The real world is much more complex than this two-country, two-product model. Trade involves many different countries and products. And it is not always clear where a country's comparative advantage lies. The basic principle holds so long as only economic motives are at work. If the United States and Mexico were at war, for instance, they would not engage in trade no matter what the advantages might be.

The principle of comparative advantage can be applied to people as well as to countries. It says, in effect, that it is best for everyone

Why might products like these be imported? Does the country they come from have an absolute or comparative advantage in making these products?

How might these people decide what their comparative advantages are? How might you decide?

when people concentrate on doing the one thing they do best. If fixing things is your specialty, for instance, that is what you should do. It doesn't matter that other people may be better at fixing things than you are. But if you are also an artist, you may have to decide which of your two skills is most needed in your world. This will depend in part on other people's strengths. You must ask yourself which of the things you can produce is worth more in trade.

ACTIVITIES

I. This activity will help you to understand better the principle of comparative advantage.

1. Split into four groups. Each group represents a country whose goal is to decide which of its resources should be developed for trade. Your own abilities, which will be tested in this activity, are the resources your country can choose to develop.
2. Economists predict four skill areas that will be useful and profitable to have in the next twenty years. The skills are service skills, sales skills, computer skills, and bureaucratic skills. Your country will determine which it should focus on by having all of its citizens tested for their ability in each of the four skill areas.
3. Each corner of the classroom should be designated as the testing centers for determining ability in one of the four skill areas. There will be four ten-minute testing sessions timed by the teacher. This will insure that you have enough time to go to all four corners to be tested in all four skill areas. Instructions explaining how the tests are to be administered follow.

Corner #1   SERVICE SKILLS
1. Your service ability will be measured by what kind of person you seem to be.
2. Introduce yourself to someone else in the corner.
3. This person must decide how much confidence she has in you and, consequently, how much you might be able to help her. She will rate you on a scale of 1 to 10, 10 being the highest grade possible.

Corner #2   SALES SKILLS
1. Your sales ability is measured by how effective a one-minute sales pitch you can come up with is.
2. Go up to one person in this corner and give her a one-minute sales talk on a product she has randomly chosen.
3. This person will rate your sales ability on a scale of 1 to 10 by deciding your effectiveness in convincing her to buy your product.

Corner #3   BUREAUCRATIC SKILLS
1. Your ability to function in a bureaucracy is measured by how accurately you can alphabetize eight words and analyze three case studies.
2. The teacher or a student volunteer acts as tester in this corner. The tester gives a copy of the test (found in the Instructor's Manual) to you and corrects it when you have finished.
3. You will receive a half point for each word alphabetized correctly and two points for each case study question correctly answered.

Corner #4   COMPUTER SKILLS
1. Your computer ability is measured by how well you perform on a mathematics test.
2. A teacher or student volunteer will have to administer this test (found in the Instructor's Manual).
3. You will receive one point for every correct answer.

Center of the classroom
You must take at least two of the skills tests. If you decide not to take the others, you can spend the testing session in the center of the classroom. While there, you must create your own job category, test, and rating scale.

4. After you have taken four ability tests, meet with the other members of your country. Everyone should fill in the following ability score chart on a separate piece of paper and drop it into a hat or box. Charts can remain nameless. If you did not take a certain test, then you should write in a 0 as your score.

	YOUR ABILITY SCORE
Service	
Sales	
Bureaucratic	
Computer	
Other	

5. Your country must now compute a productivity score for each of its potential resources by adding up the individual scores for each resource. It is not necessary to include alternative service scores unless the scores are particularly significant. Complete the following chart in the Workbook or copy the chart on a separate sheet of paper.

	YOUR COUNTRY'S PRODUCTIVITY SCORE
Service	
Sales	
Bureaucratic	
Computer	
Other	

6. Based on its productivity scores, decide what would be best for your country to concentrate on developing.
7. All four countries should next decide what it would be best for each country to produce. Copy the following comparative advantage chart on the board and fill in the necessary information.

	PRODUCTIVITY SCORES			
	COUNTRY A	COUNTRY B	COUNTRY C	COUNTRY D
Service				
Sales				
Bureaucratic				
Computer				
Other				

8. Discussion questions for each country to ask itself
   a. Should you do only what you can do best, following your comparative advantage?
   b. Should you do only what you do better than anybody else, following your absolute advantage?
   c. Should you try to be self-sufficient, producing everything?

II. This activity asks you to compute a balance of payments.

1. Take a sheet of paper and make two columns. Label one column "Receipts from Foreigners." Label the other column "Payments to Foreigners." Then enter the amount of each of the following transactions in the proper column.
   a. A Japanese auto manufacturer pays a dividend of $150 to an American stockholder.
   b. An American department store buys $350,000 worth of East German cameras.
   c. The Indian government pays a Washington hotel $25,000 for housing its diplomats.
   d. The United States government spends $2,000,000 for laundry services provided troops stationed in South Korea.
   e. An American sends $100 to a friend in Spain.
   f. A West German firm buys $150,000 worth of computer equipment from an American factory.
   g. An American restaurant buys $2,800 worth of Italian wine.
   h. General Electric pays $6,000 in dividends to foreign owners of its stock.
   i. A Swiss bank invests $900,000 in General Electric stock.
   j. An American firm builds a $15,000,000 assembly plant in Great Britain.
   k. An American buys $1,200 worth of stock in a West German automobile factory.
   l. An Englishman buys a $4,000 American automobile.
   m. An American spends $1,000 on a vacation in Italy.
   n. Israel purchases $15,000,000 worth of military equipment from the United States.
2. Discussion questions
   a. As a result of the preceding transactions, does the United States have a surplus or a deficit in its balance of payments?
   b. What is the size of this surplus or deficit?
   c. How might this surplus or deficit be financed to bring the United States balance of payments into balance?

Trade Restrictions and Their Effects

Despite the advantages of free trade, many nations impose limits on trade for one reason or another. The four main types of trade restrictions are tariffs, subsidies, quotas, and cartels.

A *tariff* is a tax placed on goods imported from abroad. The effect of a tariff is to raise the price of the imported product because the seller must charge more to cover the tax. Many foreign goods—Japanese television sets, Brazilian shoes, Mexican tomatoes—could be sold for lower prices than similar American goods if there were no taxes on them. This is because the costs of production in foreign countries are often less than they are in the United States. Due to the tariff, however, these imported goods cost the same as, and in some cases more than, American goods. This is a great advantage to American manufacturers of these goods.

A *subsidy* can be thought of as a tariff in reverse. Instead of taxing the foreign product, the government gives a subsidy (a grant of money) to the industry that is suffering from foreign competition. Those who receive such subsidies do not have to earn as high profits as they normally would. They can meet some of their production costs through the subsidy. They are thus able to charge less for their products than foreign producers can.

A *quota* is a limit on the amount of goods that can be imported into the country. A quota on shoes, for example, might limit foreign-made shoes to 10,000,000 pairs a year. If Americans buy 200,000,000 pairs of shoes each year, this would leave most of the market to American producers. Usually, quotas are imposed only when tariffs and subsidies have failed to protect native industries from foreign competition.

A *cartel* is a group of companies or countries that band together to restrict competition. The members of the cartel agree to limit the supply and to control the price of a particular good. An example is the Organization of Petroleum Exporting Countries (OPEC). Its members produce most of the oil sold in world markets. OPEC members meet regularly to decide how much oil to sell and how much to charge for it.

What are the effects of these trade restrictions? They all limit world trade, which means a reduction in the total number of goods and services produced. When production is lowered, there are fewer workers earning income. Trade restrictions also raise prices, which is usually their main purpose. Trade limits in one country, moreover, usually lead to limits being imposed in other countries. If the United States places a high tariff on cars made in Japan, for example, Japan may then impose tariffs on American goods sold in Japan.

Despite these disadvantages, nations are tempted to use trade restrictions to protect their own industries. Nations that are just beginning to develop use tariffs, quotas, and subsidies to protect their industries until they can compete without government aid. Differences in wage levels also lead to trade restrictions. Countries with low wage levels can win a large part of the market for products that require much labor and little capital. High-wage countries sometimes use tariffs and quotas to protect their own workers in these industries.

Governments are especially eager to protect what are called "strategic" industries. These are the industries, such as steel, cars, chemicals, and munitions, that are important during a war. One way of insuring that they remain strong is to protect them from foreign competition. Agriculture is another area that many

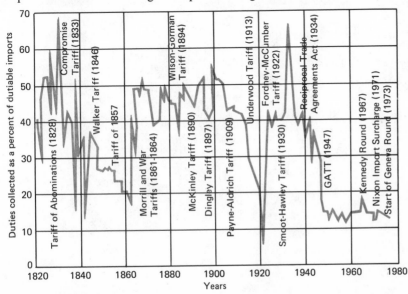

Figure 44-1 United States Tariff Rates, 1820–1976
Source: Department of Commerce
Why has the U.S. become a low tariff nation?

governments try to protect. Tariffs and subsidies help make sure that domestic farmers can earn enough profits to continue farming.

The decision to use trade restrictions is based on both economic and political factors. Trade limits help native industries, but they mean higher prices for buyers. They help the owners and workers in protected industries. They hurt the people who have to pay higher prices for the goods those industries make. They also hurt exporting industries. In the absence of competition, companies may also use less efficient production methods. This can lead to poorer quality as well.

It is in the best interests of the world economy for each nation to specialize in the goods it makes best and to trade freely with all other nations. However, this practice is not always in the best interests of each nation. Other goals may be more important.

The same is true for individuals. Specialization has its drawbacks as well as its advantages. When you can make many things for yourself, you are not as dependent on other people.

Throwing all your energies into one direction can also limit your choices in deeper ways. Perhaps, if you take the time to develop other sides of yourself, you may find some greater talents. Specialization can also cut you off from others who do not share your interests. Finally, specialization can be as risky for people as it is for countries. In a fast-changing world, you may find that your special skill is no longer valued.

The reading for this lesson is from *The Wall Street Journal*. It describes one attempt by the United States to limit its trade and be more self-sufficient. As you read it, ask yourself the following questions:

1. What are the results of this policy?
2. When should countries specialize and trade freely? When should they try not to?
3. When should people specialize and trade freely? When should they try not to?

What are some of the ways the U.S. might restrict imports like these? Why is this important?

TOMATOES AND TRADE

American businessmen complain, quite justifiably, of the nontariff trade barriers that other nations erect against U.S. goods. The U.S. will have a better chance to reduce such obstacles, however, if it stops putting up its own.

In January, for example, the Agriculture Department imposed minimum-size restrictions on all tomatoes sold in the U.S. Mature green tomatoes, those that ripen after picking, have to be at least two and $\frac{9}{32}$ inches in diameter, while vine-ripened tomatoes must measure at least two and $\frac{17}{32}$ inches in diameter.

The average consumer is likely to consider such rules pretty silly; because tomatoes are sold by the pound, not the dozen, a difference of $\frac{1}{32}$ inch or so is of little concern. But he may figure the restrictions are fair enough since they apply across the board to all tomatoes.

Actually, though, the rules discriminate against tomatoes grown in Mexico and in favor of those produced in Florida, the other major source of winter tomatoes for the U.S. market. For one thing, they are more lenient on green tomatoes, which make up most of Florida's crop and very little of Mexico's output. Mexican growers say the restrictions may bar as much as half of their crop from the American market.

One result is soaring prices for consumers. Winter tomatoes, already viewed as a luxury by many housewives, are rapidly becoming even more so—a trend that could mean smaller sales for growers in Florida as well as Mexico. The tomato rules, moreover, are another step toward worsening already shaky relations between the U.S. and Latin America.

So the restrictions imperil moves toward freer trade, irritate friendly neighboring nations, penalize U.S. consumers and may even be self-defeating for U.S. growers. We'd say that makes them look about as appealing as, say, a rotten tomato.

How might import restrictions be enforced?

Why might these images represent "strategic" industries? What does this mean?

ACTIVITIES

This is a two-part debate activity designed to help you understand the issue of diversity versus specialization. The first part will focus on an economic situation, the second on a personal one.

1. Split into two groups. Each group will argue one side of the issue, "Should a tariff be imposed?" Group A will take the side of some small shoe manufacturers. These companies are the major industries in the towns where they are located. Their workers are skilled and dedicated and are paid fair wages. Now these companies are being put out of business by cheap foreign shoes. They are asking for government help in the form of a tariff on all imported shoes. Group B opposes trade restrictions on shoes. Both groups should refer to the narrative of this lesson for the pros and cons of imposing a tariff.

2. Your discussion will take the form of a circle debate. Have each side sit in a circle. The members of each group should look at each other, not at the members of the other group. Have one student sit between the two circles and act as a recorder.

3. Group A, the group arguing in favor of a tariff, should begin. The group has one and a half minutes to write a one-sentence statement of its position. Then one person from Group A should address the statement to Group B. The recorder should write the statement on a ditto master.

4. Group B then has one and a half minutes to decide on a counter statement to Group A. Again, the recorder writes the statement on a ditto master.

5. While Group B is deciding on its statement, members of Group A should be trying to guess what the statement will be. They should also be planning their own responses one or two turns ahead in the debate.

6. The debate continues, with each side offering reasons for its position, until one side convinces the other or until time runs out.

7. When the debate is finished, run off what was written by the recorder on the ditto master. Use it to help you discuss the debate and the issues.

8. Now read the following situation and debate the diversification versus specialization issue from a personal perspective. For this debate, the groups should switch their positions.

9. "Some countries do not follow the principle of comparative advantage, because it limits what they can produce. These countries want to diversify their economies. They are willing to live without protection while they are developing a number of different industries. In the end they come out stronger."

Seth's economist mother had always used this as an analogy for the kind of career/lifestyle she encouraged him to adopt. "Don't be dependent on one skill," she would say, "life is too complicated." "Don't put all your eggs in one basket." Seth had heard this adage from the time he was a young boy from his learned, well-traveled, multilingual, more-hobbies-than-you-could-count mother. But Seth had a different idea about the career he wanted to pursue. Seth was a whittler, an old-fashioned, sit-on-the-front-porch-with-knife-and-block whittler. He was a good one too, and someday, if he worked hard enough at it, he'd be a great one. That was why college and traveling and meeting the right people and earning a lot of money didn't seem important to him. He knew the market for hand-carved items was small, but his expenses were minimal and he didn't have anyone to support or to worry about but himself. Besides, how could he be the best if he didn't spend all his time developing his skill?

10. Using the same format for debate as the previous activity, you should discuss both sides of the question: What lifestyle should Seth pursue?

Group A will take Seth's position that it is best to specialize in one skill and to adopt the kind of lifestyle that is in keeping with it.
Group B will argue that it is best to pursue a well-rounded lifestyle and to direct one's energies in a number of different ways.

11. Each group may use its imagination to expand on Seth's situation. Debaters may also make use of economic analogies, as Seth's mother did.

12. Discussion questions
    a. What were the best arguments on each side of the debate?
    b. How can a country decide between a specialized economy and a diversified economy?
    c. Do the arguments that apply to countries apply as well to individuals?

The Multinational Corporation

In the past few decades, a new factor has entered international trade, the *multinational corporation.* A multinational corporation is a firm that operates in many countries at once. Of course, firms have operated overseas for hundreds of years. What makes these so special is their enormous size and rapid growth.

Multinational corporations are by far the largest firms in the world. Table 45-1 compares the GNP of some nations with the gross sales of some multinational corporations. As you might expect, the major industrial nations (the United States, West Germany, Japan, and others) head the list. But not very far below is a company, General Motors. The sales of General Motors are larger than the GNP of Belgium and Luxembourg, Argentina, and South Africa. Standard Oil of New Jersey and the Ford Motor Company both rank higher than Austria, Norway, or Greece. IBM is bigger than South Korea. Texaco is bigger than Peru.

Multinational corporations are not only big. They are getting bigger every year. In fact, they are growing faster than world trade. They are growing twice as fast as the economies of most nations. By the year 2000, experts predict, they will account for half of all production in the non-Communist world.

The rise of multinational corporations has brought both benefits and problems. Some of the benefits are increased production, employment, and income in less developed countries. These corporations keep business activity at high levels

#	Nation/Corporation	GNP/Sales	#	Nation/Corporation	GNP/Sales
1.	United States	931.4	29.	South Korea	7.0
2.	Japan	164.8	30.	MOBIL OIL	6.6
3.	West Germany	153.7	31.	Thailand	6.3
4.	France	137.8	32.	TEXACO	5.9
5.	United Kingdom	108.6	33.	Peru	5.1
6.	Italy	82.3	34.	GULF OIL	4.9
7.	Canada	73.4	35.	WESTERN ELECTRIC	4.9
8.	India	39.6	36.	U.S. STEEL	4.7
9.	Brazil	39.4	37.	Israel	4.7
10.	Australia	29.9	38.	STANDARD OIL OF CALIF.	3.8
11.	Mexico	29.4	39.	Malaysia	3.7
12.	Spain	28.7	40.	LING-TEMCO-VOUGHT	3.7
13.	Sweden	28.4	41.	DU PONT	3.6
14.	Netherlands	28.4	42.	PHILIPS	3.6
15.	GENERAL MOTORS	24.3	43.	SHELL OIL	3.5
16.	Belgium-Luxembourg	22.9	44.	VOLKSWAGEN	3.5
17.	Argentina	19.9	45.	WESTINGHOUSE	3.5
18.	Switzerland	18.8	46.	STANDARD OIL OF INDIANA	3.5
19.	South Africa	15.8	47.	BRITISH PETROLEUM	3.4
20.	STANDARD OIL OF NEW JERSEY	15.0	48.	Ireland	3.4
21.	FORD MOTOR COMPANY	14.8	49.	GEN. TEL. & ELECTRONICS	3.3
22.	Austria	12.5	50.	ICI	3.2
23.	ROYAL DUTCH/SHELL	9.7	51.	GOODYEAR	3.2
24.	Norway	9.7	52.	RCA	3.2
25.	Greece	8.5	53.	Algeria	3.2
26.	GENERAL ELECTRIC	8.4	54.	Morocco	3.1
27.	Philippines	8.1	55.	SWIFT & CO.	3.1
28.	IBM	7.2	56.	South Vietnam	3.1

Table 45-1 GNP of Selected Nations and Gross Sales of Multinational Corporations in 1969 (in billions of dollars)

and raise the tax revenues of the countries in which they operate. Some economists claim that they also promote improved use of technology.

But critics point out that multinationals often bring uneven growth to poor countries. They get poor countries to consume their products, when such countries might do better to invest in their own plants and farms. They use automated machines, when in countries with high unemployment the need for jobs is greater than the need for complex machines. They take profits out of the countries where they do business rather than reinvesting them there. Some critics think these profits are too high and will make poor countries even poorer.

The multinational corporations bring together the work of many nations. For example, a car with parts made in Brazil might be built in the United States. A

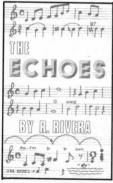

fast-food hamburger might have meat obtained from cattle raised in Mexico, then shipped to the United States. Some critics charge that these countries would be better off by producing the basic goods they require (such as food, clothing, and medicine) and not the goods required to fulfill the master plan of a multinational company.

Political questions also arise. Supporters of the multinationals argue that by operating in several countries at once they act as a force for peace. For example, there are more than 1,000 agreements in force between Western corporations and Communist countries. Such ties encourage different systems to get along.

On the other hand, the size of the multinationals gives them the power of a government without the state's sense of responsibility. A corporation, after all, is a business. Its purpose is to make profits. A government's purpose is to promote the welfare of its people. If a business gets big enough to tell a national government what to do, democracy will surely suffer.

The United Nations has a code of conduct for multinationals. Its principles include respect for the national ruling authority, obedience to the law, and noninterference in the internal affairs of the countries where multinationals operate. Whether governments will be able to enforce this code against companies much larger than themselves remains to be seen.

Within the next ten years, important changes will have come about in the world. New kinds of jobs will exist, new kinds of homes will be built, new problems and shortages will have to be faced. New discoveries and ideas will change the ways in which we think about ourselves and our world. Advances in communications will affect the way we do business and the way we relate to each other. We will have to face the growing power of multinational corporations and the demands of poor nations for a fair share of the world's resources. There will be new opportunities and new challenges for all of us.

Although no one can predict for sure what this future will be like, we can make some guesses from our knowledge of the present. The reading for this lesson is a satirical science fiction story by Marc Scott Zicree. It shows, in extreme form, what the future could be like if multinational corporations continue to grow unchecked. It pictures a world ruled by corporate power, a business mentality, and machine-made products. As you read the story, ask yourself the following questions:

1. What trends today point toward this plastic future?
2. What trends point to an opposite future?
3. What possibilities do you think the future holds for you?

THE LEADER OF THE CLUB

Tom McIntyre, the thirty-four-year-old president of the Disney Corporation, sat in his Florida office watching the President of the United States on television. So far, the President was performing up to expectations. McIntyre watched the screen intently. How fortunate it was that the real President had decided to give his State of the Union address at Disneyworld; it had made it so much easier to replace him with the robot duplicate. On the screen, the robot rambled on, sounding exactly like the original. At one point it paused and blinked its left eye twice. Damn it, McIntyre thought, that wasn't supposed to happen.

McIntyre let his gaze wander around the office. His eyes paused momentarily on the pictures of Walt and Roy mounted on the far wall. Both gone now. Directly to the left of the picture of Roy was a photograph of McIntyre taken the day he had been appointed president of the Disney Corporation, the youngest one ever. Next to that picture was a smaller one of the Dumbo ride at Disneyland in

California. Laughing children filled the seats of the flying elephants. McIntyre wondered how long the children would laugh if they knew the Dumbos were nuclear missiles with warheads concealed in their trunks.

The voices of the television commentators brought his eyes back to the screen. The speech was over. The President was back with the technicians and would soon be off to the White House. McIntyre turned the set off. He sat behind his desk, his left hand tapping a slow rhythm on the desk top. Now that the President was a Disney robot, many grave decisions would have to be made in the coming months. So far, the plan was working perfectly. The Disney Corporation had been able to work covertly, without any confrontations. He hoped it would continue to be so. He did not want to use the Dumbos, but he realized he would if he had to.

His intercom buzzed; his secretary reminded him that he was due at a meeting in ten minutes. He pushed his seat back and rose. He picked his security badge up off the desk and clipped it to his lapel. What was the subject of the meeting? He couldn't recall. So many projects were under development that it was impossible to keep track of all of them. McIntyre stepped out of his office, closing the door softly behind him.

Some of the companies illustrated here have branches in many countries. Do the people of these countries benefit in the same ways?

(facing page) Does the introduction of American products into foreign economies promote American values?

The bell chimed and McIntyre awoke. He was well over one hundred now and most of his body was replacement parts. The bed's autopump fed the proper chemical stimulants and nutrients into his blood stream. He blinked his eyes. Today was the day. Finally. He had lived for this day for the past twenty years. It was the only thing that had kept him going. Today was the Resurrection.

He reached the Shrine in just under an hour. Quietly, reverently, he made his way through the thousands of pilgrims who had held a silent vigil at the Shrine for many months. He entered the main hall. The hall alone had cost over fifteen million dollars (now affectionately referred to as "Mickeys") and had taken twelve years to build. Massive and somber, the hall was a miracle of engineering. McIntyre looked overhead at the vast network of speakers and realized that even now a subliminal vibration was being broadcast to enhance the feelings of awe and reverence.

Every line in the hall had been designed to lead the eye to the altar in the center of the hall. The altar was immense and metallic. A deep hum issued from somewhere within it. High on the altar rested a figure encased in glass. The interior of the glass was filled with liquid nitrogen.

McIntyre walked up to the podium that stood in front of the altar. The indicators on the podium showed green. All that remained was the final step. McIntyre had been retired for a long time, but the public still thought of him fondly. He had been chosen to initiate the final sequence.

McIntyre fed the proper code into the altar's computer. In answer, soft, low music began. Huge fountains of water sprang up behind the altar. A brilliant blue light fell on the figure on the altar. A red light joined the blue, and then a yellow. Together the three lights formed a blinding white light which radiated outward from the figure. Rings of flame burst from the floor and spiraled up around the altar. Slowly, the nitrogen drained from the glass. The lighting became more subdued, the flames were extinguished. A new, higher pitched vibration issued from the altar. The top of the glass case folded back. A collective gasp came from those assembled in the hall as the figure in the case sat up. The nitrogen sleep was finally over. Walt was alive.

A choir of a hundred girls, virgins, each more lovely than Walt's own Snow White, broke into "The Hallelujah Chorus." The thousands in the hall were applauding and whistling, and the sound shook the building. Walt rose from the glass casket. He walked down the altar steps and looked around at the joyous faces. McIntyre approached him, trying to maintain his dignity in spite of being completely overwhelmed.

"Welcome back, sir," McIntyre said shakily, "You've got quite a lot to catch up on. Please come with me."

Walt, looking as benign as McIntyre had remembered, followed him into the restricted area of the Shrine. Here there were no artistically fluted columns, no inlaid arches, only white walls and complex machinery as far as the eye could see.

"It's great to be alive again," said Walt, "but I feel different somehow, younger and stronger. Could I see myself?"

McIntyre brought Walt to a large mirror set within a control panel. Walt looked himself over. "Why, I look at least twenty years younger than I was. There's something else different as well. What is it? My face looks the same but . . . Why, I have a halo!" A circle of light six inches in diameter floated over his head.

McIntyre smiled. "The boys in endocrinology cooked that one up. All it took was a simple restructuring of a few hormones."

Walt chuckled, a deep, throaty sound. "Saint Walt . . ." he mused to himself.

"Everything went just as you planned, sir," McIntyre said.

"Tell me. Tell me everything," said Walt.

"It's all yours, sir, the entire planet. America, Europe, Australia, Asia—"

Why might this company find it beneficial to operate in more than one country?

"Africa too?"

"It's called Adventureland now, sir. We did away with all of the animals and replaced them with robot hippos and elephants. We did the same thing with China and Russia, only now they're called Orientland and Winterland, respectively."

"Did you have any problems?"

"Only minor ones. Population reconditioning and redistribution in Europe and Asia was the largest problem. But that's all taken care of now. There are no more problems any more, no more struggles, no more wars. Your dream is a reality, sir. Your world."

"Disneyworld . . ." One lone tear rested on Walt's cheek.

McIntyre felt a lump in his throat. "Come outside, sir. There's one more thing I'd like you to see."

McIntyre led Walt out into the open air. The sun was setting. In the distance the calls of birds were audible.

Walt smiled. "I hear birds. How lovely."

McIntyre corrected him. "Tape recordings, sir. We did away with all the live birds. Only robot birds now." McIntyre looked up. "Ah. Watch the skies, sir."

The sky darkened as night approached. A star appeared, then another and another. Soon the night sky was illuminated with stars. From on high, the familiar face beamed down at them.

"The Mickey Way," McIntyre said.

Walt was crying now. "How wonderful," he said, "How very, very wonderful."

"I knew you'd like it, sir," said McIntyre softly.

Look through magazines for pictures of products. Find at least three pictures of things that are made in the United States and three of the same things that are imported. Is there a difference between the imported and domestic things? Is this indicated in some way in the pictures? Why are the imported things imported? Are there subsidies to the manufacturers of the American products? tariffs or quotas on the imported products? Why? Do these pictures tell you anything about domestic vs. imported things?

VISUAL
ACTIVITY

ACTIVITIES

I. Let your imagination run wild as you enter into this writing activity. Perhaps some day your ideas will become a reality.

1. It is the year 2000. Pretend that you are the controlling head of a powerful multinational corporation. Write a full-page description of the world at that time and of how your corporation influences it. Elaborate on your source of power and how you achieved it. Include answers to the following questions:
   a. What are the communication and transportation systems like?
   b. What jobs are available and who holds them?
   c. How are those in power different from those who are not?
   d. What are the answers to the four economic questions?
   e. What are the living, work, and recreation spaces like?
   f. How would you describe the corporate mentality of your employees?
   g. What resources are needed and how are they used?
   h. What problems does this world have?

2. Share your vision of the world with the class and discuss it by providing answers to the questions listed above. Alternately, you may choose to base your predictions on research, using your imagination to fill in the gaps. Use *Future Shock* by Alvin Toffler and *The Futurist* magazine to get started.

II. This activity will help you to imagine how you might influence the future.

1. Divide into five groups. Each group will represent the governing body of one of the following powerful and influential forces of the future:

   - a multinational corporation
   - a country with half of the world's energy resources
   - a group with the most advanced computer technology
   - a country of two billion people
   - an international congress of nations

2. Design a proposal explaining how your group will have a major impact on the world in the future. As you will be competing with the other four groups for control, it is important that you design a proposal that is both strong and appealing. Your proposal should contain a general argument as to why your group should control the future. Later in the activity, groups will vote for one proposal.

3. List the main goals of your group. These should be more specific ideas about what your group hopes to gain or accomplish. The group whose goals are most consistent with the proposal finally chosen by the class will win control.

    a. First, list the five main objectives of your proposal.
    b. Next, distribute fifty points among the five objectives in a way that will show their importance to you. To an extremely important goal, you might give twenty-five or thirty points; to a less important one, five to fifteen points. Point distribution is for your group to decide.
    c. Submit your list of objectives and point distribution to the instructor. These will remain confidential until the end of the game.

4. Discuss what strategies your group will use to convince other groups to vote for your proposal. Take five to ten minutes.

5. *Round #1:* Each group sends out one person, who will be the negotiator for this round. The negotiator has fifteen minutes to go to each of the other four groups to try and gain their support for the group's proposal. This is the time to build alliances and make deals. Those members who remain at headquarters should plan ahead for the next round of negotiations.

6. Each group has five to ten minutes to discuss the effectiveness of its strategies and to plan for round #2 of negotiations.

7. *Round #2:* This time the first negotiator remains at headquarters, while for fifteen minutes the other members of the group go to the other four headquarters in a last attempt to win support before the vote.

8. Now each group has about five to ten minutes to revise its proposal before it is voted on by the class. This proposal should be popular with the class and should also suggest the original objectives stated by the group.

9. All final proposals should be listed on the board. Each group must decide how it will cast its one vote. Remember, the group whose objectives are most nearly represented in the proposal accepted by the class is the winning group and ultimate controller of the future of the world.

10. Groups vote. If one proposal does not win three votes, negotiations must be repeated until a proposal receives three votes.

11. When a proposal is finally chosen, the teacher then reads the list of objectives and decides if they are included in the proposal. The group with the highest number of distribution points in the proposal is the winner.

12. Discussion questions
    a. What weighed most heavily in the design of each proposal?
    b. What was your role in selecting the final proposal? What would your role be in this future world?
    c. If the proposal became a reality, what would the future world be like?
    d. To what extent do you think the real world's future will be like your proposal? How do you think it will differ?

CHAPTER 16 CURRENT PROBLEMS OF THE AMERICAN ECONOMY

Meeting Energy Requirements

The United States now uses nearly one-third of the world's total energy output. Most of this energy comes from oil. The major oil-exporting nations have formed a cartel called the Organization of Petroleum Exporting Countries (OPEC). During the winter of 1973–74, OPEC refused to deliver oil until prices were higher. Long lines formed at gas stations. Many businesses and schools closed down for lack of fuel; many homes were cold. By winter's end, OPEC's oil embargo had succeeded. Prices for oil nearly doubled, and Americans became more aware of the importance of energy supplies.

There are three questions to keep in mind in thinking about meeting energy requirements. First, how should the existing energy supplies be shared? Second, how should Americans go about finding more fuel supplies and developing new forms of energy? Third, how can the United States answer both these questions in ways that do not conflict with other economic goals, such as high levels of production and growth?

Sharing energy supplies involves decisions about the price of oil and other fuels, such as coal and natural gas. The price of fuel determines who will get it and how much of it there will be. If prices go too high, consumers and businesses without extra money to spend will suffer. Some businesses will close. Workers will be laid off. Those who rely on cars for getting to work will not have as much money to spend on other things. High fuel prices, in other words, could lead to both inflation and recession—that is, to high prices and high unemployment.

At the same time, a rise in the price of fuel means that people are apt to use less of it than they would if prices were low. Energy resources would thus be conserved for future generations. Price hikes might also encourage the owners of oil, natural gas, and coal to look for new and larger supplies.

The government has other options besides allowing price hikes. It can ration fuel in order to insure that everyone is able to get at least the amount needed to do business, run a car, or heat a home. But rationing would not encourage fuel owners to look for new supplies. In the long run, rationing might bring back the long lines at gas pumps, the closed businesses, and the cold houses.

The government could also encourage the development of new forms of energy to replace oil, natural gas, and coal. It has done this with nuclear power for many years. But there are drawbacks to the widespread use of nuclear power plants. The radioactive waste products of these plants are quite dangerous. So far, no one has come up with a completely safe way to dispose of them. The government could also encourage the development of solar power (energy from the rays of the sun).

But these new energy sources will take a long time to be fully developed. In the meantime, an old source of energy, coal, is being brought back. The use of coal declined for many years because oil was easier to use, cheaper, and cleaner. Coal is once again becoming a popular source of energy. But now the country has to decide between having costly antipollution devices in factories and homes and repealing current air quality laws. In the end, all these energy questions boil

Figure 46-1 Energy Production by Major Source
What are the most important sources of energy production? What do you think will be the most important source in the year 2000?

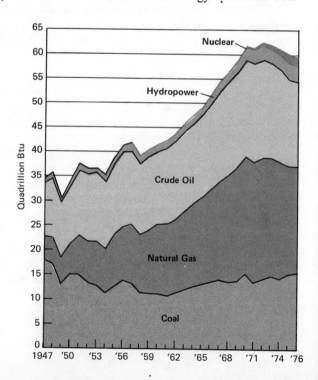

down to one. How can enough energy to run an industrial economy be found without ruining the natural environment at the same time?

As you take your place in a changing world, you must also contend with personal resource scarcity. You are young, inexperienced, and at a disadvantage in the job market. Your resources seem insufficient. Like the country, you have to find ways of achieving your economic goals in spite of a resource shortage. You do have some resources—talents, skills, ideas, energy, enthusiasm. You may have shown your ability to take care of small children, to budget time and money, to organize a group, to plan for others, to help people, to fix things, to persuade, design, or compute. You have demonstrated your strength, creativity, and intelligence. Your resources have been useful to you in your school career. But soon you will find yourself in a new situation where you will be on your own.

In order to grow, you will need additional resources. You can further develop the abilities you already have through schooling, work, training programs, or by teaching yourself. Or you can explore new fields and find new sources of power.

You can also find ways to make better use of your resources. For example, instead of babysitting for one family at a time, you could organize a play group of several children. Just as a small-scale power source may be right for a particular location, you may be right for a particular job. And, if you can show an employer how you can help him, he may be able to create a job that is just right for you.

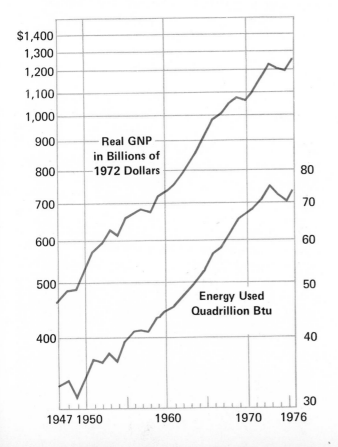

Figure 46-2   Energy and National Output in the United States
How are energy and GNP related? How can we conserve energy and have economic growth?

What might the real costs be for developing energy sources like this one? What might we save?

☐ The reading for this lesson comes from *Newsweek.* It describes two approaches to the energy crisis. The "hard energy" path, which relies on large power plants, requires an increase in energy supplies. The "soft" approach focuses on finding the right energy sources for each job. As you read it, ask yourself the following questions:

1. What are the advantages and disadvantages of the "soft energy" path for the country?
2. What are the advantages and disadvantages for you of developing high-powered skills? of using lesser skills as efficiently as possible?
3. How realistic does each path seem for the country? for you?

THINKING SOFT

Blinking in the harsh Georgia sunlight, disheveled after his fifteenth flight in almost as many days, Amory Lovins came down the ramp at Atlanta's Hartsfield International Airport. He had just flown in from St. Simons Island, where he had addressed a group of Federal energy planners. A few days earlier, he had been in Washington, conferring with top Administration officials—including Jimmy Carter, who invited him to the White House for a chat.

In the two weeks before that, Lovins had lectured, consulted, testified and debated in a dozen other cities, explaining, defending, and elaborating his controversial notion that to avoid disaster the U.S. must get off its current "hard path" of energy development and begin traveling a "soft" one. Among other reasons, Lovins was in Atlanta to see Georgia Gov. George Busbee, and he greeted his hosts with a question. "Are we going right to the governor's office?" he asked. The answer was yes. "In that case," Lovins grinned wearily, knotting his necktie, "I'd better put on my camouflage."

The image was an apt one, for there is much of the underground infiltrator about Lovins. At the tender age of 29, this baby-faced expatriate, who lives in London and serves as the British representative of the Friends of the Earth, Inc., has become one of the Western world's most influential energy thinkers. His visionary essay, "Energy Strategy: The Road Not Taken?", which appeared in *Foreign Affairs* last fall and has since been expanded into a book, is described by population biologist Paul Ehrlich as "the most influential single work on energy policy written in the last five years." "He has put a lot of things together that other people have been dealing with in pieces for years," says John Holdren, an energy expert at the University of California at Berkeley. "Because of him, the energy debate will never be the same."

Perhaps the most significant measure of Lovins's impact has been the heavy fire he has drawn, expecially from nuclear-power advocates and the utility industry. *Electric Perspectives,* the magazine of the Edison Electric Institute, the trade association for the nation's investor-owned utilities, recently devoted an entire issue to angry critiques of his *Foreign Affairs* essay. And Lovins is taken to task as much for his personal "arrogance" as for the lack of mathematical rigor in his arguments. "He is led by what he wants to find and manages to get arguments for the desired results," says Nobel Prize-winning physicist Hans Bethe. "He takes partial results of other people's work and leaves behind the numbers he doesn't like."

Lovins's basic thesis is that the hard energy path—which he defines as characterized by growing reliance on huge centralized electric-power systems that depend on fossil fuels and nuclear energy—is not only inefficient and dangerous, but also inappropriate to U.S. energy needs. Instead, he argues, the nation should embark on a soft energy path, reducing its massive energy appetite through "technical fixes" that can cut energy waste in half. What requirements remain should be filled with diverse, flexible and benign power sources such as solar and wind energy, biomass conversion

What might be some of the effects on our over-burdened environment if energy sources like this were developed?

(producing liquid fuels from farm and forestry wastes) and cogeneration (using industrial waste heat to generate electricity).

"I start by asking what are we trying to do with all this energy and what is the best way to do each job," Lovins explains. What he finds, he says, is an economy that burns 29 per cent of its fossil fuels to produce its highest-grade form of energy, electricity, when all but 8 per cent of power requirements could be filled by lower-grade fuels. This is "superfluous, wasteful and expensive," he wrote in his *Foreign Affairs* essay, "like cutting butter with a chain saw."

Not only is electricity increasingly expensive to generate—demanding a capital investment so huge it could cripple the economy—but growing dependence on highly centralized, complex power systems, Lovins says, makes the society ever more vulnerable to disruption. "A small fault or a few discontented people become able to turn off a country," he notes. At the same time, individuals will find themselves increasingly at the mercy of "an alien, remote and perhaps humiliatingly uncontrollable technological elite." The result, could be an erosion of civil liberties and the rise of "friendly Fascism."

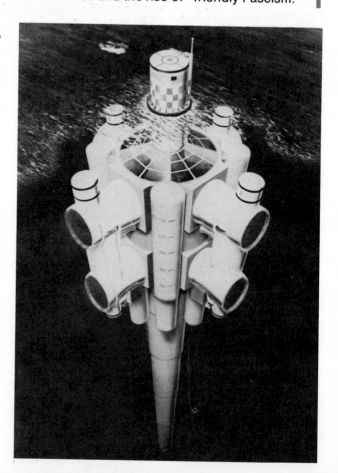

How might we best use the fuels we have until energy sources like this are a reality?

Why is it critical at this time to develop alternatives to fuels like coal, oil, and gas? How did it come to be that way?

The soft path, on the other hand, poses none of these dangers, Lovins insists. "It can be understood and controlled by the people who depend on it," he says, since it relies on a diverse array of simple (though not unsophisticated), labor-intensive technologies—neighborhood rooftop solar collectors in place of huge, remotely sited power stations, and "fluidized-bed" boilers that can burn everything from coal to garbage cleanly instead of giant coal-conversion plants producing synthetic gas and oil. And since the soft path eschews nuclear power completely, he argues, "it is the only way to come up with an intellectually consistent nonproliferation policy."

Lovins maintains that technologies on which the soft path depends are already available, and that the transition could be made within the next 50 years without forcing major social changes. What's crucial, he says, is that the transition begin soon—before the hard path's momentum forecloses all other options.

Lovins came to energy policy by way of climatology after an eclectic education that included studies in music, classics, law and experimental physics at Harvard and Oxford. His only formal degree is a Master of Arts from Oxford, which has led some to question his qualifications as a scientist. "He's impressed a lot of people who don't know anything about energy and depressed a lot of people who do," says one oil executive. Specifically, critics insist that Lovins has overestimated the costs of hard technology, while underestimating the costs of soft. They also claim that many of the soft technologies Lovins touts are actually years away from availability.

Still, Lovins's basic thesis has yet to be disproved, and his influence is widening daily. The essay has already broken *Foreign Affairs*'s record for reprint requests within a year of publication. And many of its readers are influential enough to act on its recommendations. Indeed, the day after he talked with Lovins, President Carter told an international energy conference that the world should consider alternatives to nuclear power. While it would take a capital investment of $200,000 to $300,000, to produce a nuclear-energy capacity equivalent to one barrel of oil, Carter noted, "Recent studies I have read show that we can gain the equivalent of a barrel of oil per day by conservation at very little or no cost." The author of those studies: Amory Lovins.

ACTIVITIES

I. This activity will help you to look more closely at your own personal resources and at how you might use them more efficiently.

1. A résumé is a description of the resources a person has available and is used when applying for a job. Your résumé would be based on your personal experiences and the skills you have developed. Pretend you are part of a group that has decided to make a contribution to society. Think of a cause whose goals are socially useful. Then think of something you could do to promote that cause. You must choose a job for which you would be qualified based on the resources and skills you can offer.

2. Make a list of some of the things you have done that you are proud of. These could include the following:

   helping a friend or relative   fulfilling a responsibility
   fixing something for a neighbor   teaching a younger person
   solving a problem   making something special

3. Based on your list, select a job for which you would be qualified. For example, you might do the following:

   write an article for a local paper   write letters to members of Congress
   support a politician   or others in authority
   run a summer basketball program   volunteer time in a hospital
   organize a cleanup campaign   or nursing home
                                         organize a block party

4. Write a résumé for yourself, being sure to include the following data:
   a. Name   Date of birth
   b. Address   Present date
   c. Education: course of study
   d. School activities: Member of debating team; reporter for school paper; member of soccer team for three years, now on first string; treasurer of dramatic club.
   e. Work or related experience: Babysit two afternoons a week with a two-year-old; collect money to pay for soccer team's uniforms; budget my own allowance.
   f. Job objective: To work for a telethon or raise funds.
   g. Qualifications: Speak well; have the ability to persuade others; like people; don't give up easily.

5. Trade résumés with someone in the class whom you know well. Apply Strategy #2 from Activity I to the résumé. Ask yourself how this person's skills can be presented so that his chances of finding a job in which all his resources are used will be maximized. Write your suggestions on the back of your classmate's résumé.

6. When your résumé is returned to you, see if you can revise it in a way that will show your skills and experience to best advantage.

7. Discussion questions
    a. Which special skills did you include in your résumé? Did you leave any out? Why?
    b. How do you think your special abilities will help you in the position for which you applied?
    c. Were you able to present your skills/resources more effectively after your résumé was criticized? Do you find it easier to "sell" yourself or someone else?

II. This research activity will help you to consider your present use of natural resources and how you might better use them in the future.

1. Three strategies are available to help you become more careful and creative in the way you use natural resources. You can
    a. cut back on consumption
    b. use them in a more efficient way
    c. find new sources

2. Research the cost of gasoline in your area. Think of two or three occasions when you rely on gasoline to fuel the means of transportation you use. What are the costs and benefits of using gasoline for these purposes? This should be considered in financial as well as personal terms.

3. By applying each of the three strategies, think of ways in which you could use this natural resource more sparingly or avoid using it altogether. Then determine the costs and benefits of each of the three new ways.

4. The chart in the Workbook is designed to help you complete this activity. If you don't have a Workbook, copy this chart on a piece of paper.

5. Divide into small groups and share your personal chart with others in your group.

6. Discussion questions
    a. Which strategy was most useful to you? Why?
    b. Were any of the alternatives you thought of unrealistic for you?
    c. To what other resources that you use could you apply each of the three strategies?

#1:

Present gas use	Strategy #1: Cut back	Strategy #2: Use more efficiently	Strategy #3: Find new sources
Costs:	Costs:	Costs:	Costs:
Benefits:	Benefits:	Benefits:	Benefits:

#2:

Present gas use	Strategy #1: Cut back	Strategy #2: Use more efficiently	Strategy #3: Find new sources
Costs:	Costs:	Costs:	Costs:
Benefits:	Benefits:	Benefits:	Benefits:

#3:

Present gas use	Strategy #1: Cut back	Strategy #2: Use more efficiently	Strategy #3: Find new sources
Costs:	Costs:	Costs:	Costs:
Benefits:	Benefits:	Benefits:	Benefits:

Making Cities Livable

As the American economy became more and more specialized, cities also became more important. By bringing together a great many resources, cities made it possible to produce a great variety of goods and services. But today's cities face huge problems. Not all of them are economic. Some are political and social. Yet economics can help to solve some of the problems the cities now face.

Consider, for example, the decisions of thousands of people to live in the suburbs and drive their cars into the city each day. They cause traffic jams, the spread of highways and parking lots, and air pollution. Economists can estimate the costs of these problems and compare them with the benefits of commuting by car. This could help to solve at least one major urban problem—transportation.

The concept of opportunity costs shows that each time resources are used in one way, all other uses of the resources are sacrificed. Each solution has its own price. Third-party costs, like pollution, and third-party benefits, such as parks, are other concepts that can help us deal with urban problems. Economists could suggest better ways to pay for third-party costs and to distribute third-party benefits.

The transportation problem is a good example of how economics can help people to understand the world they live in. For the past twenty years, a major question in urban transportation policy has been whether money should be spent on highways or on public transport, such as buses, subways, and trains. Ninety percent of the travel in cities is done by car. But at rush hours, the situation is different. Then, 20 to 50 percent of travel is by public transportation.

Therefore, the problem facing city governments is that public transportation is underused during non-rush hours. That is, most people travel by public transportation only during the peak periods. On the other hand, highways are used at all times of the day. When it comes to figuring how these two systems should be paid for, there is an imbalance. The cost of highways is divided among many people. The cost of subways is borne by far fewer people.

So there are two problems to solve. One is the rush-hour traffic jam on highways and in public transport systems. The other is that of paying for highways and public transportation. Economics can suggest ways of solving both problems at once. One solution might work like this. Suppose people were charged more for using highways and public transport. Non-rush-hour users would be given a free ride. Those using subways during rush hours would have to pay 20 to 50 percent more. The exact amount would depend on how much of their total use occurred during rush hours. Highway users would have to pay nearly ten times what they now pay in gasoline taxes. Clearly, this huge increase in the cost of using highways would encourage many auto users to switch to subways and buses.

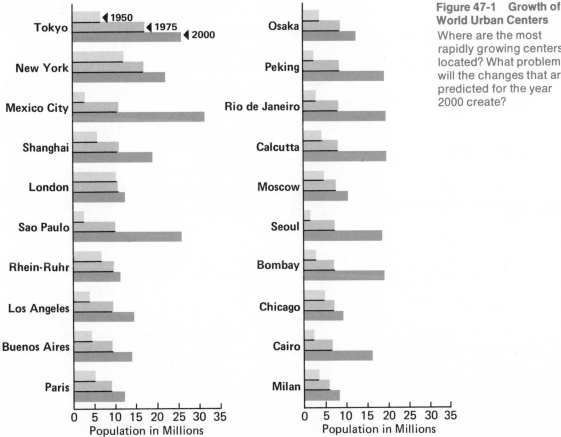

Figure 47-1   Growth of World Urban Centers
Where are the most rapidly growing centers located? What problems will the changes that are predicted for the year 2000 create?

**Figure 47-2 Percent
Urbanization of World
Regions, 1977**

Will the world ever be
totally urbanized? What
would life be like if it
were?

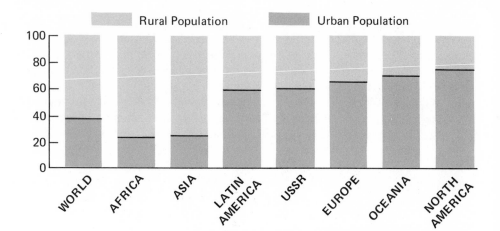

**Figure 47-2 Percent
Urbanization of World
Regions, 1977**

Will the world ever be
totally urbanized? What
would life be like if it
were?

What kinds of changes
might be made to public
and private
transportation to make
cities more livable? How
feasible are these
changes?

This would reduce traffic jams, air pollution, and the need for so many parking lots. Also, the cost of public transport would be spread over many more riders.

Other solutions could also be tried. The cost of parking could be increased. This would encourage more people to leave their cars at home and to take the train or the bus. Subsidies could be given to public transport systems. New trains, traveling at high speeds, might make cars a less attractive way of getting to and from work. The important thing to know is that economics can point out the costs

What kinds of changes might be made to cities themselves, in order to make them more livable?

and benefits of various solutions. The economist's job is to look at all the connections between problems, and to explain what each solution will cost in terms of resources, time, money, labor, and so on. But the final decision will depend on what people really want. Economics can suggest the answers. It cannot force people to adopt them.

In many ways, the cities reflect the problems of the modern economy. Poor housing, for example, occurs largely because of high unemployment in urban centers. City services, like schools, libraries, hospitals, or fire protection, are cut back because the poor and unemployed in the cities cannot pay taxes on income they do not have. Cities are also hurt by "capital flight," since the plants that close and move to other countries through multinational corporations are often found in urban areas.

Making cities livable means more than just making them clean and safe and healthy. It means turning them into the kinds of places that people want to live in. You have your own unique sense of who you want to be and how you want to live. You want a community that supports that. You want there to be people who understand you, people you can share with, people who respect what you're

"Henderson's made a remarkable adjustment to city living."

trying to do. You want a place you can feel proud of and at home in. You want a certain amount of privacy and a certain amount of contact with your neighbors. You want your neighborhood to reflect your values, both in its appearance and in the way people deal with each other.

As you look for a place that is livable, you may find an economic analysis helpful. What do you require? What are you willing to give, in terms of work, responsibility, or tax money, to get what you want? How and where can you find what you want for a reasonable price? What price does this community demand? What are the third-party costs and benefits of the various solutions to your problems? What tradeoffs does each solution require?

☐ The reading for this lesson is a photo essay, "Future Communities" (see pages 482–83). It pictures some future cities that architects have proposed as answers to current urban problems. The other visuals in this lesson present more modest solutions that are in effect now. Look at these visuals along with the photo essay.

ACTIVITIES

I. This activity will help you analyze the pictures in this lesson in both economic and human terms.

1. Choose two future cities from the photo essay and one present solution from the other pictures in the lesson. Use them to complete the chart in the Workbook. If you don't have a Workbook, copy the following chart on a piece of paper.

	City:	City:	Photo from page
What social and economic problems does this city solve?			
How might people who live here feel about their city?			
What kinds of relationships between people might this city foster?			
What tradeoffs would have to be made to produce this city?			
Would you like to live here?			

2. Share your answers with your classmates. Then discuss these questions:
   a. What makes a city livable?
   b. Which of the solutions to urban problems shown in this lesson would be worth trying? How could they be implemented?

FUTURE COMMUNITIES

INSTANT CITY   Stanley Tigerman
It is planned that these structures could be erected above existing expressways that run between cities. The bottom section of each building contains four stories, which could be used for service and parking needs. The next section of three stories could provide space for industry and commerce, as well as education. There would then be five stories of office space. There are then three other sections—each with seven stories—for residential use.

TETRAHEDRONAL CITY
Buckminster Fuller Archives
Tetrahedronal City would be built to house 300,000 families, each with a balcony and outside view. All the machinery necessary to run the city would be located inside the tetrahedron. The structure would be built so that it could float on water. Each city would measure two miles to an edge. The whole city could be floated out into the ocean and anchored at any point. The city can start with a thousand residents and expand slowly to house a million people without ever changing its shape.

HABITAT   Moshe Safdie
This version of Habitat was built for the Montreal Expo in 1967. One of the advantages of this type of dwelling is that it can be built on the construction site itself. The structure is made up of many separately built boxes. After each box is built, it is attached to the other boxes in a zigzag pattern. People get to their apartments by elevators and stairs and by covered bridges that connect them. A special advantage of Habitat is that it is built over and around existing structures, without tearing them all down first.

MANHATTAN DOME
Buckminster Fuller Archives
Buckminster Fuller has created many domes, although they are all smaller than this proposed dome over Manhattan. One of the dome's advantages is that it is extremely strong. Another is that the larger domes seem to disappear into the sky. They become transparent when it is bright outside, and opaque when it is overcast. There are problems, too. The floor area is small compared to the height, and the skin of the dome is hard to clean. Perhaps the real question the dome raises is this: can you change a city without changing the city?

ACTIVITIES

II. The object of this card game activity is to create the kind of community in which you would most like to live. The type of community you put together will depend on the cards you draw during play. The playing cards will cover the following aspects of a community:

lifestyles represented	class of residents
social norms	type of economy
public institutions	career choices available
spatial arrangements of buildings	use of resources
political structure	

There are playing cards in the Workbook. Copy the cards here if you don't have a Workbook.

GAME RULES

1. Divide the class into groups of five. Only five people can play the game at one time. Groups should take turns, or the cards should be copied for each group so all can play at once.
2. Shuffle the cards and deal six to each player.
3. Place the remaining cards face down on the center of a table. Turn the top card face up and place it next to the rest of the deck.
4. Each player takes a turn and picks the card that is face up or on the top of the deck. For each card picked from the table, one card must be discarded from the player's hand. Discarded cards are placed in the face-up pile.
5. Each player is allowed to trade one card during the game.
6. Stop the game after twenty minutes or when a player feels she has a strong workable combination of cards.
7. The players then compare their hands and convince one another of the strengths of their communities.
8. The game ends when you have created a realistic community.
9. Discussion questions
   a. What type of community did you create?
   b. Could you live in that community? Why or why not?
   c. What problems might this community have?
   d. How might this community change?

lifestyle: extended families	lifestyle: communes	lifestyle: single-parent families	lifestyle: couples without children and single people
lifestyle: nuclear families	social norm: cooperation, generosity	social norm: everyone takes care of their own	social norm: have fun
social norm: work today to provide for tomorrow	social norm: waste not, want not	public institution: to serve the people	public institution: to keep the status quo
public institution: to support government bureaucracy	public institution: no institutions	public institution: run by a few	space: communally shared
space: skyscrapers of steel and plastic	space: wilderness living	space: underwater/in the air	space: private dwellings
space: the same for all	space: Buckminster Fuller design	authority: present form of government	authority: none
authority: police state	authority: obey your parents	authority: media-governed	authority: each for himself
people: everyone welcome	people: only people with same ideas	people: rich	people: environmentally aware
people: people with different backgrounds	careers: executive positions only	careers: equal work for all	careers: all work at what they do best
careers: no work for people, automated machines everywhere	career: same as your parents	use of resources: use it while you've got it	use of resources: take it from those who have it but can't afford it
use of resources: be careful, use only what you think you really need	use of resources: rationing for all	use of resources: extensive research for new sources	use of resources: go without
economy: traditional	economy: command	economy: market	economy: mixed

Preserving the Environment

Economically, the "environmental crisis" involves two separate questions. First, what changes can be made in the natural world without doing harm to it? Second, what changes can be made in the economy without causing a high level of unemployment or preventing workers from producing the goods and services needed? Saving the environment while destroying the economy would not be much of a solution. On the other hand, letting the economy grow bigger and bigger while ruining the world would be suicidal.

People have been changing the environment throughout history. Land has been put to new uses. Wood has been taken from forests. Animals have been raised for food. Deserts have been turned into gardens. And the power of rivers has been harnessed to create electric power. Clearly, not all these changes have been harmful to the environment.

Recently, however, the changes have been more drastic. They also occur at a faster pace. For example, long ago, when all towns were small, it did not matter much if the residents of a tiny village threw their garbage into the river. The river could clean itself. But now, when cities hold millions of people, the situation is quite different. The river cannot clean itself if a million people empty filth into it. But urban residents may not realize this until it's too late. After all, they are just doing what people have always done.

Why were earlier attempts at manufacturing less harmful to the outside environment? How has this changed?

If it is hard to predict the results of actions, it is often even harder to measure them. The effects of environmental damage are especially hard to measure. For example, how does one measure the effects of air pollution on lungs? How does one measure the value of a species of tiny fish that will be destroyed by the construction of one dam?

Economics teaches people to look at such problems in a certain way. Economists would want to find out the costs of each kind of environmental damage. They would also want to know the costs of preventing that damage. For example, what would be the costs, in terms of goods, services, and jobs, of not cutting the forest for timber, or of not building the dam? What would be the costs of preventing all forms of air pollution?

About 60 percent of air pollution comes from car exhausts. Most of the rest comes from factory smoke. One way to clean up the air would be to ban all cars and factories from crowded areas where there is lots of dirty air. But what would be the costs of doing so? They would be high. Workers in city factories would lose their jobs. Local firms would suffer. More layoffs would be forced. Costly public transport would have to be built. An economist might measure these costs and suggest less expensive and less disruptive ways of ending air pollution.

One way might be to change the way pollution is paid for. At present, pollution is a third-party cost. It is paid for by people who do not cause it. Policies that made the creators of pollution pay for it might reduce it. A special tax could be put on cars that emit poisonous fumes. Factories that create lots of smoke could also be taxed. On the other hand, tax benefits could be given to those who reduced the pollution they caused.

All these suggestions are made simply to show how economists study an important public issue. There may be other economic solutions to the problems of the environment. There may be solutions that have nothing to do with economics. The country might decide to ban all cars and factories and not think about the consequences, such as unemployment. An economist could not object to that on economic grounds. All an economist could do would be to point out that all decisions have costs, whether they are recognized or not. In fact, it is the economist's dismal duty to keep reminding people that in this world there's no such thing as something for nothing.

The dilemma of preservation versus change can also be a personal one. We notice it particularly during times of transition, when we are leaving one place or phase of life for another. You don't want to stay still. Yet you need to find ways to preserve the familiar places, relationships, and traditions that are important to you. You have to decide which aspects of your past, or which parts of your environment, are most valuable. You can then try to preserve them as separate spaces—like national parks—that you can return to for refreshment. Or you can try to integrate the lessons you have learned from them into your ongoing life, building your future in harmony with your past.

But you must always consider the tradeoffs. How hard is it for you to preserve those relationships and traditions? What else are you sacrificing? Are you hanging on so tightly that it keeps you from growing? On the other hand, if you let go of too much, will you destroy the fragile environment forever in the name of growth? Will you then lose sight of who you are?

Does it have to cost more for construction to blend in with, and preserve the environment? What might we save?

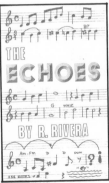   

☐ The reading for this lesson is by E. F. Schumacher. Schumacher applies the principles of Buddhism to economics and shows us a way to choose what is important. He thus gives us a new set of guidelines for applying economics to the problem of preserving our environment. As you read this selection, ask yourself the following questions:

1. How does Schumacher apply Buddhist economics to the problem of preserving the environment?
2. What other solutions to the problems of preservation and change does Buddhist economics suggest?
3. What do you like about this approach? What don't you like?

BUDDHIST ECONOMICS

"Right Livelihood" is one of the requirements of the Buddha's Noble Eightfold Path. It is clear, therefore, that there must be such a thing as Buddhist economics. Let us take some fundamentals and see what they look like when viewed by a modern economist and a Buddhist economist.

There is universal agreement that a basic source of wealth is human labor. Now, the modern economist has been brought up to think of work as little more than a necessary evil. From the point of view of the employer, it is simply an item of cost. It is to be reduced to a minimum if it cannot be done away with altogether, say, by automation. From the point of view of the worker, to work is to make a sacrifice of his leisure and comfort. Wages in this view are a kind of compensation for that sacrifice. Thus, if the ideal with regard to work is to get rid of it, every method that reduces the work load must be a good thing.

The Buddhist sees three purposes to working. The first is to give a man a chance to use and develop his skills. The second is to enable him to overcome his self-centeredness by joining with others in a common task. The third is to bring forth the goods and services needed for a pleasant life. To organize work so that it becomes meaningless, boring, or nerve-wracking would show a greater concern for goods than for people. Equally, to strive for leisure as an alternative to work would be thought a complete misunderstanding of one of the basic truths of human life. This is that work and leisure go hand in hand and cannot be separated without destroying the joy of work or the bliss of leisure.

From the Buddhist point of view, there are two types of machines which must be clearly distinguished. One adds to a man's skill and power. The other turns the work of man over to a mechanical slave so that man is forced to serve that slave. For the Buddhist, the essence of civilization is not in the multiplication of wants. It is in the purification of human character. Character is formed mainly by a man's work. And work, performed in dignity and freedom, blesses both those who do it and the products they make.

If a man has no chance to work, he is in a desperate position. Not only does he lack an income. He lacks the nourishment of disciplined work which nothing can replace. A modern economist may spend time figuring out whether full employment "pays." He may conclude that it is more "economic" to run an economy at less than full employment for the sake of greater labor mobility, wage stability, and so forth. His basic standard of success is simply the total quantity of goods produced during a given period of time.

From a Buddhist point of view, this kind of reasoning stands truth on its head. It considers good more important than people, and consumption more important than creative work.

The Buddhist is mainly interested in liberation. But Buddhism is "The Middle Way" and so is not against physical well-being. It is not wealth that stands in the way of liberation; it is the attachment to wealth. It is not the enjoyment of pleasurable things that enslaves; it is the craving for them. Consumption for the Buddhist is merely a means to human well-being, not an end in itself. The aim, therefore, is to obtain the greatest amount of well-being with the least amount of consumption. Buddhist economics, in fact, is the study of how to attain given ends with the minimum means.

Modern economics looks upon consumption as the sole end of all economic activity using land, labor, and capital as the means. The difference between the two economic systems could be stated this way: The Buddhist way aims for the greatest amount of human satisfaction by means of the best pattern of consumption. The modern way aims for the greatest amount of consumption by means of the best pattern of production.

The Buddhist way produces a high degree of human satisfaction by means of a fairly low rate of consumption. It allows people to live

What might be the costs of banning most, if not all sources of pollution? What are the alternatives?

How might these people as individuals deal with issues of change and preservation? How do you?

without great pressure and strain and to fulfill the golden rule of Buddhist teaching. This is "Cease to do evil; try to do good." As physical resources are everywhere limited, people who can meet their needs by using few resources are less apt to be at each others' throats than people who depend on a high rate of use. The same is true of people who live in self-sufficient villages. They are less apt to get involved in large-scale violence than people whose survival depends on world trade. A Buddhist economist would think that to meet human wants from distant sources rather than from nearby sources was a sign of failure.

Another striking difference between modern and Buddhist economics arises over the use of natural resources. Modern economics does not distinguish between materials that can be renewed and those that can't be. Its method is to quantify everything in terms of money. The only difference between fuels like coal and oil and fuels like wood or water power that modern economics admits is cost per unit. And the cheapest is naturally the one preferred. From a Buddhist point of view, the difference cannot be overlooked. Goods that can't be renewed must be used only if they have to be—and then only with the greatest effort to conserve them. A Buddhist economist would think that people who base their economic life on fuels that can't be renewed are parasites. In other words, they are living on their capital, not income.

Both the present condition and the long-term prospects of the modern world suggest that things are not as well as they might be. Thus, even those who believe that economic growth is more important than any spiritual or religious values could do worse than to learn from Buddhist economics. For it is not a question of choosing between "modern growth" and "traditional stagnation." It is a question of finding the right path of development, the Middle Way between material carelessness and traditional immobility. In short, it is a question of finding "Right Livelihood."

For this visual activity you can either make your own images or find pictures that you think are especially striking or important. Find at least two images (photos or drawn art) for each of the following: 1. Energy and resources, 2. Cities, and 3. The environment. What can be done to improve the situations these images portray? How do other parts of the world deal with these situations? What might images of the same type of things look like if the things were made in other parts of the world? What do these images say about the U.S. economy?

VISUAL
ACTIVITY

ACTIVITIES

Four activities dealing with the issue of preservation are included in this lesson. As a class, you may decide to do just one, or two, or all four. They are designed to help you think about the things in your world/life that are worth saving, either from an environmental or a personal point of view.

I. CLASS LETTER
1. As a class, write a letter to an influential person about an important environmental issue. Clearly state your views and explain what your goals are regarding the problem.
2. If the class cannot agree on one important issue, committees should be formed so that a number of letters can be written on different issues.
3. Discussion questions
    a. To whom did you write? Why did you choose this person?
    b. How optimistic are you that something can be done about the issue you chose?
    c. What will happen regarding this issue ten years from now? in twenty years? How will it affect you? the rest of the country? the world?
    d. What other steps can you take?

II. LETTER TO YOURSELF
1. Write a letter to yourself about the goals and values that are important to you. Pick a date (at least five or ten years into the future) when you will open this letter. Write about things that you plan never to forget or lose sight of. Explain why you believe what you do and how you plan to realize your goals. For example, you may promise to give your children more freedom than your parents have given you. You may hope never to tell a lie or always to fulfill your community obligations. You may always want to remember some of the special difficulties teenagers have in society.
2. Put this letter in a safe place and make a note to yourself to open it on the date selected by you.
3. Discussion questions
    a. What values that you presently hold do you hope to preserve?
    b. How realistic are you in believing that you will be able to preserve these values?
    c. What might happen that could force you to alter your ideas?
    d. What might give you the strength to hang on to what you believe in?

III. PICTURE CHARADES

1. Two or three students volunteer to make a list of words representing special events, discussions, activities, or days that this economics class has experienced together. This group is called the Preservation Committee. Each word should signify something important, useful, or meaningful that people in the class would benefit from remembering.
2. The rest of the class forms separate groups of four or five students. Each group should be supplied with large pieces of paper and a dark crayon or marker. For the purpose of this activity, each group should sit apart in a different section of the class.
3. One representative from each group goes to the Preservation Committee, which quietly reveals one of the words on its list.
4. The representatives return to their respective groups and, at a signal from the Preservation Committee, draw pictures which in some way symbolize the words given them.
5. It is the goal of each group to try to guess the word the representative is drawing on paper. The "reps" should not give any verbal or body clues to their teammates. Each group must guess the word purely on the basis of the drawing presented.
6. Rounds continue until everyone has had a turn or until there are no more special things to preserve.
7. The class may want to hang the drawings around the room to enhance the following discussion.
8. Discussion questions
   a. What was worth preserving? Why?
   b. What else might have been included by the committee?
   c. How might you benefit from preserving those special times?

IV. PRESERVATION ROLE PLAY

1. The class divides into groups of five or six students. Each group creates a skit about something special that has taken place in the class. It should be about an event, discussion, or lesson that was particularly meaningful and that will be useful to preserve. Each group must decide whether its role play is to be verbal or nonverbal and whether it wants the rest of the class to guess what it is about.
2. Each group takes a turn performing its role play before the class.
3. Discussion questions
   a. Why do you think each group chose its particular skit?
   b. What was worth preserving in the events, discussions, or lessons that were dramatized?
   c. Why is it important to remember things from different periods in your life?

GLOSSARY

ability-to-pay principle—taxing people based on their incomes and/or wealth without reference to the benefits they receive from the state. (*See also* benefits-received principle.)

absolute advantage—the ability of an individual, a business, or a nation to produce a larger output than a rival individual, business, or nation, using the same inputs.

acceleration principle—small changes in demand produce larger percentage changes in investment needed to meet that demand.

administrative costs—the costs of managing business activity as opposed to production costs.

autonomous changes—changes that occur independent of market forces. Events outside the economy such as war, natural disasters, etc. produce autonomous changes. (*See also* induced changes.)

automation—self-regulating machines that replace human workers are examples of automation.

balance of payments—a summary of all of a nation's economic transactions with the rest of the world.

balance of trade—that part of a nation's balance of payments that is based on its exports and imports of goods and services.

barter—exchanging goods and services without using money.

basic economic questions—every economic system must answer these questions: What shall be produced? How shall it be produced? How much shall be produced? For whom shall it be produced?

beneficiary—an individual who gains as a result of an action or policy.

benefits-received principle—taxing people based on the benefits they receive from government services. (*See also* ability-to-pay principle.)

bond—an interest bearing certificate issued by a business firm or a government. A bond is a promise to pay the bondholder a specified amount of money on a specified date. Bonds are used to borrow money, usually to finance capital expansion.

business cycle—changes in business conditions over time. The typical phases of a business cycle are depression, recovery, prosperity, recession.

byproducts—material that is the result of the production of another product. Byproducts that can not be used are considered waste products.

capital flight—the rapid movement of investment funds out of a nation where economic conditions are seen as unstable by investors.

capital gain—income received from the sale of a capital asset.

capital resources—goods such as tools, machines, or factories that are used to produce other goods and services.

cartel—an agreement among firms not to engage in price competition. Production quotas may also be set and penalties for violations agreed upon. Cartels are not legal in the United States.

checking accounts—(*See* demand deposits.)

closed shop—union membership is required before an employee can be hired in a closed shop. In 1947, the Taft Hartley Act outlawed the closed shop in the United States.

collective bargaining—when workers act as a group, usually through a labor union, to deal with their employers.

command economy—an economic system that solves its basic economic problems through central planning and control.

comparative advantage—having a greater absolute advantage or smaller absolute disadvantage in the production of a good. Nations maximize gains from international trade when they specialize in the production of goods in which their comparative advantages are greatest.

compensation of employees—wages and salaries and payments for fringe benefits such as medical care and retirement plans.

competition—two or more parties trying to obtain the business of others. Competition may focus on prices, quality, or service.

constant dollar GNP—Gross National Product adjusted for price changes. Prices that prevailed during a given base year are used to convert current dollar GNP to constant dollar GNP.

consumer—a user of goods and services.

Consumer Price Index—a price index constructed by comparing the prices of a market basket of goods and services to the prices of that market basket during a specified base year.

consumption—using goods and services to satisfy wants.

contract—an agreement of two or more parties, enforceable through legal proceedings.

corporate profits tax—a tax on the gross profits of corporations.

corporation—a form of business organization chartered by a state government or the national government. A corporation is a legal person. Stockholders' liability is limited to the amount they have invested in the corporation.

cost of living—the average amount of money needed to buy a market basket of essential goods and services at a specific time and place.

currency—that part of the money supply consisting of coins and bills.

current prices—stating Gross National Product for a given year in terms of the prices that existed in the same year.

cyclical unemployment—unemployment that is caused by the ups and downs of the business cycle.

deficit—the amount by which spending exceeds income. Often used to indicate the amount by which the federal government's spending exceeds tax revenues.

demand—the amounts of a good or service that buyers will be willing to purchase at each possible price at a given time.

demand curve—the demand for a good or service shown graphically with price on the vertical axis and quantity demanded on the horizontal axis.

demand deposits—checking accounts in commercial banks. Demand deposits are approximately 80% of the money supply. Payments by check account for 90% of all business transactions.

demand schedule—a table showing the number of units of a good or service that would be demanded at various prices.

depreciation—reduction in value of an asset; for example, a machine as it wears out in use.

depression—a period of significant and long-term unemployment of workers and machinery.

derived demand—the demand for a factor of production that is determined by the demand for the final product.

destructive competition—when some firms cut prices drastically, often driving other firms out of business. This occurs most often when excess capacity exists in the industry and all firms can not earn profits.

devaluation of currency—the reduction of the official exchange rates at which a nation's currency is exchanged for other nations' currencies.

discount rate—the interest rate that the Federal Reserve Bank charges member banks who borrow from the Fed.

discrimination—making economic decisions using non-economic criteria.

Disposable Personal Income—total amount of money that people have available for spending and saving after taxes have been paid. DPI is the sum of wages and salaries, rent, interest, dividends, income of unincorporated enterprises, and transfer payments less personal income taxes.

distribution—the process of getting final goods and services to consumers.

dividends—payments out of earnings that are made by corporations to their stockholders.

division of labor—breaking down work into different operations.

double counting—when estimating Gross National Product, economists avoid double counting, the counting of both raw materials and the goods made from these raw materials, by counting only final goods.

durable goods—goods which are expected to be used over an extended period of time.

earnings and cost approach—measuring Gross National Product by adding up the money received by all those who contributed to its production. GNP is equal to the sum of wages and salaries, rent, interest, dividends, income of unincorporated enterprises, social security contributions, corporate savings, corporate profits taxes, indirect business taxes, and depreciation. (*See also* flow of product approach.)

easy money policy—increasing the money supply, lowering interest rates, or encouraging banks to expand credit in order to make it easy for businesses to borrow and expand the economy.

economic growth—increasing a nation's production of goods and services, especially its ability to produce in the future.

economic indicators—statistical series used by economists to predict future economic activity.

economic model—a set of assumptions about important economic factors and their relationships used to explain the workings of the economy and to predict the future. Economists frequently use mathematical models.

economics—the study of the way scarce resources are allocated in order to satisfy wants. Economics looks at the way goods and services are produced, distributed, and consumed.

efficiency—a measure of how effective an economy is in using resources to meet consumer demands for goods and services.

elastic demand—when a price change results in a relatively larger change in quantity demanded.

elastic supply—when a price change results in a relatively larger change in quantity supplied.

emissions—gases and particles discharged into the air as part of production or consumption. A form of air pollution.

equilibrium—a state of balance or rest in the economy with no tendency for change to occur. Equilibrium may occur for an individual decision maker (firm or consumer), an entire market, or the entire economy.

equilibrium price—that price at which the quantity of a good or service supplied by producers is exactly equal to the quantity demanded by consumers.

equilibrium quantity—that quantity that producers are willing to supply and consumers are willing to buy at an equilibrium price.

equity—fairness. In taxation, equal treatment of people with the same incomes and circumstances.

excise tax—a tax on the manufacture or sale of a specific product like gasoline, tobacco, or liquor.

exports—goods and services sold to foreign people, businesses, or governments.

factor markets—markets for labor, raw materials, and capital, which are sometimes called factors of production.

F.I.C.A. taxes—payroll taxes under the Federal Insurance Contributions Act. These taxes finance the OASDI (old age, survivors, disability insurance) programs of the Social Security Administration.

financial capital—money used to invest in tools, machinery, and new production facilities. Real capital is the term that refers to these producer goods themselves.

fiscal policy—government taxing and spending to achieve economic goals.

fiscal year—a financial year used for accounting purposes that does not necessarily correspond to the calendar year.

fixed exchange rates—when a nation's currency has official and unchanging prices in terms of the currencies of other nations.

floating exchange rates—the price of a nation's currency in terms of the currencies of other nations is determined by market conditions. There is no official rate.

flow of product approach—determining the Gross National Product by adding the value of goods and services received. Gross National Product is equal to the sum of Personal Consumption, Investment, Government Spending and Net Exports, using this approach. (*See also* earnings and cost approach.)

foreign exchange—currencies of other nations.

foreign exchange markets—places where foreign currencies can be bought and sold.

full employment—the availability of jobs for all who want them. A certain amount of unemployment of new entrants to the labor force and workers in between jobs is expected. Economists have used 3%, 4%, and 5% unemployment as being equivalent to full employment.

functional distribution of income—income classified by the resources contributed to the productive process: compensation of employees, business and professional proprietors' income, farm proprietors' income, rental income, interest, and corporate profits.

geographical specialization—specialization based on climate or other natural advantages. Growing citrus fruit in Florida is an example.

GNP deflator—a measure of changes in prices of final goods and services. The GNP deflator is used to convert gross national product in current dollars to the constant dollars of a base year.

goods—tangible products like cars, clothing, and food that can be used to satisfy human wants.

government—in the national income accounts, government refers to spending on goods and services by all branches of local, state, and national governments.

government securities—bonds issued by local, state, and national governments in order to borrow money.

Gross National Product—the market value (sales prices) of all the final goods and services produced in the country during one year.

Gross Private Domestic Investment—all nongovernmental spending on new machinery, buildings, and vehicles plus additions to inventories of both intermediate and final goods.

hidden unemployment—this concept refers to those workers who have given up and dropped out of the labor force, those who are employed parttime who would like to work fulltime, and those who are employed at jobs where they cannot use their best skills. Official unemployment figures do not include hidden unemployment and therefore tend to underestimate the unemployment problem.

households—a statistical concept that refers to living units that function as economic units. Single persons living alone, married couples, or large family groups can be households.

human resources—the contributions made by people to the production of goods and services. Mental efforts as well as physical efforts are included.

imperfect competition—the condition in all markets where barriers prevent perfect competition. Monopoly, oligopoly, and monopolistic competition are forms of imperfect competition.

imports—goods and services brought into a nation from other nations.

import quota—a limit on the quantity of a foreign-made good that can be brought into a nation.

income—payments to people who supply productive resources, and transfer payments. Payment may be made in money, goods, or services.

income distribution—the way national income is divided among households in the economy.

indirect business taxes—taxes collected from businesses that are usually partially or entirely shifted to consumers. Examples are excise taxes, property taxes and import taxes.

individual proprietorship—a business, usually small, owned and operated by a single person. Many barbershops, bakeries, and farms are individual proprietorships.

induced changes—changes that are produced by interactions within the economic system. When production increases, income also increases, for example.

induced investment—investment that occurs because of an increase or expected increase in demand.

industrial production—the physical output of manufacturing, mining, and public utilities industries.

inelastic demand—when the percentage change in quantity demanded is less than a percentage change in price.

inelastic supply—when the percentage change in quantity supplied is less than a percentage change in price.

inflation—a rising general price level that reduces the purchasing power of money.

informal controls—the use of political pressure, threats of the use of regulatory power, etc. to encourage businesses to regulate themselves. This is sometimes called "jawboning."

input—factor used in production. Land, labor, and capital are the most commonly used input classifications.

institutions—business organizations, labor unions, government agencies, laws and customs of a society. Banks, minimum wage laws, and tipping are economic institutions in the U.S.

interdependence—in a market economy, all prices are to some degree affected by all other prices. Specialization makes trade necessary and people depend on others for vital goods and services.

interest—payment for the use of borrowed money.

international currency—a medium of exchange acceptable in payment of accounts among nations. Gold and the U.S. dollar have served that function in the past, and Special Drawing Rights at the International Monetary Fund are now being used as international currency.

International Monetary Fund—an institution that exists to provide stable exchange rates and to allow necessary adjustments to be made more easily. Members can borrow from the Fund to buy up their own declining currency, and the Fund can sell its reserves of a currency that is increasing in value.

investment—spending on capital goods. (*See* Gross Private Domestic Investment.)

investment tax credit—an amount business firms are allowed to deduct from their taxes. It is a percentage of investment purchases made during a tax period. This device is used to encourage expansion of output, employment, and income.

invisible hand—Adam Smith's theory that when people seek their own self interests in a competitive economy they automatically promote society's interests as if by an "invisible hand."

itemized deductions—the U.S. personal income tax system allows taxpayers to avoid paying taxes on income spent on specific goods or services. Charitable contributions and property taxes are examples of such deductions that must be listed ("itemized") on the taxpayer's return.

limited liability—describes the situation where owners of stock in a corporation are not responsible for debts of the corporation beyond the amount they have invested. This allows corporations to raise large sums of money from many stockholders, each of whom has a minimum risk.

macroeconomics—the study of economics that is concerned with large aggregates such as total production, total employment, and general equilibrium.

marginal cost—the change in total cost of production when output is varied by one unit.

marginal revenue—the change in total revenue which results from changing output sold by one unit.

market economy—one where the basic economic questions of what, how, how much, and for whom are answered in competitive markets. Resources, goods, and services are allocated by the forces of supply and demand, which determine market prices.

means of exchange—money serves as a means of exchange (also called medium of exchange). It allows people to exchange productive factors or goods and services for money now and to spend that money later, thus avoiding the difficulties of a barter system.

microeconomics—the study of individual economic units such as households and firms and the way that prices are determined in the market.

mixed economies—economies that contain elements of traditional, command, and market economic systems. Virtually all

economies that exist today are mixed economies.

monetary policy—activities intended to produce changes in the money supply, the availability of credit, or interest rates. In the U.S., the Federal Reserve System is responsible for monetary policy. (*See also* discount rate, open market operations, and reserve requirements.)

money—anything that is generally acceptable in payment of accounts. Money in the United States consists of currency and demand deposits. (*See also* currency and demand deposits.)

monopolistic competition—a market condition of many sellers and similar products. Since each seller is relatively small and cannot influence price, products must be differentiated to capture a larger market share. The markets for clothing and food products are examples of monopolistic competition.

monopoly—a market situation with only one seller and no close substitutes for the product.

multinational corporation—a firm with operations located in two or more countries.

multiplier effect—when an increase in spending produces an increase in national income and consumption greater than the initial amount spent.

national debt—money that has been borrowed by the Federal government to cover spending not paid for out of current tax receipts.

national income—the total amount paid for producing the goods and services produced during the year. It is computed by deducting depreciation and indirect business taxes from Gross National Product.

natural resources—factors of production not created by human effort. Land, water, and ores are examples.

Net Economic Welfare (NEW)—an alternative to Gross National Product as a measure of economic well-being. NEW subtracts disproducts that are a result of the production or consumption of goods and services from GNP figures.

net exports—goods and services sold to foreigners less goods and services bought by foreigners. (Exports minus imports.)

Net National Product—the value of new goods and services available for current consumption. Net National Product is equal to Gross National Product less Depreciation.

nondurable goods—goods that are consumed in a relatively short period of time.

occupational specialization—when an individual performs one kind of work and buys the goods and services needed using the income earned. Doctors, mechanics, and farmers are examples of occupational specialization.

oligopoly—a market that has a few sellers. The actions of such firms are interdependent, and non-price competition, especially advertising, is common. The automobile industry is an example of oligopoly.

open market operations—the buying and selling of government securities by the Federal Reserve System in order to increase or decrease member bank reserves.

open shop—both union and non-union employees can be hired to work in an open shop.

opportunity cost—what is given up by producing a good or service. It is also called alternative cost because resources used one way could have been put to alternative uses. Those uses are the opportunity cost of the choice that was made.

output—the goods and services that result from using inputs in the production process.

partnership—an unincorporated business owned by two or more persons.

payroll taxes—taxes on wage and salary income used to finance social security programs. (*See also* F.I.C.A. taxes.)

per capita—literally, per head. Whenever it is important to know what is available for each person in a society, per capita measures are used.

perfect competition—a market situation characterized by: 1. Many buyers and sellers, acting independently; 2. Identical products; 3. Perfect knowledge of the market by each buyer and seller; 4. Complete mobility of buyers, sellers, and resources. While this model rarely depicts reality, it provides a standard to compare real markets to.

personal consumption expenditures—the amount spent by households on currently produced goods and services.

personal distribution of income—how many persons or families received different levels of income. (*See also* functional distribution of income.)

personal income—the sum of wages and salaries, rent, interest, dividends, income of unincorporated enterprises, and transfer payments.

pollution—damage done to air, water, soil, and other natural resources.

poverty level—the level of income necessary to achieve an adequate standard of living. This changes with changes in the cost of living.

price controls—temporary measures taken by government during periods of rapid inflation. During World War II, for example, the U.S. government set maximum prices on many goods and services.

price index—an indicator of the general level of prices. The three most important price indices in the United States are the Consumer Price Index, the Wholesale Price Index, and the GNP Deflator.

private business firm—an economic unit in a market system where owners of capital seek to earn profits.

private property—when people and corporations have the legal right to own and control economic resources and goods within limits.

producer—one who creates goods or services out of productive resources.

production possibilities model—used by economists to explain the costs of producing more of some goods in terms of the quantities of other goods lost.

productive resources—human physical and mental labor, raw materials, and capital. They are also known as factors of production.

productivity—a measure of worker efficiency. Output per unit of input is the general measure used.

profit—the difference between a firm's revenue and its costs. Economists include the opportunity costs of the business owner's labor and capital or normal profit as costs. Profit then is revenue over and above normal profit.

profit motive—the reason producers create and sell goods and services in a market economy is to earn profits.

progressive tax—a tax whose rate increases as the tax base increases. The progressive income tax in the United States is designed to take a larger share of the incomes of people with high incomes, for example.

property rights—the legal limits governing people's use and control of economic resources.

property tax—a tax on land and structures that is collected by state and local governments in the United States.

proportional tax—a proportional tax takes the same percentage of each dollar of income regardless of the level of income.

public goods—goods that cannot be kept from one person without being kept from all. National defense and flood control are examples of public goods. Since no private citizen could force others to pay for such goods, they would not be provided privately. Only the government can provide public goods because it can tax people to pay for them. Not all goods and services provided by government are public goods, because many of them could be provided privately.

rationing—allocating available resources, goods, and services among possible uses or users. Market prices are one way of rationing. Government has intervened and used a system of ration coupons when the price system was seen as unfair.

real cost—the resources used in producing goods, and services among possible uses or available for alternative uses.

real GNP—Gross National Product measured in constant dollars. It is obtained by dividing current GNP by the GNP deflator and multiplying by 100.

real income—income measured in terms of goods and services it can buy. Money income is divided by a price index to obtain real income.

recession—a period of short term unemployment of workers and resources.

redistribution—the process by which household income is reallocated. Inflation redistributes income when it changes what people on fixed incomes can buy. Public programs which transfer income from taxpayers to people without income are another kind of redistribution.

regressive tax—a regressive tax takes a larger percentage of low incomes than it does of high incomes. A general sales tax is an example of a regressive tax.

regulation—government control of the operation of privately owned businesses. Regulation may limit entry into an industry by requiring licenses, may set maximum prices for businesses like public utilities, or may control the operation of businesses as with safety requirements.

regulatory agencies—government offices created to control privately owned businesses, especially those which have elements of natural monopoly. (*See also* regulation.)

rent—payment made for the use of land or other property such as buildings or machinery.

reserve requirement—one of the Federal Reserve's instruments of monetary policy. Expansion of the money supply can only take place when banks have excess reserves over the legal requirement. The Federal Reserve sets the legal reserve requirement. Lowering it increases excess reserves, raising it decreases excess reserves.

reserves—currency held by banks in their own vaults and deposits in reserve accounts with the Federal Reserve to meet the demands of people who want to withdraw funds and to meet legal reserve requirements.

resource immobility—this concept refers to the existence of barriers that prevent land, labor, and capital from moving to more profitable uses.

resource specialization—a situation in which land, labor, or capital is used to produce one kind of good or service. Growing only corn on a farm, treating only children in a medical practice, making only rolled steel in a factory are examples of resource specialization.

retail sales—goods and services being sold to final consumers.

revenue sharing—taxes raised by the federal government and passed on to local or state governments.

right to work laws—laws that outlaw compulsory union membership.

rival in consumption—when one person's consumption of a good deprives other people of the use of the good, it is rival in consumption. Public goods are not rival in consumption. (*See also* public goods.)

rules of the game—basic laws of a society that are necessary for economic activity. Protection of private property and enforcement of contracts are examples of rules of the game.

sales taxes—taxes on the sales price of goods or services collected at the retail level.

savings bonds—United States government securities sold to individuals .

scarcity—the basic economic problem. Human wants are greater than the resources necessary to satisfy those wants.

seasonal unemployment—the decline in the demand for labor caused by the end of holiday seasons or changing weather produces seasonal unemployment.

services—economic actions that satisfy human wants. The work of doctors, plumbers, and actors are services.

shares—the units of stock which represent ownership in corporations.

social indicators—statistical services used to assess present and to predict future social conditions.

specialization—when people, businesses, or nations produce those goods and services they are most efficient at producing, then trading their surpluses for the other goods and services they need.

stable prices—stable prices change not at all or slowly. Inflation or recession disturb price stability and government fiscal and monetary policy are used to combat them.

stock—a certificate of ownership issued by a corporation.

structural unemployment—when shifts in industry location, the decline of an industry, or other long-term changes in demand or technology result in people losing their jobs. Because these workers tend not to have skills now in demand, structural unemployment is often long-lasting.

subsidy—government financial assistance or special treatment to promote specific economic objectives.

substitutes—goods and services that can be interchanged. When a price increase in one good causes an increase in demand for another good, the goods are substitutes.

supply—the relationship between market prices and what will be offered for sale at those prices.

supply curve—the supply for a good or service shown graphically with price on the vertical axis and quantity supplied on the horizontal axis.

supply schedule—a table showing the number of units of a good or service that would be supplied at various prices.

surplus—when the price of a good or service is too high to bring about a market equilibrium, a surplus results. At the high price sellers will bring more to market than buyers will be willing to buy. The unsold quantity is the surplus.

tariff—a tax on imports.

tax breaks—special tax benefits given to promote specific economic or social objectives.

tax shelters—special provisions in tax laws that protect specific kinds of income. Taxes on that income are either eliminated or reduced.

technology—the combination of skills and knowledge used to produce a good or service.

third-party benefits—benefits of a market transaction received by people other than those who pay for the good or service. The treatment an individual receives for a contagious disease may benefit an entire community, for example.

third-party costs—costs of a market transaction not fully paid by those who purchase the good or service. Air and water pollution are examples of third-party costs.

tight money policy—restricting the money supply, raising interest rates, or pressing banks to restrict credit.

trade barriers—tariffs, import quotas, and customs regulations that discourage international trade.

tradeoff—what must be given up when an economic decision is made. (*See* opportunity cost.)

trade restrictions—(*See* trade barriers.)

traditional economy—an economic system that solves its basic economic problems by relying on the customs of the past.

transfer payments—income transferred from one group to another without an exchange of goods or services. Government transfers include welfare payments, social security benefits, and veterans' benefits. Private business transfers include retirement allowances and donations.

treasury bills—short-term government securities sold at auction.

turnover costs—the handling costs incurred at each stage of production of goods and services.

underemployment—a situation in which people are working at less than their full potential.

undistributed corporate profits—(*See* retained earnings.)

union shop—in a union shop, an employer may hire non-union workers, but those workers must join the union representing their bargaining unit within a time period specified by the contract.

unit of account (GNP)—the dollar is the unit of account in the United States. Gross National Product is calculated by summing the prices that final goods sold for during the year.

use tax—a supplement to a retail sales tax. It is applied to expensive items like automobiles that are purchased in a state that does not have a sales tax. The use tax must be paid when such items are brought into the taxing states.

utility—a measure of usefulness to a consumer. Much of economic theory relies on consumers' ability to rank their choices in order of their preference.

vouchers—some economists believe that goods and services supplied by government (public schools, for example) would be provided more efficiently if vouchers that could only be spent on such goods and services were provided to citizens. Private business firms would compete for the right to provide those goods and services.

wages and salaries—payments made for labor services.

wholesale price index—a measure of the prices of a market basket of basic raw materials and intermediate products used by businesses.

INDEX